PROPHETIC MAHARAJA

RELIGION, CULTURE, AND PUBLIC LIFE

RELIGION, CULTURE, AND PUBLIC LIFE

Series Editor:
Eleanor B. Johnson (2024–)
Matthew Engelke (2018–2024)

The Religion, Culture, and Public Life series is devoted to the study of religion in relation to social, cultural, and political dynamics, both contemporary and historical. It features work by scholars from a variety of disciplinary and methodological perspectives, including religious studies, anthropology, history, philosophy, political science, and sociology. The series is committed to deepening our critical understandings of the empirical and conceptual dimensions of religious thought and practice, as well as such related topics as secularism, pluralism, and political theology. The Religion, Culture, and Public Life series is sponsored by Columbia University's Institute for Religion, Culture, and Public Life.

An Impossible Friendship: Group Portrait, Jerusalem Before and After 1948,
Sonja Mejcher-Atassi

Moral Atmospheres: Islam and Media in a Pakistani Marketplace, Timothy P. A. Cooper

Samson Occom: Radical Hospitality in the Native Northeast, Ryan Carr

Karma and Grace: Religious Difference in Millennial Sri Lanka, Neena Mahadev

Perilous Intimacies: Debating Hindu-Muslim Friendship After Empire, SherAli Tareen

Baptizing Burma: Religious Change in the Last Buddhist Kingdom, Alexandra Kaloyanides

The Sexual Politics of Black Churches, edited by Josef Sorett

At Home and Abroad: The Politics of American Religion,
edited by Elizabeth Shakman Hurd and Winnifred Fallers Sullivan

The Arab and Jewish Questions: Geographies of Engagement in Palestine and Beyond,
edited by Bashir Bashir and Leila Farsakh

Modern Sufis and the State: The Politics of Islam in South Asia and Beyond,
edited by Katherine Pratt Ewing and Rosemary R. Corbett

German, Jew, Muslim, Gay: The Life and Times of Hugo Marcus, Marc David Baer

The Limits of Tolerance: Enlightenment Values and Religious Fanaticism, Denis Lacorne

The Holocaust and the Nakba, edited by Bashir Bashir and Amos Goldberg

Democratic Transition in the Muslim World: A Global Perspective, edited by Alfred Stepan

*The Politics of Secularism: Religion, Diversity, and Institutional Change
in France and Turkey*, Murat Akan

Holy Wars and Holy Alliance: The Return of Religion to the Global Political Stage,
Manlio Graziano

For a complete list of books in the series,
please see the Columbia University Press website.

Prophetic Maharaja

LOSS, SOVEREIGNTY, AND THE SIKH TRADITION
IN COLONIAL SOUTH ASIA

Rajbir Singh Judge

Columbia University Press
New York

Publication of this book was made possible in part by funding from the Institute for Religion, Culture, and Public Life at Columbia University.

Columbia University Press
Publishers Since 1893
New York   Chichester, West Sussex
cup.columbia.edu

Library of Congress Cataloging-in-Publication Data
Names: Judge, Rajbir Singh, author.
Title: Prophetic Maharaja : loss, sovereignty, and the Sikh tradition in colonial South Asia / Rajbir Singh Judge.
Other titles: Loss, sovereignty, and the Sikh tradition in colonial South Asia
Description: New York : Columbia University Press, [2024] | Series: Religion, culture, and public life | Includes bibliographical references and index.
Identifiers: LCCN 2023057153 (print) | LCCN 2023057154 (ebook) | ISBN 9780231214483 (hardback) | ISBN 9780231214490 (trade paperback) | ISBN 9780231560368 (ebook)
Subjects: LCSH: Duleep Singh, Maharajah, 1838–1893. | Sikhs—Kings and rulers—Biography. | Sikhs—Politics and government. | Punjab (India)—Kings and rulers—Biography. | Punjab (India)—Politics and government.
Classification: LCC DS475.2.D45 J83 2024 (print) | LCC DS475.2.D45 (ebook) | DDC 954/.550315092 [B]—dc23/eng/20240126
LC record available at https://lccn.loc.gov/2023057153
LC ebook record available at https://lccn.loc.gov/2023057154

Cover design: Elliott S. Cairns
Cover image: © The British Library Board. India Office Records R.1.1.67, Movements of Duleep Singh and Sindhanwalia.

For my mom, dad, and brother
&
For Abby, Musafir, Rogelio, and Naamras

CONTENTS

CONTENTS

ACKNOWLEDGMENTS

When we were younger and life would become difficult, my mom would take my brother and me to the public library. I was impressed at the time by the rows of authors enclosed in the stacks. Now I marvel at the communities it takes to produce a book and the multiple debts an author incurs—debts and communities that escaped my simplified calculations back then. As I sat there and read or walked and looked, my own debts grew and have continued to expand. They are too numerous to count (even though, alas, the U.S. Department of Education does have one exacting figure). I apologize in advance for my less than meticulous accounting here, but, in my defense, we must recall that debts proliferate and cannot be contained, including in these limited acknowledgments. I could never provide a full account.

At California State University, Chico, I met Edward Pluth, who took an interest in my own poorly developed ideas at the time. He has continued to listen, helping me work through arguments in this book. This project took shape at University of California, Davis. I want to especially thank Ali Anooshahr, Omnia El Shakry, Parama Roy, Michael Saler, and Sudipta Sen for their generosity and criticisms. For their support in Davis, many thanks are owed to Elad Alyagon, Blu Buchanan, Reema Cherian, Logan Clendening, Tanzeen Doha, Mark Dries, Ellie Harwell, LL Hodges, Suad Joseph, Beshara Kehdi, Chau Kelly, Ari Kelman, Jacob Lee, Shan Lin, Thomas Matzat, Caroline McKusick, Mary Mendoza, Jeremey Mikecz, Yesika Ordaz,

Pablo Silva-Fajardo, Stephen Silver, Laura Tavolacci, Juan Carlos Medel Toro, and Duane Wright. In particular, I must thank Muneeza Rizvi for all her time commenting and discussing my work—she is an ideal friend. Jamil Jan Kochai and Jalil Jan Kochai have listened to my despair about the prospects of this book with verve. Zunaira Komal provided clarity and comments for many interventions. Jasdeep Singh Brar and Naindeep Singh Chann provide care in a world void of it. I am grateful for them.

Traveling to archives incurred debts. I appreciate the care demonstrated by my family and friends in England, India, and Australia too many to name, a testament to my father's kindness in cultivating a global family, which I have inherited. Inderjit Kaur, Kuldip Kaur, Preet Kaur, Tonya Kaur, Amrik Singh Khatkar, Surindepal Singh Khatkar, Manpreet Singh Khera, Baljit Singh Mahal, Jarnail Singh Mahal, Prithpal Singh Mahal, Parminder Singh Mahal, Jag Mahal, Manjit Kaur Mann, Jaswinder Kaur Riarh, and Barinder Singh Ranu, as well as their respective families, deserve special mention as they opened their homes to us and made our peripatetic adventures worthwhile. My uncles and aunt—Nishaan Singh, Avtar Singh, and Tej Kaur—were always ready to convene and supported my project throughout. I want to especially thank Manjit Singh from Moranwali, who became a trusted comrade and ally; I am saddened by his loss. When I felt adrift academically, I met Professor Jagdish Singh, who showed me tremendous kindness and a way to think outside the confines within which I was working. I want to thank everyone at Naad Pargaas Institute, especially Sukhwinder Singh, for their assistance. In Patiala, Jaswinder Singh is a dear friend who assisted me throughout my stay and beyond.

I accumulated more debts at Columbia University and New York City. I wish to express my gratitude to Manan Ahmed, Sami Al-Daghistani, Mehr Ali, Gil Anidjar, Talal Asad, William Carrick, Marwa Elshakry, Matthew Engelke, Katherine P. Ewing, Anmol Ghavri, Navyug Gill, Samira Haj, Walid Hammam, Samaah Jaffer, Mana Kia, Mohamed Amer Meziane, Zehra Mehdi, Kavitha Sivaramakrishnan, Yannik Thiem, and S. Akbar Zaidi. Both Talal and Samira opened their respective homes to my family. I owe them much. And, of course, many thanks to Cecily.

At conferences, workshops, and elsewhere, numerous people have advised and commented upon this project and beyond. I have benefited from conversations with Mona Bhan, Naisargi N. Dave, Amrit Deol, Aaron Eldridge, Rahuldeep Singh Gill, Basit Kareem Iqbal, Randeep Singh Hothi,

Mohamad Junaid, Hafsa Kanjwal, Harini Kumar, Philippa Levine, Beatrice Marovich, Ali Altaf Mian, Deepti Misri, Milad Odabaei, Marika Rose, Megha Sharma Sehdev, Pashaura Singh, Prabhsharanbir Singh, Prabhsharandeep Singh, Anthony Paul Smith, and SherAli Tareen.

One week before the 2020 shutdown I received an offer from California State University, Long Beach. The transition has been incredibly difficult. David A. Shafer undertook the interminable task of mentoring in a time of uncertainty. His scholarly and personal support has been immeasurable. Multiple people have made the move smoother and created a stimulating intellectual environment, including Jake and Sabrina Alimahomed-Wilson, Yousef Baker, Azza Basarudin, Robert Blankenship, Emily Berquist-Soule, Justin Gomer, LL Hodges, Ali F. Igmen, Beka Langen, Marie Kelleher, Kavitha Koshy, Aparna Nayak, Carie Rael, David Sheridan, Phyllis Simon, Demetrius Tien, and Abraham Weil. My undergraduate students have been particularly inspiring, especially in their ability to grapple with difficult theoretical questions about the writing of history. Finally, I gain strength from my colleagues Isacar Bolaños, Kate Flach, Ulices Piña, and Preeti Sharma. Not only are they brimming with brilliance, but they have also helped my family create a sense of home here in Long Beach. I am indebted to them for their kindness and generosity.

Numerous people commented on drafts of this book and have made the manuscript immeasurably better. I learned much from the suggestions made by Gil Anidjar, LL Hodges, Omnia El Shakry, Katherine P. Ewing, Basit Kareem Iqbal, Harleen Kaur, prabhdeep singh kehal, Zunaira Komal, Muneeza Rizvi, Parama Roy, Joan Wallach Scott, Nirvikar Singh, and Matthew Wyman-McCarthy.

This book would not be possible without the support of Matthew Engelke, who has been a compassionate mentor. I am also thankful to the manuscript reviewers and to the editorial support of Wendy Lochner, Marisa Lastres, Alyssa Napier, and Lowell Frye at Columbia University Press. I remain terrified by the book publishing process, but Lowell, Marisa, Alyssa, and Wendy have made it as smooth as possible.

The research and writing for this book was generously supported by the American Historical Association, American Institute of Pakistan Studies, American Institute of Indian Studies, and U.S. Department of Education. At California State University, Long Beach, I was supported by the Research, Scholarship, and Creative Activities Award as well as my union, the California Faculty Association, which fights for equitable and fair working conditions.

Chapter 5 was published in a modified form as "Reform in Fragments: Sovereignty, Colonialism, and the Sikh Tradition," in *Modern Asian Studies* 56, no. 4 (2022): 1125–52. I thank Cambridge University Press for permission to reprint it.

I would not have survived without my friends and family who are removed from academia. Raul Buenrostro, Carlos Castillon, Fernando Corona, Jorge Lupian, Jesus Mendoza, Alex Ortega, Stephen Rojas, Javier Silva, and Griseyda Vargas have remained steadfast friends throughout the years. Without them, life is dull; I owe them much. In California, family has sustained me. Baljit Kaur Judge and Macie Sangha continually demonstrate the best of family as does Tía Cristina alongside her children and their families: I am thankful to Ernestina Ortega, Manuel Ortega, Maribel Ortega, Pedro Ortega, Randy Ortega, and Rosaelia Ortega. During our visits, Tía Cristina has allowed me to sit at her dining room table and type away without complaint. *Muchas gracias.* Jose Cerros will inevitably grumble if I do not mention partners of the Ortega family, so thanks to Rene, Pilar, Jose, Adriana, Lupe, and Juan as well.

I would not have completed this book without the thoughtfulness, attention, and general overall brilliance of Omnia El Shakry. She has helped me navigate a world that remains radically alienating without judgment, even when my failures strained credibility.

My mother, Surinder Kaur Judge, father, Rai Singh Judge, brother, Satbir Singh Judge have provided a whole world for me, an umbilical cord from which we can trace an entire history, an inventory of immense care and love. Their love is one that structured and sustained this work. And this love continues to grow with the addition of my nephew, Mohkam Singh Judge, who is adorable.

Musafir, Rogelio, and Naamras appear at the limits of what is sayable—limits Musafir continually exceeds in his refusals. Of course, limits are no match for Rogelio and his immeasurable curiosity. Naamras is too delightful to be concerned with limits and horizons. I love them all dearly.

And then language halts traveling toward Abby, who always remains untimely, creating life and hope—at times, from just a glance—in the folds of a presently miserable history.

PROPHETIC MAHARAJA

INTRODUCTION

Losing Duleep Singh

Both loss and the alleviating responses to loss raise profound and interrelated questions about time, attachment, ethics, and politics. Today there is a prevailing and forceful demand which dictates that loss requires recovery or restoration, that gaps produced by loss need to be filled in.[1] Consider, for example, the attempts to recover lost harmonious forms of life or the attempt to restore agency lost in the historical record. These approaches reverberate across our destroyed world. Looking to heal wounds left in the wake of loss, there is an insistence that both scholars and the communities they analyze catalogue losses as well as bind the past with the present as a way to secure against further losses.[2] But this reparative turn to history may limit possibilities rather than reinstate them. Examining different forms of life and different traditions, in contrast, can reveal relations to loss that challenge our theoretical presuppositions that losses must be redressed by recovery and restoration.[3] In the pages that follow, I think with both the Sikh tradition and psychoanalysis to reconsider varied assumptions about loss as well as to continue to question what loss entails.

This book asks: What happens when a tradition encounters the possibility of its loss, especially when that loss—not unlike the present-day losses that mount in the wake of environmental, political, and social disasters—exceeds the very possibility of narration, reflection, and redemption? How do traditions and peoples occupy and contend with loss even in the wake of destruction? I consider such questions by turning to Sikhs at the end of the nineteenth century, and in particular to Maharaja Duleep Singh and his struggle, during the 1880s, to restore Sikh rule, the lost Khalsa Raj, in what is today northern India and northeastern Pakistan.[4] The book explores Singh's efforts, and the responses of the Sikh community to those efforts, in order to highlight how a people articulated loss (military, political, and psychological). Through theological debate, literary production, bodily discipline, and the cultivation of ethical practice, Sikhs undid the colonial politics that sought to conquer, secure, and map the world. I show how a people responded to loss not solely by seeking to recover the past but also by seeking to remake the past and create change. Sikhs in the final decades of the nineteenth century were not seeking to recover the past. They engaged loss by remaking it. They show that the past was not—and is not—an inert object awaiting reclamation.

If, however, the past is not a static object awaiting scholarly analysis, then the task cannot be mere recovery of an indigenous theory of loss. My examination of Duleep Singh and his attempted revolt against British colonial rule highlights the ambiguities that emerge in both Singh himself and the images of Singh that circulated as Sikhs contested and challenged representations of Singh as well as of the colonial state. There is, I argue, no "real" Duleep Singh nor an authentic story to tell.

My goal is not to historicize Duleep Singh and the politics that surrounded him by uncovering how he aligned with "cosmopolitan networks," "messianic politics," or wider global formations that we can trace in the subcontinent—other scholars have already done this.[5] Nor is it to locate historical exclusivity or to find historical exceptions. Indeed, my goal is not to provide historical explanation at all; "there is no history lesson, one might translate: no lesson learned, not from the victors."[6] The book is thus, perhaps strangely, a historical narrative that refuses to historicize: Duleep Singh, suspended, exceeds placement.

The way Sikh rule in Punjab both came into being at the end of the eighteenth century and ended in the middle of the nineteenth century influenced Sikhs' subsequent grappling with loss in multifaceted ways. After the slow fragmentation of the Mughal Empire during the eighteenth century,

Punjab found itself organized into multiple sovereign states called *misls* within a larger Sikh confederacy. Toward the end of the century, Ranjit Singh, the heir and commander of the largest of these *misls*, the Sukerchakia Misl, created a larger kingdom by conquering rival *misls* and defeating and expelling Afghans from Punjab. With other *misls*, Singh forged alliances to build the Khalsa Raj (Sikh Kingdom) and institute a Sikh form of governance, with himself as maharaja.[7] But when he died in 1839, Ranjit Singh's successors engaged in numerous internecine struggles and court intrigues, some of which resulted in untimely and horrific deaths. These include the poisoning of his immediate successor, Kharak Singh, and the presumed murder of Kharak Singh's son, Nau Nihal, on whom a block of stone fell after he performed the last rites at his father's funeral. These conflicts had the cumulative impact of eroding the power of the Sikh state.

The youngest of Ranjit Singh's sons, Duleep Singh, became the nominal ruler of the Khalsa Raj in 1843 at the age of five. Yet struggles for power among various factions continued, which placed the waning Kingdom in a weakened state when it went into battle against the British East India Company during the Anglo-Sikh Wars (1845–46, 1848–49). The British were victorious in these conflicts, which marked the beginning of their occupation of Punjab. Though the East India Company originally declared that it arrived, as General Gough proclaimed, "not as an enemy" but to "restore order and obedience,"[8] the occupation quickly turned to annexation. Under the Treaty of Lahore in 1849, ten-year-old Duleep Singh was forced to "resign for himself, his heirs, and successors all right, title and claim to the sovereignty of the Punjab, or to any sovereign power whatever."[9] In exchange, he was provided with a fixed annual stipend for life by the British government. The Khalsa Raj had been lost, and with it Duleep Singh.

After Duleep Singh signed the Treaty of Lahore, the British placed him in the care of Dr. John Login, a Scottish surgeon (and once she returned reluctantly from England, his wife Lena Login) in Fatehgarh, Punjab. Though in Fatehgarh Duleep Singh was largely removed from the public eye, his mere presence in Punjab represented a threat to British rule, since he had the potential to serve as a focal point around which anti-British sentiment could coalesce. This remained the case even after the maharaja converted to Christianity, receiving the sacrament of baptism in 1853. Fearing his ability to unify the population, the British exiled Duleep Singh to England the following year. In subsequent years, he became a fixture in the royal palaces at London, adoringly referred to by Queen Victoria as the Black Prince.

The queen's adoration of Duleep Singh diminished as he grew older and his financial situation grew more dire throughout the 1870s and 1880s. These financial difficulties emerged largely because the Treaty of Lahore in 1849 did not account for inflation; Singh lived in London on a fixed income designed to ensure that he did not develop ostentatious tastes. In 1879, the Earl of Cranbrook, Secretary of State for India, argued it was important to "bear in mind that the Maharaja's income was fixed 23 years ago, when the position which he would assume in society could not be accurately fore-seen; that the cost of living has since very greatly increased; and that even at the time the sum of 25000*l*, a year, suggested by Lord Dalhousie, was described by His Lordship as an allowance which, though liberal, would be 'not too liberal.' "[10] Duleep Singh was not the extravagant spender that he was portrayed to be through the reproduction of tropes of the gluttonous Oriental Despot. Rather, as one official, Lieutenant Colonel W. E. West, reported, "The Maharaja's style of living appears, as far as I have been able to form an opinion, to be economical."[11] Trapped in financial straits while required to maintain a royal lifestyle, Duleep Singh in 1886 would publicly condemn the Treaty of Lahore of nearly a half-century earlier as "that iniquitous treaty of the annexation, which was extorted from me by my guardian when I was a minor."[12]

Despite Duleep Singh's exile, colonial officials recognized the dangers he posed to their rule in Punjab and remained vigilant. For the colonial state, a key to limiting Sikh attempts to revive the Khalsa Raj was an extensive surveillance network consolidated by establishing intelligence departments across the subcontinent, including one that flourished in Punjab at the end of the nineteenth century. These departments became necessary, Viceroy Dufferin argued in 1886, because of both "the facility which railway transit gives to the criminal classes" and "the growth of political as well as of religious excitement during the last few years."[13] Singh and his image were regulated by colonial political technologies and strategies that sought to still his unstable form while fixing religious identities and texts, and the rights and responsibilities of imperial citizenship. Such regulation through colonial power, as David Scott stresses, was not "merely to contain resistance and encourage accommodation but to seek to ensure that both could only be defined in relation to the categories and structures of modern political rationality."[14]

In 1884, Duleep Singh's cousin Thakur Singh Sindhanwalia traveled from the Punjab to England in order to reveal to Duleep Singh the extent of his and, by extension, Punjab's riches stolen by the British. He brought with him news of a population not only excited about the prospect of the sovereign's return, but also prepared for it. Sikh expectancy, Sindhanwalia explained, was cultivated by the extensive circulation of prophecies within the Sikh tradition. For example, oral prophecies of a Sikh revolution against foreign rule were found in the *sau sakhis*, attributed to Guru Gobind Singh, and the *Malwa Des Ratan Di Sakhis*, attributed to Guru Tegh Bahadur and Guru Gobind Singh. These prophecies found in revered texts asserted that a Khalsa Raj would emerge through the leadership of a "Deep Singh," who was the chosen one to lead the Sikhs in rebellion against the British. When the British first learned of these prophecies through the 1860s, they caused significant concern. In 1861, for example, Lord Canning argued, "it is difficult to over-estimate the influence which prophecies . . . have over an uneducated, semi-barbarous, imaginative people like the Sikhs."[15]

Sindhanwalia found sympathetic ears: living in London and quickly falling into bankruptcy, Singh was becoming ever more dissatisfied with British rule in his homeland. Moreover, before Sindhanwalia's visit, Duleep Singh's mother, Maharani Jind Kaur, had apprised him early on of both his lost fortune and the prophetic claims. Refused pecuniary aid from the India Office and urged on by Sindhanwalia, Singh in the 1880s started to demand that he be allowed to return to India to investigate the financial worth of his lost estates and live where his stipend could maintain the lifestyle to which he felt entitled. Significantly, he demanded that the British allocate him rights based on imperial citizenship, arguing that "the Government may with impunity succeed in stripping me of my property; but freedom is the right of every British subject."[16] Colonial administrators, however, refused to let Duleep Singh return to Punjab, citing a provision in the Treaty of Lahore that restricted the maharaja's residence to wherever the governor general of India deemed fit. While recognizing this regulation was "not in accordance with European ideas," Henry Mortimer Durand, the foreign secretary of India, nonetheless argued that "we cannot let the Maharaja override us, and if he forces a conflict, I would take any measures which may be necessary to show him once for all that the Government of India means to be obeyed."[17] The state's adamant refusal was predicated on the fear that the population of Punjab would rally around Duleep Singh, even though, as the Anglo-Indian newspaper, *The Pioneer*, reported in relation to his proposed return, "In dress, in language, in pursuits an Englishman for more than 30 years, he has become completely denationalized, and he probably cares as little for the Punjab now, as the Punjab, in his individual capacity, cares for him."[18]

But fear lingered. As the lieutenant governor of Punjab, Charles Aitchison, argued, although Duleep Singh's "conversion to Christianity and his long residence in England have greatly estranged him from the Punjab people," this evolution did not "remove all political danger, though it may minimize it."[19] Tensions were already heightened and colonial authorities were on edge especially in the 1880s. For example, as the Government of India noted, "prophecies and rumors among Hindus and Mahometans alike point to the current year [1883] as a season of trouble both in politics and religion." Sikhs, too, especially the Namdharis (a "sect" within the Sikh tradition), helped to create this atmosphere of anticipation. The state reported there was much "uneasiness and an unusual movement" based upon "the predictions in their [Sikh] religious books. More dangerously, there were reports in 1883 that Sikhs were "performing the same ceremonies as were observed by Guru Govind before his revolt against the Mahometan power."[20] Noting precedents for Sikh political revolution, colonial administrators concluded that if Duleep Singh entered India at a time when prophetic happenings were taking place (or believed by much of the population of Punjab to be taking place), unnecessary trouble would result. For loss was not really loss, Ranjit Singh's death was not an end, and his *samadhi* (tomb, memorial) was not a final resting point. Instead, Aitchison worried that Duleep Singh would rekindle a desire for sovereignty since there were "thousands of Sikhs who long for and expect the restoration of the Khalsa," because "the magic of [Ranjit Singh's] name is still powerful in the country."[21]

Defying the state's orders, Duleep Singh set sail with his wife, Bamba Müller, and their children for Bombay, India on March 31, 1886, on the Peninsular and Oriental steamer *Verona*. Endeavoring to thwart Singh's maneuverings, British authorities stopped him en route in Aden, where on May 25 Singh converted back to Sikhism by taking *amrit* in the presence of five Sikhs, including a cousin, Thakur Singh of Waga. Despite being foiled in this first attempted return, Duleep Singh was not deterred, and he traveled to Paris in 1886 and to Moscow in 1887 as part of his efforts to build foreign support for his cause. In Moscow, the tsar ignored Singh, but he found a sympathetic ear in Jamal al-Din al-Afghani, Mikhail Katkov, and the Kashmiri Abdul Rasul. Al-Afghani and Rasul were embedded within what Seema Alavi calls "Muslim transimperial webs that permeated the rigidly demarcated official borders."[22] Abdul Rasul organized widely throughout the Ottoman Empire and worked closely with Al-Zubayr Rahma Mansur in Sudan, who implored Duleep Singh to "throw himself entirely upon the Musalman element [in the Punjab]," which would help create "an insurrection in Egypt simultaneously with one in India."[23] With their help, Duleep Singh attempted to organize an Indian, Russian, Afghan, and Egyptian alliance against British rule that included a plot to cut access to the Suez Canal.

Meanwhile, on his return to the subcontinent, Sindhanwalia, whom Duleep Singh had appointed prime minister in exile, spread word of Duleep Singh's imminent return to Punjab and finally set up camp in Pondicherry, where he led Duleep Singh's exiled government. In this role, Sindhanwalia secretly contacted leaders of the various princely states such as Maharaja Pratap Singh of Kashmir, successor to Ranbir Singh, and Raja Bikram Singh of Faridkot, asking them to back Duleep Singh in his quest to retake the Punjab. He also met frequently with the exiled Myingun Prince of Burma, who had led an unsuccessful coup against his father, the Burmese King Mindon Min, in 1866.

Attempts at organizing a revolt in favor of Duleep Singh's return, however, petered out, and Duleep Singh eventually admitted defeat. Sindhanwalia died in 1887. The colonial state, through its extensive network of surveillance, arrested many of Singh's emissaries. Unable to find sustained support abroad for his nascent state, Duleep Singh eventually capitulated in 1890, writing to Queen Victoria from Paris, "I write to express my great regret for my past conduct towards Her Majesty the Queen-Empress of India. I humbly ask Her Majesty to pardon me, and I trust entirely to the clemency of the Queen."[24] Three years later, in 1893, Maharaja Duleep Singh passed away in Paris. The Khalsa Raj was lost, again.

This narrative has been told and retold numerous times, and the literature on Duleep Singh is vast and widely known.[25] In contrast to such historical narratives, this book centers the structure of desire in relation to Duleep Singh. What fantasies did and does he conjure about sovereignty and community? In asking about desire and fantasy, we return to questions of loss. Fantasies are themselves structured around a lost object that ignites desire and leaves us only with echoes.[26] To return to the original question, then, what does it mean to 'lose' the *Khalsa Raj* and repeat that loss decades later?[27] Rather than take a secure Sikh sovereignty and its loss as a given—a loss embodied by Duleep Singh which can be mourned or held in melancholic attachment to or recovered and restored—this book asks what it might even mean to lose sovereignty. For loss remained marked by ambiguities even as the colonial project gifted the very conditions for what could be lost—the lines on a map, for example, that are retroactively "recovered" by the postcolonial state.[28]

COMMUNITY AND SOVEREIGNTY

Who is sovereign? Over whom does one rule? Does the latter question immediately follow the former? To think about sovereignty is, commonly, to think about community. But individuals can be on a common path, the *panth*, as the Sikh tradition has it, which is never completed but always ongoing. How then can one be sovereign—transcendent—over that path and those commonly on it? In other words, how is sovereignty tied to community? This section lays out how sovereignty and community became tied together conceptually and the alternative relations that exist between them. As I will explore later in the book, Duleep Singh's attempt to reclaim sovereignty troubles easy ties between community and sovereignty.

These are political theological questions, since the normative ideal of sovereignty presupposes a Christian paradigm. We must think about how Christian presuppositions structure the normative ideal of sovereignty and community before we can think otherwise, not least about Duleep Singh.[29] In this Christian paradigm, sovereignty becomes immanent to the community. This is not any generic community, but a community that is always already constituted as such; strangely, as Roberto Esposito explains, there, "community is a 'property' belonging to subjects that join them together [*accomuna*]: an attribute, a definition, a predicate that qualifies them as belonging to the same totality [*insieme*], or as a 'substance' that is produced by their union."[30] This immanentization of sovereignty has to do with internal shifts within the Christian tradition, notably the discovery of the self, which, in turn, meant the discovery of groups, as Caroline Walker Bynum has historically described. Bynum makes clear how "the discovery of self in all its aspects went hand in hand with the discovery of models and the discovery of community" in which grace brought "about not only the conformity of the individual to God but also the conformity of inner and outer man."[31] Correspondence between inner and outer becomes crucial—a correspondence measured in likeness to God, *imago dei*, within a community.

The change in meaning leads to what Esposito calls the immunization paradigm of modernity.[32] In this understanding of community, community is enclosed, a possession. Yet, he argues, community remains unrealizable. He asks: "How are we to realize something that precedes every possible realization?"[33] Community eludes such realization because community is not something in common—a shared property or possession—but rather an obligation, a debt, a subtraction.[34] Esposito traces the meaning of community to its Latin root *munus*, which means duty or gift. This is in contrast to *res publica*, identified with the common thing, the public thing. It is this strange community, the community with that shared blood, that becomes the body politic, oriented toward immunity and immanence.[35]

Though "our collective imagination remains bloody," there are other ways to consider community and sovereignty.[36] Partha Chatterjee directs us toward some of these considerations, writing that "community, which ideally should have been banished from the kingdom of capital, continues to lead a subterranean, potentially subversive, life within it because it refuses to go away."[37] This is the case with the Sikh community, where "community" (and therefore sovereignty) is much more dislocated. But why not just call the Sikh community "the Sikh communities," if the community is not so homogeneous? My response is that the plural is no antidote to the singular. To posit a plural against the singular upholds the very logic the plural seeks to challenge. Instead, this book demonstrates how community in the singular is interrupted within; its dislocation is inherent in itself.

There is a risk in using "community" in the singular in continuing conversations about sovereignty and community. As Jacques Derrida contends, "To put the old names to work, or even just to leave them in circulation, will always, of course, involve some risk: the risk of settling down or of regressing into the system that has been, or is in the process of being, deconstructed."[38]

This is the risk this book undertakes: to center the Sikh community; to rethink the very contours of community, sovereignty, and the Sikh tradition. Such risk is one that we learn about in the Sikh tradition itself. Sovereignty in the Sikh tradition, for example, is an antagonistic, impossible, unity. As the philosopher Kapur Singh argues, though the spiritual (*piri*) is intimately bound with the temporal (*miri*), these spheres remain in antagonistic relation to each other in a state of irresolution, not harmony. Thinking with the modern distinction of church and state, he writes "the Guru does not assert that this perpetual dichotomy and antagonism of the Church and the State must be resolved, or even that it is capable of being resolved, by the suppression or subjugation of the one by the other."[39] Within such an understanding, the bloody exchange that restores "the balance of payments between the divine and human" might not translate so well, especially when the Sikh tradition foregrounds their antagonism."[40] The Khalsa—the sociopolitical order instituted by Guru Gobind Singh in 1699—centers this struggle. There is not a lost plural harmony that needs to be recovered nor a sovereignty that is immune from contaminations. Instead, this antagonism invites us to consider different (im)possibilities. One can recall here Derrida's conclusion that "pure sovereignty does not exist; it is always in the process of positing itself by refuting itself, by denying or disavowing itself."[41]

These insights are germane to the study of loss within the Sikh community. As scholars of South Asia too have taught us, sovereignty was multiple and nested in the precolonial period; there were different paradigms that governed community. There were, Norbert Peabody rightly argues, "various tensions and disjunctions in the meanings associated with political relations."[42] Much like Peabody, Purnima Dhavan also shows that the Khalsa and attendant kinship networks limited claims of individual political sovereignty from the seventeenth century to Ranjit Singh's empire in the 1830s and early 1840s.[43] Such contestations did not disappear after the Khalsa Raj, but shifted as new distinctions emerged with the advent of British rule.[44] Periodization is not law, even if it presents itself as a sovereign decision.[45] Thus there remained, under British rule, Sudipta Sen writes, "undigested remainders of indigenous regimes not fully incorporated," leaving room for more radical questionings and openings.[46] These possibilities surrounding community and sovereignty were not "something monopolized by some ruling elites and hierarchs," but "present in all," as Milinda Banerjee has put it.[47] This is certainly the case among Sikhs, for whom royal authority, with the institution of the Khalsa became, Priya Atwal contends, "diffused and spread in a radically new form [royal authority] throughout the entire Sikh *panth*."[48] This diffusion of royal power proceeded even though, as Atwal traces quite vividly, tensions around creating and maintaining sovereign rule did not dissipate.[49]

But rather than centering the loss of a prior sovereignty, this book asks: what do we make of loss *and* sovereignty? Inserting "and" defies pretensions of what Yarimar Bonilla calls sovereignty's normative ideal by asking us to consider what is being lost.[50] This is an especially important task since sovereignty is, Bonilla writes, "a category that both seduces and disappoints in its attempt at transcending its provincial origins." To speak of loss *and* sovereignty against the loss *of* sovereignty, therefore, is to wonder where sovereignty ever "was," to wonder how "we have never been sovereign."[51] Sovereignty, put differently, might not be so secured, so fastened, in the first place. It might not be something that can be lost because it might never have been something possessed; its integrity itself is in question. In the chapters that follow, I show that loss and sovereignty were always tied together, even though today sovereignty remains thought of as an ideal to be secured: if not in history (by the state, the maharaja, or the empire) then in historiography (by the historian).[52] Though sovereignty remains a "transcript of the future," offering redemption in its eschatological promise, the clocks are never synchronized as such.[53] And so loss and sovereignty become a problem for and of history.[54]

LOSS AND FAILURE

While *Prophetic Maharaja* does center a dislocation within community and sovereignty, the book does not show continuity of an indigenous form of sovereignty and community in history.[55] What is the purpose of this book, then, if not recovery? I want to consider, following Stefania Pandolfo, "invention at a time of political and cultural crisis, and on the ruins of symbolic forms, exploring the possibility of transmission for a tradition uprooted from its system of reference."[56] This book participates in examining such uprooted transmission. I grapple with a fractured inheritance and system of reference while focusing on the aftermath of the fall of the Khalsa Raj—an aftermath that continues into the present.

The problems around loss and the transmission of tradition in Punjab post–Ranjit Singh are compounded because the bid to restore Duleep Singh and reestablish the Khalsa Raj failed. Duleep Singh's abject failure, emplotted as a tragedy, dominates the standard narrative of his resistance.[57] For example, Christy Campbell, in his popular recounting of Duleep Singh's story, explicitly declares that Singh's struggle was "the true tragedy of the last King of Lahore."[58] Failure, the signaling of total loss, endures as authoritative, affirming disappointment that confirms our own certainties about what is and was possible.[59] And this disappointment, reflecting the failure of a sovereign Sikh state, creates particular modes of intelligibility in the present. One mode of fostering such intelligibility today is the repeated enunciation of failure in relation to Duleep Singh: he is, for Campbell and so many, the *tragic* king of Lahore. Yet by foregrounding Duleep Singh as a tragic king, Sikhs cultivate an attachment to Duleep Singh the person. It is this attachment that then fosters intelligibility for Sikh understandings of sovereignty, rather than vice versa. Put another way, in the process of thinking about the loss of the Khalsa Raj, the body of the sovereign becomes central as a representation of the reality of the community; Duleep Singh becomes the empty vessel in which the blood of community flows—a circulation short-circuited by colonialism.

Rather than foreground a tragic narrative that concludes in failure, thereby upholding Duleep Singh as the historical *imago*, *Prophetic Maharaja* highlights the dreams, inventions at a time of crisis, attached to Duleep Singh. This aim is difficult to realize, especially since, in Lauren Berlant's phrasing, "dreams are seen as easy optimism, while failures seem complex." Yet an understanding of the other possibilities of Duleep Singh—the inventive and contested dreams surrounding him—dissolves both Singh as an historical actor and his present-day reputation as a secure object that can be easily grasped. By pausing in the ubiquity of disputations surrounding Duleep Singh in Punjab and beyond at the end of the nineteenth century, we can halt and cultivate "lagging and sagging relation to attachment," which provides an occasion to center a vertigo in relation to sovereignty.[60] This moment, however, does not create opportunity to discover the "truth" behind Duleep Singh, to recognize Duleep Singh "accurately" as confirmed through archival recovery. Misrecognition is inescapable; as Slavoj Žižek insists, we must "fully acknowledge this misrecognition as unavoidable," since, even in its multiple valences, it provides the very possibility of an ontological consistency.[61] Dwelling in this unavoidability of misrecognition while refusing to enunciate failure or unmask a real Duleep Singh, refusing to triumph over the past, this book aims to rekindle, however briefly, what Berlant terms "a practice of meticulous curiosity" without repair.[62]

This rekindling without repair means that rather than provide a new theorization of loss—which cements a relation to loss—this book endeavors to reckon with the powerful resources that work on loss, such as mourning and melancholia, and what they have already provided. Said differently, I contend with loss instead of transcending it through recovery. But I am also wary of holding loss, which, by securing absence, further cements the past as an object to be recovered. The question arises: Is this book then really *about* loss? Or is loss simply a thread that is itself lost within the book? My answer is that I am ambivalent about loss, affirming and denying it, resisting it and acknowledging it, working through it and against it, and interrogating its nature, its ground or presuppositions, its form and its failures.[63] I do not tie a thread throughout the text that provides an adequate answer *to* loss because there might not be any answer to it. In this sense the book does not provide a theorization of loss but dwells in the various rhythms of loss. My goal is not to recognize loss and provide it taxonomic space but to sit with losses as they appear, disappear, and reappear throughout the text.

In this play of appearances I grapple with theoretical formations that were remarkable interventions in their time, even if today they appear to have "failed," much like Duleep Singh himself. These formations include psychoanalysis and subaltern studies, intellectual traditions that have robustly dwelled in loss.[64] One could say these projects themselves were (and are) not concerned with rationally dominating the world, but with working within the impasse of modernity itself against both the search of a sealed authenticity and the expertise of the rational agent. Working within this impasse, my goal, like these failed projects, is much more modest. It is to ask how these "failed" intellectual frameworks, much like the failure of Duleep Singh, reorient our normative commitments toward loss in order to demonstrate how sovereignty and, by extension, community remained open to rearticulations then and continue to do so now.

I ask these questions around loss by working within the colonial archive, papers and documents from the British Library, National Archives of India, Punjab State Archives, and newspapers from the time.[65] Though descriptive empiricism proceeds unimpeded for historians, it bears repeating that a transcendent account is not possible.[66] There are only contaminated inscriptions that conjure desires in both their presence and absence, even though scholars remain attached to "the colonial archive as an epistemic project," as Harleen Kaur and p.s. kehal brilliantly analyze.[67] Against such attachments I work within the seam of the colonial archive to trace the ambiguities that emerge in Duleep Singh as Sikhs disputed and challenged both Duleep Singh and the colonial state. By refusing adjudication into a singular and fixed form from which we can determine the colonial or native, *Prophetic Maharaja* demonstrates how societal, theological, and political revolution in South Asia remained open to numerous possibilities at the turn of the century, since loss and engaging with loss destabilized formations rather than fixing them.[68]

This is not to say that the pursuit to cohere a singular formation was absent in the final decades of the nineteenth century. Sikhs and others struggled to make sense of the world that was vanishing. Stressing these discordant struggles to reinstitute the Khalsa Raj and Duleep Singh, this book argues that people relied on the Sikh tradition to make sense of surmounting losses and struggled to work through those losses. To give one example, Sikhs centered *hukam* (order, command) in their struggle. *Hukam* disrupts sovereignty as understood within a Christian form because it requires a consent to an inscrutable will rather than a circulation between transcendence and immanence; *hukam* cannot be, then, a subject or object of knowledge. What, then, does it mean to live under *hukam* especially when *hukam* is untimely, reconfiguring what can appear possible and impossible? It means to erase the "I," the ego—a loss that requires we let go of our attachments while remaining grounded in the struggle. It is to center a loss without attachments.[69] Centering Sikh understandings such as *hukam*, this book thus establishes how loss can signal political and ethical struggle based on both prior understandings as well as emerging distinctions. That is to say, people contended with loss rather than accepting it as a given or something needing to be filled in.

MOURNING AND MELANCHOLIA?

Other scholars have located the loss of the Khalsa Raj quite differently. In particular, I want to focus in this section on two academic works that analyze Duleep Singh: Tony Ballantyne's *Between Colonialism and Diaspora: Sikh Cultural Formations in an Imperial World* and Brian Keith Axel's *The Nation's Tortured Body: Violence, Representation, and the Formation of a Sikh "Diaspora."*[70] A psychoanalytic orientation is critical for understanding the stakes of the historiographical arguments presented by these authors; I contend that Ballantyne centers mourning in relation to Duleep Singh while Axel argues that Sikhs have a melancholic fixation with Duleep Singh. I end this section by exploring an alternative possibility that permeates this book: namely, a possibility enabled by an ethics of remembering that does not require we center a stable lost object.

In reckoning with loss and how the Sikh tradition grappled with loss, psychoanalysis is necessary. It has engaged extensively with questions of loss in the metropole, colony, and postcolony through its theorization of mourning and melancholia. Today, psychoanalysis offers an inheritance that collides with the loss of Duleep Singh and a powerful site for thinking about loss. What is this inheritance? For Sigmund Freud, mourning normalizes the relation to loss. Over time, mourning frees the ego from its libidinal attachment to the lost object.[71] Though mourning reorients the longing for the lost object, there is understandable opposition to the withdrawing of such attachments. As Freud writes, "people never willingly abandon a libidinal position, not even, indeed, when a substitute is already beckoning to them."[72] Therefore, the longing for the lost object cannot be accomplished at will through an autonomous decision. At times, not even the allure of a new object can short-circuit the process of letting go—attachments to loss are never matters of choice.[73]

Mourning works as a "reparative remembering," writes David Scott.[74] One could say that mourning is the project for historians. Historians first posit the past as past but repair our relation to the past by disinterring the dead and bringing them into the present, as Michel de Certeau taught us.[75] Such a move stabilizes the present's relation to the past. This movement of reparative remembering performs, to appropriate Jacques Lacan, funerary rites in order "to propitiate [*satisfaire à*] what we call the memory of the departed."[76] This has been a goal of many scholars focused on the Khalsa Raj, Duleep Singh, and the Sikh tradition: to properly bury Duleep Singh, to mourn his lost sovereignty by situating and stitching the man into his time. Such a move suppresses the enigmatic questions raised by death. These questions remain irresolute: "What does the dead person want? What does he want of me? What did he want to say to me?" as Jean Laplanche asks.[77]

An example of metabolization of mourning in relation to Duleep Singh is useful here. Tony Ballantyne suggests that contestations around Duleep Singh reveal how "Sikh identities are constantly formed and reformed through an uneven polylogic process, whereby understandings of community continue to be formulated, performed, and reformed in response to other groups."[78] For Ballantyne this approach challenges, as he labels it, the "internalist approach" and instead highlights the multiple shifts that Duleep Singh underwent relationally in order to reveal how "Sikh identity is constantly remade through encounters with other communities and access to public institutions and the machinery of government." In so doing, Ballantyne discovers a truism: "Sikhs occupy diverse cultural locations and articulate a multiplicity of identities."[79] Recognizing this heterogeneity, the goal of scholars becomes to catalogue and metabolize these diverse movements of Duleep Singh in order to properly settle and digest a diverse past. This past is simultaneously integrated and polylogic, reduced to a historian's will. We know what the dead wanted, for their context—a diverse one—answers our questions. The historian identifies the bodily remains and localizes the dead.[80]

History, then, offers mourning in the present, a proper burial through the conquest of time. Although scholars have extensively questioned it, history has, Anidjar notes, "successfully managed to remain in fashion."[81] For even with the challenges, Anidjar continues, "one can hardly imagine, with any degree of seriousness, an *apologia pro vita historia* being written today, one that would argue that history is *not* bunk, that it is in fact important." Can we imagine "who would consciously oppose the claims of history?" Anidjar is right. As troubles increase we find continuous calls for more historicization rather than its end—concerned reminders that we need alternative genealogies, new methodologies, and better archival reading practices in order to finally create a generative history where we previously found impediments. Hope flashes as we realize those primary sources are not going to read themselves. Once we dust them off and become familiar with them (the task of professionalization), then the dead can be sewn together to produce ever more vigorous and plural histories, which we can even call "memory" now that it has been historicized.[82] Success is grasped through a frozen hold on time. In this repair, historians, like Ballantyne, can subsume difference into a singular complete reality across time and space. There is a reality out there that only requires cataloguing—a cataloguing that disavows the impossibility of such an integrative whole. The impossibility of cataloguing as such is masked as the relationship to Duleep Singh is repaired and settled in a fantasy of completed knowledge.

Though historians have argued for healing in burial, this is not so easy a task. As Lacan rightly contends, "the object here has an existence that is all the more absolute because it no longer corresponds to anything that exists."[83] One such resistant reaction to loss is melancholia, which Freud describes as a narcissistic identification with the lost object—an attempt to preserve the object by ingesting the object and the loss into oneself.[84] Melancholia, therefore, can function as an appropriation and preservation of loss itself, in which the ego defends against loss while reinscribing the very object it "lost."[85]

Mourning and melancholia, however, are not so easily divided into the normal and pathological. Tenacious attachments to a lost childhood such as Duleep Singh's, or political ideals such as the Khalsa Raj, are not so pathological as an easy diagnosis of them may imply.[86] Far from serving as a diagnosis of pathologies, examining melancholia has allowed scholars to uncover, investigate, and marshal discrepancies in how losses are experienced, inherited, and incorporated by communities, individuals, and traditions.[87] Looking at melancholia, in short, enables us to witness creative relations to loss.[88] These relations are both embodied and practiced.[89] A focus on melancholic attachments, for example, could allow us to see the colonial and postcolonial afterlives of the Khalsa Raj as well as Duleep Singh himself, and how peoples oriented toward him refuse to bury his memory, encircling the Khalsa Raj and its records.[90]

Still, conceptual troubles remain, as scholars have noted the problems of idealizing loss—especially upholding loss as a site of political possibility. Rebecca Comay addresses the oscillation between denigrating and overvaluing melancholia, and suggests an inquiry should not privilege "melancholia as somehow most responsible to the historical demands of an epoch devastated by the cumulative horror of its losses."[91] For loss can be preserved in melancholic attachment, incorporated, Pandolfo writes, as a trauma or "'phantom' [that] is transmitted across generations in the form of a crypt and a corpse within."[92] That is, Pandolfo continues, because loss can be resistant to "any possibility of experience, even unconscious experience, it cannot give rise to productive new forms and configurations of being."[93] In other words, this pathological grieving, melancholia, can preemptively deny loss by creating a fetish—a corpse in a crypt—that must be preserved.[94] In this creation, melancholia and fetishism can "collude to produce the illusion of an intact present—solitary, sufficient, immune from past or future threat" by appropriating the loss which is central to melancholia.[95] In this frame, melancholia does not signal creativity in relation to the past, but risks endlessly reproducing the present as already dead.[96] For example, one can remain attached to Ranjit Singh's Khalsa Raj, and in so doing participate in forming a community defined by its loss. Such a community would always take itself to the place of the dead in a fetishistic attachment. Or, more dangerously, the scholar, looking to recover the institution of a sovereign empire, can create the very fetish object they proclaim to be recovering and burying, cementing it as a static object through their writing.

For Brian Keith Axel, this is precisely the lesson that the act of recovering Duleep Singh illustrates. According to Axel, Duleep Singh functioned for Sikhs as a fetish object to fill the loss of sovereignty. Noting the long-lasting effects of Singh's surrender to the British in 1849, Axel cites the production of portraits of Singh after this event as reconstituting "the masculinized Sikh body" and transforming it "into an icon of the Sikh 'nation' itself subject to the Crown." The surrender and its attendant loss, Axel proclaims, is transformed and institutionalized into a new colonial Sikh subjectivity, further cemented through the global circulation and consumption of Franz Winterhalter's 1854 portrait of Duleep Singh. As Axel writes, through Winterhalter's well-known portrait, Sikhs were "at once transformed into prisoners and liberated as new colonial subjects." This transformation occurred because this new icon, the fetish, created a total body for Sikhs, collapsing difference within the Sikh tradition.[97] Winterhalter's depiction of Duleep Singh, Axel concludes, facilitated "a new process of subjectification," which constituted both an anterior point and possible futures in the emergence of the portrait-cum-fetish object.[98] Axel, then, historicizes a melancholic attachment to a fetish object for Sikhs. By centering the portrait as fetish object, Axel forecloses Sikh mourning of the surrender. Put differently, the loss leads to the fetishization of identity objectified in portraiture.

Yet despite their similar resonances, melancholia and fetishism should not be collapsed into each other as they often are, a process in which a lost object becomes a fetish object, that is, the lost Khalsa Raj becomes a fetish.

Instead, we have to remember how our understanding of fetishism itself has become fetishistic in narrowing the meaning to "fixation"—a synecdoche that occludes deeper aspects of fetishism.[99] This awareness is especially important, according to E. L. McCallum, since fetishism as a strategy neither incorporates nor annihilates the self or the object of loss.[100] Instead, McCallum argues, fetishism can help "a subject negotiate the difference between self and other(s)," as well as serve as a strategy to deal with anxiety and contradiction. A more fetishistic and less melancholic view of loss, McCallum continues, "entertains the possibility of multiple and satisfying negotiations of loss rather than reductively lump[ing] all losses indiscriminately into one totalizing loss."[101] Against this totalizing loss, the relation to loss marked by the fetish *could* also index a promise. Loss is not so easily internalized and hardened.[102]

Recognizing that fetishism could offer a robust analytic for loss, I focus on the degrees and kinds of losses that cannot be predicated on a neat distinction between subject and object, although neither can that distinction be collapsed.[103] Following this reading, a frozen and static Sikh community did not internalize Duleep Singh. Instead, in melancholic and fetishistic incorporation, the very constitution of discrete subjects and objects are challenged as we are forced to grapple with the production of meaning as contradictions and anxieties appear constantly.[104] This persistent grappling provides the opportunity to foreground reciprocity without capture. In this blur, time itself cannot be settled, since it too is discontinuous, not fixed, and retroactively able to take on different meanings as well.[105] We find the transmutation of melancholia into militancy under conditions of colonial occupation, as Frantz Fanon argued long ago.[106] Melancholia and the fetish, therefore, require we consider a fraught relationship with temporality, especially when inhabiting an unbearable historical aftermath.

In this unsettling, the fetish, such as Winterhalter's portrait of Duleep Singh, is not stable, as Axel contends. Rather, it is excessive, since the object itself reciprocates and changes as relations to Duleep Singh vacillate.[107] To call Duleep Singh a "prophetic maharaja" is to dwell in this excess. Prophecy refuses to abide by the logic in which past, present, and future proceed sequentially. Recall, as Maurice Blanchot argues, that in prophecy "it is not the future that is given, it is the present that is taken away, and with it the possibility of a firm, stable, lasting presence."[108] More simply, as a sovereign-to-come, a sovereign who was prophesized in Sikh scripture centuries before his time, Duleep Singh cannot be rooted or settled. Prophecy exceeds history. Still, to prophesize about Duleep Singh is not to leave the "fracas of history," but to dwell in the "momentary interruption of history," as prophecy to history "become[s] an instant of impossibility of history."[109] In prophecy history is no longer destiny; instead prophecy attests to a moment of what Ranajit Guha calls "self-estrangement."[110] Calculability wanes in prophecy; prophecy disturbs, what Silvia Federici calls, "the individual's spatio-temporal identification."[111] The disturbance of this identification has been critical to the Sikh tradition, as we know from the centrality of *hukam*. The intervention of *hukam* invites prophecy, which we see in Sikh texts that prophesize, to follow Louis Fenech, a "future Khalsa rule."[112] To learn about Duleep Singh as a prophetic maharaja reminds us then that the modern and the temporal reordering that modernity achieves—such as the sharp distinction between past and present—is never as stable as it presents itself. Temporality is much more fraught and volatile even though modernity renders it otherwise, exorcising its always-present ghosts.[113] This book is, therefore, in part an attempt to write a history of loss that endeavors the impossible by refusing the "carceral register of ends and meanings" central to history, even while being lodged within them.[114]

In this attempt, *Prophetic Maharaja* adds to the literature discussed in this section on how peoples have negotiated and struggled with loss. I argue that Sikhs cultivated an ethics of remembering and association around sovereignty that does not seek to settle relationships with the Khalsa Raj by forgetting it or turning it into a lost object, thereby creating a melancholic afterlife.[115] Instead I emphasize the tensions of the lost Khalsa Raj without privileging its internalization as a lost object that would only reify the Sikh tradition as an identity (an inscription of the colonial regime). This is especially important since the object of both the historian's and the historical subject's desire presents itself in vanishing, not lost, form.[116]

In the pages that follow I duly chip paint from the portrait, the fetish, of Duleep Singh. This chipping is a tedious and indifferent movement that is not concerned with exposing a "real" Duleep Singh behind the portraiture or with unmasking the empty canvas. Rather, it is a practice that takes enjoyment in the peeling of the paint itself.[117] After all, such peeling continuously reveals new formations, representing a dynamic relation to the fetish object that also marks our interlocutors' relationship to the Khalsa Raj. We can scratch the surface without end until we are "blue in the face."[118]

It might be a practice of failure, to follow Jack Halberstam, as the act of chipping away paint renders Duleep Singh and the Khalsa Raj into an infinitely unplumbable site.[119]

Chipping the portrait without end would dissipate the very frames of intelligibility that sustain it—a contingent encounter that disrupts the circulation of the symbolic mandate.[120] The Sikh tradition, too, draws our attention to this impossibility without dwelling within it and privileging lack and emptiness. For example, in the Sikh tradition it is the very immersion into the inarticulability, *naam* (the unsignifiable), through continual repetition, *naam simran* (to remember continuously), that founds and unsettles the world. The question of community also draws our attention to this unsettling, to this derailment, to this excess. Within the Sikh tradition, community is the *sangat*. The *sangat* sacrifices itself in its service (*seva*), its obligation, to all without wallowing in ego-assertion or ego-denial.[121] Sovereignty then is not tied to blood but to *halemi raj*, which Gurbhagat Singh explains is constituted by the "recognition of others without subjecting."[122] Sovereignty would be a consideration of community without constituting it as a "wider subjectivity."[123] It would be a sovereignty and community that is itself always already dislocated. It would be a drive at work within community itself, refusing to let it become immune; community cultivates its own autoimmunity.[124]

What we learn in the Sikh tradition then is that we should consider how history, such as a history of Duleep Singh, cannot be totally normalized, for history too is apertured, unable to circulate smoothly—a gap this book continuously encircles. It is this drive to chip away at the Khalsa Raj and Duleep Singh that structures this project rather than a desire to secure history, sovereignty, or—for that matter—impossibility.[125] The goal is to read the Khalsa Raj and Duleep Singh in different ways, in order to dwell in the excesses and the forms that emerge before us; as fixation itself yields a form of rupture.[126]

RELIGION AND COMMUNALISM

Questions of loss in South Asia have traditionally braided historical investigations into the encounter between colonial modernity and religion. The concept of loss is critical to understanding how "religion" has been understood in South Asia. Scholars of South Asia have argued that an imposition of colonial knowledge formations led to the loss of previously fluid religious communities, producing an afterlife of religious communalism.[127] In studies of Punjab, for instance, scholars have emphasized the colonial nature of the Sikh tradition at turn of the nineteenth century.[128] For example, Harjot Oberoi writes that during this period, "the older pluralist paradigm of Sikh faith was displaced forever and replaced by a highly uniform Sikh identity, the one we know today as modern Sikhism."[129] As the argument goes, colonialism did not create a Sikh tradition but rerouted its conceptual parameters. In the stronger version of this argument, colonialism completely stripped the Sikh tradition of its earlier syncretic elements.[130] Scholars have also noted how earlier pluralist and "fuzzy" forms of community resisted emergent forms of communalism.[131] Put differently, recognizing the ill effects of these so-called communal identities in the present, scholars of Punjab have turned to recuperating lost ways of being such as *Punjabiyat*, defined loosely as "a sentiment of belonging or attachment to Punjab and/or the foundations of a shared, cross-religious, cross-caste, cross-class culture" to challenge these hardened identities today.[132] Undergirded by a fantasy of loss, the goal of these histories of *Punjabiyat* thus becomes to recover and repair what was presumed lost, and to examine how people recover from various losses. Rather than contend with the constitutive nature of loss that makes history necessarily incomplete, scholars excavate history to settle the syncretic past (its fluidity) and the communalist present (its rigidity).[133]

Part of the significance of my project lies in arguing that contestations about the meaning of tradition in a historical moment cannot be sealed into either a recoverable prior form or the logic of communalism. My project refuses the wager of authenticity and continuity, but also, crucially, absolute and transhistorical loss. Rather than searching for a communal or golden past, I argue that debates around the Khalsa Raj in the late nineteenth century were a mode and model of ethical engagement that drew on past repositories within a tradition without hardening them. They did so in order to work through the loss of the Khalsa Raj and reinstitute Duleep Singh—a project that itself eludes clear meaning. I maintain that the various imaginings of the Khalsa Raj confound the dominant characterizations of colonialism and religion by turning our attention to disputations within tradition itself in a contingent moment. This argument directly challenges how the historiography of South Asia emphasizes stable and fluid inheritances or colonial communal demarcations. Put simply, I contend that to foreground the protean we need not argue through the multiple and shared. A psychoanalytic vocabulary provides the opportunity, as Eric Santner illustrates in the German context, to avoid the "maddening binary opposition: schizophrenic dissolution of identity/narcissistic respecularization of identity" that undergirds debates about identity in the present.[134] Eschewing this opposition, *Prophetic Maharaja* asks: Is it possible to highlight the internal alienness of Duleep Singh and the community? What is in the subject—more than the subject?

But historicist repair, further tightened through the inherent transgression posed by plurality, strips away the possibility of not only its own revisability but also its impossibility. I eschew such an approach to religion by keeping in mind the formidable work of Talal Asad. Tradition, Asad clarifies, is a site of contestation about founding texts that refuses suturing gestures that emerge from mourning, melancholia, but also, importantly, historical recovery.[135] Tradition, in other words, is not constituted through its preservation, which establishes a restricted historical temporality; it is instead engrossed in shifting synchronic and diachronic disputes that are mediated, as we saw earlier, by an authoritative vanishing point.[136] As Samira Haj perceptively reveals, though many scholars construct Islam as a reified totality, it is actually a "framework of inquiry within which Muslims have attempted to amend and redirect Islamic discourses to meet new challenges and conflicts as they materialized in different historical eras."[137] Following Asad and Haj, my point is that a Sikh "framework of inquiry," one that refuses the historical as an integrating principle, must take precedence against closure offered by communalist and pluralist renderings. There is a singular tradition, which is itself marked by discrepancies.[138]

Retheorizing tradition by placing disputation at its fore, *Prophetic Maharaja* demonstrates how temporalities continually converge and intersect, creating an assemblage that exist as contradictions, disturbances, and disjunctures. Such disturbance demands we take note of what gets elided in the singular homogenous time that privileges a particular body and historicity in which an answer to loss is easily grasped—archival recovery of the precolonial, for example, in which a temporal division is already laid bare. One way we can escape the historicist desire for closure through annihilation or accumulation (and their eventual turn to postmodern arbitrariness) is by foregrounding, as Alasdair MacIntyre proposes, tradition's "not-yet-completed narrative."[139] Inhabiting this not-yet-completed space, this book highlights the multiple different and contradictory positions that remain(ed) possible as Sikhs contest(ed) and shift(ed) positions in relation to the loss of the Khalsa Raj. This continually not-yet structure of a unified tradition, which refuses our desire for closure, requires we be more attentive, as Naveeda Khan urges, to how "time creates more movements, both actual and potential, than may be found within the historical records."[140]

Challenging expressions of a totalizing history, *Prophetic Maharaja* situates Duleep Singh in a tradition striving for coherence. By examining this striving embedded within the Sikh tradition around Duleep Singh, the book does not seek to restitute intelligibility around Duleep Singh. Instead it inhabits rather than transcends the colonial impasse by demanding we take seriously the contestations around Singh within a given but also temporally dislocated moment. This is, to repeat, a central task of the Sikh tradition itself in its emphasis on both *maryada* (conduct/ethical practice/ a limit), *naam* (the unsignifiable), and the play of different modalities.[141] Functioning as an unstable quilting point, disrupted by the Sikh tradition itself, Duleep Singh remained unable to weave his subjects into a unified body and instead provided ample opportunity for Sikhs that still considered the Khalsa Raj sovereign to (re)articulate sovereignty. The possibility for this rearticulation could be actualized through Singh's own impossibility. Duleep Singh's profound alienation from himself, sovereignty, and Punjab doubled as a profound creativity amongst Sikhs.[142]

A BIOGRAPHICAL DULEEP SINGH?
CHAPTERS AND STRUCTURE

What to make of the possibilities of Duleep Singh that are not tied to his own desires? This is a troublesome question since the possibilities need not be actual. In that sense, this book is not an explanation of Duleep Singh. There are already numerous biographies of him, since Duleep Singh the person remains an enthralling historical subject about whom narratives continue to proliferate. Narrativization, however, as Žižek writes, eliminates the paradoxes of loss noted earlier by "describing the process in which the object is first given and then gets lost."[143] In so doing, and through creating temporal succession, narrative resolves a fundamental impossibility in its ordering. And yet pure difference cannot exist, much like a pure essence or pure narrative or fantasy cannot exist. One must narrate. Recall what Gayatri Spivak has taught us: "Radical discontinuity cannot appear, like pure difference, remember, essences cannot appear either."[144] Instead, Spivak contends, "Discontinuity must traffic in minimal continua." We must "go back to *ce qui reste*, fragments of essences to reckon with."[145]

In the chapters that follow, I, too, oscillate—going back to the fragments of Duleep Singh's narrative while locating its breaks and fissures and reckoning with the organization that emerged around Duleep Singh at the end of the nineteenth century. In this sense I am simultaneously grasping and ungrasping Duleep Singh, locating both continuity and discontinuity as narrative spills across the pages.[146] I both grasp and ungrasp by driving at Duleep Singh again and again while refusing to engulf the specific coordinates of loss, the particular symbolic mandates, into a larger absence while at the same time destabilizing those symbolic coordinates.

Chapter 1, "Community," begins by examining the anxiety surrounding Duleep Singh's potential return to Punjab in relation to community. I examine the notion of community by exploring both the colonial administration's fears about Duleep Singh and the unpredictability of his travels. I also explore the uncertainty that emerged within the Sikh community through considering how portrayals and stories about Duleep Singh circulated anonymously in Punjab in print and letters. Finally, the chapter surveys how anonymity was interpreted through hidden transcripts, providing an avenue to reflect on a different form of community: a dislocated one.

The second chapter, "The Public," focuses on both the public sphere and the analytic challenges that the concept brings. How might we think about the public and publicity through the relationship between Duleep Singh and the emerging print industry in late nineteenth-century Punjab? I address this question through a detailed exploration of Duleep Singh's contested and deceptive reception in the public sphere. As I illustrate, fears persisted among colonial officials about the capacity of the Sikh "population" of Punjab to distinguish between belief and knowledge. The chapter then explores the problem of the archive in relation to the Sikh population in Bengal, where intrigues surrounding Duleep Singh had also spread. I conclude by arguing that the archive disrupts such analysis, refusing adjudication in modern historical form.

Duleep Singh himself did not only circulate through hidden transcripts and print. As noted, Duleep Singh converted back to Sikhism in Aden in

1886, at which point he also pledged to take his rightful place as a heroic Sikh sovereign. The third chapter, "Conversion," traces the possible meanings of Singh's conversion. Specifically, it explores the stakes of the conversion/ reversion for sovereignty. Rather than center Duleep Singh's intentions, I drive at the various ethical practices undertaken by Duleep Singh to prepare for his return to the Sikh fold which, importantly, would also legitimate his return into the community.

As noted, the British ultimately thwarted Duleep Singh's return to the subcontinent. His attempts to cohere opposition to British colonialism thus took him to Paris in 1886 and eventually Moscow in 1887 as he looked to take advantage of imperial rivalries. He also cultivated ties with Muslim revolutionaries and the leaders of princely states. "Rumors," the fourth chapter, explores the nature of rumors related to Duleep Singh's attempts to foment revolt in his homeland. Rumors were central in disseminating news of Duleep Singh's possible return to Punjab and spread throughout the globe. I examine how these rumors traveled and how peoples sought to organize around Duleep Singh across communities.

These very attempts to organize meant there was disputation in the Sikh tradition. Chapter 5, "Reform," highlights these disputations. I explore how the Singh Sabha, a Sikh reform movement that reached its height in the 1880s, debated, deployed, and organized around Duleep Singh. I demonstrate how religious reform was a site of intense conflict that reveals the processes of argumentation within the contours of a tradition, even as the colonial state sought to continually mediate the terms of reform. Embedded within a frame of inquiry provided by the Sikh tradition, the contestations that constituted reform within the Sikh tradition remained intimately tied to the question of sovereignty. These debates surrounding Duleep Singh therefore disclose the contentious engagements within a tradition that cannot be reduced to binary designations such as colonial construct/indigenous inheritance or religious/political.

Taken together, these chapters bear witness to how reconstructing historical relationships—between for example Duleep Singh, community, and sovereignty—forces us into the realm of impossibility, since such relationships continually exceed their placement. The abyss that constitutes both Duleep Singh and sovereignty reveals how the continual injunction to provide resolution to loss through historicization encounters its limits. In this reckoning, contested visions surround a polyvalent Duleep Singh, a sovereign who could never inhabit himself.

Revealing the difficulty of demarcating historical parameters, *Prophetic Maharaja* foregrounds how the always present failure of fantasy provides opportunity to rethink our historical-conceptual assumptions. It strives to confound the desire to produce a narrative that sanctions a neat, knowable figure of Duleep Singh that we can then catalogue, providing historical satisfaction. This means that learning about the Khalsa Raj, Duleep Singh, the Sikh tradition, and even loss is much more difficult than the accumulative social sciences have it, since, as Anidjar stresses, "learning—the deceptively simple task of taking a step toward a knowledge of self or other—does mean exposing oneself to an enormous mass of unknowns. To uncertainty and to incompleteness. Or to denial, and to the possibility of failure. Is there, in fact, a self? And is it ours? Can we really know ourselves?"[147] That is my attempt here: to learn about loss, the Khalsa Raj, and Duleep Singh without end, without satisfaction, and open to the possibility of failure.

Chapter One

COMMUNITY

What is the community made of? It is a strange enough question to ask. Yet, and stranger still, it appears to have been routinely answered.

—GIL ANIDJAR

Though central to working through loss of the Khalsa Raj, Duleep Singh's personal motive and intention, the murky corridors of historical detail, also fail to fully constitute his relation to Punjab and South Asia more broadly. Attempts to reinstitute the Khalsa Raj did not rest upon Duleep Singh's intentional actions, which then either coalesced or thwarted the possibility for action within a community, the *sangat*. I seek here to understand how a sense of community was fostered, rather than taking community as a given subject or an object to be mastered. Therefore, I ask a series of inter-related questions about Duleep Singh and community, including: How did the demands that Duleep Singh made to the colonial state forge community? How did these claims circulate in Punjab? How did this community exceed and disrupt Duleep Singh's own intentions by situating him in the Sikh tradition? How was the community around Duleep Singh interrupted, refusing clear demarcation?

My goal in asking such questions is to consider community outside the parameters of homogenous national totality versus lost diversity that dominate the historiographical landscape of South Asia. Put plainly, this chapter refuses to answer the question "What is the community made of?"[1] Though there was a shift in understanding who and what constituted a community in the nineteenth century as blood became central to kin relations in Punjab, I contemplate an alternative to the readily available questions and answers.[2] Specifically, examining the struggle around Duleep Singh offers an opportunity to refuse the very terms of community. We learn instead how people forged and reforged a sense of community that was not tied to blood or pluralism, but to questions that emerged, for example, within the Sikh tradition.

Community has been a central problem in the historiography of South Asia. As Partha Chatterjee argues, "community, which ideally should have been banished from the kingdom of capital, continues to lead a subterranean, potentially subversive, life within it because it refuses to go away."[3] How to consider this refusal, this subterranean life? The continuity of community is grounded in a mythic sense of community, as Shail Mayaram has discussed, that refuses incorporation. Myth suggests, Mayaram writes, "a culture's coding of truth-values through narrative," which provides "a space to access resistance," especially so "when it expresses communal memory and becomes a contestatory site with respect to the official memory of the state."[4] To think about myth requires we take into account the imaginative and, perhaps, prophetic possibilities embedded within an incomplete, insecure world.[5] These possibilities do not signal, to follow George Sorel, that myths or prophecies are "astrological almanacs"; it remains "possible [that] nothing which they contain will come to pass." But, even absent realized futurity, myths and prophecies serve as "a means of acting on the present" through inspiring a struggle to create an ever-impossible indivisible unity. Therefore, against relying on the conceit of a finished or lost world, by dwelling within a prophetic conception of Duleep Singh I strive to understand what Sorel describes as "the activity, the sentiments and the ideas of the masses as they prepare themselves to enter on a decisive struggle," a struggle without a definitive past, present, or future even though providing a narrative to a community being forged.[6]

Yet, in foregrounding myth, a community can become a stable entity; a community coalescing around myth can produce, for example, a communal identity. By tracing a myth around Duleep Singh, then, am I not upholding "community" in its reified sense? Is it possible to examine how the community that arose around Duleep Singh repudiates, rather than sanctions, mastery? Can such a community refuse a neat diagnostic answer that would allow us to trace precolonial authenticity or the emergence of a colonized people? I want to argue that we can avoid such troubles by centering prophecy in relation to myth. That is to say, prophecy attunes us to a second operation within the community that arose around Duleep Singh after the foundation of a community by myth, which interrupted that very community.[7] Recall what Esposito teaches: a community is not just identified with its common thing, with its "myth," but also "the hole into which the common thing continually risks falling." The myth cannot be separated from the no-thing that is the common ground.[8] That is, by studying the prophetic aspects of Singh and his following we can see myth's illusory wholeness; we can see how the myth of a community around Duleep Singh was also continuously interrupted. That is to say, if we couple myth and prophecy, then we also have to consider how there is an interruption of the self-actualization of myth, since prophecy never arrives: it cannot be fulfilled.

Occupying this prophetic conception of community, I do not uphold a mythic Duleep Singh to escape limit and loss, for Duleep Singh as a myth of community, as the common thing of a community, would function to produce a total fantasy such as a national fantasy.[9] In such a totalizing myth, Duleep Singh, as the embodiment of a unifying leader, a monument to the past, would fuse together a collective Sikh communal identity. As a traceable and fortifying object, Duleep Singh would cultivate a "being of togetherness" against "being-with," in turn producing communalism today.[10] But since the Khalsa Raj was still to come, it was not filled in by a mythic community as community was constituted through an acknowledgment of its limit, thereby continuously interrupting its own constitution, interrupting the concretization of loss, as Duleep Singh was incessantly translated back into Punjab.[11]

By studying Duleep Singh and his following, then, we also encounter incommensurable accounts of community, not the certainty of nationalism or communalism. The political maneuvering of both colonial officials and the elite remained unstable as they tried to account for the broader community and their relation to Duleep Singh—a community that refused to be bound within accepted political coordinates.

The discourse surrounding Duleep Singh is best understood by what James C. Scott calls public and hidden transcripts.[12] These transcripts exist as forms of safely deferent (public) and a sharply dissident (hidden) political culture. The public transcripts were translated into hidden ones and then back again. The Subaltern Studies Collective demands we occupy this dislocated space in the South Asian context, reminding us that colonial rule was not hegemonic in the subcontinent. For example, Ranajit Guha writes, "there was a faultline that cut across the entire society," which created different forms of dissociated mobilization.[13] Within these fault lines, however, in "the contest between two kinds of politics" (state and community), the question becomes how to dignify a "textual site for a struggle to reclaim for history an experience buried in a forgotten crevice of our past."[14] How to dignify a hidden script, which is necessarily hidden? How to be responsible toward—not recover—a lost subaltern site, hidden transcripts, that both capture and confound Duleep Singh in their silence?

Working through the bifurcation between "hidden transcript" and "public transcript" is not to reproduce Partha Chatterjee's seminal distinction between inner and outer, in which the intelligentsia in their anticolonial nationalism conceded an outer realm of Western statecraft and economy while proclaiming difference within an inner, spiritual self, grounded in cultural identity.[15] Rather, my reading of transcripts foregrounds the gap within the bifurcated political order Chatterjee aptly details to dwell in the loss that emerges within that very separation. Politics in late nineteenth-century Punjab remained unable to be neatly tied in either home or world, inner or outer, subaltern or nationalist, and instead shattered those very coordinates that created a sensible version of politics in the colonial period. As Scott argues, even in what appears to strictly follow the symbolic rules of an ideological edifice, the safe deferent public discourse can exceed its very parameters—unsettling the community, nation, or people it looks to reinscribe.[16] On the subaltern end, Spivak notes such a discrepancy in recovery, asking us to instead consider the irreducibility of the subaltern by refusing the "desire for totality (and therefore totalization)" and, thus, to fix subaltern presence, to fill that loss with the historical record.[17]

Duleep Singh recounts such an unfinished narrative. It is a narrative continually interrupting its own recitation without melancholic fixation and mourned break: both then, but also now. In other words, though understandings of Duleep Singh are located within a hidden subaltern script and public elite script, working through the loss of the Khalsa Raj also signals how Duleep Singh exceeded those parameters, providing the historian an opportunity to dwell within, rather than transcend loss.

A SAFE DULEEP SINGH

But what were those parameters? Colonial officials observed the danger of Duleep Singh's prophetic possibilities as an organizing political mechanism within the subcontinent when he made inquiries about visiting Punjab in 1882. Though there were vague rumblings of discontent prior, Duleep Singh explicitly began to pressure the colonial state to acquiesce to his financial demands in the late 1870s. His bid to return to Punjab emerged from these financial problems, which grew increasingly dire into the 1880s. Duleep Singh claimed that he was entitled to more property than he was being given—property tied to questions of political power, as the legitimacy of Duleep Singh threw the Treaty of Lahore into question. Duleep Singh threatened to return to Punjab in order to dispense of these financial difficulties. He issued such proclamations and requests privately, looking to force the state's hand into granting him a larger stipend. Officials, however, denied these requests and amassed a legion of paperwork to undermine the validity of Duleep Singh's pecuniary claims.

Duleep Singh became a threat, and the bureaucratic regime mined evidence, accumulating its own historical evidence to counter Duleep Singh's claims. But even after his requests to alleviate his pecuniary difficulties went largely unheeded, Duleep Singh still followed a safe form of political discourse tied to citizenship, which took, to follow Scott, "as its basis the flattering self-image of elites." This official discourse consisted of letters and petitions directed toward the British state using the language of British rights. Duleep Singh's argument that he be allowed to return to India was premised on the terms of citizenship. Travel was a right of all British citizens, Duleep Singh contended, that therefore could not be denied to him. Duleep Singh deployed this "public transcript of deference" in his communications with the colonial state—a discourse that not only sought to appease colonial authorities but also quelled possibilities embedded within a community grounded in the Khalsa Raj, since it was tied instead to questions of rights premised within the abstract individual.[18]

For example, in a petition written privately to the India Office on March 29, 1882, Duleep Singh asked for an increase in his income by arguing that he was a "humble petitioner" who, "throwing himself entirely upon the Christian charity and generosity of the British nation," implored that a "more equitable and just arrangement may be entered into with him."[19] Even as he became more agitated with the state's refusal to acquiesce to his demands, Duleep Singh still declined to put into writing the possibility of autonomous social action outside the purview of the state. In this refusal, Singh moved within a colonial choreography that required he continuously affirm the state bureaucracy's all-encompassing reach, which in turn precluded the very sovereignty Singh sought to reclaim.

But, Scott argues, though the "elite-dominated public transcript tends to naturalize domination," there remains some "countervailing influence" that denaturalizes that very domination.[20] These influences were not located within either a public or hidden transcript; they bled into each other creating sites of indirect speech that defied authorities publicly though remaining indefinite. Duleep Singh's indeterminate sarcastic wit was hardly absent in his communications with the state. On April 16, 1882, he derided the state's failures, writing, "an opportunity has presented itself for me to go into business as a jeweler and diamond merchant, for I desire by my own industry and frugality, as well as by strict economy to add to the provision made for my children as much as I can."[21]

Straddling the line between insubordination and obedience, Duleep Singh demanded that the state measure up to its own liberal ideals. Following these ideals would grant Duleep Singh freedom of movement and the right to sell his labor freely, thereby defying the constraints of both the Treaty of Lahore and British royal expectations, which required he maintain a royal lifestyle in exile. Shedding these determinations of the colonial state, Duleep Singh argued he should be allowed to function as an anonymous citizen; "surely, my Lord," he wrote to the Marquis of Hartington in July 1882, "as the English justice acknowledges no difference between man and man, ought I not to be treated on the same footing of equality with my servants who are allowed to retain their estates?" Deprived of revolutionary options, imprisoned as he was on the imperial island, Singh sought to use the very (il)liberal language that rendered him an exile in the first place to find an escape. As he ended his note, he remained "still trusting your Lordship's and the Home Government's high sense of justice and British liberality," a trust he hoped would return him to Punjab.[22]

Colonial officials, however, repeatedly refused to accede to his demands, which would supersede the very logic of empire in which Indians could not exist as citizens. The Marquis of Hartington did not even respond to this last inquiry. The bureaucracy churned, trying to determine the nature of private property within Ranjit Singh's Khalsa Raj in order to establish which property Duleep Singh could claim as his. Generally, in these determinations, the state ruled against Duleep Singh, reducing his claims to a fantasy. The decisions centered a law of economic calculability and efficiency as the ultimate determinate for action. This understanding served to reveal both Duleep Singh's avarice and indolence, measured through his failure to manage his royal estate. In short, the state argued that Duleep Singh was responsible for his own financial difficulties. In order to discipline and correct his behavior while weaning him from his state subsidy, colonial officials sought to morally and materially improve Duleep Singh, demanding that, for example, he institute certain changes in how he administered his estate in order to make more productive and profitable use of his land.[23] Turning this argument and its underlying logic of self-sufficiency to his own benefit, Duleep Singh would soon legitimate his sojourn to Punjab in such terms. He argued, for instance, "My sole object in return to India is to lay by money for my family, while myself fully enjoying the comforts I have been accustomed to all my life, and Delhi presents the best field for the purpose, as by advancing savings from my stipend to the *ryots* on crops of indigo in that neighbourhood as much as 25 to 30 per cent per annum can be obtained on invested capital."[24]

On August 31, 1882, Duleep Singh followed the option available to a rational autonomous individual in liberal society and took his grievances to the public sphere by publishing a letter in the London *Times*. In it he presented a similar line of reasoning as he had in his private correspondence with the state officials; he followed the official discourse albeit in a public venue. Duleep Singh noted that as a child he was innocent in the intrigues that led to annexation and, thus, was wrongly injured by being treated in the same manner as those South Asians guilty of directly defying the British. Moreover, he continued, since the colonial state took him as a dependent, he experienced more loss than others. He argued that the state allowed those beneath him to keep their estates whereas he, "who did not even lift up my little finger against the British nation," was not "considered worthy to be treated on the same footing of equality with them because, I suppose my sin being that I happened to be the ward of a Christian power." Duleep Singh ended his plea by appealing to his readers' liberal sensibilities one last time, asking, "Generous and Christian Englishmen, accord me a just and liberal treatment for the sake of the fair name of your nation, of which I have now the honour to be a naturalised member, for it is more blessed to give than to take."[25]

Duleep Singh's efforts to convince the state to either increase his revenue or allow him to return to Punjab failed, though, perhaps, still arriving at their destination, purloined by unintended eyes: the community. He was denied entry into Punjab on the grounds that, while his intentions might be limited to the official transcript (his claim toward British citizenship), a hidden transcript, in which Duleep Singh was signified outside the parameters of the liberal state, was far too dangerous. The danger emerged since it was wielded anonymously. The letter Duleep Singh published in the *Times*, which was tied to the official discourse, was, colonial officials noted, "reproduced in a number of the vernacular newspapers and caused some sensation in Lahore. The people were said to anticipate the Maharaja's arrival with joy as they considered him to be the rightful sovereign of the country."[26]

The editors of the *Times* strongly rebutted Duleep Singh's financial claims and sought to manage the reach of his assertions; they sought to deny any claim to the sovereignty of Punjab. The goal was to make sure interpretations of Singh's claims remained tied to official discourse, reducing Duleep Singh's claims to a cold economic rationality. For example, the editors contended, "his arguments concerning his *de jure* sovereignty of the Punjab is manifestly only intended to support his pecuniary claims. If these were settled to his satisfaction, he would doubtless be content, and more than content, to die, as he lived, an English country gentleman, with estates swarming with game and with an income sufficient for his needs."[27] Notably, Queen Victoria herself intervened in this debate, writing to Duleep Singh to abandon his public decrees, which blurred the line between official and mythic depending on reading practice. She wrote, "If I might advise you—it would be better not to write in the papers. It is beneath you to do so. Is there no one on whose wise and impartial opinion you could rely and whose advice in these difficult questions would be of use to you?"[28]

But Duleep Singh could not be reduced to his own individual. Worried about Duleep Singh's possible travels to Punjab, a colonial official wrote to Duleep Singh on October 23, 1882 and conveyed to him that, though he was "at liberty to proceed to India," his movement across the subcontinent had to conform with the viceroy's instructions, which meant that it was "improbable that permission will be accorded you to visit the Punjab."[29] Officials in the Government of India found the possibility of such a visit to not only

Punjab, but "Sind and Kashmir and certain districts of the North-Western Provinces and Rajputana" untenable, and argued Duleep Singh be refused entry into India altogether.[30] This position was rooted in the view, as Sir Charles Aitchison argued on August 7, 1883, that though Duleep Singh's "conversion to Christianity and his long residence in England have greatly estranged him from the Punjab people," such circumstance does not "remove all political danger [of his return], though it may minimize it."[31] Specifically, Aitchison argued that Duleep Singh's relation to both his father, Ranjit Singh, and the Khalsa in the public imagination created conditions wherein historical particulars, such as Duleep Singh's conversion to Christianity, became confounded and different understandings of community took hold. Recall how the Khalsa Raj was a formidable threat and it's expansive rule in the early nineteenth century. Colonial officials recognized this and stressed the importance of Ranjit Singh's name, a name that was no longer his alone. As Aitchison continued, there was "a whole generation still alive who were his devoted followers and who took prominent part in the events which led to the over throw of the Khalsa power after his death."[32] Although Duleep Singh's struggles were tied to his economic difficulties, we find that a community also coalesced around his absence marked by patronym—an absence marked by the possible return of Ranjit Singh.

The magical element attached to Duleep Singh, officials worried, would fashion an illusory unity among the Sikh community, which would in turn nurture the possibility for direct action against the colonial state. This possibility of unity and its uncertain potentials terrified British authorities, for it defied the colonial regime's attempted delimitation of history in which the loss of Ranjit Singh's empire was a death knell to the Khalsa Raj. Loss was no longer just loss. As Aitchison argued, "It is impossible to predict what might be the effect, under such circumstances, of the appearance of the son of Ranjit in the Punjab, especially if, as is most likely, he came with a grievance and as the claimant either of power or of property of which we have deprived him."[33]

In this reading Duleep Singh signaled a discrepancy that revealed time's openness, and thus the vulnerability of colonial sovereignty, in which a Khalsa Raj endured as a possibility, even though discussion of the possibility was quelled in the public discourse. By reopening time in such a manner, Duleep Singh's potential visit revealed the state's failure to bind temporality and inculcate conditions of predictability. The name of Duleep Singh, now turned into a common noun, challenged the colonial regime's attempt to secure its monopoly over both history and temporality within the subcontinent—its attempts to fill the gaps.[34] However, even in the face of such questioning, colonial officials claimed sovereignty over the temporal becoming of the subcontinent in order to create a proper relation between the state and population.[35] Looking to manage time in relation to Duleep Singh and the Sikh population, Aitchison argued "the appearance of any of the family in the Punjab is just a generation too soon," though "fifty years hence the son of the Maharaja might be received as a guest in Government House at Lahore like any other gentleman."[36]

In the present, however, Aitchison argued that Duleep Singh must be "kept out of Punjab, and made to amusing himself at the Calcutta Exhibition and in other comparatively harmless ways." In order to create an acceptable possible future, Duleep Singh could not appear in Punjab because, Aitchison continued, "the appearance of the Maharaja himself at this time would certainly cause great anxiety to the Government, and might easily be made use of by ill-disposed persons to create excitement and disturbance."[37] He feared this excitement would not exist within particular communities such as the Namdharis alone but would create a popular movement across the subcontinent. This concern was shared by the missionary Reverend A. Gordon, who wrote a letter to Colonel Gordon Young contending, "The presence of Ranjit Singh's heir in India just now, particularly within his known ambition might, I fear, become the occasion of a popular movement."[38] For colonial officials, even if Duleep Singh had no inclination to cause opposition to colonial rule, "it is very certain that he could not prevent mischief being done in his name, and, if he once lands in India, to detain him will cause excitement only one degree less injurious than to leave him uncontrolled."[39] Considering these organizational capacities that Duleep Singh provided the people outside his own will and intent, the administration rejected even the earlier suggested modified excursion into the subcontinent and refused Singh's travel into India altogether. Or, looking to quell the explosive nature of this mythic and prophetic Duleep Singh, that could turn the world upside down, the British state sought to manage both Duleep Singh's body and the excitable dispositions it could generate in the broader colonized peoples.[40]

ANONYMOUS DULEEP SINGH

This fear among colonial officials was not unfounded paranoia, for the name of Duleep Singh was invoked to mobilize and incite revolt among the Sikh community, even without Duleep Singh setting foot on the Indian subcontinent. As Aitchison wrote to Grant on August 7, 1883, the "Maharaja's name is already being used as a political cry!"[41] Aitchison cited in particular an incident three days prior in which anonymous letters demanding the addressee revolt against the British were sent to leading figures in Punjab. Deputy Commissioner of Lahore W. O. Clarke too noted the presence of such letters, writing that he possessed a letter "received by Nawab Abdul Majid Khan, and all the leading men here have received similar letters."[42] The letters exclaimed "India for the Indians only" while imploring the receiver to wear a piece of black cloth, which was enclosed, as a "sign of brotherhood and friendship." In the final line of the letter, Duleep Singh's name was invoked as a rallying cry to tie together the broader community: the letter concluded by asking its recipients to "Remember Surendronauth Banerjee of Calcutta / Be true to our race as Indians, strike now or never, / A Maharaja Dhulip Singh-ki-jai [Victory to Duleep Singh]."[43]

By tying Duleep Singh to the recently arrested Banerjea, the proprietor and editor of the *Bengalee*, the letter sought to link together different forms of struggle under a broader banner of resistance. Notably, the letter tied this hoped-for movement to an Indian nation—one constituted by a racial community. This form of "Indianness" was centered around Bengali political direction at the time, which also spread to Punjab. As S. C. Mittal clarifies, "it was due to its contact with the English-knowing Bengalis settling down in Punjab, that the elite in Punjab began to emulate them in their style of politics." Banerjea himself toured Punjab in 1887, when he formed the Lahore Indian Association, what Mittal calls, the "first political organization of importance in Punjab."[44] After Banerjea's arrest and imprisonment in 1883 for contempt of court for an article published in the *Bengalee*, there were multiple organized agitations in both Bengal and Punjab that clamored for his release.[45] For example, Anil Seal writes, student communities in Bengal "went into a frenzy of protest" and "held protest meetings, threw stones at Europeans, and generally followed Surendranath's injunction that they should agitate if he were sent to prison."[46] In Punjab protesters met in Lahore, decrying Banerjea's arrest. The principal speaker, Dewan Narendra

Nath, proclaimed: "We never united together for a common cause, that spirit of keeping aloof died away and now Punjabis and Bengalis shake hands with each other as brothers. Surendra Babu's imprisonment contributed towards the consummation of Indian unity, hence I call it an occasion for national rejoicing rather than national mourning."[47]

Thus it follows, as Kenneth Jones argues, that Banerjea's imprisonment was one of series of incidents in the nineteenth century that brought into focus what "proved to be 'national' questions transcending regional and religious differences."[48] The Annual Report of the Indian Association for 1883 noted that Banerjea received consolation for his imprisonment: "his misfortune awakened, in a most marked form, a manifestation of unity among the different races, for the accomplishment of which he has so earnestly striven and not in vain."[49]

But this rhetoric from Banerjea and the Indian Association, like the conclusions drawn by Jones, cultivates the notion of a particular type of community premised upon a telos of national unification rather than revealing the (im)possible range of community. Community becomes a lost object that elicits political desire—a quest for homeostasis and recovery that only elicits more desire.[50] Yet, as Sanjay Seth argues, the Indian nationalist project was exclusive, not only because of socioeconomic divisions but through a discursive strategy premised on the notion that "some Indians were not ready."[51] This apprehension of the masses and the incompleteness of the Indian project meant the community could not be enveloped within colonial, national, communal, religious, or racial formations (all of which are co-concealing categories).[52] Instead, community remained open to various imaginative, at times enclosing, possibilities. Put another way, if nationalism, as Sudipta Kaviraj contends, was "a field of ideas rather than as a doctrine—evolving, unstable, volatile, capable of sudden shifts in emphasis and political direction," then the very field of ideas that get constituted as nationalism were irreducible to a nationalist rubric.[53] Ultimately, Sumit Sarkar writes, a unified rubric would be located in "images of subcontinental unity (or at least 'unity-in-diversity') extending back into a supposedly glorious past," which even absent political unity became conceptualized through "some kind of cultural or civilization integration."[54] Within this national gerrymandering, various regional and dynastic struggles are united into a singular "Indian" history.[55] However, in 1883, what this past would include remained open, a struggle to determine what Indianness would be or if Indianness was even a worthwhile organizational mechanism.[56] Community was not yet a lost object; it was not organized around a "thing" hence the worries about race and religion. These contestations, therefore, created conditions of possibility for certain nodal points, or myths, such as those surrounding Duleep Singh, to tie together peoples with pasts and futures irreducible to Ranjit Singh's empire or emergent Indian nationalism and its accompanying racial, religious, and cultural logic.

For the colonial administration, this is precisely where the danger of Duleep Singh lay. He offered a possibility to retroactively tie what they considered the "uncivilized" and fragmentary nature of the colonized together under a broader heading that elite politics had not reached nor wanted to touch. The abstraction of a diverse colonial "population" unable to function as a unified whole had emerged as a central understanding in the colonial state's attempt to manage and control the subcontinent post-1857, in which the mutiny became rendered an anthropological failure instead of a political revolution.[57] In the late nineteenth century, Karuna Mantena details, "imperial rule was often constructed as a necessity for curtailing the tendency of native societies toward dissolution, born of endemic internecine conflict, (more subtly) from contact with modern civilization."[58] This pretext of a divided and irreconcilable "population" in the subcontinent necessitated extensive ethnographic research and documentation of native society to prolong indirect imperial rule, which would serve as a balm for the "traditional" divisions that made governance difficult in the first place.

Within these demarcations, colonial officials sought to determine the loyalty and susceptibility of segments of the population in order to structure imperial rule. For example, in 1885 British administrator and official Lepel Griffin wrote to the viceroy, Lord Dufferin, to argue that "the fighting races will, indeed, and have through all historic times have been ready to see their swords to any master for a sufficient wage. But patriotism is an unknown idea; and it would be easy to persuade a shoemaker to make shoes without payment as a Rajput or a Sikh to become an unpaid volunteer."[59] Griffin described the subcontinent as divided due to the hereditary organization of the population, which meant politics narrowly defined alongside discontent would only be tied to specific racial groups, such as Bengalis, which the state could effectively control. Griffin continued, in case of revolt:

The principal classes which would then, in Punjab, fill the ranks of the volunteers are precisely those of which the least use for military purposes can be made. Every occupation in India is hereditary, and bravery and military skill and fidelity are attached, by immemorial prescription, to warlike races, such as the Sikhs, Rajput, and Gorrkhas. The cowardice of the bania or Kayath is not, in popular repute, disgraceful, for it has been as consecrated by prescription as the prostitution of the Kanchan. Vices and failings, as well as virtues and accomplishments, enjoy in India hereditary honors.[60]

Though Griffin's ethnographic musings referenced what many understood to be irreconcilable racial and religious divisions within society, the state remained concerned with how possible unity could be forged. For even though the assumed innate sectarian nature of the population rendered unity difficult and located the possibility of politics strictly within a modern English educated elite class that could only be unrepresentative, authorities worried how new social conditions wrought under the impact of British rule could cultivate new alliances and coordination.[61] Accordingly, the question became how to control the possibility of politics or, at the very least, maintain it within the coordinates of the elite class and civilizing impact of British rule.

Therefore, in order to determine the type of unity the letter sent to prominent Punjabis in August 1882 sought to cultivate, the central task for colonial officials became to establish who sent the letters. W. O. Clarke argued that this would be quite easy since, he wrote, "the postmarks show all the letters appear to have been posted in the train at Amritsar."[62] But another colonial official, John Herdon, demurred, contending that knowing the postmark alone would not make it easy to discover who "posted the letters in the Mail Van." He continued, observing "the station is always heavily crowded and such letters might be easily thrown into the Van without the sender, or the person posting them, being known."[63] Herdon was right; officials could only conjecture who the source of the letter was. For Inspector-General C. Brune, the obvious culprits were the educated elite: Bengali *babus* who were trying to use Duleep Singh to agitate for their own gain, since their popularity did not extend into the broader population. He looked to fix authorship and wrote of the letter that it was "a very mischievous production as, although evidently the work of some *babu*, it purports to be from the Maharaja Dhulip Singh."[64] The viceroy concurred and wrote that the letter that circulated in Lahore and Amritsar was "apparently work of Bengali[s], as it is referred mainly to case of Surendra Nath Banerji in whom Punjabis are not interested."[65] On August 16, 1883, the District Superintendent of Police at Amritsar reported "he had heard privately that the letters had been sent to Lahore by Yusaf Shah, a member of the Municipal Committee of Amritsar" and "a rather pronounced reformer."[66] But fears remained that Bengalis and overt desire for reform were not to blame, and that something else was afoot. Clarke, for example, speculated that the letter was "likely done by students, but I have also I heard that it was done by the Akalis [nihangs]" who, another memorandum footnoted, were "Sikh zealots."[67] Looking to downplay the potential threat posed by such fanaticism, both the viceroy and Aitchison continually reiterated that the letter was of "no great importance."[68] But the political possibilities that surrounded Duleep Singh remained unstable and signaled possibilities as the letter indicated the "use that might be made of Dhulip Singh's name."[69]

Despite downplaying the import of the letters, danger remained since the state could adjudicate neither their aim nor their sender. Even four years later, in summarizing the affair, colonial administrators noted that the letters remained anonymous.[70] The state's insistence on unveiling the true intentions of the purloined letter by discovering the sender's identity reveals the difficulties it faced in maintaining an ever-unstable colonial order. Looking to discover the identity of the sender and the letter's content, colonial officials sought to articulate a clear relation between content and political aim, reiterating an appropriate conceptual repository for what both colonial sovereignty and community could constitute. Where was the "thing," the sender, that identified the community?

Seeking to determine the sender(s) of the letter and its content, the central task of the state and the Indian functionaries who populated the colonial bureaucracy, an emerging elite, was to manage the symbolic circuit. They looked to manage the possible roles the letter brought forth in order to assuage the discontinuities and displacements the letter also laid bare: the lack of meaning itself within the colonial order. But the existence of such a letter situated the community not only in a symbolic order in which the community could act accordingly but also, as Lacan notes in another context, in "a symbolic chain foreign to the one which constitutes loyalty."[71] That is, though the British sought to possess and assign authorship to the letters, the letters could never be possessed; they refused to be secured in their elusiveness. This elusiveness, articulated through the circulation of the letters, reveals the split nature of the community, the incompleteness of symbolic bonds, demanding we consider both determinations and their dismemberment (both thing and nothing in community). In short, the danger of being otherwise remained potent. As the viceroy acknowledged, Duleep Singh's name revealed this very impossibility within the structuring limits of the colonial symbolic, the incalculable community, thereby opening the political terrain for resignification.

And this was the case, as letters continually arrived at their destinations, thwarting the symbolic chain the British state sought to preserve. The letters remained both out of place but also arriving at their destinations. A few weeks later, on August 24, 1883, letters arrived for the Arya Samaj—a Hindu reform organization—at Amritsar and Lahore as well as the Singh Sabha—a Sikh reform organization—at Amritsar. But, now, colonial officials noted their informant, Mian Asadulla of Amritsar "could give no clue to the writers of these letters, and when asked to obtain an original letter, was unable to do so, and said he believed that the originals had been destroyed as soon as received." Thus these letters eluded police capture and could not be reduced to a sensible reality, central to colonial rule, further troubling colonial authorities. Nonetheless, even without the physical letters, officials still sought to fix their contents, arguing as one official did that they were "couched in the following terms": "The time is close at hand when the white and red faced '*Malech*' will be swept away, and the beloved of the Guru, your comforter, will arrive. Rejoice and be prepared. Your enemy will soon be removed. The beloved of the Guru will rule with splendor. Be prepared. Awake out of the sleep of sloth. Be on the alert; the day is now at hand when your expectations will be realized. (Signed) A Sikh beloved of the Guru."[72]

Likewise, authorities determined there were three distinct letters sent to each reform organization (Arya Samaj and Singh Sabha), each from a different sender though with what the state believed was ostensibly same content. The three senders—"A Sikh beloved of the Guru at Amritsar," "A Sikh beloved of the Guru at Patna," and "A Sikh beloved of the Guru at Benares"—also signed off the letter in different ways, some including

"Prepare yourselves to drive these 'Malech' [foreigners] across the sea and pray to the Immortal God [Akal—literally deathless one]."[73]

Investigating the letters and regulating their lost, but then recovered, content, the state nonetheless noted, "it remained an open question whether the letters had any real existence."[74] Aitchison, a patron of the Singh Sabha at the time, heard no inkling that such a letter existed. Moreover, officials noted that "no member of that society [the Singh Sabha], nor of the Arya Samaj, made any communication on the subject to the authorities." Still, officials continued, "the person who brought the matter to notice," the aforementioned Mian Asadulla of Amritsar, was a "trustworthy person, and was not long afterward made an Honorary Magistrate." Tenuously situated between existence and illusion, known and unknown, presence and absence, the letter, even in the state's bid to render its content legible, signaled the possibility of an uncontrolled time. The letter's expectations could not be managed through a firm grasp on reality. In this unreality of the letters, officials affirmed the colonial state's political domain, arguing "the words of the letters as reported were clearly written by one, well educated in Persian, and would not have been intelligible to an uneducated Punjabi." Thus, administrators disavowed their own version of the letter's content as unrecognizable to the broader uneducated community and instead located the content within what the state thought of as the letter's proper place: a familiar realm reducible to an elite, dangerous Persianate public.[75]

Although officials sought to reduce the letter to the linguistically sophisticated looking to incite an uneducated population—a flesh-and-blood addressee—the letter nevertheless resisted its assignment. Without a secure content and placement, the letter signaled a dangerous situation for colonial officials, for the absence of the text interrupted the hermeneutic delusions of colonial administrators and their attempt to secure meaning. In doing so, the letter also opened a space of unreadability and its effects, that is, a space for the community attuned to prophecy. Colonial officials, to close this space, repressed and displaced the community, the lack within their political order. Put another way, even though the letter was shrouded, state officials made the letter decipherable only to themselves, the Indian elite, and incomprehensible within the broader Punjab landscape. This maneuver maintained the ideological contours of a time in which the community was simply awaiting its already known contents.

HIDDEN TRANSCRIPTS

Even though the state sought to effectively block his entrance into the sub-continent, Duleep Singh arrived continuously through the circulation of both his name and image in letters. For example, Reverend Herbert Udny Weitbrecht of Batala notified Aitchison in 1885 that Duleep Singh was secretly circulating (1) his image, (2) Major Evans Bell's book *The Annexation of the Punjab and the Maharaja Dalip Singh*, and (3) the privately printed compilation *The Maharaja Duleep Singh and the Government: A Narrative*. These texts were of particular importance since they lent credence to Duleep Singh's claims and argued that the British state's treaties with Duleep Singh were unjust. Weitbrecht discovered these facts when he noticed a letter at Fatehgarh in the Gurdaspur district. The Native Headmaster of the Church Missionary Society informed Weitbrecht about the letter and his strange encounter with Sardar Sarup Singh, a distant relative of Duleep Singh. According to Weitbrecht, "Sarup Singh came to the Headmaster of our Mission School at Fatehgarh and asked him to write an English letter for him to Maharaja Dalip Singh, expressing his interest in His Highness' fortunes and asking for the gift of a photograph."[76] Once Duleep Singh's response arrived alongside the aforementioned image and books, the native headmaster assured Weitbrecht that his Christianity made him immune to Duleep Singh's plotting. The headmaster then quickly copied the letter and sent it to Weitbrecht, who in turn conveyed it to the state.

Sent on June 28, 1885, from Holland House Kensington, Duleep Singh's response to Sarup Singh agreed to his request and stated, "I have pleasure in complying with your request and have given orders to send you a copy of the 'Annexation of the Punjab' and a likeness of myself."[77] Even though Duleep Singh had been alienated from the Punjab after his conversion and exile, both Sarup Singh in his initial letter and Duleep Singh in his response used ties cultivated through kin to establish their relationship. These types of connections helped make Duleep Singh legible in Punjab and countered the narratives about him that had been perpetuated by the colonial state.[78] Duleep Singh, noting their familiarity, wrote to Sarup Singh, "although I am not acquainted personally with you yet, I am very familiar with your ancestors' names having read a great deal about the Ghania Missal. It affords me also very great pleasure to note that you are the grandson of the Rani

Chand Kower [Chand Kaur] and as such a relative of mine."[79] Duleep Singh ended by airing his grievances, noting that Sarup Singh had "no doubt read in the newspapers about the estate I claim in the Punjab as my private ancestral property." Notably, this opening of communication between Duleep Singh and his distant relation was made possible by the Sikh tradition because it fostered legibility. Blood was not enough to define ancestry, and instead Duleep Singh had to locate himself within practices that cultivated a Sikh behavior to regain what we would consider kin ties. For example, Duleep Singh argued since he would not able to obtain "justice from these Christians whose immorality (I know by long residence amongst them) knows no bounds where payment of a large sum of money is concerned," he intended to "return to India and after visiting either Abchalanagar [Hazur Sahib] or Umritsar [Amrtisar] for the purpose of rejoining the faith of my ancestors to reside at Delhi," a ceremony he requested that Sarup Singh attend.[80] Practices at gurudwaras become, then, what legitimated Duleep Singh's return to what he called "the faith of my ancestors."

On November 28, 1885, this exchange between Sarup Singh and Duleep Singh came to the attention of the deputy commissioner of the Gurdaspur District, W. Coldstream, who discovered the existence of a second letter after interrogating Sarup Singh. Sarup Singh, Coldstream explained, "showed me two letters which he had received during the last four months from Maharaja Dhulip Singh."[81] In the second letter, the Sikh tradition again helped to link Sarup Singh and Duleep Singh. The second letter, sent on August 17, 1885, this time from Elveden Hall, stated that Duleep Singh had sent "Rs. 500 for *Karrah parshad* to Amritsar by the hand of Parohit Harkishan Das" and that "Rs. 250 had been sent to Lahore and Gujranwala, respectively, for offering at the Samadhs of his ancestors." After noting that he had delayed his visit to India because he lacked passage expenses, Duleep Singh ended the letter with the Sikh salutation, the *fateh*. Coldstream sought to mitigate these links. He spoke "kindly to the young man" and reminded Sarup Singh of the "objectionable tone of the writing, and warned him not to mix himself up with any disloyalty." For Coldstream, the connections Duleep Singh sought to cultivate would amount to little. Coldstream concluded he had "no doubt I could get any information out of him [Sarup Singh] which might be considered necessary," affirming the colonial state's power over the possibilities Duleep Singh signaled.

Such exchanges, however, were not limited to Sarup Singh. Duleep Singh sent numerous letters, cultivating further links between *Sikhi* and himself in order to ingratiate himself among members of the community. For example, the *Punjab Darpan* of Amritsar on September 7, 1885, published a letter in *gurmukhi* from Duleep Singh to the *granthi* Partap Singh, dated August 13 of that year. In the letter, Duleep Singh once again referenced the Sikh tradition to make clear the shared terrain of a community both he and Partap Singh occupied, even at a distance. After expressing his pleasure at receiving letters from Partap Singh, Duleep Singh noted, "I suppose you are always employed in expounding the doctrines of the *Granth* and of other religious books." Centering the *granthi*'s religious practice (*katha*), Singh told the Partap Singh that he had cultivated similar links with the Guru Granth Sahib and had, he wrote, "sent Rs. 1,000 to the Parohit with a view of *Karah Prashad* being presented at the Golden Temple at Amritsar and the tombs of my ancestors at Gujranwala and Lahore." Once this link was established, Duleep Singh made *Sikhi* and its enunciation and practice a common project between the two. This included, as he explained in his letter to Partab Singh, making sure *prashad*—a sacred offering of food made from whole wheat, butter, and sugar—was distributed properly: "I believe the *Parshad* will be duly offered and distributed. Write me at an early date all the news concerning the distribution of *Karah Parshad*. I have written to Sardar Thakur Singh to offer *Karah Parshad* on my behalf at the Apchalnagar Temple."[82]

The letters continued arriving in Punjab. On October 2, 1885, Jamiat Rai, a pensioner of Duleep Singh from Shahgharib and a former servant of Rani Jindan, presented a letter he received from Duleep Singh to Colonel Harcourt, the Deputy Commissioner of the Gurdaspur District. In the letter, Duleep Singh "regretted he had so long neglected to pay him [Jamiat Rai] his pension, but now sent him a cheque for Rs. 4,000 on a bank." Duleep Singh then once again sought to create links between Rai and himself, writing that Jamiat Rai "would be glad to learn that he had paid certain sums to his father's *samadh*, as also to his mother's and so was again *pakka* (regular) Sikh."[83] Though colonial officials translated *pakka* as "regular," the word connotes a strong and unbreakable attachment to *Sikhi*, which we have seen is something Duleep Singh frequently highlighted in his letters to correspondents in Punjab in order to underscore his commitment to reentering the Sikh fold, the Sikh community. Furthermore, on November 16, 1885, the district superintendent of police reported that Duleep Singh had written to both Hira Singh of Sialkot, Mussamat Rami, Ranjit Singh's former servant and Pandit Ram Singh, an astrologer. Each letter asked the recipient to meet him on his arrival in the subcontinent, tentatively planned for January 1, 1886.[84] With links established, Punjabis also sent letters to Duleep Singh, inquiring about his return. In January 1887 the Punjab government intercepted a letter from Ram Chand of the Jhelum District to Duleep Singh, "regarding the return of the latter to the Punjab," a return Duleep Singh sought to sanction through Sikh doctrine and practice.[85]

The binding of Duleep Singh with the Sikh tradition that these letters sought to accomplish through referencing ethical practices such as the distribution of *karah prashad* disrupted colonial knowledge formations. For though colonial officials sought to monopolize the historicity of colonized peoples—determining what was capable of being lost—the openness of the past stifled such attempts. To take one example, the Sikh tradition at the end of the nineteenth century retroactively situated Duleep Singh within a different time—one open to contestations about sovereignty. Even Western historiography, such as Thomas Evans Bell's book sent to Sarup Singh, *The Annexation of the Punjaub and the Maharajah Duleep Singh*, facilitated this process of rethinking Duleep Singh theoretically and historically. A staunch liberal and secularist, Evans Bell critiqued the East India Company and British Empire more broadly throughout his career as an English Indian army officer and writer.[86] Bell's treatise sought to dispel the official narrative about British involvement in Punjab. Within what Bell termed this "official myth," a benevolent British government in the 1840s endeavored to reform Punjab, which, continuously thwarted by insurrectionist Sikhs, eventually required annexation. In this mythic narrative, Bell continued, Lord Dalhousie and the British state treated Duleep Singh with "great forbearance, kindness, and liberality, and endowed [him] with a much larger income than could have been justly claimed for a Prince dethroned under such circumstances." Reinvestigating this history, however, Bell arrived at a different verdict, one in which annexation was as "unjust as it was imprudent," and in which Lord Dalhousie's motives were "morally low, politically short-sighted, and altogether unworthy" of Great Britain.[87]

Colonial officials found Bell's book on Duleep Singh, like most of his work, objectionable on the grounds that it destabilized state authority and hegemony. C. L. Tupper, the secretary to the Punjab government at Lahore, argued that the book was "written in the style of bitter hostility to Government common to all his political and polemical writings."[88] On the other hand, Duleep Singh and his allies certainly felt that Bell's argument about the unjust nature of the Treaty of Lahore and the annexation of Punjab could be advantageous once circulated into a reader's domain. In reading, Bell's book could function as "a hidden transcript." This offstage, Scott demonstrates, is a space "where subordinates may gather outside the intimidating gaze of power," allowing for "a sharply dissident political culture," unreadable to the secular logic of colonial authorities.[89] Circulating the book as a hidden transcript to contest the very parameters of sovereignty the British sought to secure, Duleep Singh gave Bell's book to numerous people in Punjab. Tupper, for example, noted to H. M. Durand on December 28, 1885, that "several copies of this work are known to be in the possession of Natives at Lahore."[90] Colonial officials sought to determine the location and number of these copies, enquiring to the Punjab government "whether there is reason to believe that any large number of copies of Major Evans Bell's book 'The Annexation of the Punjab and the Maharaja Dhulip Singh' have been circulated in the Punjab?"[91] On June 18, 1886, W. M. Young reported that the book was in the hands of twelve people in the Punjab from diverse backgrounds, each of whom maintained connections with Thakur Singh Sindhanwalia, Duleep Singh's cousin and lead organizer of the revolt against the British state.[92]

For Sikhs and Punjabis, central to accessing this hidden transcript was broadcasting the text in the vernacular *gurmukhi*, as we saw with the letter printed in the *Punjab Darpan*. Indeed, the readership for Bell's work was not limited to the English-speaking elite. With the wider public in mind, Duleep Singh hoped, as he wrote in his second letter to Sarup Singh, "that it [Bell's book] might be translated."[93] Thakur Singh Sindhanwalia undertook this translation project by employing the *granthi*, Partap Singh, to translate Bell's work.[94] Once Partap Singh completed his translation, Diwan Buta Singh, the proprietor of the *Aftab-i-Panjab* press in Lahore, printed three hundred copies. The goal, Tupper explained, was to circulate the "Punjabi translation of Major Bell's book gratis to certain persons in this province."[95] This translation came to the attention of colonial administration on August 9, 1887, when Attar Singh of Bhadaur sent a letter alongside four pages of the lithographed translation in *gurmukhi* to the colonial state. He informed the British that the "object of the writer seems to me to be to turn the ears of the people of this province from the English" since after reading it many in Punjab began to believe that the British had "treated Dalip Singh with severity and injustice."[96]

It was precisely by examining colonial historical truths as an object of inquiry and revealing how, Bell writes, "historical truth differs very widely from this myth of official origin," that Bell provided an apposite opportunity to question the historiography of empire itself that was burgeoning in the late nineteenth century. This historiography functioned, as Ranajit Guha shows, as "ethnology's surrogate," reinforcing Britain's imperial project by both demythologizing and rationalizing India's past.[97] But it did not only reaffirm the colonial regime; as Sanjay Seth writes, historiography eventually "became the site of contestations," even though all such histories, including Bell's in our case, "took for their form the modern and western mode of history writing." Within this historiographical form, Guha and Seth remind us, the subject of history becomes man, which, Seth writes, is an "anthropological-humanist presumption that disqualifies many of the other forms by which peoples have conceived and narrated their past." But once situated within this genealogy, rationalist historiography cannot "accord to itself any epistemic privilege." Seth concludes that we must be alert to history's own inadequacies, in which we cannot "assume the existence of subjects who endow the world with meanings, the objectified forms of which (texts, artworks, coins, monuments) allow us to recreate their world-picture."[98] One cannot simply repaint the portrait once lost; the image that circulated with Bell, for example, could not merely recuperate a lost sovereignty. Forgoing such mastery and dwelling within these inadequacies, history becomes a site of struggle to determine the organizational possibilities of a dislocated present rather than offering a recoverable and consumable object—such as an image—to ground community. History thus becomes prophecy.

Heeding Seth's warning, we can decenter Bell from his own historical work, our *primary* source, which cannot be reduced to an objectified form of Bell's own secularist lifeworld, to the author.[99] Instead there is a limit embedded within Bell's historical work on Duleep Singh, since Singh could not be reduced to Bell's authorizations. In other words, though Bell sought to settle Duleep Singh into an authentic historical form—a form that Duleep Singh, too, tried to circulate—Duleep Singh also remained heterogeneous to it as there was translation into different forms. This vertigo is most clearly discernible when we consider the antagonism between the two restless positions, reading and writing.[100] For the readers of Western historiography about Duleep Singh did not simply imbibe the same form. They did not repeat the anthropological humanist presumptions encoded within the text that searched for an immobile true object of knowledge—an object which could then be gifted to a settled community.

Instead, readers relied upon a repository of interpretive principles that displaced the very coordinates of what we consider the written form by making the work communicate through reading, which is always already translating. Consider what Maurice Blanchot writes: the reader is engaged in a struggle with the author, in which "the reader does not add himself to the book, but tends primarily to relieve it of an author."[101] What, then, of community? Reading indicates more symbolic undoing as community is no longer authored but given (although not submitted to). Therefore, though native knowledge for the colonial regime was, as Nicholas Dirks has written, "only the stuff of anthropological curiosity," it also constituted a genuine reading practice for the community. Since the community was constituted by necessarily anonymous readers, the community relieved Evans Bell and even Duleep Singh of their intention.[102] As a consequence, the circulation within which historiography was placed produced a disjuncture. This circulation was disrupted since reading and the conceptual repository reading wielded, not writing, could possibly constitute indeterminately, what Ranajit Guha calls an Indian historiography of India.[103]

The state recognized the perils of translation and reading, for both could not be easily managed. Translation, in particular, caused consternation. On January 13, 1886, G. S. Forbes wrote, "The book which may not do much harm in English, may have a different effect translated into the vernacular and spread broadcast."[104] The threat of translation lay in the act of rendering the work into *gurmukhi*, for the translated book remained dangerous even if it followed all the conventions of Western historiography premised on impartiality and objectivity that the state accused Bell of forging. For example, Forbes and Durand noted in a memo to Tupper in June 1886, "of course, the circulation of this book in translation in the Punjab cannot but be harmful. Even if it were written, which it is not, with a strict regard to facts and in an impartial, not to say friendly spirit, the influence of such a book would still be far from good."[105]

Translating into Punjabi in the *gurmukhi* script further relieved Bell's authorship, unmooring the text from its object. It produced a contrapuntal and disruptive site, providing a script that transgressed colonial boundaries of knowledge and sovereignty. Farina Mir, to take one example, argues that as a language Punjabi defies "the narrow definition of politics routinely associated with language" and remains "the site of sustained and political engagement by its speakers." Though censuring the narrowness within which language is placed politically, Mir also limits this hidden transcript, rendering it an authentically shared affective space. This secured space is then sabotaged by duplicitous communal politics such as Sikh attempts to co-opt *gurmukhi* and Punjabi into a Sikh language. Accordingly, Mir cautions, we should not "causally link affective ties to language with state-oriented politics," which would render Punjabi a language that failed to prevent the horror of partition.[106] Though an apt insight, to limit the expression of language only to shared or communal realms goes too far. Instead, language, alongside its playfulness and affective ties, reveals the ontological impossibility of a bound ideological field, not ontological heterogeneity. As a conflicting and disputing site, language keeps politics unmoored while challenging the fixing of colonial historicity—a fixation reproduced in contemporary historicity's relation to Punjabi.[107] Colonial administrators understood this danger and, looking to control such sites through their historical mastery, such as the "known" narrative of a failed Duleep Singh, lamented that "times and troubles which are long passed should be buried in oblivion."[108]

Circulating in this space unreadable to the authorities, even physical copies of Bell's book eluded the reach of the colonial state for a time. On January 13, 1886, G. S. Forbes determined that "no copy of the book appears to be procurable here," even though he had seen a copy somewhere before.[109] Officials then requested that the Punjab government send them a copy. W. M. Young procured a copy with difficulty. On April 28, 1886, he sent the requested copy to the Government of India, writing "the volume has been obtained from a blind student in the Government College on a promise that it should be returned."[110] Even after obtaining a copy of the book, its simultaneous presence within a hidden sphere and absence in the public sphere troubled colonial authorities. Thus, they sought to determine the location of the books—both those in *gurmukhi* translation and the English original—while recognizing the limits of the state intervention, reasoning "it does not seem worthwhile for us to stop the circulation."[111]

It is important to recall, however, that Evan Bell's book was circulated alongside Duleep Singh's image. What can we learn from this circulation of the image? This dissemination and gift of Evan Bell's book in conjunction with the circulation of Duleep Singh's image and name demonstrate how circulation was neither seamless nor circular but interruptive. We cannot locate Duleep Singh's male turbaned Sikh body, then, as creating "a new relation of identification productive of a Sikh 'people.'" The image would then be perfectly translated into the community, thereby securing it. It would be the creation of a total body, as Brian Keith Axel argues. Community would be secured through the consumption of Duleep Singh's portrait —a consumption that collapsed distinctions and difference while "appropriating the significance of the turban" by rendering it an "oriental crown."[112] As we saw, Duleep Singh did use his photograph to elicit sentimental attachments toward his return and his rule; he sent his image to Sarup Singh alongside Bell's work. Nor was it only a one-time occasion. The Punjab police wrote to Chiragh-ud-din, a postal peon at Lahore, informing him that his father had a letter from Duleep Singh, which included, "a copy of his photograph." Duleep Singh wrote that "he remembered Chiragh-ud-din, with whom he used to play as a child, and requested that the likeness he sent should be kept until he came out to India."[113]

Much like the circulation of letters, this economy of gifts did not have a given destination. The community did not only receive a stylized masculine image of the Sikh, producing a communal form. Instead, the image, as a gift, demanded reciprocity, in which the conditions of possibility granted by the commodified oriental crown, its future iterability, became its conditions of impossibility, annulling the total body ostensibly given by Duleep Singh.[114] Otherwise put, Duleep Singh's gift of his image did not simply bind Chiragh-ud-din and his fellow recipients to an image of the ideal masculine Sikh: it also made them responsible to Duleep Singh himself, requiring their presence for Duleep Singh's return in order to reciprocate the gift, thereby effacing its very possibility. Within this aporia, rather than identify the commodity reproducing itself incessantly with the iteration of Duleep Singh's commodified and colonized form, we are also confronted with a fundamental impossibility that limits such an exchange—the production of "the annulment, the annihilation, the destruction of the gift."[115] This impossibility, alongside the dissymmetry of reciprocity, reveals the inconsistency and mutability of the gifted commodity, if it can be called such. This is the case even as Duleep Singh was presented within a unified eternal totality central to both Axel's and capitalist form. But by presenting itself in time the gift also revealed unpredictable contaminations, outside calculation, as the state continually confronted.[116] That is, the gifting of Duleep Singh raised the question of inheritance and community, which remained elusive and therefore remained a task in its givenness.

To center these tasks is to show how community remained unstable, disturbing the colonial state alongside its knowledge formations. Though this formation of knowledge tried to dislocate community from its interruptions and tie it to reified racial formations, the continuous arrival of Duleep Singh within the subcontinent proved irreducible to the colonial state's logic or the decolonized national community. Even though the regulation and discipline of the colonial state sought to limit these prophetic tasks of community, these tasks remained both available and interrupted within hidden transcripts. These tasks circulated outside the parameters of the colonial state in the letters and texts highlighted here. But rather than examine these texts as known and fixed, thereby revealing to the historian a heterogeneous answer about Duleep Singh, these texts circulated a gap, a constitutive loss, that led to more and more questions about Duleep Singh—and questions of community.[117]

Chapter Two

THE PUBLIC

Truth is not an unveiling that destroys the mystery [secret] but a revelation that
does it justice.

—WALTER BENJAMIN

Neither the circulation of a mythic Duleep Singh nor the organization
around Duleep Singh occurred only through secret correspondence and
accompanying gifts. People organized to reinstitute the Khalsa Raj by disseminating news of the lost sovereign's return across South Asia in the public sphere as well, most notably in the burgeoning Punjab press.

The press in Punjab boomed during the 1880s. A. P. MacDonnell, the secretary to the Government of India, recorded on August 8, 1887, that "in
recent years a considerable expansion of the Vernacular Press in the Punjab
has taken place," and that "77 periodicals in the Vernacular are now published in the Punjab."[1] This boom in print coincided with the dissemination
of new technologies, such as the telegraph. As Amelia Bonea reveals, "the
press took advantage of this situation by sending more and increasingly longer telegrams," allowing for the wider dissemination of "news."[2] These
emerging technologies alongside the centrality of the public sphere within
liberal doctrine were central to how Duleep Singh built and maintained
support, and how his image spread throughout the 1880s. Officials, too,
noticed the difficulties the medium presented. As one colonial administrator, Henry Mortimer Durand, lamented, "We cannot prevent Dalip Singh
from communicating with the Press."[3]

Native elites who owned and ran the presses—proprietors and editors—
did not simply embrace Duleep Singh uncritically but sought to maintain

a space for native elite politics. They wanted to preserve both their position as native informants and political inheritors of the British Empire. But the position of proprietors and editors remained unstable; their legitimacy was tied to community—a community itself racialized by colonial officials. Those who ran the press, therefore, sought to walk a fine line between showing loyalty to the colonial state and avoiding state censure or accusations of sedition in their printing of material related to Duleep Singh. Their struggles to negotiate political demands through and against Duleep Singh reveal innumerable tensions—between subaltern and elite, Anglo-Indian and native elite, public and private, loyalty and sedition, as well as the colonial state's racial designations between, for example, the Punjabi and the Bengali.

Although they looked to assuage these tensions, the press in Punjab brought tensions to the fore by cultivating a symbolic coherence through Duleep Singh—a coherence that was itself an impossibility. The community, as an unruly question, refused the determinations and coherence sought by the native elite, who managed the press. The community created unpredictability that denied capture—an unpredictability most notable in Duleep Singh's intrigues in Bengal.

THEORIZING THE PUBLIC

The public is a notoriously slippery concept. As Barton Scott and Brannon Ingram remind us, "'the public' is a term that is most often defined in terms of what it is not—a marker of conceptual instability if ever there was one."[4] Most famously, Jürgen Habermas argues that the fully developed bourgeois public sphere conjoined private individuals into a public in order to regulate and legitimate public authorities through critical and rational deliberation, the deployment of the "critical use of their reason." According to Habermas, this sphere was in contrast to the intimate private human realm, which, historically in Europe, came to include religion.[5] Scholars have noted, as has Habermas himself, the shortcomings (and strengths) of his classifications and distinctions.[6]

The public becomes even more difficult to define and conceptualize when studying non-European contexts.[7] As scholars of South Asia have noted, the public sphere cannot be reduced to modular forms emanating from the West. Consequently, many have tried, as Scott and Ingram write, to "further historicize the concept and practice of the North Atlantic 'public' by asking how this notion travelled to South Asia and how it was adapted from within particular institutions and power structures."[8] Broadly, the public in South Asia is conceptualized within the historiography as both countering and acclimating to the Eurocentric ideal of the public in three different ways.[9] First, scholars argue that earlier forms of Indian publics continued into modernity and that these publics, like European publics, displayed the public use of reason.[10] Second, scholars have argued that in the late nineteenth century there emerged new and distinct forms of the public arena—an arena divided between "state-focused institutional activities and the collective action of public arenas," as Sandria Freitag writes.[11] These alternative collective realms, left to their own accord, became increasingly central venues of political participation, as they were more legitimate than colonial institutions, drawing as they did from indigenous performative and religious aspects of collective symbolic activities. Finally, scholars argue that a split "public" emerged in the late nineteenth century that included both a public realm mirroring that of the West and a site cultivating private difference that resisted colonial domination. As Partha Chatterjee writes, the promise of "a neat separation between a private sphere of diverse individuals residing in bourgeois patriarchal families and a public sphere inhabited by homogeneous citizens was not available to Indian nationalism." This exclusion meant that the private, spiritual, and inner domain became the place where nationalism fashioned its authority through cultural difference and resisting the sway of colonial institutions while conceding the "material" realm to the British. There existed, therefore, Chatterjee concludes, two political domains in tense relation to each other: civil society and the community.[12] The press oscillated between these worlds.

What do we make of the continuation, inauguration, or entanglements of Indian public(s)? Do we need to account for their historical differences with European publics by providing an explanation, which functions as a palliative to the problem of "unreadiness" within a normative public? The key to understanding the public in the colony becomes to determine the coordinates of diverse content, revealing the always present capacities for varied, though different, *public* engagements. Once articulated within these parameters as knowledge, or as Freitag writes, once scholarly endeavor "makes clear the [multiple] characteristics of South Asian understandings of 'the public,'" this knowledge can create "an analytical vocabulary (as well as systematic methodologies and range of evidence) serviceable for comparative purposes as well."[13]

In contrast, what does it mean to center a deadlock within the form of the public rather than tracing diverse content? This knotting is tied to the role of the unstable community in relation to the distinction between public and private—a problem compounded in the colony, where the colonial state's racialized logic decrees the people "not ready." Indeed, colonialism is premised on racial difference, indefinitely postponing entry into citizenship.[14] Or, as Freitag argues, "an imperial state cannot function in the same way as a nation-state, nor can it create a role for its subjects that approximates that of a citizen."[15] Consequently, within this logic, colonial officials thought the public in India incomplete and unable to handle the responsibilities of a developed public. A developed public, in colonial eyes, would be one that could cultivate active knowing as, what Jodi Dean calls elsewhere, "the public-supposed-to-know." In contrast, following the rule of colonial difference, colonial society was stuck: It was trapped as a "public-supposed-to-believe," trapped in its immaturity, unable to fulfill the requirements of what was considered a civilized public that could produce knowledge. Thus, colonial officials understood the Indian public sphere as, to appropriate Dean, "a flux of conflicting opinions" and "easily seduced and unable to judge its true interests" because "its judgments stem[ed] from trust ('belief in the belief of the other') rather than knowledge."[16]

Yet this split between the two publics—the supposed-to-know and the supposed-to-believe—also exists in the West, where the "public-supposed-to-believe" occupies a central role in theorizing the public as well. As Scott and Ingram argue, "the British 'public' was never a totalising sociological reality" but existed as "an unstable assemblage of shifting ideas and institutions, defined as much by its internal contradictions as by its normative force."[17] Dean recognizes this aspect of the public and contends that these contradictions that emerged within the public were assuaged by the "secret."[18] The secret is essential because it functions as a presupposition that sustains the entire order of things. It domesticates the disorder embedded within the "public-supposed-to-believe." How so? Publicity is critical because it provides what Dean refers to as "the information [about the secret] that will enable 'the public-supposed-to-believe' to believe that someone knows." In this sense, publicity "holds out the possibility of good judgment to the public-supposed-to-believe" by providing "the guarantee of knowledge that stabilizes belief" and, thus, sustains the premise of the public. To elaborate, "publicity holds out the promise of revelation, the lure of the secret," even while the community is considered outside knowledge.[19] Therefore, within what Barton Scott calls "an epistemology of exposure," the secret, which can be revealed, binds together a possible unified public.[20] This binding occurs when the secret fills "out the gap between two competing notions of the public [supposed to know/believe], compensating in advance for the public's failure to serve as the unitary subject of democracy."[21]

But how does the "secret" work in colonial societies? Here is a central difference: though the public-supposed-to-know is a presupposition in the West, it was decreed by the logic of imperialism to be absent in the colony. When the community is conceptualized outside the very parameters of the "public-supposed-to-know," when judgment is always already contaminated—rendering knowledge otherwise—then it was feared by colonial authorities that publicity of the secret could create unconstrained belief. Publicity would disrupt the very structure of the public. This possible disruption necessitated intervention. In the rule of difference that underpinned colonialism, colonial officials watchfully regulated the public while looking to inculcate an acceptable form of knowing, to make the presupposition of knowledge a possibility, through its disciplinary institutions and strategies of governance. In other words, this system of distrust was racialized. Colonial administrators regulated the public by creating a typology of racial difference that could allow them to police belief in the public. The very terms of regulation created an acceptable rendition of publicizing the secret by neutralizing belief and, thus, the racialized community. Absent knowledge, revelation of the secret was not located within the practices of unconcealment and disclosure of a presupposed disciplined knower, but rather within the censuring machinations of the colonial state.

Though the state sought to regulate the press in late nineteenth-century Punjab, since revelation was removed from knowledge and managed within belief itself—through the multitude of hidden transcripts outside the reach of the state—the community remained a threat, a site to misread even censored publicity. Revelation therefore had to be continually monitored and censored so as not to create unpredictable possibilities for alternatives to the secret, such as, in our case, through Sikh practices and principles. The secret can be viewed in a way that allows us to rethink, as Dean writes, "a spatial model of a social world divided between public and private spheres" and to center "the system of distrust, the circuit of concealment and revelation, that actively generates the public."[22] Against further historicization and discovery of an indigenous or colonial public, this circuit of concealment and revelation is key; the failure to regulate, disclose, and retrieve secret presences and promises comes to the fore. Such failure requires scholars, following Anjali Arondekar, to "complicate the very stakes of our archival mediations" on the public by trying to inhabit "an archival approach that articulates against the guarantee of recovery,"[23] what Spivak calls "a reaching and un-grasping."[24]

HIDDEN TRANSCRIPTS, AGAIN

Denied access to Punjab as well as pecuniary assistance, Duleep Singh himself embodied unpredictability. Though Duleep Singh had employed liberal ideals and rhetoric (such as in framing his rights as those of a British subject) to advance his cause, in 1885 he began to abandon this strategy in favor of directly challenging liberal ideals by centering the Sikh tradition. For example, his anger reached a climax on November 2, 1885, when he wrote to the secretary of state, Lord Randolph Churchill, that he was flattered that the state considered him "worthy of its notice" and made "a martyr of me in the eyes of my countrymen and now co-religionists."[25] By highlighting his prominence in the Sikh community when addressing the state, Duleep Singh began openly deploying what had hitherto been a hidden transcript—a transcript that already utilized him anonymously. Duleep Singh's threat was apparent. Even his letter to Churchill, that was printed for public consumption in the *Times* and designed to appeal to liberal sensibilities in Britain, spread quickly in Punjab, creating anti-British agitation in Lahore in particular. Now, renouncing his former deference to the imperial state, Duleep Singh used the hidden transcript provided through the Sikh tradition against liberal ideals to enunciate his vision for his future in his conversations with British officials.

Instead of appealing to liberal sentiments about the autonomous self, Duleep Singh foregrounded the *sakhis* to articulate his demands, which dislocated the rational subject as the harbinger of action. He mocked the state's efforts to manage and control human action through secular law. He argued that neither he nor the state could claim sovereignty over the actions of individuals, since both followed a predetermined destiny as foretold in the *sau sakhis*, in the prophecies, by the tenth Sikh Guru, Guru Gobind Singh Ji (1666–1708). In a copy of the written prophecy obtained by the British state, the prophecy read:

The last Sikh Gooroo, or teacher, died about the year 1725.

Being asked upon an occasion by his disciples whether he would ever again visit the world, Gooroo Govind Singh replied in the affirmative, adding that he will take birth again in the household of a Sikh who will marry a Mohammedan wife, and that his name will be Deep Singh, of which Duleep Singh is a corruption. Although the Sikhs can possess as man Mohammedan women in their harems as they can afford to support, yet Maharajah Runjeet Singh was the only Sikh, as far as I am aware, who went through the regular marriage ceremony with one.

The Gooroo went on to say that this Deep Singh, after becoming dispossessed of all he had inherited, and residing for a long time alone in a foreign land, will return and correct the errors into which the Sikhs will have fallen in their worship of God and by neglect of his (the Gooroo's) tenets, but that before the latter comes to pass Deep Singh will suffer much persecution and will be reduced to absolute poverty.

The Gooroo further predicts that Deep Singh will marry a Christian wife, and his children by her the Gooroo calls Englishmen in his prophecy.

The Gooroo foretells that there will be a war between the two dogs Boochoo and Dultoo (presumably the bear and the bulldog), in which Deep Singh will take part, but that he will be defeated and will take refuge at a certain village (the name of which cannot at present be identified), and when there self-knowledge will be revealed to him.

About that time "Dase baitche ooth Jaa-ay Furrunygee, Tow Gaajeu Gay more "Bhojhanggee," i.e., "The English after selling the country will quit the land. Then will thunder my snakes or disciples."

It is further predicted that Deep Singh and his descendants will reign for three generations over the land lying between Calcutta and the Indus.[26]

As a prophetic maharaja, Duleep Singh did not control his destiny, but it was foretold in the past toward a sovereignty to come. His present, too, had been foretold, one that led toward his current persecution, but this was now a present undone, since it also led to the destruction of colonial rule.

Authorities were befuddled at Duleep Singh's increasing propensity to situate himself and his political cause within Sikh tradition. British major-general Owen Tudor Burne could not even begin to interpret this new conceptual repository. In a series of interviews conducted in early 1886 in which Duleep Singh discussed the financial wrongs he incurred, Burne wrote that his interviewee "entered into a somewhat rambling statement" about the Sikh tradition and even gave him a copy of the prophecy in the *sau sakhis*. In response to Duleep Singh's centering of the prophetic claims, Burne stated that he warned "the Maharaja that all this was merely dreaming, as to which he might some day have a sad awakening."[27] Though Burne reduced the prophetic claims to "dreams" that could be counterposed to the reality of British sovereignty, the prophetic claims threw the distinction between "reality" and "dreams" into question. Specifically, it was precisely the present and claims of a secure sovereignty that could not be taken as a given in light of the prophetic claims. And that is where the danger lay, as prophecy signaled the possibility of new coordinates to dislocate sovereignty outside official discourse. Burne dismissed Duleep Singh's financial claims on these grounds as well; there was no possibility of change. British sovereignty was firm and could not be rethought. "You, on your part," he told Duleep Singh, "signed away your kingdom with alacrity[;] you could say nothing at the time against the justice then dealt out to you."[28] The present, for Burne, was not open to question.

Defying the state, Duleep Singh embarked on his return to India. By this point, Duleep Singh's proclamations had completely shed the servile tone of liberal discourse. On March 29, 1886, two days before he was set to travel to Bombay, a letter from Duleep Singh was published in the *Evening Standard*. In it Duleep Singh foregrounded Sikh concepts in order to explain his actions. Renouncing the ego as the motor of historical action, Duleep Singh instead posited that the Guru was now in charge of his destiny; he was merely, as he told Burne, "a fakir." The understanding that one is not in charge of time but under the divine command and order (*hukam*) of the Guru is central to the Sikh tradition. *Hukam* arbitrates temporal law obliterating its currents. *Hukam* is always present, reconfiguring what can appear possible and impossible; it is untimely, reconfiguring what can appear possible and impossible, what can appear as historical and ahistorical.[29]

Drawing from the Sikh tradition, Duleep Singh argued, the Guru's *hukam* determined his being. For example, Duleep Singh wrote: "It was not my intention ever to return to reside in India, but Sutgooroo [*Satguru*], who governs all destiny, and is more powerful than I, his erring creature has caused circumstances to be so brought that, against my will, I am compelled to quit England, in order to occupy a humble sphere in India. I submit to His will, being persuaded that whatever is for the best will happen."[30]

Here, destiny governed by the True Guru, by *hukam*, becomes a destabilizing force, which undercut the official form of political discourse. In fact, *hukam* dislocated "Duleep Singh" from himself by going against his own will. In his anonymous being, Duleep Singh revealed the productive capacities of the secret hidden transcript, grounded in submission to *hukam*, to create new historical conditions that defied known parameters. Simultaneously an English gentleman, deposed Maharaja, and erring creature, Duleep Singh himself refused categorization, defying colonial officials and their desire to manage and control him and, therefore, community. Within his layered movements, Duleep Singh, intertwining public and hidden, departed from the self and its attachments, creating opportunity for a different horizon.

On March 31, two days later after publishing his letter in the *Evening Standard*, Duleep Singh and his family set sail for Bombay on the Peninsular and Oriental steamer *Verona*, leading to the ire of the British. Indeed, making this hidden transcript public had severe consequences. A telegram from the secretary of state to the viceroy of India noted that the state had to do whatever was necessary to regulate Duleep Singh. The telegram stated, "Maharaja laid stress on test of alleged prophecy, announced successive steps by which he is to be restored to power, He no doubt intends to circulate this in India. Affair, if neglected, might possibly give serious trouble, but I have no doubt you will take whatever measures you may deem necessary to prevent any dangerous feeling being excited among Sikhs."[31] Looking to manage both this hidden transcript and Sikh dispositions, the state took decisive action, issuing a warrant for Duleep Singh's detention at the British crown colony of Aden. It also looked to control his communications, declaring that the "Maharaja should not be permitted to communicate with outside world."[32] On April 21, 1886, Duleep Singh was arrested in Aden.

Despite his arrest, Duleep Singh, dislocated as he was from himself, continuously arrived in Punjab. Officials noted that "his adherents and well-wishers have quite recently been circulating, in the north of India, pamphlets favourable to his pretensions."[33] But more than through pamphlets, Singh's arrivals were kept visible, colonial officials complained, through the press. Duleep Singh's published letter in the *Evening Standard* was "republished in most of the vernacular newspapers, printed copies being received direct from England by some of the editors."[34] Though critical of Duleep Singh's maneuverings, the press could not control its readership. The police recorded that "the Maharaja's letter to his countrymen as published in the newspapers, is frequently discussed, and the impression seems to be that the Sikhs will acknowledge him as their Chief."[35] After his detention, even the press criticized the state's treatment of Duleep Singh, with most papers expressing some version of their "disapproval of Dalip Singh's detention at Aden" and claiming that he was being "badly used."[36]

THE LETTERS, ANGLO-INDIANS, AND NATIVE ELITES

Newspaper editors did try to distance their publications from Duleep Singh. Reproducing colonial notions of the community and belief, Sanjay Seth argues, both the English and vernacular press conceptualized "the ordinary people as 'ignorant rustics' in thrall to 'superstitious' beliefs, and practicing 'filthy habits' and prone to violence once aroused and desperate."[37] Let us move back in time from our chronological sequence. One example of this comes from August 1883, when both the Anglo-Indian and native press reported on the letters discussed in the previous chapter that circulated in Punjab that drew links between the recently arrested Surendranath Banerjea and Duleep Singh. The press heavily criticized this attempt to draw parallels while echoing the state's concern with determining the senders. For instance, on August 4, 1883, the native paper *The Tribune* hastily noted that the letters had begun circulating and strongly denounced their dissemination. *The Tribune* argued: "These letters purport to rouse people to false patriotism and are replete with the most mischievous insinuation. The whole thing must be due to some evil-disposed person—an unquestionable enemy of the Native community. We draw to the matter the attention of the authorities, and hope the mischief-maker will be brought to condign punishment."[38]

The "people" referenced here are precisely the ordinary people that would be duped by falsified letters. The people did not have the faculty of reason and, thus, could be easily seduced since their trust, to return to Dean, emerged from their belief in falsehoods. Publicizing the fact that the letter was false was not enough for *The Tribune*, since the masses could still believe in its authenticity. The question lay in their judgment. The letters, therefore, required state intervention, and *The Tribune* called upon the authorities to take action. In this way the public sphere—the circulation of newspapers—was used as a site to call for the intervention of state authorities rather than a site for the public use of reason.

On August 9, 1883, the semiofficial Anglo-Indian newspaper *The Pioneer* concurred, reporting one letter was "distinctly seditious." Yet *The Pioneer* was prescient in predicting that the letter would help ensure Duleep Singh's name would become a slogan for natives with grievances, such as among the native elite who looking to expand their political clout, creating difficulties for British rule. Referencing the colonial trope of the manipulative Bengali, *The Pioneer* posited that Duleep Singh would "infallibly be used as a watch-word by any class of natives that may have a grievance at the time; and the consequences are sure to be pernicious, and might be deplorable."[39] Again, reporting and exposing the secret of the letters held no possibility for challenging Duleep Singh's name since the public itself was considered an impossibility. South Asia was, to repeat, too tied to belief, unable to engage in the public use of reason.

A week later, on August 11, 1883, *The Tribune* continued its scorn of the anonymous letter writers, noting "the letters seem to be written in feigned hands" and "concocted by some bitter enemy of the native community."[40] Instead of tracing the letter to Bengali elites, as their counterparts in the Anglo-Indian press had done, *The Tribune* argued that Anglo-Indians sent the letters to sully the reputation of native elites. The tensions between Anglo-Indians and the native elite had reached a highpoint in 1883 with the controversy over the Ilbert Bill, which allowed Indian judges to try Europeans, outraging Anglo-Indians.[41] Considering these tensions, *The Tribune* provided three reasons as to why the publication believed that an Anglo-Indian was the anonymous letter writer. First, it argued, "if the letters were intended to rouse the people or any section of the people to sedition, it would never have been addressed in such a way as was most like to lead to a speedy detection." Second, *The Tribune* noted that Duleep Singh and Surendranath Banerjea would not have been mentioned together since the *Bengalee* paper had recently criticized Duleep Singh. Finally, the paper determined that "the letters appear to be written in Anglo Indian rather than in native hands." Based on these clues, *The Tribune* concluded that the letters were actually "a subtle trick devised by some mischievously disposed person or persons—who disdain to call themselves natives of the country—to disgrace the native community and discredit the government of Lord Ripon in the eyes of the British public." *The Tribune* still demanded punishment, but now with a slight revision, writing "[we] pray that the offender, whoever he may be, whether native or non-native, be brought to condign punishment."[42] *The Tribune* thus provided clues about the identity of the letter writers, but revealing this secret required state intervention and discipline.

The Tribune extended blame to Anglo-Indians in order to preserve the limited political advances that Lord Ripon's reforms had granted to native elites.[43] Following the logic of liberal rule, Lord Ripon used reforms "as an instrument of political and popular education."[44] But questions remained about whether the reforms conceded too much to the native population, and worry about the community's preparedness for liberal politics grew more vocal. These questions were especially disconcerting to the Anglo-Indian community, who found the reforms a challenge to the prestige and economic opportunities they were afforded and which were denied to the native population.[45]

The dispute between the natives and the Anglo-Indians about the rights and privileges afforded to each group worsened when aspects of community that had been presumed lost, such as the Khalsa Raj and Duleep Singh, continually erupted into public discourse. One London correspondent to a Bombay newspaper wrote that Duleep Singh was dangerous because "Lord Ripon has excited among the people of India such fantastic ideas of independence that they only want a leader to assert in a very awkward manner their claim to self-government."[46] *The Pioneer*, as well, reported that even if Duleep Singh had no intention of creating intrigues, his advisors had "accurately gauged the temper of the times when they select[ed] a period of restless, undefined anticipation among the masses of the Punjab caused by the movements in their midst of busy agitators for more advanced legislation."[47]

To prove their readiness for liberal politics, the native elite sought to distance themselves from the broader and elusive political organization of the community, which remained too unpredictable within the parameters of liberal politics. Or, to put it another way, Duleep Singh brought together peoples who were not believed to possess the correct racial and thus political disposition to engage in the public use of reason. The letters were unsettling for precisely this reason—the inclusion of Duleep Singh with Banerjea expanded the political beyond the comfort of both the native elite and colonial state to those deemed "not ready" for liberal governance. *The Tribune*'s pronouncements on the alleged Anglo-Indian intrigues thus sought to confine political possibilities to an intelligible elite realm in order to reassure the British state of the letter's illegitimacy. Once the state could locate the presumed senders, the "perfidious Bengali" or "mischievous Anglo-Indian," the letters could effectively be managed as the state could then properly intervene to curtail the possibility of revolt. For the press, exposure, then, was tied to state intervention; it was not tied to persuading a public or working within the parameters of a given tradition.

RACE AND BELIEF

The enunciation of *any* possibilities, however, threatened the colonial state. Colonial officials argued that even exposing the true senders of the letter to the state in the public sphere could be integrated into a destabilized form of belief within the community. Moreover, information could have a destabilizing effect and threaten the colony with violence. This is not to say there was not any support for Duleep Singh in the press. There was, especially in vernacular newspapers. William Mackworth Young, the secretary to the Government of the Punjab, argued, "but for the Native Press we should never have had any trouble with Dalip Singh."[48] The danger of the press, Young continued, lay in how it spread "unfounded rumours," which were "freely circulated in the vernacular newspapers accompanied too often with thoroughly seditious sentiment." The press was then, as Young wrote, "the main causes of whatever excitement and disaffection has been produced by the proceedings of the Maharaja." For Young, editors were "instigators and suggesters of disaffection."[49] The lieutenant governor of the Punjab, J. B. Lyall, concurred, writing that vernacular newspapers had "no doubt largely assisted to create and spread excitement in the Punjab by frequent false and exaggerated statements about Dalip Singh."[50] Some even crossed the line into sedition. Also in agreement with these understandings of the newspapers were military personnel. General Channer, for example, wrote from Rawalpindi on February 6, 1887, that "as regards Dalip Singh, till this was put into the heads of the people by the vernacular papers they never dreamt of him: he could of course be used as a tool to work upon by seditious agencies and the local native papers, who are at the bottom of half the mischief we hear in India."[51] Dewan Gobind Sahai, the former prime minister of Kashmir, provided the same information to the state, arguing that, though there was "a great deal of talk about Dalip Singh," it arose from only "frequent mention of him in the vernacular papers and not from any special interest in his person or fortunes."[52]

Colonial officials argued that since the public did not have the capacity for knowledge and, instead, existed as possible believing subjects—and, therefore, excitable subjects—the law had to intervene and even regulate the parameters of information and its publicization. That is, since the "secret" and its publicization could not properly regulate the public, the state had to create an appropriate, though stunted, public realm. This regulation of the press occurred in order to manage what were seen to be the excitable, racialized dispositions of colonized races, such as the Punjabis. For the state, ossified and racialized temperaments created particular forms of belief that defined the different peoples of the subcontinent. These ossified dispositions meant that communities were, as Chatterjee explains, "singular and substantive entities in themselves, with determinate and impermeable boundaries, so insular in their differences with one another as to be incapable of being merged into larger, more modern political identities."[53] Therefore, the goal of colonial authorities was not merely to manage conflicting opinions through the secret; the problem was not simply the existence of different forms of belief within dissimilar ideologies or traditions. Instead, belief itself became tethered to clashing races and communities.

For colonial officials, therefore, the Indian "public" was one in which belief, much like race, required close regulation. They sought to make sure the public sphere did not inflame racial sentiments, catalyzing racial violence. Lyall recorded in June 1887, "In a country like India where the community consists of so many distinct races, living apart though intermixed, the law ought in my opinion to empower Government to prosecute criminally any persons of race or nationality, who in any book, or newspaper, published insulting or defamatory."[54] W. M. Young made the same argument to Lyall, positing "measures should be taken to prevent this despicable body of men [native elites] from playing on the sympathies of the people. One or two prosecutions conducted to conviction would produce an excellent effect."[55] On July 28, 1887, an official in the Foreign Department concurred, writing that the state needed "a firm hand in dealing with seditious, insulting, and defamatory statements in newspapers and books—English or Native." This, the official argued, would be the "best way of quieting the people."[56]

Writing about the Royal Commission and the New Poor Laws in England, Mary Poovey contends, "the use of an apparently disinterested apparatus of fact-gathering produced abstractions about an aggregate whose social components could be isolated from its political and economic dimensions." These now disinterested empirical observations fashioned "an avalanche of new information that mandated more—and more far-reaching—fact-gathering, inspection and legislation."[57] In the colonial setting, this aggregation generated abstracted yet codified ethnic identities and stereotypes. Working with these abstractions, Lieutenant Colonel G. C. Ross argued, "I have been told that on several occasions Bengalis have been talking in a seditious manner with Sikhs in civil life, and picturing all sorts of advantages to them under a new rule, but a Sikh is not easily dazzled."[58] Yet though Ross noted that Sikhs stoically refused such interferences, Bengali *attempts* to cultivate a false unity would have pernicious effects. Colonial officials concluded that they would inflame differing beliefs—racial dispositions—that were irreconcilable. Therefore, the state had to deal most firmly, officials argued, with Bengalis whose presumed racial disposition (effeminate and cunning) sought to tie together the fragmented races of India in order to gain privileges for themselves. To the British, different forms of belief, now centered on racial classifications, had cemented irreconcilable cleavages within society, creating violence and resentment. The question was: How would one discipline these different races through state regulation since knowledge of the "secret" could not do the trick? In this formation, the attempt to produce knowledge within the community in a public sphere could create only incongruity, since it could not overcome racialized temperaments that fueled belief.

The presumed hostilities between racial groups in the subcontinent required the state to manage the press. In a letter sent to general Sir F. Roberts, General Dillon outlined these incongruous effects, relaying the words of "one of the well-known Punjabi natives" who argued, "You are ruining us by education. You take the sons of the menial races [Bengalis] and having educated them you put them over their own superiors. They cannot ride, or shoot or command men. Why do you not educate them and place them in their proper sphere. The menial race is not fit to rule and know it."[59] Mirroring the state's own encyclopedic projections that guaranteed an always unready community, these differences, based in both inherent racial characteristics and in belief, paradoxically tempered the state's concern with Duleep Singh. For example, General Channer argued that despite the efforts of the native papers, his name could only "be circulated amongst seditious bazar folk," for "the mass of the agricultural Jat Sikhs are content, are at peace."[60] In general, however, regulation and standardization of peoples and spaces remained central in quelling the potential power of Duleep Singh's name. Within this logic, the unruly and corrupt nature of the bazaar alongside the racialized Bengali required continuous and extensive regulation, even prosecution, which was placed in contrast to the ordered and peaceful nature of the Sikh and Jat agricultural society—both formations reflecting back the ethnographic state's own distinctions.[61]

WORDS BETWEEN LOYALTY AND SEDITION

But the press could be dangerous to the state for precisely this reason: it tried to bridge what were thought to be opposing racial classifications, disrupting the neat divisions sought after by the state by exposing excitable forms of belief to the danger of an impossible unity through the name of Duleep Singh.[62] The press indeed published about Duleep Singh. The *Aftab-i-Hind* paper in Jalandhar, for example, wrote on May 16, 1885, that "the British Government committed a gross act of injustice in depriving Dalip Singh of the Punjab when he was a minor, and urged that the Maharaja should be restored to his kingdom." Nine days later, the *Aftab-i-Punjab* in Lahore continued such rhetoric, arguing that Duleep Singh had "proved that the British Government took advantage of his minority to ease him of his ancestral property" and therefore that his allowance should be increased. In the *Akhbar-i-Am* of Lahore, an editorial appeared from "a member of the *Khalsa* community" that implored the colonial state to reconsider its treatment of Duleep Singh. The editorial stated, "It is very surprising that this minor, aged nine years, of which the Government was the guardian, should have been exiled and his jewels, &c., valued at several millions, should have been forfeited, merely because some relative of his, committed some fault against the government." The writer demanded the state "confer on him his rights." Moreover, the editorialist also noted that since the original terms of the agreement between Duleep Singh and Lord Dalhousie had meant that "The *Khalsa* kingdom would be allowed to exist," the Khalsa remained a form of legitimate government.[63] Other rebellious actions became tied to Duleep Singh through the press. For instance, one official noted "a seditious proclamation having been anonymously published in Punjab" that "was reported in the papers [*Times*, September 8, 1886] to have been prompted by the Maharaja."[64]

Relying on the public transcript, the press did put pressure on the colonial state to accede to Duleep Singh's demands. As noted earlier, though colonial administrators sought to limit Duleep Singh's movements when he arrived in India, the press vigorously debated the merits of the state's intended intervention. By publicizing information to a believing public, the press provided opportunity to organize belief outside the sanction of the state and its knowledge formations. Early on, in 1883, *The Tribune* noted that Duleep Singh should be allowed to visit Punjab because "amidst all the gravities of Elveden Hall, and the pleasures of an English married life, it was impossible for him to forget that he was by birth a native of India. And that we think is reason to impel him to visit the country of his forefathers."[65] After disallowing his presence in Punjab, colonial officials debated where he could go within the subcontinent. They debated between several options in the Madras Presidency, including Ootacamand and Kudai Kunal, as possible suitable destinations for Duleep Singh.[66] Although this was all for naught once Duleep Singh was arrested in Aden for rebellious statements, the conclusion was clear: Duleep Singh would be kept out of Delhi. The press challenged this decree. The *Koh-i-nur* of Lahore relayed that it "did not believe the rumour that Dalip Singh would have to live at Ootacamand, as he was said to have purchased land and houses at Delhi." Another Lahore newspaper, the *Rafik-i-Hind*, reported on March 27, 1886, that "the order forbidding the Maharaja to enter the Punjab cast a great slur on the loyalty of Punjabis and was sure to irritate them."[67]

Duleep Singh's name further remained in the press thanks to his 1886 letter to the *Times*, which he also had sent to vernacular and Anglo-Indian papers including the *Pioneer, Civil and Military Gazette, Tribune*, and *Koh-i-nur*—all of which published the manifesto. Though colonial officials argued that the opposition to Duleep Singh's arrest in Aden in

April 1886 en route to India was muted, it still provoked outrage in the press. As *The Tribune* of Lahore observed on April 17, 1886, "the refusal of the Government to permit Duleep Singh to live in the Punjab or even to visit it, is casting unjust slur upon the loyalty of the brave Sikh." The editorial concluded by lamenting his state: "Poor Duleep Singh! your countrymen can weep only for you."[68] *The Shamsher Akhbar* in Madras on May 24, 1886, printed a long article on Duleep Singh, which stated that he had been "harshly treated and confined on a desert island near Aden, and that his detention is a mad act on the part of Lord Dufferin."[69] On July 26, 1886, the *Aftabi-i-Punjab* of Lahore further criticized the state's responses to Duleep Singh, arguing that "fear of his being able to stir up a rebellion in India was unfounded" and that the "Government of India should conciliate him by granting him an increase of pension." Yet, as the earlier *The Tribune* article demonstrates, though proclaiming support for Duleep Singh in his return to Punjab, the press simultaneously declared Sikh loyalty to the colonial state. This tactic was a common enough for colonial officials to note that "most of the Punjab vernacular newspapers dwell on the fact of the loyalty of the people."[70]

The loyalty to the state, the public transcript, however, was at times mainly performative. The *Aftab-i-Punjab* highlights the contradictions that owners and editors negotiated to maintain space within the censored public sphere. On September 20, 1886, for example, after the *Civil and Military Gazette* had accused natives of circulating a seditious placard by Duleep Singh, the *Aftab-i-Punjab* responded that "Natives have not yet seen any such placard. It is simply impossible that the Sikh should foolishly court their ruin by intriguing with Dalip Singh. . . . The spread of such mischievous rumors cannot be too highly condemned, inasmuch as they are calculated to embitter the feelings of a class of natives who are most loyal to Government."[71] Though outwardly proclaiming Sikh loyalty toward the state and maintaining a moderate tone toward colonial rule, the owner of the *Aftab-i-Punjab* newspaper of Lahore, Diwan Buta Singh, a member of the Namdharis (an emergent tradition within the Sikh fold), played a central role in assisting Duleep Singh in his rebellion against the colonial state. He held organizing meetings in preparation for Duleep Singh's arrival and was one of the few to receive a direct telegram from Singh when he boarded the *Verona* toward India from London. Preparing for Singh's return, Buta Singh argued privately to friends and associates that the state should allow him to roam freely in the subcontinent. Duleep Singh's failure to land in India was a blow, and Buta Singh became "deeply incensed at the detention of Dhulip Singh at Aden."[72] Still, after Duleep Singh's arrest, Buta Singh continued to organize and became a key fulcrum between Punjab and Pondicherry—the new site for Duleep Singh's allies to congregate—providing funds and information for a would-be revolution.[73]

The difference between Buta Singh's public and private maneuvering reveals how loyalty to the state was performative, allowing its performers to both remain outside the regulatory apparatus of the state as well as put pressure on the state to accede to demands, which could cultivate further possible action within a broader coalescing community. On October 29, 1886, Buta Singh's *Aftab-i-Punjab* reiterated Sikh loyalty to the colonial state, observing that "no one could be a greater enemy of Government than one who tried to alienate its heart from a brave and staunch race like the Sikhs, who had given ample proof of their courage and loyalty on many occasions." Yet after lauding the loyalty of Sikhs, the *Aftab-i-Punjab* proceeded to make demands upon the state itself, writing that Sikhs were "deserving of the highest consideration at the hands of the Government." This was especially the case since "they merely wished to see Dalip Singh in order to find out his present condition," even though "they had no sympathy with him, nor did they expect anything from him."[74] The paradoxes here are apparent. Sikh loyalty to Empire required reciprocity from the colonial state. One way to demonstrate this reciprocity was allowing Duleep Singh's return. But this return undermined that very loyalty by providing symbolic coherence and organizational capacities outside of colonial rule.

Dyal Singh Majithia, the owner of *The Tribune*, offers a similarly illustrative example. Majithia refuses to be neatly categorized—a trait he lent to *The Tribune* both in the newspaper's content and organizational structure. Though *The Tribune* wrote about Sikh loyalty to the colonial state, Majithia supported Duleep Singh's sought-after rebellion and nationalist politics in the early 1880s. He was a key member of the aforementioned Indian Association, eventually becoming president of the Lahore branch in 1890.[75] Surendnranath Banerjea even claimed to provide the impetus for the founding of the *Tribune* in 1881, writing that he had "persuaded him [Majithia] to start a newspaper in Lahore" that would be "the faithful organ of Indian public opinion."[76] These connections among the elite of the subcontinent were reflected in the decidedly nonparochial *Tribune*. The editors that Majithia hired were themselves Bengalis who were also involved in nationalist politics. The editor of *The Tribune* in 1887, a Bengali, Sitalakanata Chatterjee, was "corresponding with the Indian Association about getting up some political meetings in the Punjab," as Andrew B. Bernard from the Calcutta Police Office noted.[77]

The Bengali connection went deeper, undoing the normative racial divisions that sustained colonial rule. Beyond the Indian Association, Majithia organized with Bengalis in favor of Duleep Singh's return. The district superintendent of police in Lahore noted on July 27, 1886 that two Bengalis, Pratul Chundra Chatarji [sic] and Jogendra Chandra Basu [sic], were "stirring up agitation in favor of Maharaja Dalip Singh."[78] Chatterji was quite close to Majithia, having been first introduced to him in 1876.[79] Chatterji wrote that they became familiar after Majithia moved back to Lahore and that, in general, Majithia was "on the warmest terms of friendship with the leading members of the Bengali community in Lahore."[80] Their friendship was such that both Chatterji and Bose became principal advisers to Majithia when he started *The Tribune* in 1881. Alongside these alliances and their accompanying intrigue, Majithia sent "Rs. 50,000 to the Maharaja" while noting "his wealth was at the service of Dalip Singh." Moreover, one official concluded, Majithia was "a prime mover in the conspiracy, in connection with Dalip Singh, to tamper with Sikhs in the British Army."[81]

The discovery of an anonymous letter circulating in Calcutta in June 1887 left no doubt that Majithia was tied to these affairs and gave the state cause to intensify its watch of Majithia, Chatterji, Bose, and *The Tribune*. It was again Andrew Bernard from the Calcutta Post Office who reported that "a letter in English, without date or address, was seen last night in the house of Nilamber Mukerji [sic], who returned from Kashmir last year."[82] Mukherjee had been a central figure in Kashmir—the chief justice of Kashmir—for nearly two decades. He had also worked in 1867 at the Punjab Chief Court in Lahore.[83] While in Kashmir, Mukherjee frustrated the British state with his sharp legal mind, using legal pretext to enable the Kashmiri princely state to avoid complying with British suggestions. That the letter was seen at his home signaled further intrigue, since it was signed "Dalip Singh, true king of the Punjab." In terms of content, Bernard reported that the letter stated that Duleep Singh, now in Russia, had been "promised that the Russians will put him on the throne of the Punjab, if he succeeds in inducing the Sikh soldiers to desert from the British on the eve of battle, and if he can arrange for all British soldiers to be prevented from going to Afghanistan by creating local disturbances all over India, by means of dacoities, riots and arson. . . . And the letter ends by hoping that his friends in India will help in these matters." The letter, Bernard argued, though first appearing in Punjab, "now appears either to be in circulation, or else copies are being sent to the friends of Dalip Singh about the country."[84]

Duleep Singh's arrivals, now in Kashmir and Bengal, caused further worry to the colonial administration. In response, in June 1887 the state enhanced its surveillance of activities tied to Duleep Singh in the subcontinent in order to obtain the information needed to dissolve all possible connections that compromised the race-based stereotypes and hierarchies that buttressed the colonial system of governance. To do this the state sought to monitor those who functioned outside their ethnographic fashioning. The letter came to fix such misbehaving subjects. For example, Barnard argued, "I think that if a strict private watch was kept over Sardar Dyal Singh, Proprietor of the Lahore Tribune, and Pratul Chundra Chatterji, N. L, a Pleader of the Lahore Chief Court, something more might be found out about it."[85] But letters tied to Duleep Singh continued to circulate, though for the most part clandestinely. Just one month later, in August 1887, the Punjab police discovered another letter about Duleep Singh's revolts on its way to Majithia. This letter also noted that Jemadar Atar Singh sent two letters from Pondicherry on the same topic, one to Sardar Jowala Singh of Kapurthala and the other to Sardar Dial Singh of Majithia [sic]."[86]

As we have seen, this hidden agitation troubled colonial administrators not because it sought to uphold the Indian nation-state, a nation as community, against colonial rule. The colonial state's ethnographic assumptions revealed the community not to be capable of holding knowledge outside their particular racial groupings; the secret of the nation could not fashion a national public. Therefore, the state was principally worried that the struggle to cultivate "unity" in the public sphere would create chaos through internecine conflict as beliefs would attach themselves to an attempt to cultivate knowledge of a not-ready nation. Regulating attempts at unity, then, was essential until proper knowledge, itself based on what were considered the irreconcilable differences between races, was inculcated within the community. This paradox, however, denied the possibility of a unity altogether. Functioning within this logic, the owners and editors of newspapers recognized they were constrained. In this constraint, they remained

mindful of the fine line between sedition and loyalty. For example, if Majithia and Buta Singh discarded the public transcript that required incessant
enunciation of Sikh loyalty to the colonial state and instead used a hidden
transcript capable of performing different types of loyalty within the public
sphere, as Duleep Singh did through a renunciation of the self in his upholding of *hukam*, then they too would face censure and arrest. Facing these
constraints, proprietors such as Majithia and Buta Singh sought to keep
their efforts to cultivate a broader politics hidden from the watchful eyes of
the colonial administration. As we have seen, they did not always succeed.

Within the public terrain of contested knowledge, where the contours between sedition and permissible critique were increasingly muddled, colonial administrators continuously intervened, looking to con-
strain the parameters of belief by determining which words constituted
sedition—determining which words excited belief. For example, the
Aftab-i-Hind had harsh words for the Calcutta-based Anglo newspaper
the *Englishman*, which sought to delegitimize Duleep Singh's claims by
casting doubt on his parentage. The *Aftab-i-Hind* responded, writing
"Now that Dalip Singh has asked Government to redress his grievances
Englishmen have the audacity to question his legitimacy. These pale faces
are capable of anything."[87] But deploying such acrimonious and language
was risky. For instance, the *Rahbar-i-Hind* was reprimanded for an article that appeared on May 7, 1887, that mocked English capacities for governance by inverting the Darwinist logic that the state itself used to justify imperial rule. Writing about incomes of religious institutes and their
taxability, the article stated:

> There is a scarcity of politicians among the English now; and it must neces-
> sarily be so, for the brains of the drunkards' children become naturally
> weaker and weaker in each succeeding generation. Lord Dufferin should be
> sent to Russia as Ambassador, so that His excellency may mismanage affairs
> there. There are many ways of earning money. If the Government were to
> take the monopoly of prostitutes in its charge like the monopoly of opium
> and wines, it would create a fruitful source of income for itself.[88]

For Lyall, articles like the one in the *Rahbar-i-Hind* were "not uncommon."
The danger of such articles, Lyall claimed, consisted in both their "exciting
disaffection to Government" as well as "promoting race or class hatred."[89]

This language made the *Rahbar-i-Hind* open to prosecution under section 124A of the Indian Penal Code for defaming a particular race and thus exciting race hatred. In this case, however, authorities decided not to prosecute but to issue a stern warning to the editors and publisher.

Like other publications from Indian elites, *The Tribune* sought to negotiate boundaries between subversion and loyalty to avoid such censure in a variety of ways. On May 21, 1887, *The Tribune* published an article written by a Punjabi who came across Duleep Singh in Paris—where Duleep Singh absconded after his detainment in Aden—in December 1886. *The Tribune* qualified its reasons for publishing the piece in order to circumvent accusations of sedition. Specifically, the editors noted, "We publish the account without the least hesitation because we are fully convinced that it can do no harm—it contains nothing new; and many things foolish, which are also not new and can harm him [Duleep Singh] only. Moreover, we believe, there is not a soul in the Punjab who cares for Dalip Singh." The article then disclosed the conversation, which built affective ties between the broader community and Duleep Singh without explicitly tying the *Tribune* to the cultivated ties. The author of the account noted that the "strong and stout" Duleep Singh's "manly and handsome countenance bore the impress of thought anxiety." They spoke together in Punjabi, leading the author to note that Duleep Singh "speaks very fluently and much better than I."[90]

The conversation that the article recounted focused mainly on Duleep Singh's pecuniary difficulties and what Singh avowed was his aversion to politics. *The Tribune* reported that Duleep Singh told his interlocutor that "I never dreamt of the Punjab throne." His letter in *The Evening Standard*, Duleep Singh proceeded, was "a friendly letter only," which was "taken for a political letter by the shortsighted Government, and the words, '*Wah Guru ji ki Fatteh*' was taken as a war cry when it was only a complimentary phrase." By placing the misreading on the state, its incorrect coupling of the political and religious, Duleep Singh argued that the state had failed to live up to its own ideals. Duleep Singh further appropriated liberal discourse by telling his interlocutor that "a subject of England was deprived of his liberty without any cause and without a warrant" since "the warrant [for his arrest in Aden] was obtained long after my arrest."[91]

For a publication to show outward loyalty to the state but also advance arguments to undermine it was not always easy, and it could lead to reprimands from colonial officials who watched the press closely. In *The*

Tribune Duleep Singh's words were echoed in a European voice on June 11, 1887, in an article entitled, "A European's Estimate of Dalip Singh's Influence in the Punjab." Written by Andrew Hearsey, a British lieutenant colonel, the article mocked Britain's self-presented evenhandedness and argued that Duleep Singh's financial and political claims were not only merited but also presented a real and credible danger to British rule. Hearsey argued that Punjab was a "powder magazine, so long as it is carefully kept and guarded there is not fear, but even a single spark inside is liable to cause danger." For Hearsey, Duleep Singh was that spark. Touching on his own grievances, he noted that Sikhs would not be the only ones to revolt if armed conflict ensured, since they would be joined by "numerous young gentlemen in India, Anglo-Indians, and Eurasians to whom the Government will give no employment whatsoever, and who would therefore willingly join the Russian army" against the British Empire.[92] To the aforementioned secretary to the Government of Punjab, W. M. Young, Hearsey's open letter offered an opportunity for the state to make an example of how it would deal with sedition like this in the future: the letter, Young wrote, "would have this advantage[,] that the arm of the law would be brought to bear in a case in which the primary offender is not a native."[93]

Lyall, however, argued that although Hearsey's editorial was clearly seditious, it would not "be taken seriously by the natives" because "the suggestion of a Sikh force organized against the British government and commanded by Eurasians and discontented domiciled Anglo Indians will strike them as absurd."[94] Sedition, remember, was tied to specific racial groupings which could effectively manipulate the population—something Lyall deemed laughable in the case of Hearsey. Based on colonial assumptions about different ethnic groups, even with evidence to the contrary, Lyall concluded that peoples of different races could not unite together; thus, Bengalis were the segment of the population who posed the only real risk to British authority. Punishment for sedition, then, if any, should be meted out to that particular mischievous community. Sharing this perspective, one official in Punjab, Herbert Charles Fenshawe, concluded that even though "a seditious letter from Captain Hearsey did no doubt appear in the *Tribune* of 11 July 1887. . . . Dyal Singh has really nothing to with the editing of the paper, which is entirely in the hands of Bengalis, and this cannot be imputed to him."[95]

IMPOSSIBLY SEDITIOUS

Lyall singled Bengalis out in particular for possessing a seditious disposition. As treasonous as some of the things published in the Punjabi press were, material published in the Bengali press went further: Lyall maintained the articles about Duleep Singh were not "so distinctly seditious as many that are published against the British government in Bengal newspapers."[96] Bengalis could more freely express their views if they published newspapers outside British jurisdiction in Chandernagore, a French colony at the time. *The Dhumketu*, for example, a native paper based in Chandernagore, published a seditious article extolling Duleep Singh on June 17, 1887. In it Dayal Chander Bose, the author, wrote, "O wicked Englishmen, do you remember the insults which you have heaped on the lion (the son of Ranjit Singh)? Can Dalip, the son of the King of the Punjab, quietly cherish such fearful anguish in his heart?" The message the Bengali Bose wanted to impart was clear: Sikhs needed to awaken and reclaim their sovereignty through Duleep Singh. He continued:

> From a far distance and with the fire of hope burning in his heart, he [Duleep Singh] is from time to time roaring out, "Awake ye Sikhs." Hark, he is still roaring deeply: Ye Sikhs! quit your beds and awake. How do you bear so much insult? Look you—a fire is burning within him and tear drops stand in the corners of his eyes. Look about you, Ye Heroic Sikh bands and put that fire out by sprinkling water upon it! . . . Don't you, brother, sleep no longer. Open your eyes, call forth fresh energy and break off the insupportable shackles of bondage and slavery.[97]

Bose concluded his article by denouncing colonial rule in sharp terms, notably by employing the language of liberty that Britons of the period would have readily understood: "To live in bondage is to live in hell. To live in bondage is to suffer cruel oppression. To live in bondage is only to live in the body and not in the spirit. Snap asunder the cruel fetters of bondage."[98] Still, outside both the geographic and discursive jurisdiction of the British state, Bose's anticolonial message was not couched merely in the language of loyalty. Instead he appealed to a community both within and outside the grasp of the public, relying on a hope that a revived spirit could undo the chains of time and dispense colonial rule altogether.

When coming from outside British jurisdiction, such oppositional writing posed a problem for authorities since it was difficult to legally prevent. As Durand himself noted, even though Bose's letter was "a deliberate appeal to the Sikhs to rise in favour of Dalip Singh," the state was limited in its ability to respond. Durand argued, "if the paper were published in British territory I believe the writer or publisher or both might be sentenced to transportation for life under Section 124A of the Penal Code." But, he continued, in Bose's case all that colonial authorities could do was to punish "the dissemination of the paper in British territory though it is printed elsewhere in Chandernagore."[99] Colonel P. D. Henderson claimed the paper was "probably published by British subjects from what they consider to be the safe asylum of French territory."[100] The only recourse, Henderson believed, was to appeal to the governor of the French Settlements and pursue action through that route. Durand agreed and wondered "whether the French authorities should not be asked to take steps for putting an end to such open attempts to excite rebellion in the territory of a friendly power."[101] Eventually, the officials decided against such action since the French too would make reciprocal demands, compromising British sovereignty itself.

But in order to counteract overt opposition to British rule, the state claimed Bose's letter was motivated by individual profit and gain. For example, Young argued that Duleep Singh's "cause had been taken up by the down-country papers not because of general interest in the subject but as an excuse to abuse the authorities and further sales. Very few of the editors of the Punjab newspapers have a real interest in the Maharajah's case." Young put the profit motive behind mentioning Duleep Singh in print in even more explicit terms elsewhere: "seditious matter," he wrote, "is imported merely, because it provides a certain amount of excitement and secures a certain sale of the issues."[102] Donald McCracken, assistant to the Punjab inspector general of police, echoed this view and singled out the *Akhbar-i-am*, noting that the paper "varies its tone from day to day with a view most likely to read sale, rather than from disloyalty."[103] In this context, it is unsurprising that Bose's article in *The Dhumketu* was likewise identified as motivated primarily by profit. Specifically, colonial officials argued *The Dhumketu* published its seditious verses in favor of Duleep Singh because they hoped they would "attract Dalip Singh's and Thakur Singh's [Sindhanwalia] attention, and thus would be the means of bringing some fortune to them."[104] Patronage and sales, then, motivated Bose's rhetoric, rather than questions about sovereignty.

SECRETS IN THE ARCHIVE

Another paper in Chandernagore, *The Beaver*, unsettles the focus on individual intention tied to profit and in a roundabout way returns us to the theme of the loss of sovereignty, if we ever left it. This is especially so since loss requires we consider what we are recovering when we trace the intentions that drive the writing and circulation of letters especially in relation to the press. History, too, can hold out the promised revelation of a lost object—an object discovered in the archive. Publicization in a narrative form then offers repair in the discovery of a secret in the archive—a secret that repairs while furthering binding one to the archive.[105]

At first, *The Beaver*'s proprietor and editor, Sashi Boshan Mukherjee, sought to assist Duleep Singh.[106] The plan the two of them agreed on called for *The Beaver* to function, one colonial official noted, as "a channel of communication between him [Duleep Singh] and the natives"—a plan, Irwin thought, that required surveilling in order to "look out for any further correspondence with the Maharaja."[107] Irwin's concern was well founded, for Mukherjee did indeed inform Duleep Singh that he could provide him with an audience with the former king of Oudh alongside other native princes and many Bengalis, which would enable him to spread his feelings of discontent deep into the subcontinent. After Mukherjee received £2,000 from Duleep Singh to defray the costs of running a press, *The Beaver* published several of Duleep Singh's letters and sought to bring other editors to his cause—a project Mukherjee undertook until the paper went out of business quickly thereafter in 1887 and Mukherjee returned to Calcutta. Even after this failed venture, Mukherjee wrote to Duleep Singh under the pseudonym U. Gupta, informing him that he still had a "literary connection with many other papers" that Duleep Singh could "depend on."[108]

Even though he pledged his loyalty to Duleep Singh, Mukherjee's alliances were shifting. A memorandum in the archive notes that the inspector of the Calcutta police, J. C. Mitter, met with Mukherjee in 1887 and "took him into his confidence and through him opened correspondence with Dalip Singh."[109] This correspondence eventually led to the arrest of Duleep

Singh's close confidant and ambassador Arur Singh, who was lured out of Chandernagore to Calcutta, the memorandum relayed by Mukherjee's machinations.

Or at least that is what one particular memorandum in the archive, written on September 22, 1887, disclosed, after determining that Mukherjee's primary motive in building a relation with Duleep Singh must have been financial.[110] In contrast, Colonel P. D. Henderson and the inspector who arrested Arur Singh provided a different account of Arur Singh's arrest, obstructing, or perhaps scattering, the essential role Mukherjee played in the archive. Namely, Henderson noted that Duleep Singh gave Arur Singh instructions to visit Mukherjee at Chandernagore to meet with the editor of *The Beaver*, Boshan Mukherjee, who would give him further instructions on how to proceed. But, Henderson writes, "Arur Singh did not know that the publication of *The Beaver* had been stopped" and went onward to Chandernagore on August 1, 1887, expecting to find *The Beaver*'s office. After discovering it was closed, he went to the post office to find Mukherjee's address, "on Beadon Street in Calcutta, British territory."[111] Already under surveillance, Arur Singh left French safety to venture to Calcutta in search of Mukherjee. Once in British jurisdiction, Inspector J. C. Mitter watched Singh go into the houses of both J. Ghosal and the aforementioned Nilamber Mukherjee in Calcutta. On August 4, the inspector made acquaintance with Arur Singh by playing the "part of a sceptic" and telling him that "before I trusted him with my secrets, he must convince me that he was not a member of the secret force." Trusting the inspector, Arur Singh then presented him letters from Duleep Singh alongside a blank check signed by the Maharaja. Arur Singh was soon after arrested for revolutionary activities. Mukherjee, in this narrative, was not the cause of the arrest. Yet he remained implicated in the investigation into Bengali connections to Duleep Singh, for the inspector asked that "Ghosal, Nilamber Mukerji, and the late proprietor of the Beaver should be left altogether untouched for any proceedings against them would seriously interfere with my future work."[112]

Unlike the imprisoned Arur Singh, who divulged his seditious intentions, the shrewd inspector and Mukherjee evaded such grasp in the archive. One colonial administrator, John Ware Edgar, disclosed on August 7, 1887, that the inspector himself was pretending to collaborate with Duleep Singh. Edgar wrote, "it appears that some months ago a detective officer under

Barnard wrote to Dalip Singh a dummy letter expressing sympathy, and a desire to aid him." This unsigned letter, Edgar continued, "indicated the writer was employed in the Bengal police, and might be heard of through friends of Dalip Singh's at Chandernagore." For Edgar this explained Arur Singh's arrest: Duleep Singh, taken in by the letter, sent his emissary Arur Singh with a letter to this anonymous writer. Mitter detected his arrival and watched him until he came to Calcutta. Once in Calcutta and outside French jurisdiction, the inspector, Edgar details, "found out Arur Singh, introduced himself to him, wormed out his secret, and finally had him arrested."[113] Though securing the circulation of letters between Mitter and Duleep Singh, in Edgar's retelling Mukherjee is conspicuously lost, though, perhaps, existing as one of the unknown friends who could vouch for the anonymous letter writer.

Though the inspector ultimately had Arur Singh arrested, colonial officials were suspicious of claims that Mitter's letter to Duleep Singh was always meant as a fabrication designed to entrap Arur Singh. For instance, Barnard suspected Inspector Mitter himself of plotting with Duleep Singh. He further noted that at the time of Arur Singh's arrest he was "sleeping in the inspector's house, believing that officer to be a well-wisher of Dalip Singh's."[114] Though the arrest appeared to vindicate the inspector, the arrest itself still seemed too easy. As Durand argued, Arur Singh's proceedings "were so simple that they almost suggest a 'plant' on the other side."[115] But numerous interviews with Arur Singh to determine the nature of his activities yielded very little additional information, as "reports of another unsuccessful interview with Arur Singh" were the norm among officials, causing Henderson to write, "the case looks hopeless." Henderson labelled Arur Singh "obdurate" and "pretend[ing] ignorance,"[116] even though he was "a dull heavy man, and to all appearance about as bad a messenger as Dalip Singh could have chosen." Even so, certainly during his interrogation, Arur Singh did not incriminate Ghosal, Nilamber Mukherjee, or Sashi Boshan Mukherjee. Instead, Henderson noted, Arur Singh "would not admit that Soshi Boshan had any communications to him, but says this man [Boshan] told him to go Chandernagore as it was not safe to make any disclosures on British territory." Though finding information difficult to procure, Henderson affirmed his own ethnographic knowledge, writing, "I was not mistaken in my fear that a Sikh would not be easily brought to peach."[117] Arur Singh did, however, send a note to Duleep Singh on September 8, 1887, concealing his own missteps and informing Duleep Singh that "he was given by Mukherji and his other friends in charge to the Calcutta Police."[118]

Much like the archive, then, Arur Singh simultaneously divulged too much and not enough information, refusing to allow the administration to quell its anxieties.[119] Mukherjee, too, discloses these archival graspings, remaining both a threat to revolt and mischievously self-serving. Two years later, in 1889, after discovering four more mysterious proclamations from Duleep Singh, the state once again sought to determine Bengali involvement in their circulation. After listing possible suspects, Henderson wrote, "another possible agency in Calcutta is Soshi Voshan Mukherji of the now extinct 'Beaver.'"[120] The deputy commissioner of police in Calcutta, however, found this difficult to believe since, he argued, Mukherjee's connections with Duleep Singh's intrigues had ceased because "the Sardar's party suspected Soshi" was responsible for Arur Singh's arrest.[121] Now, once again, Mukherjee was dislocated from police maneuvering and reduced to a suspect character in the eyes of both the colonial state and Sikh exiles.

Still, though, the archival record refuses intent and content; even with these losses it produces a particular form of knowledge as well as sociality in its promise to disclose the secret. Either Mukherjee, as a site of a mischievous untrustworthiness, defected to the British, reaffirming the state's own racial fantasies of the Bengali character, which became further codified in state records, or Arur Singh, failing in his important mission, blamed Mukherjee and thus also confirmed the state's presumptive partitions of community, which continued into 1890. At the very least, the archive confirms the possible use of such divisive racial classifications though the state officials claimed no partiality towards or against individual groups. Though the inspector's duplicitous letter apparently led to Arur Singh's capture, Durand argued that he did not "quite like the 'dummy letter' business," hoping it was "not found out." He wanted it to remain a secret since knowledge of state duplicity could undermine both the self-assured knowledge of the community and the logic of waiting that undergirded liberal governance.[122] Race and religion, then, were central for the state to provide an object to community, even if these organizational webs did not function within the parameters of state control and oversight.

Although its racial demarcations were confirmed, colonial administration remained marred by difficulties. These came to the fore when Duleep Singh sent one of his followers, a Sikh, to check on the arrested Arur Singh.

Bernard recounted that on September 13, 1887, "an elderly Sikh, stoutly built, with whiskers, turning grey, and calling himself Dhurm Singh, came to the house of the late editor of the *Beaver* newspaper and asked where Arur Singh was." Mukherjee told him he did not know where Arur Singh was but took him to the inspector's house. Luckily for Dhurm Singh, the inspector was out at the time. All attempts to locate Dhurm Singh afterward were unsuccessful even though officials inquired about him through their expansive networks all over Calcutta and at Chandernagore. As Barnard wrote, "no trace of the man could be got," largely owing to his "extremely meagre description." Moreover, it was "impossible to tell whether he left Calcutta by train, as there are now-a-days so many Sikhs travelling to and from Calcutta." All Barnard could report was that he had "very little information about the man referred to," since "he was not seen by any officer of his department."[123] Both meager and many, lacking and copious, absent and present, Dhurm Singh had arrived at his destination and disappeared.

Empirically determined through imperial classification, but also elusive—lost, Dhurm Singh reveals the limits of colonial knowledge and surveillance. Or, as Anjali Arondekar reminds us, "even as an 'empire of knowledge' expanded its taxonomical gaze, its instruments of surveillance and classification seemed continually incommensurate to the landscape it sought to map and measure."[124] Dhurm Singh reveals such incommensurability, directing our attention to the untraceable and unaccountable presence of Sikhs within an ordered colonial space. For even with the Bengali's mischievous intent defined and Sikh obstinacy known, the community still remained outside such contours. Intent proved difficult to determine. People could (mis)read intent because they were unconstrained by knowledge and its secrets. Unconstrained, they could even appear at those who the state ostensibly considered under their watch and control. This was precisely the danger. The community, not bound to colonial forms of knowledge and their determination of intentions, would be unable to discern whether the press deployed Duleep Singh for profit or to foment revolt, and instead could render him in unpredictable and indiscernible ways outside the surveillance of British rule and within traffic across the space of colonial difference.

With this danger in mind, the colonial state determined, Young argued, that it had to actually consider the people on India as capable of understanding colonial forms of knowledge. The instability of information free-floating within the South Asian landscape, unattached to intent, required authorities to create conditions where people could properly adduce the correct meaning of Duleep Singh. Once the translation of Evans Bell's book into Gurmukhi had begun, this was Young's reaction as well. Young suggested that "an authentic statement of the Maharaja's case should be communicated to the newspapers." This was precisely the end goal of colonial officials: to render Duleep Singh a fact not susceptible to belief, to dispel any secret Duleep Singh harbored by foregrounding knowledge. For colonial officials, there was hope because these conditions of proper knowledge and its associated interpreters were slowly starting to emerge, though not quickly enough to bring about the end of colonial rule. Colonel W. I. Bax, for example, noted on June 11, 1887, from Nowgond, Bundelkhand, that "an occasional article in a vernacular paper is read out by someone (often a boy from the school) and discussed. But there is no dwelling on the subject, nor is Dalip Singh's name constantly on their lips or talked over in gatherings. In fact, the subject is treated very much as any other piece of news."[125] Rendered as "any other piece of news," a secret revealed to the people, this empirical and known Duleep Singh then could, the state hoped, sustain the very contours of colonial rule—contours that could perhaps enclose the lost Dhurm Singh within an appropriate frame, even if the colonial state was unable to apprehend him physically. Yet still Duleep Singh eluded, for, Spivak perceptively notes, within this reading aloud of newspapers, "the range of speculative possibilities becomes even more seductive," entrapping even the investigator and interrupting our certainties.[126]

Therefore, although publicity is central to liberal understandings of the public, since it provides so-called information to create a knowledgeable subject, thereby holding out possibility for a redeemable community, the secret continued to be elusive in the colony. Whereas "the secret" sustains the public in the West through the guarantee of knowledge, since the colonized community was conceptualized outside the very parameters of the "public-supposed-to-know" and judgment was always already contaminated, knowledge could never be stabilized in relation to belief in non-European and nonsettler societies. Publicity of the secret, in this rendering, could create unconstrained belief, disrupting the very structure of a secured public sphere under colonial rule.

The secret of Duleep Singh forged alliances in Bengal, and these alliances yielded loss, revealing the difficulties of ordering the community most notably highlighted in the figure of the malleable Sashi Mukherjee and the unverifiable movements of Dhurm Singh. Within this disrupting archive, the public emerges as a knot, unable to be adjudicated into historical form and instead requiring that we inhabit the uncertainty and instability that the stories and machinations of Duleep Singh bring to the fore. Indeed, there is no secret to be revealed.

Chapter Three

CONVERSION

I have this sense that claiming something as modern is a kind of closure.

—TALAL ASAD

Perhaps we have gone too far, evading Duleep Singh in a manner that, as Jacques Rancière notes, disqualifies "the verbiage of every proffered message in favor of the mute eloquence of who is not heard."[1] Proposing loss as the final demarcation of Duleep Singh can function in such a manner, reducing his historical being to an impossibility, always already unable to be signified.[2] It would monumentalize, fetishize, the very attachment to loss as the fixation on failure takes root. But this too is unfair, for we are trying to dwell in the impossibility of finality, to refuse to synchronize clocks as we continue to chip away at the fetish object. We are not reductively revealing a singular nondetermination in what remains a hyperinvestment in the past.[3] That is, loss does not remain as such, but, as Žižek writes, "the void of primordial repression has to be filled in" and masked by fantasy. This void, then, as the condition of impossibility for the historical landscape, provides the very conditions of possibility for historical consistency.[4] Or in other words, constitutive loss gives rise to the symbolic, our mediation of this traumatic impossibility, which always colors our relation to loss while never allowing the subject, Žižek argues, to "ever fully and immediately identify with his symbolic mask or title."[5] Instead of disqualifying the historical subject, to think about loss requires we inhabit the unstable structure of the subject's eloquence, reintroducing dynamism in time while challenging the totalizing nature of a particular ideological constellation.

I have gestured to this dynamic throughout the book thus far, considering how the colonial subject oscillated between contradictory interpellations, noting how these contradictions revealed the perseverance and failure of symbolic coherence, occurring through both conscripted public transcripts and persistent hidden transcripts that refuse easy determinations even regarding causality. Here, too, I will emphasize the tensions and contradictions of Duleep Singh by dwelling within coloniality's unruly "epistemic murk."[6] For Michael Taussig, epistemic murk occurs in conjunction with the systemization and failure of ethnographic fabulations and fantasies; it is a failure that both unravels and creates difference. As the following chapter will show, this uncertain reality made out of fiction clouded the colonial state and Duleep Singh's attempts to become sovereign once again. Enclosed within the contradictions that arose in these fantasies and their incumbent murkiness, Duleep Singh, much like the colonial project and indigenous politics, offers no cathartic resolution even while the world wavered and allowed for the possibility of a decisive and instant moment.

But how did judgment cohere around Duleep Singh? Though we have examined the double move in community (its organization and then its own impossibility), how did the *sangat*, the community, come to judge Duleep Singh central to itself and politics? This question is posed not to provide an origin for Duleep Singh's legitimacy within the community, which would, Foucault reminds us, assume "the existence of immobile forms," creating the very neat historical teleology we have tried to avoid.[7] Instead it grapples with a question central to local communities: how to determine the parameters of credibility? The answer is a muddled one. The question of cohering community is complex, a philosophical question about indebtedness, responsibility, and ethics. Under colonial rule, however, attempts to cement reality made representations of community more than just a philosophical problem: they also became "a high-powered medium of domination."[8] Yet local credibility, conferred as it is through negotiation and skill, cannot be reduced to colonial maneuverings. But neither was the colonial order absent, as we have seen, continuously intervening to determine the nature and role of community while introducing new parameters for judgment and settling reality through its representations.

Duleep Singh's conversion back, or perhaps reversion, to Sikhism reveals an interplay between a colonial order, the individual, and the *sangat*. That conversion did come to indicate an authentication of one's belief—an inner realm—a shift in epistemic coordinates wrought by colonial rule.[9] As Charles Taylor writes, there was an understanding that developed in the West in the late eighteenth century in which "Each of us has an original way of being human." A moral importance becomes attached to "a kind of contact with myself, with my own inner nature, which it sees as in danger of being lost."[10] Duleep Singh centered this inner nature as conversion came to indicate authenticity.

Conversion cannot be limited to this frame, however. For example, how did *amrit*—the nectar one imbibes to join the Khalsa—dislocate the individual and require sanction from the community—a sanctioning not grounded in property? How do we inhabit a fractured inheritance? Thus, I do not provide a definitive rendition of the parameters of Duleep Singh's conversion around his return. Rather, I foreground the "murk" central to conversion in which cultural concepts and ideological forms are cracked apart, erupting indefinite meaning even though, as Peter van der Veer writes in relation to conversion, "it is very hard to escape from the play of memory and forgetfulness in the colonial and missionary archive"—an archive that narrates Duleep Singh's conversion to us.[11] Put another way, the very questions Duleep Singh's reversion raises, the reality of "conversion," mocks understanding and rationality even though the archive and the written word seek to make conversion admissible as an object of inquiry.

What to make of Duleep Singh's reversion to the Sikh tradition? In exploring this subject, we are in murky and uncomfortable territory, especially considering, as Talal Asad writes, that "there was a time when conversion didn't need explaining."[12] Duleep Singh converted to Christianity at the age of fourteen under the auspices of Reverend John Login and Bhajan Lal in Fatehgarh. But then, as we have seen, Duleep Singh increasingly made overtures to *Sikhi* in the 1880s, eventually taking *amrit* in 1886. How did Duleep Singh try to become legible within the community through his conversion/reversion into the Sikh fold—a legibility tied to ethical practices such as *khande di pahul* (initiation into the Khalsa by taking *pahul/amrit* by the *khanda*, a double-edged sword)?[13] I reflect on Duleep Singh's conversion and reconversion not to authenticate his renewed engagements with Sikhism nor to deny his earlier commitments to Christianity. Such a fixation on the confessional identarian concerns of an inward self would violate the very terms of the Sikh tradition and uphold Christian ones, inadvertently affirming a particular form of religiosity, which, in its very name, must be a Christian one.[14]

In the Sikh tradition, the very question of conversion is upended, since the purpose is not for an individual to reach a proper destination or to change direction toward a legitimate path, as the term conversion in the Christian context implies.[15] Instead, within the Sikh tradition, the community is asked to inhabit a dislocated space of *nimrata* (loweredness, humility). Within *nimrata*, the navigating subject on their path to true consciousness is interrupted and sheds both their identity and direction. There is no reconciled subject that the logic of conversion entails. The teleological direction that conversion necessitates thus is undone in favor of a never-achieved vanishing of the self and consciousness—a state of being that differentiates (*gurmukh/manmukh*) but remains undifferentiated.[16] Conversion cannot account for this vanishing, since such a vanishing cannot be a declaration, confession, or destination. Rather, the Sikh tradition cultivates *rahit*, "repository of the customs and practices of Sikhs," through practice and discipline, creating conditions of possibility for a Sikh, for learning.[17] The question then asked in the Sikh tradition—what does it mean to be *dharmi*, that is to practice dharm—does not provide easy answers to help us situate Duleep Singh and conversion. But, in its responses, the Guru Granth Sahib certainly questions the logic of navigation offered by conversion, reminding us, "The entire world chants '*Ram, Ram*,' roaming one place to the next, but *Ram* cannot be discovered in this manner.[18] Instead, one dwells in the world within which, through *shabad*, the Word, the Word as Guru, and its accompanying *rahit*, it becomes possible to consider the impossibility of the self in order to, perhaps, become Sikh.[19]

Put this way, to understand Duleep Singh's return we must place ethical practices in the Sikh tradition at center stage to understand how one learns to be Sikh, even when looking at a very particular circumstance of an elite conversion. There is no easy recovery of practices that allows us to ward off the losses that accumulated across colonial rule. Understandings within the Sikh tradition shifted as they became entangled within a colonial and capitalist logic. This entanglement rescripted *Sikhi* as a new colonial emphasis altered practices that went against the self to fostering a private self-identity through consumption. Under colonialism a relation between self and others became reduced to a relation between self and things, both a depoliticizing and privatizing gesture. In the colonial condition, endowed with newfound magical powers, both the self—now itself a commodity—validated private consumption and confession as the legitimate modes of expressing religious transformation and identity.[20] This change is explicitly, though not totally, reflected in the strategies deployed by Duleep Singh and his elite supporters to appeal to the broader community. Duleep Singh and his supporters, indeed, still appealed to the *sangat* in order to work toward sovereignty because *Sikhi* was not an individual depoliticized matter but required approval from the wider community, even though the new parameters of conversion sought to invert these relationships between the community and individual.

AN AUTHENTIC IDENTITY

We last left Duleep Singh in Aden, where colonial officials had arrested him. They sought to prevent him from advancing toward Bombay, where Duleep Singh wanted to take *amrit* in order to rejoin the Sikh fold. However, what this return meant was unclear, and Duleep Singh's understanding of conversion oscillated between centering the "known self" and "lowered self," drawing as he did from both longstanding Sikh and modern Western concepts to make sense of his world. This contradiction created what Tony Ballantyne calls Duleep Singh's "idiosyncratic vision of Sikhism."[21] Duleep Singh did dislocate the self, as we have seen, shedding his identity in favor of a non-self, and we learned how this was read in the *sangat,* the community. But the very possibility of an idiosyncratic theology reveals the emergence of the bourgeois self, in which the possibility of being standard *contra* idiosyncratic now constituted new epistemic coordinates.[22] That is to say, the question shifted from correct and incorrect behaviors within a collective, to individual idiosyncrasies and self-fashioning of an individualized form of life.

For instance, Duleep Singh wrote to the Khalsa in 1886, stating "I submit to His [the Guru's] Will [*hukam*], being persuaded that whatever is for the best will happen. I now, therefore, beg forgiveness of you, Khalsa Jee, or the Pure, for having forsaken the faith of my ancestors for a foreign religion; but I was very young when I embraced Christianity."[23] Occupying a position of both submission and decision, Duleep Singh's proclamation to Sikhs reveals the difficulty of demarcating conversion and identity under the conditions of colonial rule, since "authentic" belief could always be perceived as inauthentic by situating it in time, revealing prior immature judgment. The community, as well, did not just inhabit a paradigm in which *nimrata* constituted an ideal being, for the community, too, existed within epistemic conditions of the modern, which valorized the self-conscious cultivation of a private identity. From this perspective, the community reflected Duleep Singh's understanding as well, for the police recorded in May 1886 that Sikhs "state that they are quite willing to receive him back into the Sikh faith as his conversion to Christianity was effected when he was a child and not possessed of proper reasoning powers."[24]

Replicating missionary logic by declaring his previous belief in Christianity inauthentic due to his being a mere child at the time of his conversion, Duleep Singh looked to validate his new proper "belief" and rejoin the Sikh tradition. To return to the letter in 1886, he wrote to the Khalsa collective that it was his "fond desire on reaching Bombay to take the Pahul again, and I sincerely hope for your prayers to the Sutgooroo on that solemn occasion."[25] Taking *pahul* in itself, however, was no longer enough to reveal the proper orientation. Rather, one had to authenticate belief—which required rationality and reason; it required the mature individual subject who could discern fact from superstition. Duleep Singh presented himself to the community as such, and by extension his conversion as a mature one, largely through juxtaposing his decision with what he framed as the community's backwardness, highlighted in their deviation from the true teachings of the Sikh Gurus. For Duleep Singh, the community at the moment was misguided, led down a stray path by generations of leaders who introduced errors into Sikhism. In the same letter, he wrote:

But in returning to the faith of my ancestors, you must clearly understand, Khalsa Jee, that I have no intention of conforming to the errors introduced into Sikhism by those who were not true Sikhs—such for instance, as wretched caste observances or abstinence from meats and drinks, which Sutgooroo has ordained should be received with thankfulness by all mankind but to worship the pure and beautiful tenets of Baba Nanak and obey the commands of Gooroo Govind Singh.[26]

Inhabiting this pure and secure inheritance, Duleep Singh argued that his conversion back to Sikhism occurred because of his newfound ability to distinguish right from wrong—to establish the true object that constituted the Sikh community. Creating an identity as an object to be obtained and viewed from nowhere then, enabled him to recognize that consumption of meat and alcohol were permissible in the Sikh tradition. Against the constitutive role of difference in the Sikh tradition, which cultivated distinctive forms of practice irreducible to a singular form—that could not be objectified and viewed from an Archimedean point—Duleep Singh sought to authenticate his belief in *Sikhi* through such an object. In doing so he functioned within a static rendition of the Sikh tradition in which tradition itself was reduced to an object to be obtained rather than a struggle. Once rendered as object to be collected, authentic belief could then be substantiated by the knowing individual, who through reason alone could decipher truth from error, creating an authentic conversion.

The script then shifted from the impossible and unanswerable question "Who am I?" centered in the Sikh tradition to the emphatically modern answer "I am a Sikh" as a truth about the subject became a historical possibility. How to authenticate this truth? Proper self-constructive reasoning was insufficient to reveal temporal progression from a previous false consciousness to an enlightened one. Instead Duleep Singh had to substantiate his inner belief through action. Here, gender was crucial in securing the boundaries of the answer "I am a Sikh." For instance, once Sindhanwalia elicited the proper approvals from the community to Duleep Singh's return, as the Punjab police noted, he "sent letters announcing that the Maharaja has re-embraced the Sikh religion in England"—a conversion marked by the betrothal of "his daughters to the Buriya *sardars* in the Amballa district."[27] Though marriage ties legitimated sovereign rule in precolonial South Asia, securing the intricate alliances of nested sovereignty, in the colonial period women became a key means through which to establish the very parameters of Sikh identity—in this case, Duleep Singh's "Sikhness." Women, for Duleep Singh, helped to reveal the authenticity of his inner belief, an authenticity required by the logic of identity in the colonial period. Duleep Singh then, to bind this new Sikh identity tied to inner authenticity, betrothed his daughters to the sardars in Amballa. It was through his daughters that Duleep Singh demonstrated his "faith," since women were central in revealing the boundaries of both one's inner colonial subjectivity and tradition in the subcontinent, as Partha Chatterjee, Lata Mani, and others have forcefully shown.[28]

Duleep Singh's planned return was gendered in myriad other ways. Once establishing his return to the Sikh fold, Duleep Singh argued that he embodied a virile masculinity denied to his previous Christian self. In his rallying cry secretly sent to rulers of the Native States, he reminded his fellow native princes while imploring them to join him in revolt that "though we invite you thus to take part in this grand and glorious both work and duty, yet do not for a moment suppose, that we seek any aid from you, for God has otherwise made as strong who were once utterly feeble."[29] Upholding his own masculinity and personal maturation, he chastised the other princes for their naïve belief in British justice—a belief that emerged through their failure to protect their masculine sovereign selves, which, he argued, let effeminacy seep into their polities. He argued, "Friends, if you have not yet entirely degenerated into cowards and become effeminates nor turned into mere puppets in the hands of your deadly enemies, then rise up and make common cause with us and share with us also in the glory of liberating our mother country."[30] In Duleep Singh's rhetoric, and building on colonial demarcations of racial and gender roles, the key to liberating the "mother country" lay in cultivating the boundaries of the masculine Sikh self while warding off effeminacy—boundaries partly secured in his case through the strategic marriage of his daughters, now deployed in order to protect his "mother country" and reclaim sovereignty. Community and sovereignty thus become things that can be lost as they become authentic objects to be discovered and then confirmed within; the goal becomes to secure the object of identity and, therefore, community. Once this object is clearly defined, the distinction between Sikh and non-Sikh, for example, becomes crucial to defining the subject.

Duleep Singh had to continually authenticate the boundaries of his return to *Sikhi* because colonial officials argued that the Sikh tradition was lost to him; they, too, argued about the success, to borrow from scholarly parlance, of the colonial episteme. Colonial administrators emphasized the power of the European civilizing mission in transforming colonial subjects. Duleep Singh's Christian past remained a prophylactic against prophecy, against the impossibility of history. Instead, officials insisted that rupture governed a sequentially moving time. Since time was constituted by breaks in which the past became a distant object, then Duleep Singh could not return to his Sikh past. His earlier conversion to Christianity was important for this very reason. In 1851, upon receiving news of Duleep Singh's conversion at the age of fifteen, Lord Dalhousie argued, "Politically we could desire nothing better, for it destroys his possible influence forever."[31] Dalhousie argued that he would have preferred that Duleep Singh defer his conversion until he was older, "since at present it may be represented to have been brought about by tampering with the mind of a child." Still, however, Dalhousie noted that it was Duleep Singh's "own free act," representing "his own firm resolution." On September 14, 1853, J. Lowis made similar conjectures, writing that a trip to England would further Duleep Singh's break from the community by deepening his Christian ties, as well as "make him a man and gentleman" rather than "a thing" only known to South Asia.[32] By 1883 colonial administrators continued to hope that this rupture that was catalyzed by Duleep Singh's conversion to Christianity would hold. C. Grant, for example, wrote, "As he is a Christian, and has been entirely estranged by his long residence in England and his Europeanised habits from his own race it is conceivable that the Sikhs may attach little importance to him and his movements."[33]

According to colonial officials, even after his conversion back to the Sikh tradition, Duleep Singh could not become a true Sikh, tied as religion was to identity. Duleep Singh, the argument went, only displayed outward Sikh actions/rituals, and did not undergo a real spiritual conversion and therefore could not be recognized by the community as fully Sikh. Colonel Bonness Fischer, a British consular agent in Pondicherry, speaking to a French official, argued, "He is not unlike one of Alphonse Wandito [Daudet] 'Rois en éxile' [Kings in Exile] with this exception[:] that as he came to England when he was merely an infant he is much more of an Englishman than a Punjabi; and has as little in common with a Sikh as a Paris Boulevardier or a London man about town, both of whom he rather resembles in habits."[34] Referencing Daudet's novel about the idiocies of exiled monarchs, Fischer highlights the impossibility of Duleep Singh becoming Sikh since colonial rule instituted a break in time and, in so doing, created a hybrid subject who could no longer fit easily as within the Sikh community. In the eyes of colonial officials, Duleep Singh, in his efforts to overthrow empire, was an absurdity, one created by colonial rule.

Duleep Singh challenged this proclaimed success of the colonial project by contending that the colonial state was wrong in denying the possibility of such conversion. Gauri Viswanathan affirms this function of the colonial state, arguing, "Even when Hindus or Muslims were converting to Christianity, the decisions made by civil courts denied that such conscious change occurred, and the Christian convert was treated as essentially someone who had *not* converted."[35] Duleep Singh noted this discrepancy and argued that his arrest at Aden reflected the impossibility of his previous conversion to Christianity. Though he was, he argued, both a "naturalized Englishman" and a "Christian," the colonial administration placed him under arrest "without a warrant" and did not allow a "public trial" or even offer funds to obtain legal advice.[36] This differentiated treatment revealed, Duleep Singh stated in another letter to the community in 1887, that "there exists one law for the favoured Englishman and another for the hated Indian, though he might even be Christian." He contended that his experience was one of many for "their Christian immorality knows no bounds." The examples of Christian immorality that he provided were numerous. "What has taken place lately in Burma," he noted of the Third Anglo-Burmese War and the loss of Konbaung dynasty's sovereignty, was one more sign of this immorality. He asked, "In spite of the declarations of the Queen's Proclamation of 1858 to the contrary, does it appear that the days of annexation have come to an end?" Taking into account this Christian and colonial duplicity, Duleep Singh argued that the doors to an authentic Christianity remained closed, ruled as he was by a colonial state predicated on an irreconcilable difference between colonizer and native. In so doing, however, Duleep Singh upheld the interiority of the subject, which as Rupa Viswanath writes, made exposing an original interior central to determining the possibility of conversion and, therefore, also determining the possibility of community.[37]

A SPACE FOR CONVERSION

But this conclusion is too easy, too clear, evading the very murk that constituted colonial rule and conversion. More dangerously, in writing about Duleep Singh's bid to authenticate his identity and the colonial state's efforts to thwart such a possibility, we are replicating that very colonial frame, revealing inauthenticity in Duleep Singh's conversion and his attempt to cultivate *rahit* in *Sikhi*. We are upholding his selfhood to public scrutiny, which, in turn, provides a new site from which to regulate community. Seen from this perspective, taking Duleep Singh's inner life as central to his conversion(s) upholds the possibility of authentic representation in relation to a secure reality—now an inner one.[38] We cannot, however, reduce Duleep Singh's gestures to the actions of a self-conscious private individual because becoming Sikh, by taking *amrit*, is irreducible to such a logic. Taking *amrit* requires protocols of legitimation tied to a *sangat*, the *panth*, rather than the beliefs of the individual. But there is murk. Within this murk, *amrit* also confounded epistemic coordinates central to modernity, for it necessitated community, the *sangat*, in which the steadfastness of the modern conscious subject endowed with a personality became dislocated from within. This dislocation forces us to consider the possibility that perhaps *Sikhi* was never Duleep Singh's to lose and find again.

By taking *amrit*, Duleep Singh dissolved himself within the space provided by the broader community. As a space of debt rather than recognition, community confounds the self-certainty of the subject. The *sangat* muddled Duleep Singh's own attempts to substantiate his inner conscious life—a verification that looked at the tradition from a place of nowhere, an objective viewpoint. Instead, there were questions of responsibility that evaded the decision of a self-enclosed subject. Indeed, others were critical to the conversion. Once it became clear he would take *amrit*, Duleep Singh garnered further support from the community and did not simply dwell in his own subjecthood. The Punjab police, for example, reported in May 1886, "The Sikhs of Firozpur at first appeared to take little interest in Dhulip Singh, and to be indifferent whether he remained in England or not, but there was great rejoicing amongst them when they heard that he intended to take the *pahal* at Amritsar."[39]

Writing about conversion in colonial contexts has tended to revolve around the consciousness of the individual convert, focused as it is on the missionary experience predicated on the emancipatory powers of the reflective self and personal conviction. As Catherine Hall argues, "faith was at the heart of the missionary endeavor: a belief in the depravity of mankind and the absolute necessity of a change of heart with Christ as the only route to salvation."[40] Most famously, John and Jean Comaroff critique the naïve use of conversion as a conceptual tool, suggesting that within the European colonial project "'conversion' has always been part of its apparatus of cultural coercion."[41] Specifically, the Comaroffs show how the conversion process extended "the European system of distinction over Africa, drawing its peoples into a single scale of social, spiritual, and material inequality" even though at the time "the Tswana did not concede to the universalistic ethos of the mission, or to its discriminatory logic." Instead, the Comaroffs write, "the very nature of consciousness was the object of struggle." Conversion, therefore, fails as a heuristic device because it cannot account for this challenge and resistance practiced by the Tswana and other colonized people refusing to conform to European preconceptions and creating, as they did, spiritual bricolage and cultural change.

Though recognizing the importance of this intervention, Talal Asad and Ruth Marshall question the Comaroffs' conclusions, albeit in different contexts. For his part, Asad notes that, "what is now identified as the *object* of struggle in the Tswana setting—consciousness—has a specific Western genealogy, partly rooted in the Christian concept of 'conscience.' "[42] He continues:

> The changed epistemic structure brought about by the conversion to modernity articulates a range of new possibilities not adequately captured by the simple alternatives of passive reception by subjects or active resistance by agents, of unoriginal reproduction or synthetic originality. The politics of consciousness, like the politics of personal identity of which it is part, is an entirely modern Western possibility. The self-conscious selection and integration of new elements into that identity (which many anthropologists refer to as syncretism or hybridity) is central to that possibility.[43]

Bricolage and idiosyncrasy as conceptual tools then concede the very terms of the debate to the logic of consciousness, reinforcing the very strategies the missionaries engaged in to establish those very parameters. Ruth Marshall similarly writes, "the very *possibility* of 'religious identity' and the self-conscious inclusion of various elements within it—was produced for indigenous society for the first time through the encounter with the mission." Therefore, the notion of a "syncretic form or *bricolage*," Marshall contends, "does not do justice to the nature of these solid and permanent effects, nor the historical process that brought them into being," creating as they do room for agency and identity.[44]

But even with such warnings, the desire to find a fluid identity in historical actors remains strong, especially in scholarship on colonial South Asia, a form of longing all too pronounced in the present. For example,

Timothy Dobe foregrounds "code-switching" as a conceptual tool to understand the individual creativity at work within the new discursive contexts that had hardened religious boundaries in the late nineteenth century, such as missionary logics. For Dobe, following Ayesha Jalal, we need to consider the "important role played by individual consciousness and other dimensions of the religious in their contexts."[45] Gauri Viswanathan posits a similar resistance within conversion. She argues, "conversion ranks among the most destabilizing activities in modern society, altering not only demographic patterns but also the characterization of belief as communally sanctioned assent to religious ideology." But, Viswanathan claims, the determining reach of the colonial state strived to restore "a fixed, unassailable point of reference from which cleavages within communities are addressed," undoing the possibilities within belief itself.[46]

Viswanathan continues and argues that in colonial South Asia in the late nineteenth century, the state faltered, unable to adjudicate fixed points clearly and creating forms of belief that existed in an "uncolonized space." This in turn created political agency outside liberal horizons of the colonial regime. Viswanathan highlights the relational and adaptive aspects of conversion, arguing that "the power of conversion as an epistemological concept is that it reclaims religious belief from the realm of intuitive (nonrational) to the realm of conscious knowing and relational activity." This is hopeful for Viswanathan because "conceived in these relational terms, conversion is defined not as a renunciation of an aspect of oneself (as it is in the personal or confessional narrative form), but as an intersubjective, transitional, and transactional mode of negotiation between two otherwise irreconcilable world-views."[47]

As is clear in the very terms, however, conversion remains tied to consciousness, though now a fluid and shared one. In contrast to these concerns over the individual and consciousness, the interplay between Duleep Singh the individual and Duleep Singh within the *sangat* provides an opportunity to consider how conversion was both within and outside the parameters of a bourgeois self, fluid identity, and coerced subject. Although belief cannot be reduced to "propositions demanding assent," since it remains, as Viswanathan astutely writes, "a form of dynamic activity capable of producing assent," it also does not reject normative propositions and practices altogether.[48] For activity is not assented to or produced through individual belief tied to self-fashioning, but is also located within the broader contested parameters of a unified tradition, which strives toward its own coherence outside scholarly demands for both intelligibility and admissibility.

This dynamic activity outside the individual is clear in Duleep Singh's case, since he could not make a declaration of his return to *Sikhi* through a conscious decision and declaration. Such propositions repudiated the very parameters of the Sikh tradition and, therefore, legitimacy in the *sangat*. Instead, he had to be reestablished within the Sikh community through the realm of the intuitive—the grammar within a form of life—which required the vanishing of the self, a process finalized by taking *amrit* in the *pahul* ceremony. That is, the individual and state were not the only variables in arbitrating conformity and breaches within community. There existed conceptual and embodied ethical practices within *Sikhi*, for example, to determine violation and return.

This is not to say that consciousness was absent in conversion prior to colonial rule, a denial both Asad and Marshall would caution against. But we cannot reduce Duleep Singh's reconversion to a decision made by himself only, to his own demarcation of a new authentic truth tied to an inwardly oriented religious identity. Instead, his "consciousness," if the term is adequate, still had to conform to the ethical practices and bodily disciplines prescribed by within the Sikh community in which the experience of learning was valued above individual decisions. Duleep Singh himself recognized such conditions. Before his voyage to Bombay, Duleep Singh contacted the Earl of Kimberley, requesting Thakur Singh Sindhanwalia be allowed to meet him in the destined port city in order to administer *amrit* and reinitiate him into the Sikh tradition. Duleep Singh wrote to the Earl of Kimberley on March 11, 1886:

> As my cousin Sardar Thakur Singh Sindhanwalia informs me that he fears permission will not be accorded him to go to Bombay by the Lieutenant-Governor of the Punjab, and as I particularly desire to be re-baptised into the faith of my ancestors by some relative of my own, may I therefore beg of Your Lordship kindly request His Excellency by telegraph on my behalf, or permit me to do so, that the Sardar be allowed to meet me on reaching India.[49]

For colonial officials, it was imperative to stop Sindhanwalia. Henry Mortimer Durand argued, "the Sardar is a troublesome person, who has visited Dhulip Singh in England, and has since been doing mischief on his behalf out here. I would not permit him to see Dhulip Singh."[50]

One of the principal dangers of Sindhanwalia's perceived mischief—and Duleep Singh's return—lay in its legitimation of a form of sovereignty premised on a community without object, which posed a challenge to colonial authority. But more than that, Sindhanwalia was seen as especially dangerous because of his ability to navigate through networks that conferred a legitimacy to Duleep Singh amongst the broader community outside the contours of the individual self. In other words, Duleep Singh's conversion did not provide a proper subjectivity from which the community could revolt; rather, the community afforded opportunity for Duleep Singh to dislocate his own self. Even before Duleep Singh's return and conversion, C. L. Tupper detected these openings that Sindhanwalia and the community provided and wrote to Durand on October 6, 1885, noting that "the vernacular newspapers in the Punjab have begun to discuss the Maharaja's return to India, and congratulate Sardar Thakur Singh on his success in prevailing on His Highness to re-embrace the religion of his forefathers."[51]

Cultivating this space within the *sangat* while deindividuating Duleep Singh, however, was no easy task. Before he left for England to visit Duleep Singh, Sindhanwalia had already begun working to create conditions for his cousin's return to the Sikh tradition. For instance, he traveled to the four *takhts*, Sikh temporal authorities located in Amritsar, Patna, Anandpur, and Nanded, and sought their approval to bring Duleep Singh back to reestablish the Khalsa Raj. After his return from England in 1885, Sindhanwalia continued the arduous task of building support. First, he headed to Hyderabad to garner sympathy from Sikhs there, meeting with Raja Narender Bahadur, the Peshkar to the Nizam of Hyderabad, as well as the Nizam himself. Sindhanwalia fostered friendly relations with Sikhs in Hyderabad mainly in order to build favor for Duleep Singh at Huzoor Sahib in Nanded, which was located in the Princely State. For Sindhanwalia, Huzoor Sahib provided an appropriate site to perform the *pahul* ceremony because of both its proximity to Bombay and the takht's historical importance. Tupper reported to Durand Sindhanwalia's intentions, writing, "The Sardar is reported to have the intention of conducting Dhulip Singh to Apchalnagar, if he makes certain, beforehand that the priests of the Sikh shrine there will give him the 'Pahul.' Thakur Singh's chief desire just now is said to be to bring about the performance of the 'Pahul' ceremony for the Maharaja, and get him publicly accepted as a Sikh." Sikhs at Huzoor Sahib welcomed Sindhanwalia and accepted his offering of "Rs 125 worth of *Karah Prashad* on behalf of Maharaja Dalip Singh." The head *granthi* then made an announcement, declaring, "Maharaja Dalip Singh has offered *Karah Parshad* and has again become a Sikh of the Guru." In celebration, "guns were then fired, drums beaten, flowers strewn and saffron sprinkled on the assembly."[52]

A contingent of Sikhs from Nanded accompanied Sindhanwalia to his next destination, Indore, where he again sought to build support for his cousin's return and a return of the Khalsa Raj among the local Sikh community. In this mission he was largely successful, as "when he left that place a large deputation of Sikhs was present at the railway station to see him off, showing the high consideration in which he is held." From Indore he further promoted Duleep Singh across the subcontinent from Ajmere to Rewari in the Gurgoan District to Dadri in the Jhind State, eventually finding himself at Patna Sahib. Throughout his journey, Sindhanwalia carved a space for Duleep Singh's acceptance into the Sikh tradition, reentering him into the parameters of the *sangat*—a return that did not rest solely on Duleep Singh's intentions but that rested to a large extent on the will and acceptance of the awaiting Sikh community, a community preparing for his return. Sindhanwalia bypassed Duleep Singh's intentionality and agency altogether, arguing, he would go back to England "to inform the Maharaja when all was prepared, and of forcing him to come to India."[53]

Bringing Duleep Singh back into the *sangat*, however, did not occur only through Sindhanwalia's travels and labors, but required approval from various Sikh bodies and the community, as well as Duleep Singh's own surrender to *Sikhi*. Individual consciousness was only one aspect of a broader apparatus that framed conversion or return. First Sindhanwalia had to get approval from the Sikh Guru, the Guru Granth Sahib, to determine if an individual could even return to *Sikhi* after converting to Christianity. Sindhanwalia wrote to the *granthis* and as one of Sindhanwalia's supporters, Jowala Singh eventually confessed to the police, "asked them to explain the passage in the Granth about Guru Gobind Singh's having joined the Muhammadans at Machiwara and also whether a Sikh, who has embraced

Christianity, can be re-admitted into Sikhism."[54] The *granthis* determined that it was possible for Duleep Singh to return into the Sikh tradition and informed Sindhanwalia of their conclusion.

Like the *granthis*, the community also had to legitimate Duleep Singh's conversion for it to take place. The forms of reasoning the community employed, like the *granthis'* appeal to the Guru, produced *nimrata* (loweredness, humility) within the *sangat*, for the question centered on this: Who are we to say Duleep Singh cannot convert? This is precisely what the British authorities monitoring Duleep Singh's following understood to be the position of the community, for the Punjab police reported in April 1886 that "the Sikhs are in favor of his being allowed to re-embrace the Sikh religion if he desires to do so."[55] These efforts to bring Duleep Singh into the Sikh fold, thus, reveal the limits of the divide between public institutions and subjective consciousness in which conversion was confined only to the individual. Instead, the debates about Duleep Singh's conversion demonstrate the importance of Sikh concepts and institutions outside the logic of individual consciousness and rational calculation in delimiting conversion. Or, as a native official of the Patiala Princely State argued, "although the Sikhs would be much disgusted to find Dalip Singh with short hair and dressed like a European, and also to know that he was a Christian, yet all that was necessary for the Maharaja to do, in order to regain popularity and rouse enthusiasm, was to bathe in the holy tank at Amritsar."[56]

ETHICAL PRACTICE

We have thus far hinted at how ethical practices and bodily discipline also reveal the limits of individual consciousness as a determining factor for conversion as it must be accompanied by outward manifestations and performances for the community. Unable to be uprooted or transferred to a different space, practice, Michel de Certeau tells us, is not only tied to what he calls an "operators' way of operating," in which production and consumption reflect infinitely into each other. Instead, de Certeau argues that practice as "modes of operation or schemata of action" requires us to consider "the non-autonomy of its field of action." Practice provides a strategy to ponder ways in which one evades, de Certeau writes, "the mute processes that organize the establishment of socioeconomic order."[57]

Everyday practices, therefore, such as Sikh ethical practices, tear apart the surface of authentication within the colonial order, rendering it a sieve. Taking *amrit*, to give one example, did not make manifest Duleep Singh's intentions or legitimate his royal genealogy in the *sangat*. Instead, as we will see, *amrit* and the practices it entailed undid Duleep Singh's intentions and desires to authenticate and reestablish Ranjit Singh's empire. Taking *amrit*, *amrit* as practice, provides an opportunity to reroute Duleep Singh's individual identifications toward a sovereignty irreducible to colonial rule and blood ties—a sovereignty bound to an already dislocated, impossible community.

We do not have to overvalue the consumer's creativity within a particular moment, as de Certeau does with practices of the everyday, in which expressions of the subjugated challenge the ordering strategies of the powerful. Instead we can also consider how the consumer could cultivate such a challenge through repetitive ritualized practices without resorting to internal and intentional transgression. Or, in other words, repetition itself is by no means stagnant or uncreative, cultivating as it does specific capacities and dispositions. As Saba Mahmood demonstrates, "bodily behavior does not simply stand in a relationship of meaning to self and society, but it also endows the self with certain kinds of capacities that provide the substance from which the world is acted upon."[58]

Jacques Lacan's distinction between *l'action* and *l'acte* from his Fifteenth Seminar is fruitful here. As Adrian Johnston explicates, "the former [*l'action*] is simply some sort of natural and/or automatic process (for instance, the body's motor activities). The latter [*l'acte*], by contrast, involves a dimension over and above that of something like mundane material occurrence." So, Johnston goes on to highlight, "whereas an action is part of the normal run of things, act disrupts the predictable cycles governing particular realities, forcing transformations of regulated systems in response to its intrusive irruption."[59] Within colonial rule, even repetitive practices such as taking *amrit* and the recitation of the *akhand path* (continuous reading of the *Guru Granth Sahib* from beginning to end) interrupted the seamlessness of the colonial order. The repetitive and consistent habituated practices of the colonized that cultivated ethical virtue took on new roles. Whereas ethical practices would function only as actions (*l'action*) prior to colonial rule, in the colonial symbolic order they operated to continuously disrupt colonial rule as possible acts (*l'acte*).

How is this so? We know the act is not necessarily spontaneous. Edward Pluth explains that, in Žižek's reading of the act, the negation of the symbolic order appears in a refusal of transgression and spontaneity alongside the refusal to provide content in the denial, for example, Bartleby's enunciation of the declaration "I would prefer not to" that rejects the compulsion to enjoy. Though Alain Badiou's conception of the act rejects Žižek's focus on negativity, it too remains antispontaneous, though articulated as "destructive consistency" rather than just negation.[60] The quotidian ritual practices of subaltern communities, even if not framed as willful opposition to the colonial order, functioned as potential acts, for these consistent actions continually refused the contours demanded by the conceptual logic of colonial modernity through a repetitive and unacknowledged "I would prefer not to." Practices such as the *akhand path*, then, offered the possibility for Sikhs to traverse the colonial order without demanding spontaneity or a wholly new future. Or, as Peter Gratton writes, we must "resist a dominant modus of thinking the event [act] as wholly new, as wholly 'to-come,' as wholly unsymbolizable . . . because our very facticity suggests what is 'to come' has always already arrived." Thus "the event [act] may even be something passé, that is to say, not something futural or ever-new, but coming from what we have deemed comfortable and from the past as a 'known entity.'"[61]

Khande di pahul itself was such a known act, for *amrit* continually allowed the community to reestablish debts within itself, dissolving the contours of the self within the Sikh tradition. Within the *pahul* ceremony, Kapur Singh elucidates: "Amrit is administered to a Sikh, when he is knighted a Singh, enrolled as a member of the Khalsa, in accordance with the procedure laid down in these rules, which substantially represent the procedure formulated and adopted by Guru Gobind Singh on March 30, 1699, when he enrolled the first Five Beloved Ones, as the Khalsa."[62] Following Kapur Singh, this procedure, a way of operation, is not an individual affair but requires the presence of the Guru Granth Sahib and "at least, six adult Singhs as officiants." Constituting the *sangat*, within the ceremony "the sixth one should sit on the throne in attendance of the Guru Granth, and the other five should cooperate in preparation and administration of *amrit*. They all should have had a full bath, including the washing of head-hair, and should be dressed in clean and proper clothes. These Singhs may be of any sex, male or female." Once these conditions are in place, *amrit* can be administered to the aspirant, repeating the process at Anandpur in 1699, in which, as Puran Singh writes, "a new language was born in the Akali camp at Anandpur, out of the poor Punjabi dialect." After this process, Puran Singh notes, "No Akali said 'I,' he always spoke of himself as 'The armies of the Khalsa.' "[63] Deathless and timeless, the Akali in the *khande di pahul* ceremony is an instant of creativity; the taking of *amrit*, as Puran Singh writes, is a "moment of creation whose full fruition requires the lapse of aeons."[64]

Taking *khande di pahul* seriously as an act, and not as a vehicle reflecting a society's cultural beliefs, provides opportunity to reconsider the revolt of Duleep Singh anew. Ram Singh, a constable of the Gurdaspur District Police, for example, noted that "on the 7th April the Sardar received a letter from the Maharaja Dhulip Singh announcing his arrival at Aden and requesting him to entertain 10 or 12 old and trusted Sikh retainers of his family and to make them take the *pahul* again in token of fidelity to the Maharaja and his cause." After Sindhanwalia received the letter he held a secret conference in the Jamadar's Bagh at Amritsar, where he was residing at the time. At the conference, *karah prashad* was distributed and, as Ram Singh explained, "every Sikh present was required to take the *pahul* afresh." For Sikhs, *khande di pahul* provided the conditions for a creative undertaking, in which the repetitive practice of gifting *prashad* continuously without return signaled immense possibility. Sindhanwalia expressed this to his fellow Sikhs and told them "to be hopeful, and be prepared for whatever might happen."[65] Afterward, Thakur Singh Sindhanwalia alongside a host of Sikhs moved onward from his current destination in Delhi to Bombay to await the arrival of their returned sovereign in order to bring him back into the Sikh fold.[66]

In the lead up to Duleep Singh's arrival in Bombay, ethical practices created a wider *sangat*. *Khande di pahul* was not the only such practice that did this. *Ardas*, too, functioned in a similar fashion. *Ardas*, a Sikh prayer amongst the assembled *sangat*, developed through what Kapur Singh calls the "common consensus of the Sikh community." It was and is recited within a *sangat*, which can be constituted, Kapur Singh continues, by "any suitable member of the congregation, irrespective of sex or social station, for, there is no ordained priestly class amongst the Sikhs, many lead the prayer."[67] Grounded in the Sikh tradition, the *ardas* has continually centered the struggles of the community while recognizing the dislocated sovereignty of individual humans—a sovereignty fragmented by *hukam*. Put differently, *ardas* communicated in memory an unfinished narrative. The *ardas*, that is, does not historicize or unearth meaning but continuously translates memory into an unmoored and unsecured present.

After the *ardas*, *karah prashad* then is distributed, served from a common bowl to the entire *sangat*. In this moment time itself is expanded and exploded, for, as Puran Singh writes, "all pass through the inspiration of the whole Sikh history on this occasion and are thrilled and activated."[68] *Ardas*, therefore, simultaneously invokes the parameters of the Sikh tradition while revealing the limits of human's sovereignty over that tradition, of that very memory. Inhabiting all time and no time, the fundamental aspect of recitation is to dwell in both the Sikh community and the impossibility of such a sovereign historical subject bound as it is to the Guru's *nadar* and *hukam*. Most notably, then, proclaiming sovereignty while remaining unbounded geographically and temporally, *ardas* shifts attention to the Guru's *hukam*, which resides outside the parameters of the autonomous subject privileged in the framing of Duleep Singh's conversion.

These practices of *khande di pahul*, *ardas*, and the distribution of *karah prashad* were essential to Sindhanwalia and his allies as they prepared for Duleep Singh's return. They engaged in such Sikh practices, making offerings in the name of Duleep Singh. One such person, the *purohit* to Duleep Singh's family, Harkishen Das, colonial officials reported, "applied to the Punjab government" for sanction to make offerings at Amritsar, saying that "he was desired by the Maharaja to offer *Karah Prashad,* on behalf of His Highness, at the Golden Temple at Amritsar, at the tomb of Maharaja Ranjit Singh at Lahore, and the tomb of Sardar Mahan Singh at Gujranwala." On receiving approval between August 20 and 22, 1885, "*Karah Prashad* to the value of Rs. 250 was presented at the Golden Temple, the Akal Bunga, and the other Gurdwaras (Sikh temples) at Amritsar on behalf of the Maharaja." Accordingly, on those days, "Twenty-one trays of *Karah Prashad* were daily distributed among the people present on the occasion, and Rs. 250 was in addition devoted to offerings at the Gurdwaras and to making gifts to the attendants at the Golden Temple and to the poor." Finally a prayer was recited that stated, "May the Maharaja Dalip Singh, who has sent presents, money and *Karah Prashad* enjoy good health and *Sikhidán* (blessings of the Sikh faith)."[69]

Though the translation provided by colonial officials for *Sikhidán* was "blessings of the Sikh faith," it is more accurate to conceptualize *Sikhidán* as "to receive the gift of *Sikhi*." This timeless gift without a sender, self-interest, or calculation forged an inclusive community by helping members forget the binds of the ego, which over time is destroyed within an irreducible One. In the gifting, these ethical practices, these ways of operating, were not limited to Sikh elites such as Harkishen Das. Within these conditions established through the irruptive disinterest of *hukam*, *Sikhidán* tore coloniality and its centering of an identarian logic that provided the community with a cohesive identity—a martial Sikh—or an intention that could be fastened to individual intrigue.[70] Operating within such tearing and gifting, these practices around Duleep Singh took precedence. On March 6 and 7, 1886, Sindhanwalia, colonial officials noted, "celebrated a *bhog* [ritual observances at the end of a prayer from the Guru Granth Sahib] in the Golden Temple at Amritsar on the behalf of Maharaja Dalip Singh." Later, Sindhanwalia "held an *akhand path* to the value of Rs. 25 at the Tarn Tarn Sikh temple on hearing that the Maharaja had actually started for Bombay."[71] This was a quotidian occurrence and not taken to be threatening. As the Punjab police noted on March 27, 1886, that "*karah parshad* to the value of Rs. 5 is offered daily on his name at the Golden Temple in Amritsar."[72]

Colonial officials, however, counteracted the creative ties of community in the *khande di pahul* ceremony and this cluster of ethical practices discussed earlier by foregrounding the privatized religious nature of the ceremony. By emphasizing the religious nature of the ceremony, officials reconstructed the ego and framed the ceremony as occurring through an inner privatized identity. But the colonial state's very logic of noninterference in religious affairs of the community rerouted the terrain, creating distinctions between religious and nonreligious that were previously nonexistent, alongside the continuous need for colonial officials to create exceptions. Put differently, the very presumptions of noninterference formed a privatized self that could remain untouched, redirecting practices in *Sikhi* that annihilated this very self.[73] Or, within our example, the colonial officials gave approval to Harkishen Das to conduct the aforementioned rituals after determining "the ceremony was a purely religious one and of simple character." Reduced to a religious private realm, Harkishen Das did not need to obtain Government permission, even though "the Deputy

Commissioners of the three district [were] informed of his intentions."[74] The response to Duleep Singh's official request to take *amrit* was similar. Lieutenant Governor Aitchison determined that "refusal would be misunderstood and might cause irritation as interference with freedom of religious convictions, it would also magnify his importance."[75] The state deemed that intervention in a private religious ceremony would violate its claim not to interfere in religious affairs.

In order to avoid getting embroiled in issues (and potentially controversies) surrounding religious practice, the lieutenant governor of Punjab suggested, "I would not advise that Resident [at Aden] be present" at Duleep Singh's own *khande di pahul* ceremony he wished to undertake.[76] But the very conditions of the *khande di pahul* ceremony, as we have seen, challenged the British policy of noninterference. For example, Thakur Singh of Waga, Duleep Singh's cousin (not to be confused with Thakur Singh Sindhanwalia), alongside Jawand Singh of Barki, arrived in Aden on May 8, 1886, to meet Duleep Singh and, they hoped, administer *amrit*. The viceroy ordered that although Duleep Singh could see Thakur Singh, it had to be "in the presence of an English officer who understands the[ir] language" and that the "Punjabis [Thakur Singh and Jawand Singh] should be recommended to return as soon as possible."[77] Duleep Singh, however, as he wrote to the viceroy, wanted to "take advantage of my cousin's presence here to be re-initiated into Sikhism."[78]

The viceroy reiterated that although Brigadier General A. S. T. Hogg, the resident at Aden, could "allow the ceremony to be performed," it was "not desirable that you yourself should be present, or that any of our officials should have the look of countenancing the proceedings."[79] This then was the paradox. Thakur Singh could not see Duleep Singh unless an English officer was present, but an English officer also had to avoid the *khande di pahul*. This episode neatly illustrates the lesson that Nandini Chatterjee has drawn about the colonial rule in India: in "colonial India demands for 'freedom' and for 'non-interference' by the state usually meant, especially in the case of personal laws, demands for positive state action."[80] Though the English officer had to accompany visitors in their meetings with Duleep Singh, he also had to avoid the very reason for the accompanying the visitor: the *khande di pahul*. The viceroy recognized his contradictory instructions and, creating an exception, allowed the resident to do as he wished and interfere within the *khande di pahul* ceremony. The exception centered a bourgeois codes of ethics tied to decorum and sensitivity. As the viceroy argued, "it would be well to prevent any private communication between the Maharaja and the Punjab gentlemen. I dare say your tact and skill will enable you to arrange the business in a desirable manner. I have myself witnessed it."[81]

On May 25, 1886, after a delay, Duleep Singh took *amrit* in Aden. Hogg did not attend the ceremony, nor did he sanction it—though, he explained, he "took steps to ensure there being no objectionable conversation with the five Sikhs who were present."[82] Hogg assured officials that Duleep Singh had "no communication with the Sikhs (except at the ceremony) save in my presence." Again, however, the very project of securing the conversion and noninterference required state intervention. Since Duleep Singh was detained and could not take *amrit* in India per his plan, the colonial state had to provide conditions for *amrit* in Aden itself in order to not infringe upon his religious liberties. Hogg, therefore, had to find enough Sikhs to form a *sangat*, as well as provide Duleep Singh with the Guru Granth Sahib. He did this by detaining Sikhs who landed in Aden for that purpose. For example, Hogg found "a man by name Arar Singh [*sic*]" whom he "detained here to assist at the ceremony." Rur Singh of Kohali was joined by "two Sikhs from a transport ship which touched at Aden," who became part of the *sangat*. Moreover, the *sangat* had to be quickly dissolved, requiring further state intervention. Hogg notified authorities, "I am sending off by the Mecca tomorrow His Highness's cousin, Thakur Singh."[83] Thus, "Thakur Singh left on Wednesday for Bombay in Sural. Two other Sikhs left on Monday in Laipura, via Karachi."[84]

Yet, though Hogg claimed that he regulated the *khande di pahul* ceremony through his intervention to make *amrit* a strictly private ritual affair, the practice exceeded those regulations and refused this placement. That is to say, *khande di pahul* remained a site for community engagement and political significance for Sikhs outside the private realm. By July 3, 1886, Thakur Singh of Waga had returned to Punjab and was letting the *sangat* know that Duleep Singh had returned to the Sikh fold and "received a revelation from the Guru that he was destined to rule at Lahore." This news reportedly excited the *sangat*.[85] Soon after, at the end of July 1886, one follower of Duleep Singh and former servant of Rani Jind, Jamiat Rai, informed the community that "before dismissing the men who gave him the *Pahul* at Aden, the Maharaja conferred on each the 'Dalip Shahi,' an order of his own creation, and directed them to make known his grievances and the fact that Russia had promised to aid him to all the *Khalsa,* as he felt confident the Sikhs would submit to any sacrifice for his sake."[86] Defying the state's control of communication and ethical practice, Duleep Singh's *khande di pahul* reveals the difficulties of reducing the practice strictly to the individual—as well as caste and kin ties—since he could now make direct entreaties to the entire body of the Khalsa, which the community in turn would consider. Put another way, as we see with Thakur Singh and Jamiat Rai, the *sangat* and broader Khalsa remained essential in making sense of Duleep Singh's return and the complications it wrought. The question of conversion, even in its ties to belief, did not just authenticate the private self. When he entered the Khalsa, Duleep Singh and his grievances were fragmented, unable to be contained within either the parameters of the colonial state or his own self.

Even after the *khande di pahul,* problems continued for officials in their attempt to regulate *Sikhi* as a private affair since Duleep Singh sought to live within the conditions of being a Sikh, or what colonial administrators deemed "his new capacity as a Sikh."[87] He demanded both that his meals be prepared differently and that he have constant access to "a Sikh Grunthi [*sic*] and an attendant with copy of the Granth." As noted, upholding his own precedents that required state noninterference in religious proceedings, the viceroy found it difficult to avoid positive state action. Once again creating an exception, the Viceroy agreed to Duleep Singh's religious demands with one qualification: that the state would monitor and restrict the movements of the *granthis* themselves. As William Mackworth Young wrote to Henry Mortimer Durand on May 31, 1886, "I am to say that, subject to one condition, Sir Charles Aitchison regards the matter [of *Khande di pahul*] as a private one, and would recommend that the Maharaja should be allowed to employ whom he likes. The condition is that the men should be distinctly given to understand that they will share the Maharaja's fortunes, and will not be able to go backwards without permission of Government."[88] Even though the lieutenant governor of Punjab, Charles Aitchison, determined that Duleep Singh's conversion and the changes it brought were private affairs that did not require state intervention, administrators recognized the volatility of this privatization. To keep private and public realms separate, the state inhibited the *granthis'* movements, forcing them to function as only private *granthis* to an individual rather than as knotted within a *sangat*. Such policies then rerouted the very terms of the Sikh tradition in order to uphold the paradoxical policy of noninterference.

COMMODITIES AND ETHICAL PRACTICES

Is this reading of colonial murk too neat? Does it strive for alternate truth, providing hope for an essence where there is none? Puran Singh cautions against this modern neatness, arguing that the *Akali* (Timeless One) cannot exist in this disciplined space. He contends, "Alas! The Akali is gone. His language is dead, his self-realization too has volatilized!" Still, even with this colonial loss, Puran Singh contends that an anonymous Sikh remained, "suffering, and beaming with song both at home and in prison." Imprisoned within the contours of representation, *amrit* too remained murky in the colonial logic. For much like Sikhs became embedded within capitalist relations of production, discarding the Akali in favor of "money-makers" and "tax-gatherers," *amrit* too became predicated on individualized consumption of a commodity.[89] Ethical practices cultivating submission within the *sangat* were transformed into a relation between objects.[90] Within this logic, feudal forms of servitude as well as the submission of the subject become repressed, and the concern shifted to "free subjects whose interpersonal relations are discharged of all fetishism," in which servitude and submission are now disguised as relations between things.[91]

For Duleep Singh, recording the monetary amount he donated to produce *karah prasad* was central in cultivating relationships with the *sangat*. As noted in chapter 1, he wrote to Sarup Singh in 1885, informing him that he, "sent Rs. 1,000 to the Parohit with a view of *Karah Prashad* being presented at the Golden Temple at Amritsar and the tombs of my ancestors at Gujranwala and Lahore."[92] Within these terms we are left to ask: Is the *sangat* cultivated through *amrit* which bring Sarup Singh and Duleep Singh into a community, or is it cultivated through money, functioning as a universal equivalent of value that ties together two atomistic individuals? Once money becomes the mediating equivalent, consumption takes precedence vis-à-vis *amrit*.

Within such a relation, where money is the universal formula, Duleep Singh foregrounded the thing itself rather than the relations it produces to understand the *pahul* ceremony. Let us consider a central ingredient in the *karah prashad*: sugar. In 1886 Duleep Singh informed Sindhanwalia "that the white sugar sold in bags was unfit for consumption by Hindus."[93] Learning of Duleep Singh's wishes, Thakur Singh wrote to Sardar Man Singh, superintendent of Golden Temple, and told him "not to use this sugar for *karah prashad*."[94] But differentiating between types of sugar in order to determine the proper mode of consumption can uphold relations between things. Or, in other words, *karah prashad* comes to embody its own source of value dependent upon the correct formulae of ingredients outside its relation to the *sangat*. This shift to *karah prashad* as a fetish covers the very impossibility of the subject centered by the *khande di pahul* ceremony. Instead, as a fetish, *karah prashad* comes to jettison relationality, and in contrast the correct production, exchange, and consumption of a commodity outside relations in the *sangat* create value in and of itself and the appearance of a self-reconciled bourgeois society.

Again, the theoretical movement occurs too quickly, diagnosing the colonial and historical parameters of *amrit*. Perhaps the goal is not to determine how capitalist relations within coloniality produce a false *amrit*, to detect behind *amrit* the machinations of a colonial official and emergent bourgeois *sardar*. Instead the ideological procedure would be, as Žižek argues, to beware ideology's most cunning feature: "an over-rapid historicization."[95] This covers the fundamental ontological impossibility of the subject, which eludes symbolization—a being cultivated in the *khande di pahul* ceremony. Oscillating between historicization and its impossibility, both defining the structure of *pahul* at the end of the nineteenth century, we are left with the ambiguous nature of the commodity form that ties together a community irreducible to the logic of market exchange of autonomous individuals as it goes in and out of commodity form.[96] This was C. A. Bayly's lesson about cloth: namely, that market value could not obliterate other forms of value.[97] Is the relation between sugar and the *sangat* then so secure, bound to a monetary equivalent? Or does it exceed that very frame tied to questions of eating and ingestion that trouble equivalence? After all, there is no "bodiless body" in the sugar exchange as its sensibility remains crucial.[98]

This ambiguity of the commodity, Arjun Appadurai argues, refuses "excessively dualistic" tendencies in order to determine "the magic distinction between commodities and other sorts of things."[99] Instead, Appadurai demands that we consider how "things can move in *and* out of the commodity state." This shifting in between, in and out, produces what Appadurai calls a "constant tension between the existing frameworks (of price, bargain-ing, and so forth) and the tendency of commodities to breach these frame-works." This tension arises because "not all parties share the same *interests* in any specific regime of value," which in turn creates the political. Even with the commodification of *amrit* and *karah prashad*, they still remain recalcitrant to the logic of the market, retaining their transformative char-acter. Following Appadurai's general rule, "commodities whose consump-tion is most intricately tied up with critical social messages are likely to be *least* responsive to crude shifts in supply or price, but most responsive to political manipulation at the societal level."[100]

This continual unevenness and malleability of *amrit* and *karah prashad* formed an untenable situation for colonial administrators, who tried to stop ethical practice in relation to Duleep Singh altogether. A report from the district superintendent of police at Amritsar on February 10, 1887, claimed that "prayers were offered for Maharaja Dalip Singh in the Golden Temple at Amritsar every morning." Colonel Lang, the deputy commissioner, requested the practice be terminated. The superintendent of the Golden Temple, Sardar Man Singh, acquiesced and ordered the discontinuance of the prayers—a turn of events Colonel Henderson approved of, writing that it was satisfactory "to note that some influence *can* be brought to bear in this direction."[101] However, though Man Singh caved to the regulatory inter-ference of the state, reports indicated that in 1887 "prayers were now offered for Dalip Singh at every Sikh Gurdwara (temple) throughout the Punjab." The state sent out enquiries to determine the nature of these prayers and ascertained "that in *public* assemblies of Sikhs, prayers were not offered for Dalip Singh but that *individuals*, such as 'Granthis,' 'Pujaris,' Kukas, and 'Nihangs' did pray for the restoration of Sikh rule and openly invoke a bless-ing on the Maharaja!"[102]

Highlighting prayer reveals the difficulties the state faced in determin-ing the nature of Sikh ethical practice. Within their determinations of value, colonial officials created a typology of good and bad Sikhs, looking to reg-ulate the governability of the population, about which more follows. This logic reduced the *ardas* for Duleep Singh's return to a privatized individ-ual realm governed by nefarious characters such as the *nihungs* contra the public assemblies of prayer of Sikhs in general, which were rendered decid-edly unpolitical. This inversion of where the danger of religion resided, the private space of autonomous choice contra the public recitation of prayer, discloses how *ardas*, like *amrit* and *karah prashad*, undermined colonial demarcations. For *ardas*, like the distribution and consumption of *karah prashad* in conjunction with these prayers, refused the neat classifications central to colonial rule. Sikh ethical practices, in their cultivation of both a nonself and its accompanying *sangat* through repetitive practices such as "public" and "good" prayer, demonstrate an indeterminate creativity premised in relationality. Within this indeterminacy and relationality, we have the opportunity to consider both Duleep Singh's return into the Sikh fold and the fragmentation of colonial rule and the body it sought to sew together.

Duleep Singh's body reflected this impossibility that *ardas*, *karah prashad*, and *amrit* presented, disrupting colonial political technologies and their determination of the Sikh "essence." Once a Sikh takes *amrit*, their body too reflects this change, losing its individuality, engulfed with the Khalsa. For the colonial state, this presented a problem since colonial technologies of knowledge production such as photography, functioning as visual modes of surveillance, failed to accurately codify and archive Duleep Singh's body to make sense of both his intrigues and the colonial world. Though Colonel E. R. C. Bradford forwarded enclosed photos of Duleep Singh to the colonial state, officials found the documentation worthless. Irwin argued the photos "can be of no use to us" because "since he became a Sikh, the Maharaja has probably grown a beard and is not much like this now."[103] The file was archived and of no use to the state as they waited patiently for "'different photos.'"[104]

In embodying Sikh practice, one could say that the lost Maharaja returned to his inheritance. But is the opposite not the goal in this chapter: to unsettle this unity within the subject altogether by refusing to dialectically reproduce it within our search for that very unity's fragmentation? In my reading of conversion, I refused authenticating and reifying gestures by turning to Sikh modes of existence such as *sangat* in order to reject a logic that crafts a utopian subject—a Sikh who abandons the impossibility of mapping the Guru's *hukam* for an absent but abiding and authenticating sovereign. Such a task created a narrative of disappointment, though certainly not apathy.[105]

Chapter Four

RUMORS

> By contrast, rumour is necessarily anonymous and its origin unknown (even though on occasions, as we shall presently see, a fictive source may be assigned to it).
>
> —RANAJIT GUHA

We have thus far strayed from the subaltern by what can appear to be an intensive focus on elite maneuvering. Although it has allowed for symptomatic readings, our reduction of Duleep Singh to an elite realm to this point in the book risks upholding the very class structures of nationalist thought of the time—a structure that reduces the subaltern, as Ranajit Guha has taught us, "to a mere embellishment, a sort of decorative and folklorist detail serving primarily to enliven the *curricula vitae* of the indigenous and foreign elites."[1] In order not to privilege the dominant elite of the dominated class and their failures, is it possible to inhabit a space of articulation within a subaltern realm, a hidden script? How did Duleep Singh and the tales of his return (both to *Sikhi* and the subcontinent) enter the community through gossip and rumor?

Rumor and gossip contest the tightknit relationships between public and private, outer and inner, world and home, central to both colonial rule and nationalist thought. As Allan Feldman succinctly summarizes, "resisting this cohabitation of the state and private life takes the form of rumoring."[2] James C. Scott ably reveals how this resistance develops within a hidden transcript, which is "a site where social links and traditions can grow with a degree of autonomy from dominant elites."[3] In the South Asian context, the Subaltern Studies Collective has thoroughly examined the nature of the relationship between this hidden transcript and rumor, what Guha calls the "truly ubiquitous form of insurgent communication in many lands at many times." As a spoken utterance, rumor, Guha argues, was central in creating rebellion in the colonial era, since rumor spread more urgently and dynamically than the written word. Moreover, unlike proprietors and editors who the state easily traced to verify their information, rumor was, Guha contends, "necessarily anonymous and its origin unknown."[4]

Exchanging rumors around Duleep Singh was one way that Sikhs worked through the loss of the Khalsa Raj. This activity reveals that loss was not simply confined to the consuming reader, but could be a productive force, creating information itself within a vacillating community. Through rumor, the anonymous community without a fixed place did not wait for the production and publication of news about the Khalsa Raj in order to properly mourn Duleep Singh; reading reproduced distinctions between author and reader while also sedimenting meaning and law. Instead, within rumor, transitivity took precedence and disrupted settling because, as Guha puts it, the "encoding and decoding of rumour are collapsed, unlike news, at each point of its relay."[5]

But our attempt to inhabit this hidden script, what Scott refers to as a "cryptic and opaque" site, is not an effort to locate a discernable subject, nor to overvalue oral transmission as providing evidence of a 'real' or 'authentic' Duleep Singh; we are not seeking to make the community present. It is important to note that the subaltern corrective is not to locate the consciousness of a speaking subaltern subject. Gayatri Chakravorty Spivak famously deconstructs this historiographical gesture, reminding us of the Collective's own phonocentrism situated within its strategic deployments of the subject and the consciousness of a collectivity. Revising such assumptions, Spivak submits, "it is more appropriate to think of the power of rumor in the subaltern context as deriving from its participation in the structure of illegitimate writing rather than the authoritative writing of the law" sanctioned by the very phonocentrism Guha upholds. I have tried to heed Spivak's reminder throughout this work so far, noting how writing confounds a singular authoritative self-present voice. Within this confounded space of writing in the general sense, there emerges not an "authoritative truth of a text" discernible in a voice, but rather a refusal of theoretical orthodoxy.[6] Inhabiting this strategic rather than unveiling space (recall, knowledge is never adequate to its object), anonymity and transitivity surround rumors about Duleep Singh.[7] These rumors, both open and free to improvisation, undo the certainty demanded by colonial identarian logic, historicist desires, and efforts to determine the parameters of ideological concepts.

Though open to improvisation, rumor remains grounded in local credibility, within the parameters of tradition; Guha writes, "A rumour can be improvised only to the extent that the relevant codes of the culture in which it operates permit." Therefore, Guha concludes, "this pre-formed setting, scheme, or pattern is utilized in a completely unreflecting, unanalytical and unwitting manner," relying as it does on a pre-formed code of political thinking.[8] Luise White, on the other hand, challenges such an all-encompassing understanding of rumor, reminding us that rumors, rather than existing as a modular pre-formed code, reveal "passionate contradictions and anxieties" about, for example, the encroaching colonial state, which are irreducible to a singular formation. Importantly, then, White reminds us, "asking, let alone deciphering, what a rumor is about makes a rumor about one thing," which "turns rumor into something that it is not, something much less rich and complex."[9] This complexity, Homi Bhabha prompts us to consider, occurs through a time-lag, creating a "space of cultural and interpretive undecideability" within the colonial moment, which occurs in between the "social-symbolic ordering and its iterative repetition as the sign of the undecidable."[10] Rumor, then, is not simply about local credibility or precoded political thinking, but about disjuncture and displacement, which both creates and restricts possibility for political struggle.

Yet such a reading of rumor and its function need not be opposed to Guha's. Following Talal Asad, disjuncture and displacement should not be understood as oppositional to tradition, since tradition itself is a series of simultaneously affirming and displacing contestations within a historically continuous argument between assumed narrators and audience.[11] Learning is crucial, which undoes but also reaffirms the very code, what is called a form of life. This play between raveling and unraveling demands Duleep Singh assume a space in an already displaced community; a displacement does not occur through Duleep Singh.[12] In other words, these struggles grounded in tradition are not simply anticolonial, but, Jennifer Wenzel argues, "acolonial," in which they are "impossibly, simultaneously, pre-and postcolonial."[13] My attempts to analyze anonymous rumor at the end of the nineteenth century do not then aim to conjure "a coherent framework organized around class, consciousness, contradiction, and confrontation," as Richard Fox strived to provide in his recounting of Sikh identity formation in the colonial era.[14] Instead, I explore the futility of securing the boundary of this framework through a focus on the spread of rumors about Duleep Singh, rumors grounded within a contested and discrepant tradition rather than an ossified script.

Duleep Singh's attempted alliance with Russia is a case in point. In 1886, disguised as Patrick Casey, an Irish revolutionary, Duleep Singh traveled to Russia with hope of securing a meeting with the tsar and a land route to Punjab. Duleep Singh had contacted Russian authorities to find this route to India, asking for "a letter of authority to pass my baggage and sporting guns and ammunition both at Batoum and Baku on the way to Teheran in Persia."[15] In January 1887, he sent a letter to Sardar Hira Singh of Amritsar "stating that he will shortly invade India with the help of Russia."[16] During his time in Moscow in 1887, Duleep Singh met with numerous officials, although he never obtained a meeting with the tsar. Still, the possible alliance created a whirlwind of information. The September 5–17, 1887, edition of the *Moscow Gazette* reported, for example, that after trying to obtain justice from England, Duleep Singh had "abandoned that country entirely, and finally threw himself into the arms of Russia." The article concluded, "The Maharaja has decided to break off all relations with England and to settle in Russia. We welcome him with the conviction that he will find among us all the sympathy which his fate demands."[17]

GOOD SIKHS, BAD SIKHS, AND FASHIONING UNITY

"Concerns about the martial prowess and rebelliousness of Punjab's inhabitants, specifically the province's Sikh population, preoccupied the early colonial state in the aftermath of the Second Anglo-Sikh War," as Mark Condos relays.[18] Rumors cultivated this anxiety by both settling and unsettling colonial typology, revealing the incommensurability of Sikh life and colonial categorization. These rumors that circulated in the community centered on Duleep Singh's return; colonial officials recorded numerous examples of them. For instance, once Duleep Singh made initial inquiries into returning to Punjab in 1883, colonial administrators observed that "all through the months of February, March, April, May, June, July, and August 1883 unusual activity was noticed among the Kukas [a sect within

Sikhism]."[19] These rumors and the "unusual activity" that officials detected were in many ways grounded in the Sikh tradition. For example, colonial administrators worried about the "many meetings" in which "seditious talk [was] indulged in; frequent 'Bhogs' and other religious ceremonies were held." These ceremonies predicted the end of British rule and the rise of the Kuka leader, Ram Singh, which would occur "simultaneously with that of Maharaja Dalip Singh."[20] Therefore, unlike scholars who trace the conscription of Sikhs into the racial typology of the colonial state, colonial administrators were troubled by Sikh reliance on Sikh teachings, using this to call into question their supposed loyalty.

The British assiduously catalogued potentially subversive activity, observing the increased hearsay about Duleep Singh's intentions and future movements throughout the 1880s. The cataloguing of rumors and subversive activity among Sikhs paralleled the broader and more ambitious aim of the imperial state to catalogue Sikhs themselves—to understand different groups within Sikhism and to determine the characteristics and "nature" of members of each group. In this cataloguing of Sikhs, the state parsed Sikhs into different categories. Creating these divisions, officials detailed that "orthodox Sikhs and other residents of Amritsar were said not to entertain any such feelings" of disloyalty to Britain even though, as we have seen, Thakur Singh Sindhanwalia succeeded in organizing around Duleep Singh in Amritsar. Educated Sikhs were deemed uninterested in Duleep Singh's affairs, since they "had no feeling in common with him."[21]

But these divisions were of course unstable. As speculation about Duleep Singh's future abounded, officials determined that religious sentiments became unwieldy, undermining the state's previous categorizations and suggesting that a much wider revolt was possible. Otherwise put, though colonial officials had once assumed that only the unruly "bad Sikhs," the Namdharis, would participate in a revolt against British rule, the persistence and power of rumors led many to conclude that even orthodox Sikhs, previously categorized as loyal and "good Sikhs," were dangerous. Under the crucible of Duleep Singh's potential return, certain group demarcations were no longer tenable. Sure enough, as news of Duleep Singh's return spread, Kukas and orthodox Sikhs did indeed call for boycotts to show their displeasure at the colonial state. In Lahore specifically, Kukas and orthodox Sikhs united to argue that "the people of the Punjab should show their grief at the action of Government in forbidding the visit of Maharaja Dalip

Singh to his native country by abstaining from the use of salt and sweetmeats"—a deployment of boycott against the colonial state that had typically been spearheaded by Namdharis alone.[22]

Like rumors themselves, the locations in and occasions during which rumors were disseminated, bazaars and *melas* respectively, served to fracture the state's categorization and demarcation of colonized Sikhs. Guha has studied how "in India the bazaar was clearly identified in colonialist thinking with the origin and dissemination of rumor."[23] This is because, Dipesh Chakrabarty writes, "the bazaar, the street, and the fair (*mela*), it seems to me, have for long formed a 'spatial complex' in India," combining "the different purposes of pilgrimage, recreation and economic exchanges."[24] Early on, when the East India Company took the reins in Bengal, the company state had tried to design a different and ordered form of market that would be, Sudipta Sen argues, "a neutral, much more sequestered, and uncontested space; a space, that could at least, in economic terms, be 'exposed' to the rising flow of imperial commodities, speculation and investment."[25] Although colonial administrators continuously sought to cultivate this exposed and visible geography, their efforts to order space failed. At the end of the nineteenth century, Chakrabarty continues, the British still conceptualized the bazaar as "a den of lies and rumors, bazaar *gup*, through which the ignorant, superstitious and credulous Indian masses communicated their dark feelings about the doings of an alien *sarkar* (government)." They were partially right. The bazaar or the *mela*, Chakrabarty concludes, was the site "where conspiracies were plotted and carried out," though in a coherent manner not reducible to ignorance and superstition.[26]

Looking to provide classificatory order to an unruly site, the watchful and attentive colonial state produced an archive that overflows with documentation of rumors that circulated in bazaars and during *melas* about Sikh rebellion. This archive reveals the serious threat Sikhs posed to colonial rule. Or, as Guha argues, "sensitivity to 'bazaar gup' was, of course, at its most acute among the officials when the regime felt seriously threatened by enemies abroad as in times of war or by those within as in times of popular revolt."[27] Sikh organizing brought these two elements together as rumors revealed ongoing Sikh alliances with the Russian state, a process whereby Sikhs became both an external and internal threat.

Diwali was one *mela*/festival around which rumors continually coalesced, creating opportunity for the Sikh community to cohere a politics around

Duleep Singh and a corresponding danger for the colonial state. Colonial officials recorded, "in October 1883, it was rumoured in Jhelum that Maharaja Dalip Singh and his wife would reach Amritsar in time for the 'Diwali' (Feast of Lanterns) and that rooms had been prepared for them at the Golden Temple."[28] Again, two years later, once Duleep Singh began to articulate his return in earnest, *Diwali* was central. On December 12, 1885, C. L. Tupper wrote to Henry Mortimer Durand and noted: "Quite recently it was reported that the Maharaja's return and restoration to power were freely spoken of by the people attending the great *Diwali* fair at Amritsar in the beginning of November last, and his expected arrival in Delhi is said to be exciting much interest there." Kukas were, once again, especially vocal. Colonial officials reported that "Kukas were said to have expressed a hope that the British government would be overthrown by the Russians, and they were also reported to be looking forward to Dalip Singh's coming with pleasure," since it would coincide with Ram Singh's return.[29]

Revolt brewed at other festivals as well, for example *Baisakhi*, which celebrated the formation of the Khalsa. *Baisakhi* was a crucial celebratory event that drew multiple communities together as it occurred alongside harvest. Colonial officials documented: "In April 1884, a Kuka, named Chanda Singh of Saharan in Gujranwala district was found to be reciting an inflammatory poem at the 'Baisakhi' Cattle Fair at Amritsar, which is largely attended by the Sikhs."[30] Poetry was an essential mode of literary expression in Punjab that took multiple forms, including the *ragi* or *dhadi jatha* modes of expression.[31] Kukas in particular deployed poetry in their political struggles, but the mode of expression was far from limited to this group. As Joginder Singh details, Ram Singh, the founder of the Namdharis, "employed professional singers (*ragis* and *dhadi jathas*)," who "sang the songs of bravery of the Sikh heroes in the religious congregations."[32] There was room for improvisation as well. Michal Nijhawan documents such improvisation in relation to *dhadi*. Though continuing within an inherited form of tradition, cultural performers still engaged reflexively within that very tradition, which does not allow us to reduce performances to stable ideologies advocated by institutions such as reform organizations.[33]

Chanda Singh, too, weaved a heroic and subversive tale for his listeners during *Baisakhi* at Amritsar. This tale was not limited to delineating past valiant exploits, but also to unfolding time in the present central to *barah mah*, a genre of Punjabi folk poetry that captures the changing moods and emotions in the course of a human year over twelve verses. Within the Sikh tradition, the form is used in the Guru Granth Sahib by two Gurus, Guru Nanak and Guru Arjun. Within this form, each month signals a longing for reunification with the infinite, which, due to one's temporal constraints, is reduced to a longing and waiting for the beloved (*birha*). In the literal translation of his *barah mah*, as recorded by the state, Chanda Singh recited the following:

> The Sat Guru (True Guru) further remarked that the martyrs had already been sent by him to fetch Russia, with instructions to deliver the order of God to her, and compel her to obey it.
>
> Having delivered the written order to the messenger, the Guru told him to deliver the following message to Russia:—"Thou art ordered by God to conquer Lahore for us."
>
> When the Czar held his court, he called his Minister, and offering him a seat, told him that in the night he had seen the *Khalsa* in a vision at which he was alarmed as they had asked him to march on Lahore.
>
> The Minister reflected on the arduous and hazardous nature of the journey, but finally ordered preparations to be made for the army to march, with drums beating.
>
> When the Russian troops invade the country, agitation will prevail in London, and the British army will march to India.[34]

Chanda Singh's recitation inverts the very temporal structure of colonial rule. Beginning with the month of Chet, Sikh time is a dream time that transcripts a stage within a stagnant European time, which is governed by the reality of the stalemate of the Great Game—not the progress promised by the civilizing mission.

In his rearrangement of time, in his retranscription, Chanda Singh centered divine intervention (*hukam*). This intervention superseded colonial authority and the Russian state, highlighting the contingency of a particular historical period. This was a central point Chanda Singh made throughout his performance by revealing how even the most concretized time is always prone to alternative figurations through one's yearning as different visions kept materializing. Yet this opening was not one which accelerated toward a new time, but the continuity of an earlier time marked by permanent loss, a central understanding with the Sikh tradition and the *barah mah* seasonal form. In other words, catastrophe itself continuously became destiny, which the seasonal logic of the *barah mah* entails.[35] Inhabiting this sense of cataclysmic loss in the present, Chanda Singh disclosed how the historical moment was not a stable site, creating onward progress or a continuation of a prior stability, but one of irrevocable violence as is the case in the cyclical rendition of *karma*—the repetition of life itself. Chanda Singh continued and recited in the *mela*:

> Many battles will be fought, and there will be much lamentation, mothers will weep for their sons, and wives for their husbands.
>
> Bishen Singh, the Guru's precious jewel and martyr, who has a large following, has entered into negotiations with others, who have expressed their readiness to join him.
>
> The future rests with God.
>
> The Pathans will rise when they see that the English have withdrawn from Peshawar to defend Lahore.
>
> They will take counsel together, but the decree of God will surely be fulfilled.
>
> When Russians enter the Punjab, famine will rage and make havoc in the country. People will die in terribly large numbers and crime will be without limit.[36]

Bliss and fulfillment, therefore, lie not at the end in the recognition of the infinite, but in a horrid calamity brought forth by the Great Game in which Russia too offers no salvation, but only disaster as famine and havoc reign.

The key then to revolt, according to Chanda Singh, was to fully ally neither with Russia nor Britain. The poem rejects full alliances with either power and counsels instead to play themselves off of each other to create a space of Sikh autonomy between the two—a challenging if not impossible task. It mirrors the longing for a unification, a space of vanishing not available within the colonial impasse. Still, recognizing that he was bound to this temporal world, in this recitation of violence and loss Chanda Singh deftly interlaced concrete evidence into his narrative about impending revolt and the need for any future Sikh polity to distance itself from both Russia and England.

The Bishen Singh referenced in Chanda Singh's poem was presumed to be an Arora trader at Kabul and in Central Asia who, in 1884, came to be in Russian service in Samarkand. He served as the linchpin in communications between Namdhari and Russian officials and was assumed to be the one who would "guide the invading Russian forces to the Punjab."[37] But Bishen Singh himself was no Russian pawn in his dealings with them, which explains why Chanda Singh referred to him in the poem. Communicating with a fellow Kuka, Bishen Singh "sent word that he had been obliged to eat with Russians, for which he hoped to be forgiven."[38] But the alliance with Russia was necessary in order to thwart the British, Bishen Singh believed, who would be "treated with ten times more severity [than] they showed to the blacks!"[39] Within this logic, Chanda Singh's performance not only destabilized the given temporal coordinates through a fatalism rendered in seasonal form, but also disseminated information about the Russian alliance and its possible consequences to the broader crowd. Like Bishen Singh before him, Chanda Singh refused to concede the parameters of a war between Russia and Britain in which Sikhs would be pawns. Instead, both men advanced an alternative political vision in which Russia and England were pawns in a much greater game—that of independence for colonized peoples, but also a play with *hukam*.

The colonial archive records the recitation of Chanda Singh's poem twice during Baisakhi in Amritsar in 1884. In the second archival recording, however, the reciter was not Chanda Singh, but "one Dewa Singh of Shahbazpur in the Firozpur district." Dewa Singh, it was reported, also recited the same stanza about Bishen Singh: "Bishen Singh, the Guru's precious jewel and martyr, who has a large following, has entered into negotiations with others, who have expressed their readiness to join him."[40] There also appears difficulty in determining who Bishen Singh precisely was. There were two reports from Hoshiarpur district about a Bishen Singh, but colonial officials struggled to determine if he was the same Bishen Singh referenced in earlier reports. The problem was that the Bishen Singh the reports referenced arrived before the letters proclaiming that Bishen Singh was going to arrive. As the report stated, "It seems probable that these two Hoshiarpur reports refer to Suba Bishen Singh, whose intention to visit India was communicated by letter. The letter may have been delayed in transmission if it came by hand, and Bishen Singh arrived before it." Another report claimed "that this Bishen Singh is a different man altogether." Yet, in a surprising twist, in trying to determine the truth of Bishen Singh, the colonial spy confirms the prophecies instead, writing that "he was the same

Bishen Singh mentioned in the 'sakhis' or prophecies of Guru Govind Singh."[41] The prophetic Bishen Singh, thus, becomes "real" as colonial officials struggled to place "Bishen Singh."

Such archival lapse—as we have the same recitation ascribed to two different authors and the trouble of identifying Bishen Singh—reveals the difficulty in demarcating anonymous performance and words that were weaved within it, traveling as they did in networks of rumor. It would be remiss to limit this performance to Chanda Singh or Dewa Singh or Namdharis in the *mela*. Instead, the mela created a space where the anonymous community gathered and stitched together a broader organization. As the colonial state's difficulty at naming the reciter reveals, this network could not be easily divided into individualized parts, for recitation at the *mela* confounded such logic, as did the very form of the performance.

The performative structure of the recitation in the *mela* cannot be reduced to an affective style that would only appeal to a singular community. Such a reduction would uphold the divisions of the colonial state's classificatory paradigm and limit the reach of revolution. Instead, the state's attempt to codify divided communities in the Sikh population in order to distinguish "Good Sikhs" from "Bad Sikhs" was troubled by both the spatial order of bazaars and *melas* and the form of performative culture. Yet this common discursive site does not suggest the *mela* alongside the performative structure was a plural and heterogeneous space cultivating a broader common understanding. Within these sites that resist such clean demarcations, the very terms of ethical being were negotiated and contested. To return to Chanda Singh, he questioned the contemporary meaning of *Sikhi,* its ethical-political order, and its coupling with the colonial state. Disagreements over what politics would entail and the ability of Sikhs to be persuaded that a singular political form was possible did not signal separate divisible communities. Rather, they revealed contested visions about the correct form of Sikh being that did not remain static as a heterogeneous form. And this is a central aspect of performance as well, for, Nijhawan argues in relation to *dhadi*, "The persistence of the *dhadi* genre as a form through which to articulate a pious Sikh self has been due to the influence of core traditions within the Sikh fold, which have assigned agency to the religio-aesthetic forms associated with *dhadi* representational practice"—including practices that cultivated Sikh political and ethical institutions and being.[42]

The central task for Chanda Singh and Dewa Singh's recitations in the *Baisakhi mela* was not to sustain their own particularity within a heterogeneous Punjabi milieu. Rather, the goal was to consider the emancipatory potential of *Sikhi* to disrupt the very parameters of historical context that cultivated such specificity in the first place. Though there were, Farina Mir argues, "a cross-section of the Punjab's inhabitants" who frequented such Punjabi literary performance at the end of the nineteenth century, such performances also offered differing and contesting articulations of proper ethical behavior that would castigate some of the attendees for failing to behave ethically.[43] Chanda Singh ended by reciting:

> He alone will be saved who will seek their protection of the Guru, and devote his whole attention to God.
>
> The Sat Guru will then return to Punjab and disestablish all former systems and set up new standards, causing the name of God to be repeated by everyone, even the demons.[44]

That Chanda Singh ends by unambiguously dislocating sovereignty from "Man" further challenged the very distinctions central to maintaining colonial rule, the binary divisions essential to the Great Game, and the harmonious plurality that sustains liberal desires for recuperation today. For in Chanda Singh's poetic voice, all former systems would be disestablished— including colonialism—and the Guru would return. This return is marked "new" but is also a repetition. His public performance rejected what Farina Mir considers "notions of religious identity that could accommodate multiplicity" in the Punjab landscape.[45] Instead, Chanda Singh highlighted the failure of his listeners to inculcate an ideal that demanded they follow the Guru's *hukam* outside their wills and desires. Or, put another way, Chanda Singh claimed authority over Sikh practices and the Punjab terrain whether others concurred or not. The key was to make others cultivate the very same orthodoxy they strived to practice in themselves. Yet this orthodoxy was not just given but a struggle.

This is not to say that the bazaar, *mela*, and rumor did not help fashion unified senses of community between traditions as well. They did, but without providing an essence to identity. Three years after the earlier reports, in April 1887, a colonial official's report from Lahore documented that "one Devi Dial was going about the bazars saying the throne of England had been shaken and that Dalip Singh would return and Hindus and Muhammadans unite, when he would become himself again!" Devi Dial's rumor breaks the apparent neat divisions between tradition that Chanda Singh tried to cultivate through the very same invocation of Duleep Singh. This pronouncement of unity was not a unique iteration. In December 1885, in Gurdaspur, rumors spread and reports came in that "the Maharaja's approaching visit was exercising the minds of both Hindus and Muhammadans a great deal, and that both sects expressed a hope that Dalip Singh would again rule over the Punjab." Once again, in May 1887, facing this imminent threat of Duleep Singh, colonial officials recorded rumors that abounded about Muslim-Sikh unity: "People were said to be of [the] opinion that if the Maharaja accompanied them to this country, the Sikh[s] and even the Muhammadans would desert the English and flock to his standard."[46] Rumor, thus, reveals the wide range of disputations in time, in which unity can neither be presumed nor dismissed outright. What we learn is what Ann Stoler has already taught: "Rumor was a highly ambiguous discursive field: it controlled some people, terrorized others; it was damning and enabling, shoring up colonial rule and subverting it at the same time."[47]

Colonial officials, however, sought to delimit the unifying possibilities of rumor, terrifying as rumors were to the ordered classificatory system of the state. Durand argued that "no doubt the Punjabi Hindus have some fellow-feeling for the Sikhs, but this feeling is, I think not of such a nature as to arouse any enthusiasm in favor of Dalip Singh. It is caused in great measure by dislike of Muhammadans, and need hardly give us much uneasiness." Seen as possible foreign agents by colonial officials, Muslims—and in particular a suspicion of them—reconstituted irreconcilable differences in Punjab while it also created the possibility for a purified 'Indic' unity. Durand argued, "Punjabi Muhammadans are of necessity the enemies of the Sikhs, whom they outnumber by five to one." Political allegiances stemming from the precolonial era, Durand argued, would also hamper possibilities for unification. He argued "that more than a third of the Sikhs in the Punjab belong to the Feudatory States, and the bulk of the Feudatory States are traditionally opposed to the Lahore family."[48] Historicizing life, which could then be classified and codified, colonial officials sought to limit the possibility of broader types of dissonance. Notably, certain types of connections became worthwhile (Sikh and Hindu), while coeval relationships were judged insignificant (Sikh and Muslim).

Colonial administrators quelled discordant facts that did not match their schemas of thought by investigating rumors. Through these investigations, the state concluded that Muslims and Sikhs could not be as allied as rumors of unity suggested. Early in January 1886 in Delhi, one colonial official reported "Muhammadans of the Punjab looked forward to the return of Maharaja Dalip Singh with anxiety, believing that things would go hard with them if he came into power." Young too argued that "Nearly half the province is Muhammadan and Muhammadans are of course not favourably disposed towards him."[49] Young's use of "of course" here unwittingly reflects the state's certainty in its own ethnographic demarcations, even despite evidence that Muslims were deeply involved in Duleep Singh's affairs—from Jamal al-Din al-Afghani to Abdul Rasul, a Kashmiri Muslim. In order to legitimate this certainty, the state employed Munshi Aziz-ud-Din, a Muslim spy in Punjab, to gather evidence while discrediting rumors. On April 9, 1887, Aziz-ud-Din reported about Sikh plotting around Duleep Singh, revealing the extent of organization around Duleep Singh though claiming that Muslims had "no sympathy whatever with the Sikhs and their would-be leader." But Aziz-ud-din also divulged that in April 1886, when Takhar Singh had arrived in Bombay, Husen Khan, a Muslim, who was at the time "employed as teacher in Ahmedabad School, whose father Ewaz Khan was the personal elephant driver to the late Maharaja Ranjit Singh," joined Sikhs in their congregation.[50]

The paradoxes of revolution, then, were not so easy to classify. Since Aziz-ud-din was a colonized Muslim subject, his impartiality remained in question; he was susceptible to the very same rumors the state demanded that he investigate. As Parama Roy writes, there is an uneasy link between "native permeability, malleability, and lack of essence" and "the notion that the native is an opaque entity who must be known, categorized, and fixed in the most complete way possible." Colonial knowledge, though striving for completion, Roy reminds us, nevertheless remained tied to "a system of representation that simultaneously entertains a profound anxiety about the native's slipperiness and inscrutability."[51] This impossibility at the center of colonial knowledge meant that Aziz-ud-Din could not to be trusted in making the Other transparent; Aziz-ud-Din's narrative provoked caution among the colonial authorities who received it. On May 2, 1887, Durand argued that the information provided by the Muslim spy itself was suspect, noting "the writer is a man of intelligence; but he is a Punjabi Mussalman, and he is, I find, hasty in jumping at conclusions, so his assertions must be taken *cum grano.*"[52]

Colonel Henderson as well questioned Aziz-ud-din's conclusions, but still placed faith in the state's ability to codify colonial subjects by collecting even more ethnographic data. Indeed, for Henderson, any gaps in existing knowledge about colonized subjects and their thoughts and activities could be redressed in the future by obtaining more data about them. This data would be provided by Aziz-ud-din, which the state could then decipher through its reading practices, unfastening the particularity that colored the colonized reporting. Employing this reasoning, Henderson argued that Aziz-ud-din should be: "required to send in frequently, perhaps daily, a diary of his movements recording minutely the observations heard by him, the persons from whom heard &c., &c. No doubt there would be a good deal of rubbish, but the mere fact of having to send such a record makes a man careful as to the conclusions state in the general report made at the end of his tour."[53]

For the colonial state, Roy perceptively notes, though "natives [had] a capacity (an imperfect one) for mimicry, they [had] no capacity for self-examination or self-representation or for offering up their subjectivity in any way that [would] usefully mesh with the colonizer's various information systems."[54] To counteract Aziz-ud-din's opaque nature that rendered his information suspect, Aziz-ud-din had to provide his own personal autoethnographic reflections to authorities in order to properly play the part of native informant. His reflections could then be read and archived by colonial observers to discern the truth of his reporting. For Henderson, Aziz-ud-din existed simultaneously without "any significant subjective autonomy," but, lacking a coherent self, was also unaccountable for his own reporting. Even while fearful of the opaque colonized subject, the state still trusted its knowledge-producing mechanisms grounded in keen observation of the colonized, in which self-reporting, though much of it "rubbish," could be disciplined and read to glean from it truth, producing a knowable albeit untrustworthy colonial subject.

Russian intrigue in the Great Game further intensified these fears about the population and territory. The British state, Simanti Dutta contends, "conjured the fearful future of annihilation, the dreaded end of imperial time."[55] For the colonial state, Russia excited the racialized nature of the colonial subject. In 1887, by then Lieutenant Governor of the Punjab, James Broadwood Lyall argued "the idea of an invasion of India by Russia has more or less disturbed and excited the native mind in the north of India."[56] Cataloguing what they took to be the excited and disturbed native mind, colonial administrators fragmented the native mind itself, categorizing it according to gendered and racialized markers.[57] Russia, Lyall argued, terrified the effeminate Bengali population who needed the order and protection provided by a strong state to prevent being overrun by "stronger" races—a logic that appeared and reappeared in the colonial setting. He wrote: "The idea of an invasion of India [by Russia] in the shock of which the British Power might be overthrown, and a time of tumult and anarchy succeed, has a very sobering effect upon the disaffected or dissatisfied natives in the greater part of India, where the people generally, and the educated classes in particular, feel they are soft and unable to hold their own in war against the stronger races."[58]

The Bengali was in stark contrast to the Punjabi. Lyall continued, "But in the Punjab, the Sikhs and some Hindus who go with them, and the warlike tribes of Muhammadans think, I believe, that they could hold their own well enough whatever happened; and regard the chance of a crash with more excitement than alarm."[59] For Lyall, the excitable warlike nature of the dissatisfied Punjabi meant that Russian invasion could topple British rule, threatening both the British and the educated natives of the region. Russians, to Lyall, had to be stopped in order to protect both the British and their adversaries the Bengalis, who together valued order over chaos—a sober familial sensibility in contrast to the excitable nature of the Punjabi population most visible in the figure of the fanatic. Though the figure of the Bengali troubled colonial authorities vis-à-vis the press, he could still be ordered within a framework.

Consider, for example, how Lyall catalogued a range of possible scenarios in case of Russian attack. He contended that natural divisions between the Punjab population would manifest themselves if Russia invaded; he suggested that "hostility between Hindus and Muhammadans in Punjab has become hotter and more pronounced in the last four or five years," which was "partly explainable by the drawing together due to Russian scares."[60] The excitement inaugurated by this possibility of a Russian invasion coupled with what Lyall argued was a preexisting "strong jealousy and antagonism between Hindus and Muhammadans in the Punjab" caused members of both groups to "wake up, and look forward to see how they would stand if they were left face to face and had to depend on themselves only." Islam posed problems to the state because Muslims were bound to a realm that was irreducible to a known Indic territory, in which temporal progress and civilization, though still pending, was possible. Lyall argued:

> But if Russia with Muhammadan troops in her pay was fighting us in Afghanistan and we met with a disaster I imagine that the fidelity of our Punjabi Muhammadans would be as shaky as that of the Sikhs would be, if Dalip Singh was with the Russians. For the Muhammadans, if they thought our power was collapsing, would be under great temptation to join the northern invaders in order to plunder India and to tyrannise over the Hindu.[61]

The Punjabi Muslim remained dangerous, for his fidelity remained in question because of the weight of Islam, which threatened the security of the Punjab—a reproduction of a British fortified history in which Muslims were foreign invaders and the British merely custodians of a presumed Indic unity.

Within Lyall's framework of colonial populations and the threat that each posed to British rule in Punjab, Sikhs became tied to Hindus. Lyall proposed, "the Sikhs and Hindus who go with them, remember that the last Native Raj was a Hindu one, and feel the necessity of drawing together so as to be strong if left alone: some revival of sectarian and political enthusiasm is required for this end and is also the natural outcome of the feeling." Tying Sikh claims to sovereignty to only the prior political state of Ranjit Singh rather than to the founding of a tradition, Lyall concluded that this excitement was not seditious but merely nostalgic. He wrote, "The excitement among the mass of the Sikhs is, I think, of this kind only, and not of a seditious kind, but it of course tends to heighten their traditional ideas of the glories of Ranjit Singh's days." Still, this nostalgia posed threats since Sikhs would, Lyall continued, "regard Dalip Singh with greater interest and sympathy, than they would otherwise have done."[62] Or, as Lyall noted beforehand, fidelity toward British rule would break down with the emergence of Duleep Singh on the frontier with invading Russians.

In order to make sense of these scenarios, Lyall sought to divide Sikh subjects into "Good Sikhs" versus "Bad Sikhs."[63] He argued that alongside a generalized nostalgic feeling toward Ranjit Singh, which was a "general excitement of a mild kind," nostalgia could also take a negative turn toward fanaticism when it was coupled with political demands against the British. He wrote: "There is a mixture of strong seditious feeling in the person of a few fanatic Sikhs, Kukas, or orthodox, of men of broken families who have lost jagirs or estates, and of a few educated, free-thinking enthusiasts, who have been inoculated with the inner doctrines of the Arya Somaj and whose sentiment is Hindustan for the Hindus and hatred for all outside the Hindu pale, and for the English in particular."[64]

For Lyall, then, the danger of a past that was not past was quelled by locating political claims by Sikhs in a subjunctive mood produced through the *failure* of time. Within this formulation, claims to sovereignty were dislocated from previous conceptualizations of the political. This dislocation rendered the current claims illegitimate within the Sikh tradition—an illegitimacy that secured colonial sovereignty over knowledge itself. Marked by crisis, time became measurable to the rational colonial observer who recognized that the past only haunted the present through a nostalgic longing. This nostalgic structure then required the community, as Arjun Appadurai writes, "to miss things they have never lost."[65] Within this structure, claims to sovereignty indicated an always inauthentic desire: nostalgia rather than history, for example. The present was rendered in an always already inauthentic relation to both past and future, creating, according to officials, a necessarily corrupt politics.

Determining types of Sikhs still presented difficulties. Though the "population" became a key site to regulate difference, community was a collective and unstable formation. In this sense, the population in colonial knowledge functioned as an unobtainable object of desire, always eluding British grasp, while also functioning as the object cause of that very desire—to know and control the population was the foundation as well as the ultimate aim of colonial knowledge. Remaining uncomfortably near and present to colonial officials, the very idea of the population then threatened the colonial state. Finding Sikh elites generally trustworthy, Lyall maintained that though "Sikh peasants enlist freely [in the military] and are generally content with their lot under our Government, I suspect that they are in a frame of mind in which it would not take much to make them dangerous and unreliable."[66] Both known and desirous, but also inscrutable and perilous, the Sikh "population" and the Sikh "native" simultaneously structured colonial knowledge and rendered it meaningless. For the unknowable native was always unable to be fully symbolized while remaining far too near to the colonial state.

RUMORS, AGAIN

The Sikh tradition did still hold importance for Sikhs, though not as a past history that needed to be recaptured. This was not a melancholic fixation or a nostalgic longing. People did prioritize a prior sovereign who they thought could manage territorial boundaries effectually—namely, Duleep Singh—without rendering him in the past or subjunctive tense. This too is reflected in rumors.

The dread of colonial officials is palpable in the reports on the rumors about Duleep Singh's return and an impending war with Russia that they penned. Rumor presented difference to the colonial state, a difference not able to be quelled and ordered through the temporal and spatial logic the state perpetuated. Condos has addressed these problems within the state, writing that "authoritarian crackdowns and draconian legislation borne from panic and fear" were not "effective measures in suppressing what were often sophisticated and complex acts of anti-colonial resistance."[67] Rumor reveals this sophistication alongside the anxiety that accompanied sovereign power, the failings of disciplinary power, and the contested nature of resistance surrounding Duleep Singh.

The rumors that generated worry among colonial officials ranged in content, since the past was not dislocated from the present for the colonized, but an actively contested terrain of organizing society. Prior to Duleep Singh's capture at Aden, rumors were rampant that the British would recognize their own previous errors and make Duleep Singh sovereign once again. These rumors became enflamed as Duleep Singh pressured the colonial state to let him return to Punjab, and also because the British did indeed give in to some of his demands, such as letting Thakur Singh Sindhanwalia visit him in England. Rumors swirled that the state had "deputed a Granthi from Amritsar to England for the purpose of reconverting the Maharaja to the Sikh religion"—a rumor the colonial state traced to "the fact that Partap Singh, Granthi of Amritsar, having gone to England with

Sardar Thakar Singh, Sindhanwalia." This rumored conversion back into the *sangat* meant Duleep Singh could once again lead Sikhs, and affirmed that "Sikhs were said to be looking forward to his visit with great pleasure." A rumor in a similar vein was reported in circulation in Ludhiana on August, 1885: once the war between Britain and Russia commenced, the rumor went, Duleep Singh would be appointed to "the command of the Sikh troops and sent against the Russians" by the British themselves. In the Firozpur District and Amritsar, rumors spread of "Dalip Singh's restoration to the throne of the Punjab" and "it was stated that he would be appointed Commander-in-Chief of the Sikh army." A month later, rumors seemed to expand to suggest that he would not only "be sent against the Russians," but also that "he would assist Government to obtain Sikh recruits for the army, assisted by Sardar Thakur Singh." This rumor remained alive through February 1886, when it was reported circulating in Gurdaspur and Gurgaon in Punjab.[68]

As noted, rumors revealed the contested nature of politics at the end of the nineteenth century. The continual discord between Duleep Singh and the British state also meant that competing rumors tied Duleep Singh to Russia intrigues. Or, as Spivak notes, "any reader can 'fill' [rumor] with her 'consciousness,'" thereby creating indefiniteness.[69] In May 1885, in Ludhiana, rumors emerged that "Russia demanded restoration of the Punjab to Maharaja Dalip Singh, and of Delhi to the ex-Imperial family, and that war could only be averted, if England complied with these demands." Such rumors offered that British rule in Punjab would be overthrown once Duleep Singh returned to the frontier with Russian troops, upon which territory would be ceded to him. Moreover, the rumors continued, "the Maharaja was also said to have announced that, with the assistance of the Russians, he would rule in the Punjab." There emerged a line of continuity in these rumors, though one that did not imply established coherence within a singular essence, but an always emergent cohering within an established tradition. In one instance, for example, the state recorded, "at the close of the year 1886, the rumour that Dalip Singh was with the Russians on the Afghan frontier was current in many districts of the Punjab and one district, *viz.*, Firozpur reported that the Maharaja was accompanied by Bishen Singh, the Kuka *Subah* in Russian territory."[70] Rumor and prophecy thus come together.

These rumors spread. In Jalandhar, one colonial official reported that "speculation was rife as to when the Russians would invade India now that Dalip Singh had joined them."[71] In January 1887, Shahab-ud-din Khan, a horse trader in Ghazni, informed colonial officials that he had heard that in Ludhiana "Dalip Singh was with Russians, who intended to invade India in the summer." In Delhi as well, one colonial official observed, "there appears to be a general belief that Dalip Singh and Thakur Singh are in Russia, and that the massing of troops by the Russians will lead to an advance on Heart before long." Kukas were central in disseminating these rumors of alliances with the Russian state. In Ludhiana, the Kuka Jiwan Singh of Kindwal in the Jalandhar District arrived at Sri Bhaini Sahib in Ludhiana and informed people that "while he was in Hazro, in the Rawal Pindi district, about five months ago, Khan Singh (? Kuka) of that town received a letter from Dalip Singh announcing that he would invade with a Russian army" in February–March 1887.[72]

Rather than consider conflicting rumors about Duleep Singh's plans and possible British responses as contestations about the nature of possible politics, colonial officials believed that opposing ideas about Duleep Singh signaled the "wildness of the people of Punjab." They refused to consider the possibility of rumor outside the certainty of their law. Shifting the encyclopedic determinations of the colonial state, contestations became a sign of the population's inability to decipher objective truths from the wide range of information available—a sign, Bhabha writes, of "too much meaning and a certain meaninglessness."[73] On October 6, 1885, C. L. Tupper wrote to Durand, arguing that "the news of the Maharaja's expected return to India has given rise to a number of more or less wild rumours in the Punjab."[74] In March 1886 the state once again reported that "anxious enquiries were said to have been made in the Hoshiarpur district about the Maharaja, and wild rumours were current as to the powers that would be conferred on him."[75] In Ambala, too, the state reported that "Sikhs are anxiously looking forward to his appearance."[76] Paradoxically, the state found the population anxious because the population could not adjudicate between the wide range of information flooding the terrain. Or, to rephrase, rather than consider Duleep Singh as a struggle to constitute meaning, the state assumed the "population" was unable to properly conceptualize the right way to settle Duleep Singh.

The cryptic nature of Duleep Singh produced, as Roy writes in relation to *chapatis* and 1857, "a blockage in an Anglo-Indian information order" that had "a curiously powerful and hystericizing effect upon Company officials."[77] These hysterics were also displaced onto the population, whose assumed inability to classify information properly meant that, for colonial administrators, rumors could begin anywhere. This included in the press. One official argued that rumors in Lahore about Duleep Singh coming to India to "settle in Delhi and live as a Sikh" because land was "being acquired there for him" began in the pages of the *Aftab-i-Punjab*. On September 2, 1885, a report in the *Aftab-i-Punjab* newspaper stated, "Hira Singh, a Motamid (agent) of Maharaja Dalip Singh's, had visited the *Rakhs* (jungle or forest land) in the vicinity of Delhi, and reported to the Maharaja that they were worth buying. He also informed him of different rates at which tents could be had at Farukhnagar and that the Maharaja's houses at Farukhnagar and Musoorie were being repaired, furnished, and set in order." For colonial officials, the "population," unable to properly discern fact from fiction, took Hira Singh's testimony as a fact. Since the already determined future of colonial knowledge located Duleep Singh outside sovereignty, the "population" could only misread a future in which Duleep Singh incited violence. Attempts to signal Duleep Singh's return as sovereign, as Hira Singh attested to and actively organized, could only remain fictive with the colonial state's logic. Rumors, therefore, existed as false hopes, lies that needed to be watched and ordered toward an acceptable future. As incorrect hopes, rumors about Duleep Singh led to one main conclusion: that Duleep Singh's projected visit was getting "a good deal of attention in this Province [Punjab]," revealing an anxious "population" prone to unruliness.[78]

It is this wildness, which revels in its illegitimacy, that, Gayatri Spivak reminds us, makes rumor "accessible to insurgency."[79] The indeterminacy and accessibility it cultivates, Homi Bhabha demonstrates, produces a "communal adhesiveness" and "contagious spreading." The iterative function of rumor links it to panic—one central affect tied to insurgency in which an "old familiar symbol," in our case Duleep Singh, "develops an unfamiliar social significance as sign through a transformation of the temporality of its representation." Bhabha argues that we must foreground this panic and indeterminacy, for by disavowing it "the collective agency of the insurgent peasant is given a simplistic sense of intentionality" in which "the mutineers are located in a semi-feudal time-warp, the playthings of religious conspiracies." Bhabha contends that his rendering enhances our understanding of political struggle, mapping how the familiar becomes the unfamiliar. Within rumor, the native order of signs become "circulating signs of an 'English panic.'" Yet such a reading can also uphold the very grammar of the colonial order in divorcing expectations from experiences; expectations tied to the undecidable are critical in this line of argumentation. For Bhabha, rumor's contagion creates a "contingent borderline experience . . . a space of cultural and interpretive undecidability produced in the present of the colonial moment," in what is the "disjunctive 'present' or the 'not-there' of discourse."[80]

A problem, it seems, appears in the reduction of tradition to a conspiracy in which insurgents are located in a time warp. What of a tradition's striving toward internal coherence as a mode of organizing that does not induce panic? For Bhabha this would constitute a "binary opposition of racial and cultural groups" as "homogenous polarized political consciousnesses."[81] Following Ashis Nandy, Bhabha cautions against an unalterable past moving toward an inexorable future, and instead shifts our attention to indeterminate choices in a disjunctive present. But for Nandy, as Bhabha notes, this temporality is a problem of historicity, not of rumors. Nandy argues that a "refusal to acknowledge the primacy of history, thus, is also the refusal to fetter the future in terms of the past."[82] Providing a different grammar against historicity, Talal Asad invites us to consider how tradition constitutes "socially embodied and historically extended argument" that rejects the contextualization central to history.[83] A discursive tradition troubles, as Omnia El Shakry puts it, "a temporal unfolding," and instead allows us "to contemplate the convivial presence of the past in the historical moments that we are analyzing, as well as its co-presence in the present and in the future."[84] Within this threaded space of tradition, removing panic does not necessarily dislocate indeterminacy; there are ways of conceptualizing indeterminacy without upholding the panic of the present time striving toward a not-there.[85] Though hesitant to use tradition as a concept in order to maintain India as heuristic unit, Nandy points to Asad's argument about tradition, writing that for "the little cultures of India . . . the past shapes the present and future, but the present and the future also shape the past."[86] This, then, is not a temporality of panic but a form of temporality within a tradition that allows for the working through of coherence without demanding historical intelligibility. This is precisely the work of rumors.

Rumors around Duleep Singh were marked by neither panic nor inauthenticity but were part of a legitimate form of contestations within a tradition about what constituted sovereignty. Rumors were tied to the Sikh tradition itself, yet rumors were also located in the realm of the indeterminate. Think back, here, to the *barah mah* in the *mela*. Moreover, rumors began to coalesce around Duleep Singh and Russia, which worked in conjunction with Duleep Singh's return to the Sikh fold. Rumors spread that Duleep Singh's reconversion—his return to the Sikh tradition—meant that soldiers would be ashamed to fight against him. In October 1886 the state noted that "Nihal Singh, Zaildar of Ajnala in the Amritsar district, was heard to say that the Russians had gained a great advantage in being joined by Dalip Singh as the Sikh soldiers would be ashamed to fight against him."[87]

These rumors rejected broader pan-Indian understandings about caste such as the fears around caste pollution that incited indigenous and colonial panic in revolutionary attempts. For example, in what was imagined to be the reconstituted army of Duleep Singh, the military was not to be divided according to caste and race. Instead, rumors spread that "Sardar Thakur Singh had written from Patna to say that Maharaja Dalip Singh was in Russia and to encourage all castes of Punjabis to enter the Russian service."[88] By October 1886 rumors repudiating the polluting divisions in colonial and Indian society spread further: it was "rife that Maharaja Dalip Singh was at the head of a large Russian force and was about to invade India." These rumors were met with great approval. On January 8, 1887, one administrator registered that "From Amritsar came a report at this time that people at village Satiala were heard to say that Dalip Singh had issued a proclamation in English, Urdu, and Gurmukhi offering Rs. 2 per diem with free rations and clothing to every Punjabi who would go to him for service." And worry grew that "a great many people secretly entertained the idea of going to him!"[89]

Perhaps here we can make a provisional conclusion: Sikh rumor in both its form *and* content rejects the immediacy of consciousness central to speaking. Even though "oral," rumor becomes instead a generalized form of writing that is, as Spivak writes, "always in circulation with no assignable source."[90] In rumors about Duleep Singh this point is made clear by the failure to ascribe rumors a singular source. The nonpossessive nature of rumor disrupted the possessive nature of colonial rule, for rumor highlighted the British state's weakness through the circulation of information about British failures. This was a refusal of both territorial and conceptual mapping. Or, put another way, rumor revealed the unstable nature of Empire since rumors continually challenged both the state's territorial consolidation and its military reach by spreading across borders while providing evidence (real or imagined) about the state's pending failure.

On September 13, 1886, a proclamation in the vernacular was affixed "to the rear wall of the 'Kup' Police barrack in Multan city." The decree written by a purported yet unnamed Russian spy highlighted several rumored activities in which Russia functioned as the linchpin in order to reveal the instability of the British Empire. The author of the proclamation claimed that they "had left Russian territory three months ago" and had come "to the Punjab for the purpose of viewing the administration of the army and giving notice." The author noted they had been joined by another spy who informed them "that Italy and Turkey have allied themselves with Russian monarch." Italy and Turkey were joined by the Amir of Kabul who, the declaration stated, "had allied himself with the Russian monarch. All the inhabitants of Kabul are very much pleased with the alliance." The declaration then reached out to the Punjabi population. It read, "The Russian monarch, having the welfare of the inhabitants of the Punjab and Hindustan at heart, warns them to recover at once all monies they may have in the hands of Government, or else they will regret it." The written notice appealed to Punjabis through Duleep Singh himself, informing the community that "Maharaja Dalip Singh has for some time past been with the Russian monarch, and has now been placed in command of 75,000 troops at Paina."[91]

The direct confluence of rumor and writing in this notice also reveals the irreducibility of insurgent organizing to a singular cause. Highlighting the failure of the British state, the written form produced openings for a broader Middle Eastern, Central Asian, and South Asian connection. The notice also relayed that "The Khedive of Egypt has given notice to the Government that he will rule the country by himself. The ill-fortune of the Government is known to everyone." Alongside the Khedive's independence, the proclamation rumored that in Sudan, "the Mahdi too has established himself" and "a message has been sent to the Mahdi to come to the Punjab at once, as the Muhammadans are yearning for him." This rumored rebellion was said to draw in participants from Central Asia as well, since the note declared, "in Bokhara [in present day Uzbekistan] lakhs of *maunds* of food for soldiers and animals have been collected. Englishmen in high positions are sending their families home."[92] Within the written form, rebellion is left open for the determination of peoples outside the singular logic of an empire such as Russia, as well as the closings of an ethnic community tying in, we can see, broader global Muslim politics while recognizing other forms of difference.

The danger of the rumored insurrection lay in the unpredictability cultivated by rumors in which the spy dealt as well. The spy, however, enunciated the rumors to provide them a specific form and even asked the population to enter organized resistance in Bokhara, writing "whoever has a wish to enter Russian employ can get it at Bokhara according to his abilities. The Russian language is more prized that the English. It is now spoken in Bokhara."[93] But the capriciousness of resistance, rumors, and writing revealed that there could be no such centralized or stable site for resistance against British rule. Indeed, the rumors divulged the ability to collectively organize and confront the British at will outside any centralized organization. On the other end of the subcontinent, the declaration noted that "In Burma thousands of Government servants have been killed in battle." In the Sudan too, the spy noted, "The [British] Government is at present a mark to be fired at by all" and that "No Government ships can pass through that country."[94] Collective violence against the British Empire cultivated through rumor, then, could not be attributed solely to Russian efforts, but instead revealed multiple possibilities within a discrepant situation.

These possibilities centered around Duleep Singh as well. The spy also revealed how rumors stated that "on the 8th September 1886, the things [clothes] which were purchased at Lahore for Maharaja Dalip Singh arrived" in Moscow.[95] Organizational capacities around Duleep Singh did indeed strengthen after Duleep Singh embarked for Moscow from Paris in March 1887. Once in Moscow, even efforts to reconcile the return of Duleep Singh while acquiescing to British officials became an impossibility. Duleep Singh himself enflamed sentiments against the British. Leaving Aden, he wrote a letter to the *Times of India*, writing "although the Indian Government succeeded in preventing me from reaching Bombay lately, yet they are not able to close all the roads that are to India; for when I return I can either land at Goa or Pondicherry, or if I fancy an overland route that I can enter the Punjab through Russia."[96]

Through these rumors, Duleep Singh started to consolidate his resistance across the Punjab and South Asia more broadly. Rumors were spreading, the colonial state recorded, that "Dalip Singh is now in Germany and Russia has offered to help him with an army to conquer Afghanistan."[97] In Punjab, rumors spread of Sikh sympathy with Duleep Singh, strengthened by the porous nature of the frontier. Rumors circulated that Sikhs could navigate the frontier with ease, crossing the space that the British found difficult to regulate. Rumors in Muzaffargarh in Punjab relayed that "several Sardars and well-wishers of Dalip Singh had gone to meet him in Russia." These cross-frontier connections, spread through rumors, led to further rumors that Sikhs "fully sympathize[d] with him and were sorry he had not come to India." Rumors disseminated strategy and looked to cohere a community. Rumors proliferated that "in the event of war [Sikhs] would not fight against Dalip Singh." This circulating and questioning talk created dissensus through the recognition among the colonized that the colonial state's horizons and frontiers did not govern the community. Within this dissenting space, rumors of the people's union with Duleep Singh spread, as did rumors that Sikhs were ready to "aid the Maharaja" as well as "make any sacrifice for him."[98]

The anonymity and transitivity of rumors make conclusions about them difficult, especially when trying to avoid the very historical closures the colonial state continuously enacted by foreclosing its own limitation. Historians can indeed mirror this anxiety, overwhelmed by the feverish promises of the archive. But against this anxiety, the overwhelming promises of origins and presence, I have tried to inhabit rumor's loss—its indeterminacy—without dwelling comfortably in the colonial state's lost objects, rendered prior in a temporal lag.

To put the matter another way, a weak state overwhelmed by information denies two things: a particular form of knowledge that orders information, and the possibility of resistance within that state outside its own paranoia. Reading rumors about Duleep Singh discloses contestations about a sovereignty within the community without privileging his individual authority. We find only a subaltern maharaja, vacillating and shuttling within a turbulent although cohering community.

Chapter Five

REFORM

Traditions may reconfigure themselves without necessarily engendering historical ruptures and epistemological crises that lead to their demise; in fact, such
reconfigurations may lead to the revival and renewal of the tradition.

—OMNIA EL SHAKRY

Though the encounter with Duleep Singh at the end of the nineteenth century has tried to dislocate him, dwelling in his loss and his vacillation, the
Sikh tradition, in our analysis so far, functions as totality, integrating all
logics within itself. The dangers of such totality are apparent as tradition
becomes the site to memorialize loss—incorporating loss. But the tradition
refused such totalization. It could not be easily bound and remained caught
in a struggle both within itself and with the colonial state to constitute its
parameters rather than persisting as a given that we can mourn today. Such
struggles are most clear in the emergence of Sikh reform organizations at
the end of the nineteenth century, which sought to correct the tradition,
revising it by removing bad practices that denied the politico-ethical imper-
atives of the Gurus.

The impetus for the reformist impulse can be dated in part to 1873, when
four Sikh students at the American Mission School in Amritsar—Aya Singh,
Attar Singh, Sadhu Singh, and Santokh Singh—announced that they wished
to convert to Christianity, creating widespread distress among fellow Sikhs.[1]
This uproar added to existing unease in the Sikh community fostered in
part by encroaching missionaries and the outgrowth of multiple socio-
religious movements in Punjab, which had led to numerous attacks on the
Sikh gurus and the Sikh tradition.[2] Confronting these threats, on October 1,

1873, a diverse assortment of Sikhs assembled in Amritsar to found the Sri Guru Singh Sabha Amritsar, which sought, Jagjit Singh writes, to "provide the Sikh tradition a correct and coherent mode of ethical being," to cohere an orthodoxy for the Sikh tradition that could lead to improvement.[3] A Singh Sabha emerged at Lahore six years later and other branches of the movement would spread across the Punjab in the coming years.[4]

But the nature of coherence within the movement remained tentative, since each Singh Sabha branch developed, N. Gerald Barrier argues, its "own personality and peculiar interest despite similarity in composition and programme."[5] Indeed, these organizations were not a site of unified agreement about what constituted orthodoxy and correct conduct: as Teja Singh notes, "the[ir] meetings, lectures, and discussion were held in an atmosphere of controversy and denunciation."[6] Still, striving toward coherence through these disputations, Sikhs eventually centralized the Sabhas under a larger umbrella organization, the Amritsar Khalsa Diwan, in 1883. Controversies and conflict, however, continued and in 1886 the Khalsa Diwan fragmented into two separate organizations: the Amritsar Khalsa Diwan, which was constituted by the Singh Sabhas in Amritsar, Faridkot, and Rawalpindi, and the much larger Lahore Khalsa Diwan.

As significant sites of mobilization at the end of the nineteenth century, the Singh Sabhas and Duleep Singh's intrigues were imbricated. There was no distinction between "religious" and "political," and political sovereignty, "religious" reform, and proper conduct were inextricably intertwined.[7] The link between sovereignty and correct ethical conduct, however, has gone largely unexplored by scholars. For the most part, historians and theorists of reform in colonial India have focused on the consolidation and construction of religious boundaries by colonial technologies, changes in communications, and rampant commercialization of the rural countryside.[8] In their analyses of the struggle to reinstitute political sovereignty, scholars have emphasized purification of religious communities in relation to colonialism and how this process negated dissent. They highlight how reform movements instituted a modular and reified religious form. In doing so, scholars construct a colonial epistemic totality that overcomes a similarly totalized, but fluid and hybrid, past.[9] By emphasizing the "religious" nature of reform within Sikhism at the end of the nineteenth century, scholars not only leave the questions of political sovereignty and its ties to tradition unexplored, but also uphold the very binaries central to the colonial state between, for example, religious/political, urban/rural, elite/subaltern, and good/bad.[10]

The organization around Duleep Singh offers a different narrative in which the struggle over political sovereignty is not a lost one, but an unplumbable site for struggle that would eventually cohere into further political struggles.[11] The formations, argumentations, and fragmentations within the Singh Sabhas disclose the vibrant nature of the Sikh tradition as the Sabhas and Khalsa Diwans soon became both an object of derision as well as praise, revealing the wide terrain of orthodoxy at the end of the nineteenth century. Therefore, the central point of inquiry into reform, I will argue, is not to determine if a tradition became lost and therefore bounded due to colonial power or to determine the superficiality of the colonial order. Rather, the goal of exploring reform is to understand how, David Scott queries, "claims about the presence or absence of boundaries are *made*, fought out, yielded, negotiated."[12] Debates about Duleep Singh in the Sikh tradition in the late nineteenth century are important precisely because they show how Sikhs struggled toward coherence within particular rules of engagement about political sovereignty, even as the authority to intervene in such matters shifted to the colonial state from the Khalsa itself.[13] Put another way, the contradictions in the pursuit of coherence, both political and religious, reveal how reform did not inaugurate a rupture, losing the Sikh tradition. Instead, reform remained a site of contestation, Talal Asad contends, between "narrator and audience," between so-called elites and the community. In this struggle, a subject, elite or subaltern, could not speak in total freedom from the community, no matter how silent or elated they claimed they were.[14]

These contestations around reform require that we center questions of sovereignty. In the Sikh tradition, the spiritual (*piri*) is intimately bound with the temporal (*miri*), and the gurus denied their separation while recognizing that they remain in antagonistic relation to each other.[15] One could never become sovereign because even those who claimed sovereignty remained subordinate to *hukam*—a lesson from the gurus. Colonial officials, as we will see, conceptualized these struggles around Duleep Singh within the Sikh tradition suspiciously, reducing them to nefarious individual motives. Though the colonial state reduced these disputes to individual maneuvering, these debates, occurring within native networks, were a site to conjoin divergent aims. Although Sikhs tried to keep maneuvering around Duleep Singh a secret, the colonial state became an arbiter within the Sikh tradition as institutional authority, *miri*, increasingly became located with colonial officials. Sovereignty, in other words, became a possession of the colonial state.

RETHINKING REFORM

Since the political and religious were braided together, to contest "religion" was to simultaneously contest sovereignty and vice versa. These constant formations, contestations, and fragmentations within the struggle to secure sovereignty reveal the political nature of reform as the Sabhas and Khalsa Diwans refuse easy adjudication into archetypes that analyses of reform in the subcontinent typically entail.[16] Reform largely remains understood as a sanitizing gesture rather than a struggle; reform is understood to cleanse particular historical conditions. For one group of scholars, reform safeguards a formerly lost past by eliminating accumulated foreign contaminants in Sikhism, leading to revival.[17] For others, reform annihilates earlier progressive but heterogenous conditions within Sikhism, in turn preserving colonially inflected formulations of identity.[18] Both understandings of reform reveal how previously surpassed Sikh pasts themselves were already developed to match contemporary visions of progress, necessitating recovery. For example, as the arguments go: (1) reformers reified boundaries in a previously authentic amorphous and polyglot landscape, or (2) the undisciplined community introduced foreign practices into a formerly pure Sikh tradition, thereby requiring reform. Progress emerges as a concept, then, not in the temporal organization of colonial modernity, but in the actions of reformers or the prior practices of a heterogenous community. Though dislodged from modernity's horizons, historical perfectibility remains located and accessible within the modern's very temporal form, in which authenticity, signaling a historical end, remains both the organizational frame and the desirous object of discovery.[19]

Numerous scholars have emphasized the closures of reform. For example, scholars have argued that efforts by the Singh Sabhas, especially in the Lahore version, to consolidate a Sikh identity signaled a triumphant movement in Sikh history as Sikhs organized themselves to overcome decline wrought by foreign elements; this is the second tendency I outlined earlier.

As Harbans Singh argues, "the Singh Sabha was a great regenerating force" for it "rescued the Sikhs, awakening in them a new awareness of their past and of the excellence of their faith," thereby opening "the doors of modern progress." Nripinder Singh continues where Harbans Singh ends. Noting the prodigious output of the Singh Sabha, he claims that "the guiding principle of Singh Sabha regeneration was the endeavor to discern what is moral and to what was considered right and good."[20] The Singh Sabha's attempt to cultivate morality, Nripinder Singh relays, did not lead them astray from Sikh values. Instead, what emerged was a "desire to provide fresher insights into the nature of the Sikh ethos—an ethos which [the Singh Sabha] did not challenge, but which it clearly wished (given the terms of late-nineteenth-early twentieth-century religious life in the Punjab) to infuse with newer meaning." This newer meaning, Nripinder Singh compellingly demonstrates, did not challenge or change the Sikh tradition but rather "reinvigorated the basic principles enunciated in Sikh Scripture and by the Gurus themselves," for the moral motifs highlighted "by Singh Sabha writers in the twentieth century were essentially the same as those culled by Bhai Gurdas in the sixteenth/early seventeenth century."[21]

In contrast to such scholarship and following the first tendency I outlined before, scholars such as Harjot Oberoi have argued "historians are at fault when they simply reproduce these value judgments and employ categories invented by a section of Sikh elites to discredit specific beliefs and rituals." By not interrogating the categories, Oberoi argues, scholars can "fail to pursue any implication of the fact that the Sikhs were not a homogeneous social group." In contrast, Oberoi maintains that though the Amritsar Singh Sabha early on was "at home with the traditions of Sanatan religious culture" and kept "the Sanatan episteme intact," eventually the formation of the Lahore Singh Sabha would create a new episteme through "the powerful discourse of the Tat Khalsa." This Tat Khalsa discourse and its emphasis on purity, coupled with fundamental changes in Punjabi society wrought by colonial rule, Oberoi writes, first dismantled and then redefined "the entire phenomenology of Sikhism and what it implied to be a part of that tradition." This discourse represents, to Oberoi, a change in the episteme within the Sikh religion from an amorphous, fluid notion of Sikhism to a rigid and uniform conception of Sikh identity. Or, as Oberoi writes, "the older pluralist paradigm of Sikh faith was displaced forever and replaced by a highly uniform Sikh identity, the one we know today as modern Sikhism."[22] Within this logic, for Oberoi, the Singh Sabha cleanses; Oberoi mourns the lost past in need of redemption.

The vibrant and political nature of reform, as the Sabhas and Khalsa Diwans demonstrate, means we cannot reduce reform in the Sikh tradition to a form of closure that eliminated a heterogenous past, a ruptured contemporary moment that signals the advent of a colonized tradition and the emergence of modernized religious identity, or the differentiation into a multiplicity of minor "traditions."[23] Instead these contestations were singularly tied—hence the singular use of "Sikh tradition" in this book—to each other. My use of the term "Sikh tradition," however, does not imply that it is a static essence. That is, as Talal Asad teaches, an authentic essence cannot be retrieved from a nonperspectival position; rather, it is "the search for what is essential itself [that] provokes argument."[24] These arguments about what is essential are efforts to cohere orthodoxy; this is especially so, Asad writes elsewhere, since "it is too often forgotten that the process of determining orthodoxy in conditions of change and contest includes attempts at achieving discursive coherence, at representing the present within an authoritative narrative that includes positive evaluations of past events and persons."[25] Contestations and debates about the nature of Sikh praxis underscore how contradictory positions remained possible as Sikhs contested and shifted judgments in relation to the internal grammar of the Sikh tradition and new emerging historical injunctions. Such disputes reveal a singular albeit fragmentary form that marks, Anand Pandian writes, "the impossibility of a whole and seamless horizon of experience" that still strives toward its own coherence within particular rules of engagement.[26] In other words, though Sikhs took oppositional stances towards what constituted orthodoxy in the late nineteenth century, their goal was to persuade fellow Sikhs of their position within a tradition that remained a site of learning—learning which is necessarily an opening.[27] And "another Asadian word for learning is, of course 'tradition,'" as Gil Anidjar underscores.[28]

To use a metaphor to elaborate on the workings of tradition, contestations in Sikh tradition were a complex interplay that created an intricate and, at times, concealed and disruptive network from which orthodoxy, directly tied to sovereignty, mushroomed—but never as a totality, since it struggled both with and against itself.[29] The metaphor is illuminating since mushrooms do not emerge from an essence, to return to Asad, but grow and organize from disorder. For Anna Tsing, mushrooms force us to consider how indeterminacy is a process that learns the landscape—a landscape that might be ruined even as the fungi themselves remain both generous and exclusive.[30] Or, as Slavoj Žižek notes in relation to Hegel, mushrooming, the arising of necessity out of contingency, functions through autopoiesis, which signals a "process of the emergence of necessary features out of chaotic contingency . . . contingency's gradual self-organization, of the gradual rise of order out of chaos."[31] Or, as Asad has phrased it, contestation within the form of tradition creates "the possibility of changing elements of circumstances that are changeable" in which tradition itself provides "an invitation to change contingent aspects of one's tradition, the circumstances in which it is embedded, or both."[32] Importantly, these contestations, this chaos, does become ordered; they do not remain fluid or dead matter.[33] Rather, to return to mushrooms, within the chaos a coherence arises as the landscape rearticulates itself within its own loss. It is this discord at the heart of orthodoxy that continually orders itself even as loss mounts, that refuses our scholarly closures within reassurances of static heterogeneity or authenticity.

This struggle to dispute and authorize sovereignty also occurred through the Sikh tradition's "framework of inquiry," its generative principles, which provided a form in which Sikhs could contest the meaning of politics and reform.[34] Rather than an abstract inquiry into Indian sovereignty or Sikh sovereignty, such an approach requires that scholars engage a tradition from which debates about sovereignty mushroomed without reducing the tradition to either a stable inheritance or fluid matter. As previously stated, the spiritual (*piri*) is intimately bound with the temporal (*miri*), remaining in antagonistic relation to each other.[35] What we find, then, is not a reconciliation within a shared space or a firm grounding of sovereignty, but a tense space of conflict. Even in the reign of Ranjit Singh, tensions abounded as the relationship between Sikh institutions and the Khalsa Raj remained fraught with such conflict.[36] Just as there was not a unified view of orthodoxy coming from the Singh Sabhas, there was, put another way, no singular authorized version of the Khalsa Raj or Duleep Singh, or even a settled relation between *miri-piri*, awaiting subscription.[37]

MONITORING THE SINGH SABHA

A focus on Duleep Singh reveals these aporias because he became a sharply contested node in debates about the Sikh tradition precisely because he intersected with predominant questions of the time, which centered on political sovereignty and reinstituting the Khalsa Raj. These challenges were not simply radical undertakings, as we shall see, but also led to collaborations with the colonial state. There was, Omnia El Shakry contends, "an array of possible responses to the range of historical negations created by the colonial experience."[38] One possibility was political violence, but also obsequiousness. Sikh elites, for example, were not singularly tied to Duleep Singh as they renegotiated their own roles in the colonial regime. Against the simmering violence looking to reinstitute political sovereignty, Attar Singh of Bhadaur, the founding president of the Sri Guru Singh Sabha, Ludhiana, and patron of Khalsa Diwan Lahore, looked to gain the favor of the colonial state, which he regarded as legitimate sovereigns, and denigrated Duleep Singh. He argued that Sikhs were decidedly loyal and offered intelligence on Duleep Singh's proceedings in Punjab. Attar Singh wrote to H. M. Durand, the private secretary to the lieutenant governor of Punjab on August 9, 1887, arguing these accounts were the result of other communities maligning Sikhs vying for favor with the colonial state. He wrote, "among rival communities attempts are constantly being made by members of one sect to set the Government against members of another, and I am also aware that attempts are being made to blacken the character of Sikhs."[39]

The colonial state did not take Sikhs to be so passive as Attar Singh claimed and continually sought to arbitrate and manage the Sikh tradition. Its management hinged on efforts to improve the Sikh population. It also required the state to monitor, as Brian Hatcher explains, "the relationship between reform as an expression of the quest to purify religious truth and reform as a slippery slope leading to dissent, viewed with suspicion as a source of competition, enmity, and ill will."[40] The danger of reform in the colonial imagination prompted the state in the late nineteenth century to become an intervening intermediary of the Sikh tradition. Indeed, colonial officials remained uncertain and troubled by the proliferation of the Singh Sabha. In November 1886, the colonial state undertook various enquiries "to ascertain if possible whether the *real* object of these 'Sabhas' was political," or if it was "a moral, social, and religious" one. Attempting such a classification proved difficult; according to one official recorded, "nothing was elicited confirming this view [that it was a political affair]." Nevertheless, William Mackworth Young, at the time the secretary to the Punjab government, noted in June 1887, when government officials attended the Singh Sabha meetings, they commonly found Sikhs uttered "strong expressions of opinion," at times "verging on seditious." Young lamented the situation, concluding "these societies are very little under our control."[41]

Young's disquiet about the state's lack of control rested on its inability to firmly demarcate the Singh Sabhas as political organizations, thereby precluding overt official interference due to the British Crown's policy of noninterference and neutrality in religious matters.[42] Unable to distinguish whether the Singh Sabhas had a political or religious mission, the colonial state had to take the Singh Sabhas at their word: the Singh Sabhas existed to reform Sikhism, which, in colonial terms, was a matter of private custom. But the state nonetheless feared religious reform would catalyze political upheaval, especially since ethnographic knowledge at the time suggested that a particular ethnic community was predisposed to being excitable, such as Sikhs.[43] With this tension in mind, Young argued that although many district officers upheld the policy of noninterference in religious affairs and therefore did not seek to regulate the wide array of opinions and expressions at the Singh Sabha meetings, the colonial state could not "afford to allow an organization of this character to proceed to the length of organization against Government measures or in favor of opponents of Government." To prevent such disaffection and tumult, Young concluded that even though he did "not think that Government could in accordance with law take any direct measures for interfering with such societies," district officers, through loyal allies in the Singh Sabha, had to "keep themselves acquainted with their proceedings, and to endeavor to control the tone of their debates" and "keep discussions within proper bounds."[44]

The attempt to indirectly manage the Singh Sabhas took on particular urgency because of rumors about Duleep Singh, especially since he claimed sovereignty on "religious" grounds through citing Sikh "prophecies," the *sau sakhis*. As we saw earlier, the state had remained concerned about Duleep Singh's deleterious effect upon the Sikh community throughout the 1880s. The question of sovereignty, albeit presumed dormant, in the community required the state to maintain constant vigilance in order to determine, in Young's words, "whether anything is now going on which distinctly fosters it [claims of sovereignty]" even though it was impossible to eliminate the interest in Duleep Singh since the irrational community could never be trusted.[45] For the colonial state, the Singh Sabhas were one such organization that threatened to revive interest in Duleep Singh and the Khalsa Raj among the Sikh community by fomenting debate around the nature of the colonial state's sovereignty. Many Sikhs themselves made such arguments. A pensioned *havildar* (sergeant) in Ludhiana, for instance, argued that the institutions of the "Singh Sabha" alongside the expected return of Maharaja Duleep Singh were key indications of the "re-establishment of the Sikh kingdom." Tying the two together, Young reported "there is no doubt that considerable activity has of late been manifested among the 'Singh Sabhas' or Sikh societies, partly in connection with the Maharaja Dalip Singh's affairs."[46]

Religious reform was indeed tied to sovereignty in the Singh Sabhas. On April 5, 1886, Gurmukh Singh, the superintendent of branch schools in Hoshiarpur, sent a letter to Duleep Singh, writing that he had established the Sri Guru Singh Sabha at Hoshiarpur. (This Gurmukh Singh should not be confused for Bhai Gurmukh Singh, whom we will encounter later.) He implored Duleep Singh to find a route to India as the people looked forward to his return. He concluded by noting, "I have shown a picture of your Royal Majesty to the members of our Sabha which they all bowed down and prostrated, and paid thanks to God for your Royal Majesty's return to the Punjab." As news of Duleep Singh's rumored return spread through organizations such as the Singh Sabha, tumult manifested in Punjab against the British. Captain John Paul Warburton, deputy superintendent of police, Amritsar, reported, "The rural people (Punjabi Sikhs) make no attempt at concealing their sympathies for Maharaja Dalip Singh, who, they say, will very soon come and assume the government of this country." Warburton continued to relate that a "Mission Lady" had assured him that "of late the behavior of the Sikhs has quite changed in the villages." They had become "defiant and insolent now to Mission ladies and order them out of their houses saying—We do not want you: in a short time you will see what will happen." Warburton concluded by cautioning colonial officials against allowing the Singh Sabhas and other such organizations to operate, arguing they were a "dangerous political elements, and movements intended to increase disloyalty among the people against the British Government, and it is impossible to say when the volcano we are sitting on, with a feeling of security, may break out."[47]

Therefore, the political nature of the Singh Sabhas was not a figment of colonial imagination.[48] The threat to the colonial state was not an imaginary one but had been ongoing for several years, since Sikhs did not capitulate. Nor did they consider the political and religious separate entities; rather, Sikhism functioned as a repository to think about sovereignty even within a newly emerging political context.[49] Elaborating on these ethics that refused to separate the spiritual from the temporal, numerous high positioned members of the Singh Sabha had actively cultivated ties with Duleep Singh. Most famously, Thakur Singh Sindhanwalia was a founder and the initial president of the Singh Sabha at Amritsar and, as we know, an ardent supporter of Duleep Singh. As we have seen, Sindhanwalia traveled to meet Duleep Singh in England in 1884–85. After his return, Sindhanwlia continued his travels, this time across the subcontinent. He visited central Sikh temporal authorizes, *takhts,* at Huzar Sahib in Nandair and Patna Sahib, organizing on Duleep Singh's behalf (see chapter 3). Eventually, "after a stay of about three months at Patna," the British spy Munshi Aziz-ud-din reported, "Sardar Thakur Singh returned to Punjab" where "he carried on preaching Dalip Singh's case." Sindhanwalia found a sympathetic response from fellow founding members of the Amritsar Singh Sabha such as Khem Singh Bedi and Raja Bikram Singh of Faridkot and the president of the Lahore Singh Sabha, Diwan Buta Singh.[50] Soon thereafter, in 1887, recognizing that the British discovered his plotting, Sindhanwalia, with Duleep Singh's sanction, formed an exiled Sikh state in Pondicherry as the newly appointed chief minister of the Khalsa Raj.[51]

Even though Sindhanwalia engaged in widespread documented revolt, he sought to keep his maneuvering a secret, continually paying sycophantic respect to colonial authorities hoping to obscure his objectives. The revolt of 1857 played a central role in affirming his dissimulated allegiance to the Crown, for just as that event functioned for colonial authorities as a sign of the danger of the Indian population, Sikhs used 1857 to demonstrate their loyalty. In the aftermath, many Sikhs trusted that this demonstrated loyalty would help them not only to remain outside the watchful eye of the colonial state, but also to receive favors—both monetary and otherwise, such as job placement in the civil service. Asking for such financial aid in a letter to the viceroy, Sindhanwalia pointed out that he was "one of the most loyal and faithful subjects of Government," which he demonstrated when "on 31st July 1857, during the Mutiny, I and my late brother Sirdar Pratap Singh rendered very valuable services to Mr. Cooper, then Deputy Commissioner of Amritsar."[52]

However, despite participating in flattery of the colonial state, in other venues Sindhanwalia argued that the colonial state read natives too literally, leading it to put too much stock into expressive flattery as a way to determine native intent. Since his flattery was deemed insufficient, Sindhanwalia deduced, it meant that he did not receive compensation from the colonial state and additionally faced sabotage from corrupt colonial officials. To quote Sindhanwalia at length:

> Of course I am wanting in one quality, and that is of flattery. I do respect the officers, but I never like to do such acts that would disgrace my family. I was thinking in vain that I have rendered good services, and that I am a real loyal and faithful subject of the Government, and that I need not flatter the officers. Those officers who were given to hear tales of people and liked flattery were always disinclined to have any regard for me. I accepted the Government employment for sake of maintenance and was allowed a very low rank of an Extra Assistant Commissioner, but I had to forgo it because the local officer would rather like me to serve as a mere slave.

His stoicism misread and unable to face continued disgrace by colonial officials, Sindhanwalia decried British rule, arguing, "I do not know where is the English justice so famous everywhere. I have never seen or heard of it."[53]

Sindhanwalia made appeals to the British state for funds even while in Pondicherry as the head of a newly minted exile government in the name of Duleep Singh. He hoped, in essence, that the British would provide the very financial tools to destroy their empire. In another letter continuing his pleas, he argued that he moved to Pondicherry not to overthrow the British state, but because of his pecuniary embarrassments emerging from internecine familial struggles. These familial struggles centered on a financial dispute with his adopted son, Bakshish Singh, which the state refused to adjudicate even after his numerous appeals. Facing financial difficulties and persecution from corrupt colonial officials, Sindhanwalia argued "as men prefer death than disgrace, we came here in French India." The state's misdiagnosis of the situation by proclaiming him seditious, Sindhanwalia claimed, emerged from rumors circulated by his enemies. He wrote, "I feel very sorry indeed to find that our arrival at Pondicherry has produced a wrong impression in the press . . . I think some of my enemies have caused the origin of this impression." Against this maligning, Sindhanwalia argued that he and his sons were "really loyal to the British Crown," while quipping they looked forward to Lieutenant-Governor Lyall's "first act of benevolence," which depended on his "kindness and love of justice."[54]

Colonial officials recognized that Sindhanwalia's claims were duplicitous. His son Bakhshish Singh, the state noted, also "supplied him [Sindhanwalia] money to enable him to make his way to French territory."[55] But rather than consider Sindhanwalia's intrigues as the mobilization of a wider threat, the colonial state reduced them to a backward act by someone who carried "no weight in the Punjab" and was not "worth powder and shot."[56] Oberoi presents precisely such a conclusion, arguing that men such as Sindhanwalia—the elite class displaced by colonial rule—"cannot be expected to lead cultural revolution. They could at best preserve what they inherited" while "striving to freeze the pace of time" in a passive revolution.[57] Yet the colonial state itself detected the incremental but notable increase of Sindhanwalia's supporters through the 1880s. The British consular agent in Pondicherry reported, "Thakur Singh's followers here have been increasing, of late, by ones and twos, and that they now number about 30 persons, but what this means I do not know."[58]

Opposition to British sovereignty that was starting to coalesce at Pondicherry reveals the difficulty of demarcating the parameters of Sikh resistance to British rule, as Sikhs sought to hide their intriguing from the colonial state. That Sindhawalia and many of his allies flattered the state while seeking to undermine it makes it difficult to read the archive, for the archive itself presents both a stymied resistance and a burgeoning one. Within this archival doubling we must hesitate and recognize that contestations refuse simple adjudication into given categories of analysis such as "elite" and "subaltern" or "religious" and "political." That is to say, such deception does not imply that the "religious" was a ruse to obtain or preserve political or economic ascendancy. Nor did financial incentives render religious or political claims inauthentic, unable to constitute a political revolt. Rather, Sindhanwalia's efforts to reform Sikhism through the Singh Sabha, to reclaim Duleep Singh's throne, and to alleviate his pecuniary troubles are overdetermined. The efforts refuse our attempt to map his desire onto a singular nodal point signifying either a political, religious, or economic determinant—a determinant that can then be located and mapped.[59]

But, as Hussein Ali Agrama reminds us, the secular forces us into such a mapping, for "it is secularism itself that makes religion into an object of politics."[60] Once made into objects of politics, religious claims produce only suspicion, potentially deceiving both the scholar and the state. In our example, Sindhanwalia's advocacy for a return of Khalsa Raj through Duleep Singh became a pretense presented to the colonial state, hiding Sindhanwalia's economic or another personally suspect motive. In centering a hidden interior motive, the state continually remained vigilant even over institutions it sought to partition into a religious realm like the Singh Sabha. On guard, the state reduced Sikh contestations within the parameters of tradition in the Singh Sabha, which necessarily included disputes about the political, to *inauthentic* religious claims that were only disguised power ploys undertaken for political gain.[61] The danger lay, as we saw earlier, in the ignorance of the community, since deceitful political ploys could succeed on a gullible population.

Suspicion about the underlying motives of religious discourse surrounded the Singh Sabha, were further entrenched as Sikhs sought to hide their revolutionary activities from the British.[62] This deception posed particularly difficult problems when determining the intent of *granthis* (readers of the Sikh Guru, which is in text form known as the *Guru Granth Sahib*). Bhai Sumer Singh, for example, the head *granthi* at Patna Sahib, one of the four temporal Sikh authorities, was involved in Duleep Singh's intrigues as well. He was in Faridkot in 1887, engaged in a project funded by the Raja Bikram Singh of Faridkot to produce a counter-exegesis to Ernst Trumpp's translation and analysis of Guru Granth Sahib. A native agent of the colonial state, Amrik Singh Hasanwalia, traveled to Patna on March 22, 1887, to garner more information about Sumer Singh and met with Bawa Bir Singh, Bedi, the deputy of Bhai Sumer Singh and Bhai Gulab Singh, *ardasi* of Patna. He advised colonial authorities that Gulab Singh, unsuspecting of Amrik Singh's duplicity, divulged that "Bhai Sumer Singh is only ostensibly employed in translating the Granth at Faridkot."[63] This admission, Amrik Singh concluded, meant that Sumer Singh's purpose in being in Faridkot was not a religious but a political one—one in which he could use the guise of religion to manipulate others for political purposes. Exegesis, in this logic, was rendered inauthentic in relation to the political—proper

exegesis would be one, in these terms, that did not engage in overt anticolonial politics.

Inhabiting the interstice between what were thought to be two distinct realms—religious and political—*granthis* such as Bhai Sumer Singh
played a particularly important role in trying to bring back the Khalsa
Raj. This was especially so since they were embedded within the subaltern community (the *sangat*) while remaining outside the purview of the
colonial state—engaged as they were in now putatively defined religious
affairs. In this narrowly defined space, the colonial state could only read
exegesis as inauthentic preaching that *granthis*, under guise of religion,
engaged in to advance political ends.[64] Within the state's secular understanding, exegesis, or *katha*, which intertwines narratives from *sakhis*
through persistent questioning of a sociopolitical context while creating
a *sangat*, could not function in itself as providing an anti-British context,
since *katha* refused divisions between the religious and political. Instead,
katha became rendered a duplicitous tool deployed by self-indulgent
granthis. Put another way, *katha* was first stripped of political meaning
and then, if political meaning was attached to it, as it is in the Sikh tradition, this politicization was rendered as artful cunning.[65] This is precisely how Sindhanwalia and Sumer Singh's attempts to intervene in the
Sikh tradition functioned from the perspective of the colonial state,
reducing the overdetermined nature of the political to an originary
moment located in individual intention. Amrik Singh argued that he
was not only positive of these connections but also considered "Sumar
[sic] Singh as at the bottom of all intrigues." He was influenced, Amrik
Singh continued, by monetary gain and duplicity from Sindhanwalia,
reporting, "Thakur Singh had been very generous to Sumar Singh in
Patna, *and he* had a persuasive *tongue*."[66]

For the state, the key then was to allay individual concern in order to
ward off collective action. Recognizing the central role Raja Bikram Singh
of Faridkot played in both the formation and growth of the Singh Sahba
and his involvement in exegetical affairs, the colonial state argued that these
"religious" engagements became dangerous when coupled with discontent.
Young, for example, contended that Bikram Singh's engagements with "Sikh
religious observances" coincided with "a considerable amount of discontent in the mind of the Raja of Faridkot." Young continued that "although
such cases of discontent cannot always be avoided, every opportunity

should, I think, be taken to reassure such Chiefs of the friendly disposition of the British Government towards them."[67] The need to quell this discontent emerged because nefarious plotting by individuals could unite discontent into a common front.

Even though the colonial state noted there was a split between the Sabhas in Punjab since different Sabhas had different agendas, the state argued that these sides could come together only due to nefarious individual maneuvering, harnessing the discontent. This was the case in relation to Duleep Singh as well, as one report assessed that there was no "agreement between the Sindhanwalia people, the Faridkot Raja and Bawa Khem Singh about the matter of Dalip Singh." In fact, Amrik Singh reported that it was Sumer Singh himself who brought about an agreement between disparate parties—Khem Singh Bedi, the Raja of Faridkot, and Thakur Singh Sindhanwalia—after being awarded the *gaddi* at Patna. Khem Singh Bedi, for example, did not back Duleep Singh's revolt until he became convinced by arguments made by Sumer Singh and Sindhanwalia. As his conversion illustrates, disputations that revolved around matters of religion and religious authority had the power to bring together individuals who went into discussions with conflicting views. In another example, Amrik Singh visited Maharani Jind Kaur's *dasi* (favorite maid), Mangala, who served in a motherly role to Duleep Singh. According to Mangala, Amrik Singh reported, "Bawa Khem Singh, Bedi, was not originally mixed up with Dalip Singh intrigues, but has since been persuaded to join the Maharaja's cause through the efforts of Bhai Sumer Singh of Patna."[68] Mangala's information coincided with the evidence Amrik Singh gathered at Patna, where he learned that Khem Singh Bedi affirmed his ties to Duleep Singh at a marriage ceremony. He reported:

During the marriage festivities at Faridkot, a compact was made between the Raja, Bawa Khem Singh, Sardar Bur Singh of Mangheria (Hoshiarpur District), Motabir of Shabzada Sha deo Singh, and other persons to the effect that they would aid in bringing back Dalip Singh. This compact, they said, was made on the day after that on which Bhagu Mall had publicly alluded to Dalip Singh. In an open Darbar, Bhagu had risen and said, on the previous day "while we are all feasting here, Dalip Singh is in distress in Europe, get him back, put up some prayers for his sake." Khem Singh replied publicly "He will come: we are with him."[69]

Although the British sought to demarcate between the political and religious—the latter always already defined by the secular—Sikh contestations exceeded these placements. A marriage ceremony, in this example, was not simply a private affair for merging familial ties but also served to solidify political allegiances.[70]

The challenges and shifting placements signal the important role of native networks in conjoining divergent aims. Numerous *granthis* took charge, supporting Duleep Singh. The colonial state documented that "*granthis* of the four principal Sikh shrines" were both circulating and furthering Duleep Singh's cause among Sikhs. One report concluded that at least sixteen *granthis* and *nihungs* from the four principal *takhts* at Amritsar, Patna, Anandpur, and Nander and Akal Bunga and Baba Atal Gurdwara in Amritsar were involved in the intrigues by 1887.[71] *Granthis* were especially difficult to confront and through their *katha* remained embedded within the community broadly. Rather than be limited only within cosmopolitan networks or temple officiants, the community was therefore central in working within this framework of *miri-piri* and coalescing orthodoxy in order to make sense of political sovereignty.[72] Or, to follow Partha Chatterjee, "religion to such a community provides an ontology, an epistemology as well as a practical code of ethics, including political ethics."[73]

Denying the possibility of this political ethics, colonial officials argued that the organization around Duleep Singh was only elite manipulation, even when tumult existed in the community. To take one example, Major General M. Dillon took note that an officer of the Fifteenth Sikhs reported that one of his officers, Bishun Singh, mentioned "there was much excitement amongst the people respecting Dalip Singh" because "these people are uneducated and believe anything."[74] The community, Bishun Singh concluded, was "in a state of 'expectancy'" rather than active disloyalty, since it had been disturbed by agents at work. These agents, another officer of the Punjab Frontier Force confided to Dillon, were Sikh *granthis* with whom Duleep Singh organized through Sindhanwalia. This held revolutionary potential as Duleep Singh asked Sindhanwalia to "warn the Pujaries at Amritsar, Anandpur, Patna, and Nandair [*sic*] to keep arms in temples in serviceable order. They will be very shortly required by my loyal subjects."[75] Colonel F. E. Hastings, too, revealed that his troops remained embedded within these networks, challenging the presumed loyalty of the native Sikh army. He provided information that "Sikhs invariably amongst themselves speak of him as their 'Maharaja' which custom shows the light in which they regard him." Hastings argued that this left "no doubt that Dalip Singh's presence with a Russian army engaged in hostilities on our North-West Frontier would have a most prejudicial effect on the loyalty of the Sikh community." Hastings noted a conversation with a Sikh soldier attesting to this danger, since he "freely stated that under such circumstances there would be risings among the Sikhs, though he was of opinion they would fail for want of due organization."[76] What we find then is a form of sovereignty that circulated through *granthis* and *katha*, all of which disseminated a code of practical and political ethics.

SECRETS EXPOSED

Singh Sabhites did not simply use preestablished Sikh networks to circulate the code of practical and political ethics. They also relied upon new modes of communication, most notably the printing press. The Raja of Faridkot would print books and pamphlets, for example, and then would distribute them to the community, which fellow Sikhs lauded.[77] As Rachel Sturman notes, within community struggles "the limitations of colonial political space encouraged the parties to adopt the forms and modalities of colonial civil society—petitions, pamphlets, newspaper articles, public meetings, and the like—and colonial institutions provided multiple venues for jockeying over community claims."[78] Relying on these new networks meant that these internal contestations about sovereignty also became visible to the colonial government, especially the publication in 1885 of the work in Urdu of Bawa Nihal Singh, a *thanadar* in Kalsia State, the *Khurshid-i-Khalsa*. In this publication, Nihal Singh caused controversy by referring to Ram Singh, the leader of the Kukas, as Guru, as well as proclaiming that Duleep Singh should be restored to his throne. Nihal Singh argued that John Lawrence had deposed Maharaja Duleep Singh through unlawful threats against members of the court and that "the people are now in hopes that by the royal and imperial favors of the Empress of India, the throne of Lahore will be restored to Maharaja Dhulip Singh . . . Sardar Thakur Singh, Sandhanwalia, who has, by his perfect belief in the Sikh faith and by his excellent undertakings, exonerated himself from the disgrace attached to his family, is expecting to be made a Wazir."[79]

The Singh Sabha was closely tied to Nihal Singh's seditious publication, as Surmukh Singh, the author's brother and secretary of the local Singh Sabha, oversaw the printing of the book at the press of Diwan Buta Singh, founding president of Singh Sabha Lahore, in Jalandhar. Moreover, the work garnered favorable reviews, printed on its final two pages, from "Sardar Harnam Singh, Rais and President of the Singh Sabha, Kharar; Sahib Singh, Secretary of the Singh Sabha, Fatehgarh; and Jodh Singh, Secretary of the Singh Sabha, Nawashahr." It also received praise from Sumer Singh from Patna and Kartar Singh of Kartarpur, who like the other endorsers considered that the work "would be useful to the Khalsa community."[80] Soon, the book began circulating even within the military, prized by the British as a bastion of loyalty. One official reported that "early in November 1886, it was ascertained that men of the 9th Bengal Lancers and 23rd Pioneers had subscribed for the Khurshaid-i-Khalsa," even though, one memorandum conjectured, the soldiers were "without intimate knowledge of its contents."[81]

Since the political constituted a site of disputation about sovereignty, the central location assigned to Duleep Singh in the *Khurshid-i-Khalsa* did not go unopposed. Following the publication of Nihal Singh's work, on October 23, 1885, Bhai Gurmukh Singh, a lecturer at Oriental College in Lahore and the secretary of the Singh Sabha Lahore, circulated a notice through the Khalsa Diwan, challenging the printing of the positive reviews as well as the content of the *Khurshid-i-Khalsa*, especially the post-Guru period. The public notice read that after contacting the reviewers in the Singh Sabha, they stated that "they were cognizant of that part of the book alone which contained an account of the Sikh Gurus, and that the author was responsible for the historical portion from the time of Banda [Bahadur] up to the present period, and for the genealogical trees inserted in the book." Gurmukh Singh continued, noting that the reviewers had not given "any opinion on the historical sketch (of the Sikh conquests after the death of Guru Gobind Singh) and on the genealogical trees, and they are not, in consequences, responsible for them." Following this inquiry, Gurmukh Singh advised that Bawa Nihal Singh be "asked why he published the reviews of the aforesaid gentlemen as applying to the entire work (when the said reviews only referred to a portion of the book)."[82]

On February 8, 1886, Gurmukh Singh issued a further notice stating that Nihal Singh had been called to the Singh Sabha to explain his "expressions against [the] Government and of statements calculated to bring the *Khalsa* faith in disrepute."[83] When Gurmukh Singh determined that the author had "not replied to any of the questions put to him," he asserted that "the author should be excluded from the Singh Sabha."[84] Failing to "give a satisfactory answer," Gurmukh Singh noted, "the case would be placed before the Khalsa Diwan."[85] On February 14, 1886, the Khalsa Diwan met, with members coming "unanimously" to the "opinion that the author should be given another opportunity to acquit himself of the blame." Yet despite this second chance, Nihal Singh did not respond. Instead, Nihal Singh, Gurmukh Singh continued, "joined in opposition to the Sabha in several matters."[86] In April 1886 "a notice was issued under the same signature, declaring the book to be unauthorized on behalf of 15 Sabhas, and the author to be excluded from the Singh Sabhas."[87] Likewise, "it was also decided that anybody, whether a Sikh individually, or Sabha collectively, who might hereafter express disapproval of this proceedings of the Lahore Khalsa Diwan would be dealt with in the same manner as the author of the book in question had been treated."[88] This decree was a not-so-veiled threat to the Amritsar Khalsa Diwan in particular as the dissension between the two bodies was widening.

This public notice assured the colonial state of Sikh loyalty. On May 24, 1886, Young wrote in a letter to Durand that "the issue of the present notice excluding Bawa Nihal Singh from the Singh Sabhas is noteworthy, inasmuch as the objections taken to the Khurshid-i-Khalsa are professedly on the account of its disloyalty to the Government."[89] G. S. Forbes, junior undersecretary to the Government of India, concurred, noting how Nihal Singh's excommunication was "a gratifying testimony to the loyalty of the leaders of the Sikh Community."[90] Yet doubt remained about where institutional authority to disbar Nihal Singh emerged. Even though, for example, as *The Pioneer* reported, the Khalsa Diwan was "the last Court of appeal in matters connected with the Sikh religion and ordinances,"[91] the state was suspicious that Bhai Gurmukh Singh "circulated it on his *own* authority, since it was known that dissensions had lately arisen in the society."[92] Once again the question of individual manipulation came to the fore.

Within the dissensions of the Singh Sabha, the opposition to Gurmukh Singh, too, contacted the colonial state. Looking to cohere their own authority against Bhai Gurmukh Singh and his vision of the Singh Sabha, in October 1886, even though they were actively plotting against the colonial state, the Raja of Faridkot, Khem Singh Bedi, and Sardar Man Singh, superintendent of the Golden Temple at Amritsar, sent a letter to the lieutenant governor "repudiating the acts of Gurmukh Singh." They too conferred authority to themselves, conveying to the lieutenant governor that "no document purporting to come from the Khalsa Diwan should be considered authentic, without the signatures of at least two of its members."[93] Importantly, following Nihal Singh's excommunication from the Sikh fold, the Amritsar group countered and excommunicated Gurmukh Singh from the Sikh fold in March 1887. The Khalsa Diwan Amritsar, through the Akal Takht and Darbar Sahib, issued a *hukamnama* excommunicating/separating (*alhida kita*) Gurmukh Singh from the Khalsa Panth.[94] The *hukamnama* announced that Gurmukh Singh affronted the Guru Granth Sahib in his writings and lectures, which went against the entirety of the Sikh tradition. This was grounds for Gurmukh Singh's isolation; the *hukamnama* went on to state that if anyone persisted in associating with Gurmukh Singh, that person would meet a similar fate.[95] With two excommunications in play, one issued from the Khalsa Diwan Lahore against Nihal Singh and the other issued from the Akal Takht through the Khalsa Diwan Amritsar against Gurmukh Singh, there emerged a political vacuum from which Sikh institutions were unable to draw authority. The possibility of cohering tradition became an impossibility as sovereignty became located as a "thing" in the state.[96] Otherwise put, the temporal (*miri*) and spiritual (*piri*) became dislocated from their antagonistic and intertwined relation within the Sikh tradition to a resolved one with the colonial state using its sovereignty to determine spiritual matters.

On April 16, 1887, the *Khalsa Akhbar*, the main organ of the Singh Sabha Lahore, reported on the controversy and the split between the Singh Sabhas, tracing it to the publication of Nihal Singh's book. The *Khalsa Akhbar* explained that Gurmukh Singh's extended efforts in the Singh Sabha Lahore had created a vibrant Khalsa Diwan, which became eroded by the Khalsa Diwan Amritsar. This erosion became exacerbated, the *Khalsa Akhbar* continued, when Nihal Singh published the *Khurshid-i-Khalsa*, which challenged much of *gurmat*, such as identifying Ram Singh as a guru. The *Khalsa Akhbar* chided Nihal Singh for recommending to the English state that all Sikhs had reached a uniform agreement that Maharaja Duleep Singh should receive the *takht* of Lahore and Sardar Thakur Singh Sindhanwalia should receive the vizier. For the *Khalsa Akhbar*, upholding Duleep Singh signaled a breach, creating irreconcilable differences between the Singh Sabhas that the column details vividly. The central concern in the article around this breach, however, originated in Khem Singh Bedi's ties to the colonial state. The Khalsa *Akhbar* reported that Khem Singh Bedi went to Lieutenant Governor Aitchison and told him that he was "the hallowed and main Guru of the Sikhs [*Sikhan da vada and pavittar Guru*]" and that he was "all of Punjab's *vakil* [delegate/custodian of tradition]." The *Khalsa Akhbar* lamented this self-proclaimed authority that challenged both Sikh tenets and the parameters of authority in Punjab. The writer asked: When was he named *vakil*? How did he become authorized?[97]

The *Khalsa Akhbar* report therefore reveals not only internal discord within the Sikh tradition but also the role of the colonial state in adjudicating *Sikhi*. Bedi's declaration of being a representative of all Sikhs was dangerous because it could unduly influence the state, which in turn would authenticate and arbitrate between practices such as further entrenching caste practices in the Sikh community—practices Gurmukh Singh and others vehemently opposed. But in refusing to allow dissension and contestation within the parameters of tradition, authority shifted from Sikh institutions, which cultivated multiple strands of argumentation—as we saw with the exegesis on the Guru Granth Sahib in Faridkot—to the colonial state. The shift was crucial since the colonial state sought to sanitize disagreement through, for instance, the management of Sikh institutions and the creation of encyclopedic knowledge—the translations of Attar Singh for the state are but one example. Political and theological matters around the publication of Nihal Singh became the backdrop to a wider struggle that looked to fix where institutional authority, sovereignty, lay. In this struggle, disagreement became routed through individual authority tied to the colonial state's legal apparatus, which sought to eradicate difference through the uniformity of law. *Miri-piri* thus became separated from each other. This separation, then, led to fantasies of both a state (*miri*) that could control "religion" (*piri*), but also the fantasy of an eventual reconciliation and balance between *miri-piri*.

In response to intruding state jurisdiction, Singh Sabhites attempted to maintain some autonomy by circulating documents secretly. As we saw earlier, Diwan Buta Singh and Thakur Singh Sindhanwalia organized to publish and distribute books in Punjabi hidden from the watchful eye of the state, such as Major Evans Bell's book entitled *The Annexation of the Punjab and the Maharaja Dalip Singh* (1882), as well as the privately printed compilation *The Maharaja Duleep Singh and the Government: A Narrative* (1884).[98] Sindhanwalia undertook to translate these texts by employing *granthi* Partap Singh to translate Bell's work.[99] Once Partap Singh completed his translation, Diwan Buta Singh, the proprietor of the *Aftab-i-Panjab* press in Lahore, printed three hundred copies in order to circulate, C. L. Tupper noted, the "Punjabi translation of Major Bell's book gratis to certain persons in this province."[100] Using memory to reclaim the narrative of *Sikhi*, the Singh Sabhites sought to reclaim sovereignty from the British (see chapter 1).

Though trying to maintain secrecy while cohering to an orthodoxy in order to remain outside the purview of the British state, the Singh Sabha's contestations could not avoid its encroaching jurisdiction. Since the state had become the arbiter of tradition through its ability to grant favors, thus demonstrating its sovereignty, Sikhs then could make direct appeals and expose their fellow Sikhs to the colonial state and legitimate their own hold over the tradition. For example, Attar Singh of Bhadaur wrote to the lieutenant governor of Punjab in 1887, divulging the secret circulation of Evans Bell's work by sending "four pages of a matter lithographed in Gurmukhi character and Hindi language which is intended to show up the hardships suffered by Maharaja Dalip Singh at the hands of British Government."[101] Attar Singh notified the colonial authorities of the possible danger of having the work circulate, decrying that "the object of the writer seems to me to be to turn the hearts of the people of this province from the English. Now-a-days it is being discussed here and partly believed that the British Government have treated Dalip Singh with severity and injustice."[102]

Using the same demarcations between Good Sikh and Bad Sikh as the British employed, Attar Singh lauded "the good sense and loyalty of the members of the Singh Sabha of Lahore who sent me the enclosed pages." In contrast to these loyal members, Attar Singh argued that it was likely that intriguing lay with "Amritsar people" who were "greatly exercised by the prophecy contained in the *Sakhi* book that Dalip Singh will come to the Punjab and will be victorious over his enemy." Instead of engaging in contestations within the Sikh fold itself, that were necessarily fractious, Attar Singh appealed to state power to adjudicate these claims—to uphold *piri*—providing them with the context in which they could intervene. He held that the statements of the Amritsar Sikhs could be "satisfactorily answered" and, moreover, enclosed "a list of references to the *Sakhi* book for His Honor's kind attention to the contents of the small volume." Attar Singh continued on to say that armed with this knowledge, it was incumbent on the government to respond to Diwan Buta Singh's possible publications by "showing the fair character of their dealing with Dalip Singh has no good cause of complaint."[103]

Within these disputations in the Singh Sabha Lahore about the location of arbitration, Diwan Buta Singh resigned his position in the Singh Sabha although he was a founder. *Khalsa Akhbar* reported his resignation on July 1, 1887. Though denigrating Diwan Buta Singh in other contexts, *Khalsa Akhbar* did not publicize the particular reason for his resignation, looking to keep such matters internal. Instead, it reported that "for a long time, the Sabha has been separated [from Diwan Buta Singh], the reason which we will report some other time. This separation, however, has meant that Diwan Buta Singh has taken a position against the Sabha." The writer asked, "how does one resign, if one is not even a member?"[104] Attar Singh, however, made the internal separation visible to the colonial state, so the state could properly intervene. He promised that though "the Government will hear more of this all before long," the "real cause of the expulsion of Buta Singh from the Singh Sabha" was the Duleep Singh matter. Attar Singh acknowledged that this information was a secret, noting that "some of the members of this society did not consider it wise to give this out. It was reported that 'owing to the hostility of the Singh Sabha, Lahore, to the Raja of Faridkot and Bawa Khem Singh and other causes, Buta Singh resigned his place.' "[105]

Like Attar Singh, Bhai Gurmukh Singh also continuously appealed to the state, exposing disloyalty within the Sikh community. On November 25, 1886, he enclosed a copy of a purported letter posted to the village of Chaudhar from Duleep Singh addressed to the Khalsa. Sent from Mul Singhan district Amballa, the letter read:

One om.

Vaheguree jiki Fathe [*sic*]
Vaheguree jiki Fateh [*sic*] to the whole Khalsa community.

The Khalsa will reign—no[ne] will be independent of them.
All (who oppose) shall submit through disgrace.

Only those shall be saved who take protection.
Month Kartiq, 7th of the dark half moon Sumbat (Bikram jit) 1943.

Signature Maharaja Dalip Singh.
Tell to all Sikhs and remain firm in your faith that is all.[106]

Gurmukh Singh argued that the letter appeared forged and seemed to have been written by a partisan of Duleep Singh. But the letter's importance lay in its potential impact among the villagers. Though he was not able to determine the identity of the letter's author, Gurmukh Singh learned "from the tenor of its contents that the adherents are making such communications in [Duleep Singh's] name to spoil the ignorant villagers."

The use of Duleep Singh's name went against the logic of improvement central to colonial rule. Gurmukh Singh lamented the dangers of a so-called ignorant population exposed to backward ideas by troublesome Sikhs, arguing that he regretted "to see that, while we are making attempts to take advantages afforded us by the blessed rule of Her Majesty to turn out our brethren, learned, polished, and civilized, an opportunity has been taken by some devils to do such mischievous, unlawful, and sinful actions." This presumed unconstrained faction of the community, Gurmukh Singh argued, required the state's intervention, and he asked the state explicitly to intervene against these "bad Sikhs." He noted, "Although I feel sure that such communications are very insignificant and cannot be considered to make effect or produce some consequence, yet it seems necessary that efforts be made to stop such nonsense." Gurmukh Singh directed the state's attention toward Sikhs who deserved intervention, arguing, "Kukas are the persons who most probably write such letters in such a tone" alongside the other "few malcontents who hope for Dalip Singh, and do not shrink to produce secret excitement in his favour."[107]

Duleep Singh's pursuit to reclaim the Khalsa Raj was used by the Singh Sabha Lahore to denigrate and expose Khem Singh Bedi's secret attempts at revolt to the colonial state. Toward the end of January 1887, one memorandum records that "rumours were in circulation that Baba Khem Singh Bedi, CIE, was suspected of intriguing against the Government and had been placed under surveillance." Still, the state remained reluctant to enter religious affairs, especially with such high-powered leaders in the mix. The conclusion reached by this memorandum about Bedi is one stark example:

"these rumours are spread abroad by his enemies, most likely the party opposing him in the Khalsa Diwan."[108] Furthermore, Donald E. McCracken, assistant to the superintendent of the special branch for *thuggi* and dacoity, argued that he doubted whether it was possible for the leaders of the "Khalsa Diwan" or "Singh Sabhas" to be involved in the affairs of Duleep Singh, although he conceded that "it's not impossible." McCracken concluded that while the state could only "watch their proceedings," "it might become necessary to detain some or all of them if we are to put a stop altogether to Dalip Singh intrigues out here."[109]

Still, the state had to get involved. This intervention is evident in the libel case that emerged after Gurmukh Singh's excommunication by the Amritsar faction. Khem Singh's nephew, Bawa Udey Singh, funded by the Raja of Faridkot, sued Giani Ditt Singh, the editor of *Khalsa Akhbar* and associate of Gurmukh Singh, for writing a play entitled *Svapan Natak*, a satire that mocked the Amritsar group and their excommunication of Gurmukh Singh.[110] Udey Singh argued that the figure of Kabudh Singh, "an associate of slanderers, thieves, &c.," before whom "*Shaitan* even trembles," was intended to depict him, which constituted libel. The libel case was tried in the court of W. A. Harris, subordinate judge, Lahore, who ruled in the favor of Udey Singh, arguing that "no man on finding his views opposed was at liberty to vilify, in public print his opponents or to bring them into ridicule and contempt." However, Harris argued that "the work was a well written one and tended to reform," and since the authors were "carried away by religious feelings" he gave them only a slight punishment, fining Ditt Singh fifty-one rupees or a thirty-two-day imprisonment, which enabled an appeal.[111]

In the initial case the defendants sought to use Khem Singh Bedi's intrigues with Duleep Singh in order to convince the colonial state to rule in their favor. As the *Civil and Military Gazette* reported, "The counsel for the defence distinctly states that there is sufficient evidence on record in the case to show that there exists an organization for the purpose of influencing the Sikhs in favour of Dalip Singh, and that the Raja Faridkot and Bawa Khem Singh are the heads of this organization."[112] Evidence in a legal proceeding was more than enough to convince Colonel P. D. Henderson of Bedi's guilt. He noted of the trial that "I do not suppose that such evidence could be procured by the defendant without a good deal of watching and enquiry." The chief court, on appeal, revised the lower court's decision and

acquitted Ditt Singh. The revision of the decision by the chief court further made visible the ties between the Amritsar faction and Duleep Singh's
revolt, for, Henderson argued, "to a certain extent it places the Faridkot and
Bawa Khem Singh party in the wrong." Moreover, as Amrik Singh argued,
since "for good or for evil Khem Singh is the most influential man perhaps
in the Punjab," the colonial state had to remain vigilant, remaining "in a
position to know something like certainty how far they can depend upon
his loyalty."[113]

Here, then, we find the reach of the colonial state and extent to which it
was able to enclose *miri* to itself. Even though both sides sought to use Sikh
institutions such as the *takhts* and Khalsa Diwan to excommunicate their
respective opponent, it was the colonial state that became the final arbiter
of the disputes within the Singh Sabha through its legal and state appara-
tuses. The trouble here lies in the attribution of authority to the colonial
state, for Attar Singh, Gurmukh Singh, Bedi, and others, as we have seen,
continually turned to the colonial state to legitimate their positions on Sikh
orthodoxy. In placing their hopes with the colonial state, the Sikh tradition and the *sangat* came to occupy a space beneath the colonial state's
sovereignty—as an object to be adjudicated by the legal apparatus. In his
final ruling, Lieutenant Governor Lyall concluded that "no secret enquiries should be made regarding the Raja of Faridkot, Bawa Khem Singh, and
that party which may cause uneasiness, and make them feel that they have
fallen under suspicion," even if Gurmukh Singh provided evidence to the
contrary.[114]

DISSIMULATING CONTESTATIONS

While there were indeed controversies in which Sikhs appealed to the state
to settle scores, overvaluing Attar Singh's and Gurmukh Singh's rendition
also creates an unnecessarily stark division within the Singh Sabhas writ
large. This division removes the possibility of cohering a common position
between the two, which had remained a distinct historical possibility even
as the two sides jockeyed for position in relation to the colonial state. Conceptual trouble emerges from our desire to locate clearly demarcated subjects in
relation to colonial authority, a problem David Arnold has diagnosed.[115] The
problem is exacerbated when, as Verne Dusenbury cautions against, we
"read directly from the programmatic texts of the reformers to actual Sikh

behavior" since "one of the mistakes of an earlier orientalism was to assume that South Asian social life corresponded to how it was represented in the classical texts and elite discourses."[116] Yet what emerges underneath the essentialized elite discourse is not just the heterogeneity of South Asian religious life but attempts to achieve coherence about life through struggle, argumentation, and organization.

Therefore, although the locus of institutional power did shift toward the colonial state, the colonial state's reach remained incomplete, failing to grasp its desired totality. In this sense, when studying reform we cannot privilege the elite as the site that reveals the Other. Instead, we must recall, as Gayatri Spivak trenchantly demonstrates, "the colonized subaltern *subject* is irretrievably heterogeneous," an impossibility. We encounter then in our efforts to demarcate reform an unplumbable site, what Spivak calls "an undifferentiated preoriginary space" that supports both the histories of authenticity and coloniality that structure theories of reform (to return to the earlier typology).[117]

Both authenticity and inauthenticity, which includes our own pursuit to historicize claims to discover what lies behind them, remains grounded in, as Ethan Kleinberg explains, an ontological realism—the certainty that an event occurred even while routed through an epistemological uncertainty.[118] But perhaps positioning the subaltern community as a site of impossibility that remains irretrievably heterogeneous can turn our attention to the fact that constructing orthodoxy always encountered a limit, an impossibility, from which orthodoxy emerged and cohered (mushroomed), though never as a closed totality. This is, we must recall, the very logic of *miri* and *piri*; the two are never enclosed in their relationship but constantly bloom unstable forms as well as limits.

Centering such limits in both our own and past historical possibilities, the antagonistic relation between *miri* and *piri* in *Sikhi* undoes the totality of the Singh Sabhas and their eventual subsumption into an episteme. A concrete historical example might be helpful here. Institutional meetings of the Singh Sabhas, for instance, are not as stable as they appear at first glance, especially when situated in relation to the Sikh community—a community that sought to reinstitute Duleep Singh's rule by bypassing the colonial infrastructure. Such meetings sought to remain autonomous and defied the overtly nonpolitical stance ascribed to the Singh Sabhas and desired by some elite Sikhs. These meetings were, then, to follow Ranajit

Guha, "an autonomous domain," since they did not originate from elite politics nor did their existence depend on it.[119] Colonial intelligence gathered that "at a meeting of about 2,000 Sikhs held in the house of *Chaudris* Lehna Singh and Jiwan Singh of Amballa city, in the first week of June 1886, it was given out that the Maharaja would soon arrive at Lahore."[120] Again, on January 8, 1887, the aforementioned Bawa Nihal Singh, *thanadar* of Kalsia, argued that "there was no doubt that Dalip Singh would ascend his throne at Lahore this year."[121]

Singh Sabha meetings such as these ones undermined the neat divisions between the political and the religious laid out by the colonial government. Early in 1887, an official recorded that a Namdhari Sikh had started to offer prayers for Duleep Singh during their meetings. Sikh meetings in Amballa were similar. Seventy Sikhs assembled on December 11, 1886, to hear the Guru Granth Sahib and, after its reading, "it was given out that Dalip Singh would come to Lahore in 1887, and the people would place him on the throne." This happened again during another meeting on December 16, 1886, when Tara Singh, a *granthi* from Amritsar, noted that "Dalip Singh was at present with the Russians, who would assist him." Another *granthi*, Natha Singh, offered similar prayers. He prayed publicly at a Singh Sabha meeting in Ambala that "Guru Gobind Singh would bring Dalip Singh back to the Punjab and set him on the throne at Lahore."[122]

As noted previously, *granthis* played a significant role in cultivating political aspirations not only among the elite but also in the broader subaltern community because of their itinerant nature. Tara Singh, for example, was "an agent of the 'Singh Sabha,'" deployed "to visit all the places in the Amballa direction where the society had branches, and to direct them to collect funds [and] submit a complete list to the President of the Singh Sabha of Lahore of those who had been admitted to the Sikh religion during the previous month and enrolled in the 'Singh Sabha.'" Though traveling ostensibly to gather empirical data for the Sabha, Tara Singh was in a unique position to spread rumor and intrigue among the community in his *katha*. Undeniably, these prayers were not confined to Amballa, for Tara Singh traveled from Amballa to Chachrowli to Hurdwar and then returned to Amritsar via Bassi in Kalsia territory, Kharar, Kotehra, and Sohana. Furthermore, Sikhs that attended such meetings like the ones Tara Singh presided over were from diverse backgrounds. For example, though members of the Amritsar Singh Sabha such as Khem Singh Bedi notoriously upheld caste distinctions, affiliates of the Amritsar Singh Sabha also promoted caste equality. One colonial official recorded that, a member of the Amritsar Singh Sabha, Nihal Singh and his allies "advocated (unsuccessfully) the cause of the Mazhabi Sikhs [rendered 'untouchable' under the dictates of Hinduism, but a central part of the Sikh tradition and history], by trying to induce the general body of Sikhs to admit them on equal terms to all social gatherings."[123] Contestations about what sovereignty meant in such an autonomous domain, as a consequence, opened multiple questions about difference and inclusion that did not echo the programs and policies of the institutional authorities in Amritsar or Lahore.

Mirroring broader debates on religious reform in South Asia, the historiographical consensus in Sikh studies remains that one particular strand of reformist thought, advanced by the Lahore Singh Sabha, gained ascendency in the late nineteenth century over competing strands of reform. The Lahore Singh Sabha did so not through its organizational prowess or the direct intervention of the colonial state but because of the "immense seduction of their discourse" which captured the "restless and upwardly mobile Sikh elite" propelled forward by changes wrought by colonial governance, as Oberoi has written about in detail. This "seductive" discourse conjoined local sabhas with the Lahore branch. Oberoi argues, "in conformity with the metropolitan paradigm, local sabhas convened annual and weekly meetings, organized processions, marked the anniversaries of the Sikh gurus, employed missionaries to propagate the faith, printed and distributed Sikh histories and literature, and often backed the official line as it emerged from Lahore." Oberoi makes his argument by pointing to discourse, noting that "the proceedings of these local Sabhas are well documented in the *Khalsa Akhbar*."[124]

Against these static demarcations, however, the debates and circulation of information around Duleep Singh reveal a much more tenuous historical terrain, as the meaning of "reform" could not be stabilized so easily. Indeed, meaning cannot be reduced to mere coloniality or criminality.[125] The most salient evidence of the Sabha remaining marked by contestations emerges from an account of their meeting in Amballa on February 15, 1887. Namely, the district superintendent of police at Amballa reported that a meeting of the "Singh Sabha" was held in the house of Lehna Singh, Chaudri of Amballa City, on February 5, 1887, where about fifty Sikhs were present. There Sardar Harnam Singh, *rais* of Kharar, made a speech claiming "the time for Sikh rule was close at hand, and that Maharaja Duleep Singh would sit on the throne at Lahore." He exhorted the community "to be faithful to their religion and told them to join the subscription that was going to be started."[126]

Colonial officials made numerous enquiries as to the veracity of this report, looking to determine the reach of Duleep Singh's intrigues and the amount of financial support he had gathered. On May 10, 1887, the district superintendent wrote that "his informant had given a correct version of what happened and that a notice in the *Khalsa Akhbar* of the 12th February 1887, of the meeting was incorrect and misleading, and intended to hoodwink the authorities."[127] Oberoi, however, explicitly points to this edition of the *Khalsa Akhbar* to uphold his argument that Singh Sabhas fomented a singular episteme that followed colonial demarcations. When arguing that many Sabhas emulated the Lahore Sabha, he footnotes the Ambala Singh Sabha as a prime example and asks us to consult the *Khalsa Akhbar* of February 12, 1887, as proof.[128] The *Khalsa Akhbar*, however, does not reveal the hegemony of a particular vision of *Sikhi* in the reproduction of the meeting's proceedings. Instead, rather than imbibe colonial categories, members of the Singh Sabha used them—the state's own demarcations between the political and religious—to create another space to reinstitute a relationship between the religious and political. The report of the meeting sent to the papers was falsified through this very distinction.[129] Namely, in the report, Lehna Singh and Jiwan Singh of Amballa gave the meeting the appearance of "a purely religious meeting" to deceive the authorities who they knew were monitoring the newspapers. Instead of backing the official line as it emerged from Bhai Gurmukh Singh, the Singh Sabha at Amballa concluded to send money to Diwan Buta Singh in order "to form a fund to cover all expenses for printing and sending letters, &c., about the country, and paying their different agents."[130]

What do we make of this discrepancy between the *Khalsa Akhbar* and the spy's report? We might need to rethink efforts that provide historical depth to Sikhs through native vernacular writing and their rhetorical strategies—attempts that challenge the colonial state's technologies that read and fixed martial bodies, an ethnographic surface, one then mirrored by Sikhs themselves.[131] The problem is that such depth precludes the possibility of a fragmented body by mirroring the authoritative gaze inward. By foregrounding the community, which spread information about Duleep Singh and the Khalsa Raj without an originary center through itinerant *granthis* and Sikhs in the Singh Sabha, the supposed authority of a particular discursive regime is undone and irreducible to an authoritative center in Lahore or Amritsar. As Florencia Mallon has argued about peasant communities in Latin America, these communities were "never undifferentiated wholes but historically dynamic entities whose identities and lines of unity or division were constantly being negotiated."[132] Within these negotiations, the community could adjudicate and spread information without recourse to the visions of either the Lahore or Amritsar Singh Sabha while denying the state and scholars the ability to fix and integrate the community, as the false report in the *Khalsa Akhbar* demonstrates.

The Singh Sabha, therefore, also reveals the absence of a dichotomous divide between Amritsar and Lahore, for people continually contested and debated what now appear as stable and oppositional positions. For instance, Bawa Nihal Singh did not set himself in opposition to the Lahore Sabha. Instead, on May 2, 1887, he sent "a notice to the Singh Sabha that Dalip Singh was the real Raja of Punjab, and that this fact ought to be proclaimed in all the newspapers, and that it would be a good thing if Government allowed Dalip Singh to return to Punjab, and all Sikhs would be pleased, and that possible Government might grant permission, if the above notification appeared in the papers."[133] Though the Singh Sabha rejected Nihal Singh's assertions, on May 18, 1887, the previously mentioned Sarmukh Singh, Bawa Nihal Singh's brother, continued his travels and was "itinerating and taking down the names of persons belonging to the 'Singh Sabha'" while organizing for Duleep Singh. Though organizing on behalf of Duleep Singh, Nihal Singh did not reject the Singh Sabha but sought to change the very parameters of its own coherence by continuing to work within Singh Sabha networks.

Though labeled a reform organization, the Singh Sabha unravels our desire for a fixed placement of tradition in a historical setting, a point inaugurating purification. By foregrounding the Sikh tradition, which spread information through itinerant *granthis* intimately tied to the Singh Sabhas, the supposed authority of a particular discursive regime, indigenous or colonial, becomes undone. Moreover, the debates and organizing attempts within the Sikh tradition around Duleep Singh offer an important corrective to how we understand the encounter between religious traditions and colonial rule more broadly. The fragmentary nature of reform challenges narratives that locate reform as expressions of a colonized mindset or as continuities of an authentic precolonial practice, either heterogeneous or homogenous. They demonstrate how tradition remained a question, refusing easily assigned binary designations that then confront each other in a dialectical movement of history in which the Lahore Singh Sabha overcomes the Amritsar Singh Sabha, thereby inaugurating a new historical moment.

But these contestations within the Singh Sabhas in relation to Duleep Singh are not a historical footnote to the eventual triumph of the Lahore version, which, following the scholarly consensus, reformed the Sikh tradition from a previously heterogeneous and fluid indigenous identity into a homogenous and distinct identity, what Oberoi calls the Tat Khalsa episteme.[134] As we have seen, these boundaries within the Singh Sabha did not emerge immediately nor as a totality and, instead, offered multiple untold possibilities, including political ones.[135] Therefore, rather than neat breaks and divisions, these subaltern networks persevered, struggling with (and against) presumed narrators of orthodoxy, thereby cohering and dissolving it.

Sikh reform "does not freeze into an 'object of investigation, or worse yet, a model for imitation."[136] Against this freezing (the detailing of a colonial *Sikhi*) or imitation (the discovery of a past plural *Sikhi*), we must try to hesitate within the disruption of a historical moment. Our hesitation will not seek to explain the community's actions but rather to pry open our own need for certainty through the very object that fixes—the archive. Recognizing that explanation, as Ananda Abeysekara argues, "cannot make im-possibility available; explanation kills im-possibility,"[137] the tensions embedded within *miri-piri*, political and religious, narrator and audience, elite and subaltern as well as the community and Duleep Singh force us to consider how attachments are not static, since meaning itself is not inherent in a sovereign or a tradition. Put another way, an attachment to a sovereign is not mystification or nostalgia but continuous struggle and an attempt to persuade—a site of learning that is necessarily out of joint.

CONCLUSION

Failure

Nothing could be worse, for the work of mourning, than confusion or doubt: one has to know who is buried where.

—JACQUES DERRIDA

Contestations over Duleep Singh endure to this day, dead and buried though he has been since 1893. In 2017 *The Black Prince*, a movie directed by Kavi Raz and starring Satinder Sartaj, was released worldwide. Telling the story of the life of Duleep Singh, *The Black Prince* found enthusiastic support in both Punjab and its diaspora. For Raz the film was important because it was "a story that was begging to be told—the end of a glorious chapter for the Sikhs in their short but rich heritage of the Khalsa kingdom." Raz's claim is a fairly common refrain that highlights the lost past of a once great Sikh history that needs to be excavated and retold. For Raz, the film provided "an opportunity to set the record straight and give voice to the boy-king of a powerful yet lost kingdom." While acknowledging that many good books and periodicals recount Duleep Singh's narrative, Raz "knew Duleep's life had a purpose far greater than what was expressed in the written words I came across."[1] Raz's goal was not to present conventional history in film form, but rather to eschew the parameters of conventional history altogether. When a reporter asked Raz, "Is the film based entirely on fact?" Raz responded that his film "goes beyond—to the heart and soul of the man. It's not the persona advanced by the distortions of history."[2]

Raz could be accused of presenting alternative facts, altering the underlying truth of history—an accusation that proliferates as the imperative to tell history factually is increasingly urgent especially with the global rise of violent appropriations of history. On the other hand, one could say that Raz is quite perceptive, recognizing that some things elude the narrative form, an absence that continues to haunt us in our relation to Duleep Singh. Yet for Raz, much like the historian, the goal remains to fill in that absence, that loss, in order "to make the record straight" in Raz's words, in order to give voice to the boy-king of that lost kingdom, the Khalsa Raj.

For Jasjeet Singh, the executive producer of *The Black Prince*, working through loss was also a crucial motivation for his involvement in the film—a loss history could help recover. For example, he argued that the film represented "a missing chapter of Indian history. . . . It's not in the textbooks, even in Punjab."[3] The film's purported goal, then, though outside historicity, was to provide the absent chapter of a narrative that we all know, to fill the gap, especially for children, in order to secure a future for Sikhs within the contours of an Indian history.[4] Jasjeet Singh continued, "I felt this story needs to be told because our children do not know much about the last king of the Sikhs—Maharajah Duleep Singh. . . . We should realize his efforts to regain his kingdom that eventually resulted in a Gadar Movement and the contribution of Sikhs in Indian Independence."[5] The precise movement of history, at its promised end, culminates in the desire to suture its own tears.

Raz's and Singh's target, to get to the heart and soul of Duleep Singh by going beyond facts, is not to dwell in loss. Rather, it is to mourn the Khalsa Raj and Duleep Singh properly. In order to achieve this mourning, the film tries to provide an authentic portrayal of Duleep Singh's inner life—the richness of his inner symbolic life. The thrall of Franz Xaver Winterhalter's 1854 painted portrait mentioned in the introduction to this book massages this desire, continuously re-presenting Duleep Singh within the abysses he tumbles into. When remarking on the casting decision of novice actor Satinder Sartaaj in the role of Duleep Singh, Jasjeet Singh commented that "he was struck by how much the young singer's eyes resembled those in the paintings Victoria had commissioned of the maharajah, resplendent in jewels and embroidered clothes. 'How tall are you?' Singh asked. At 5 feet, 7 inches, Sartaaj was the same height as the king. Singh decided he was the perfect man to play him in a film, even though he had never acted before."[6] To capture the authentic life of Duleep Singh, arrested in portrait form while distorted by historicity, became the central aspect of the film and of Sartaaj's embodiment of Duleep Singh himself. One could call this aspect of the film a melancholic attachment as Raz and Singh attach themselves to the lost object (Duleep Singh and the Khalsa Raj), striving to stage it accurately as they descend back in time.

I do not wish to dismiss Raz and Jasjeet Singh's difficulties in portraying Duleep Singh as simple mystification—to uphold fetishism as fixation. Instead, my musings about their film and their stated goals are to highlight how desire for Duleep Singh settles more difficult questions—questions of community, publicity, conversion, rumors, and reform—into his bodily form. The desire then that Raz and Jasjeet Singh articulate for Duleep Singh might not be so oppositional to history as they present it to be. Recall that historians strive to give voice to absented diverse bodies through narrative form, reading the lineaments of the archive to produce a more encompassing narrative. Indeed, the goal for many historians, similar to Raz and Singh, remains to reach the heart and soul of Punjab—a heart and soul that challenge the distortions produced by communal historians, to name one instance.

Wonder dissipates as the past is mapped, lost, in time. Scholars posit a "past" lost from the "present"; the task of the historian is to surgically repair that relation through the act of writing, after which a proper burial ensues as loss is filled in. In this burial, stories are no longer stories but facts to be accumulated, hoarded, and partitioned; a law emerges. Historical exploration is conquest, Ranajit Guha teaches us, as curiosity for discovery and mapping takes root. The child is no longer listening to the stories but pointing "at the uncharted regions on a map to say, 'When I grow up, I will go there'" with an "aura of providentiality."[7] And we then occupy these inscriptions in time, searching, for example, for the lost part of the map.

But filling in such loss, healing the injuries wrought by time, presents a difficult task since a symbolic order is, Slavoj Žižek notes, "always and by definition in itself 'decentered,' structured around a central void/impossibility."[8] This is a point at which, as Guha contends, "the jungle begins," emerging as a foil to the civilization that repairs. One can acknowledge such points in one's writing—as narratives of conquest do—but there is also an alternative way of recounting conquest: the story of conquest told by the conquered. This alternative structured by the "cult of mourning" is one that "spiritualizes subjugation by calling upon its victims to immolate themselves in a different kind of fire from the one lit by the subjugators to celebrate and sacralize their triumphs." This fire, nationalism, perpetuates mourning, Guha tells us. History is once again "spiritualized as destiny."[9]

Questions of time are indeed troublesome. As Johannes Fabian ponders, is the very denial of temporal coevalness strictly a sign of domination?[10] Or can coevalness also be refused as an act of liberation? Think back to the dichotomy between jungle and civilization: can one claim the jungle? Or is the demarcation of the two already domination? The trouble continues: how does one even begin to refuse coevalness in a mode of production in which temporal crisis is internalized and normalized, what Žižek calls "the endless postponement of its point of impossibility?"[11] In other words, we must recall that "we suffer," Marx writes, "not only from the development of capitalist production, but also from the incompleteness of that development."[12] Conservation and heritage beckon as an industry unfolds.

The fragmented originary moment of capital itself, what Marx termed primitive accumulation, laid the groundwork for this perpetual incompleteness. Capital continually repeats its originary moment—more "accumulation by dispossession"—but assuaged by the riposte that redemption is already here.[13] Primitive accumulation, therefore, to follow Sami Khatib, is "the non-historicizable origin and starting point of each state of capitalist accumulation," which is "repeated in the dehistoricized space of the present."[14] And rather than signal a site of its own impossibility, a contradiction, incompleteness is arrogated through the promise of historical becoming that is already here. Incompleteness itself offers inclusion in and recognition of a past—the amassing of cultural difference flowing into a historical present. In this sense time becomes marked by both postponement and discovery, the grasping toward an illusory wholeness or originary plenitude—salvation with difference.[15]

A *different* history then signals the possibility of redemption as we accumulate alternative content while multiplying time itself.[16] Historians in this sense are practitioners of orthopedics.[17] But perhaps this is too unkind. The goal of thinking with the past, thinking with the dead, after all, is not to forget—what is in question is recovery and the boundaries erected to facilitate it. Therefore, even if it does function at times as a strategic historicism, the plea to write history of course has its own history. What we forget in our zeal for recovery is that, as Gil Anidjar argues, "the recurring appeal to history as some form of scholarly panacea is itself entangled in a history that conceives of itself as soteriological, as the critical blessing that heals the curse of ahistorical essence."[18] Or, as Prathama Banerjee holds, the very "act of historicization, an administrative and inquisitorial act," placed the Santhal *hul* into chronology, creating a measurable event that could be deemed historical.[19] In this delirium, historians wonder how the historicization of history itself can be properly historicized. Intellectual history beckons as the salve. Still, to undo history, the world has to become precisely what the colonial project demanded: historical. Given this historical disposition, a past of community is settled.

The promise of a rehabilitated and mastered history, offered to us by an archive, whether in image, digital, or narrative form, remains ever alluring in its promised closure. Eschewing the possibility of disturbing a symbolic field, the move toward "true" knowledge precludes any risk of an encounter with alterity by producing future promises of completion within the rules of the archive's own temporal and spatial taxonomy.[20] Perhaps then the new positivist turn that is engulfing the discipline of history is not a turn at all, but an ending: a posthistorical writing of history.[21] This posthistorical collecting annihilates the logic of struggle and, in its place, introduces a nightmarish detailing.[22] This "descriptive empiricism" presents only foregone conclusions such as that society is complex, which, as Gary Wilder perceptively writes, "masquerades as theoretical insight." In the hegemony of descriptive empiricism, the purpose of theory is reduced to a mere technicality: "a means for refining research methods in order to reconstruct the past more accurately."[23]

One can imagine this complex posthistory: a truly postmodern form detailing the minutiae of everyday Sikh life from the past, simultaneously rendered lifeless. It would be a lifelessness that required that we eventually remove the all too coherent adjectival modifier of "Sikh" to a much more diffuse and complex Punjabi descriptor. But here is precisely where we see a glimpse of possibility in the very detailing itself. Why continue detailing what we already know? Put another way, is it possible to consider that "just as the ultimate failure of communication is what compels us to talk all the time (if we could say what we want to say directly, we would very soon stop talking and shut up for ever)," that what compels us to continually write Sikh history is the impossibility and failure of truly and fully narrating *Sikhi*?[24] Is it possible that the very need to continually produce narrative, alternative or otherwise, is to quell tradition, to quell something that exists in tradition that refuses our enclosing efforts?

What if we were to take instead incompletion seriously by refusing the gesture of temporal inclusivity—historical or otherwise? We could consider how, as Saidiya Hartman poignantly argues, "the very conditions that have produced the broken and disciplined body and the body as object, instrument, and commodity ensure that the work of restoration or recompense is inevitably incomplete."[25] Redress, in other words, signals the inadequacy of the remedy itself. There is no possibility of inclusion, we must remind ourselves. History is lacking. Time, then, does not offer an ointment, a last word, or the accumulation of even more words, but only further fissures. Put another way, the past itself refuses the authority of history, heritage, or even coherence, remaining decidedly unreasonable or, to be strategically essentialist, even ahistorical, not there for our easy grasp.[26] Here too we can return to Hartman, who notes that her approach to memory when writing about *juba* is "not to recover the past but to underscore the loss inscribed in the social body and embedded in forms of practice."[27] Recognition, after all, can further tether and bind one to oppression.

This is not to conflate absence with the historical losses caused by slavery, which Dominick LaCapra cautions against.[28] Rather, it is to consider how historical methodology runs into trouble when confronted by historical as well as constitutive absences. It is to ask: in a constitutive loss, anguish not mollified by time, are there other relations to the past that refuse the demands of *Homo historicus* so central to both colonialism and decolonization?[29] Are there relations to the past that are not necrophiliac, forcing the dead to speak through archival intimacy—the historian's hand reaching around time in the thrill of discovery or lamenting their failed tactics? To be more explicit: What does it mean to be "coeval with the dead" who are neither buried nor present? This is an especially important question since unilinear time marked by events, recuperated or mourned, as Talal Asad writes, is "only one kind of time people imagine, respond to, and use."[30] Is it possible, then, to think of a time that is not historical, that refuses its recuperative and inclusive gestures? Is it possible to rethink another relation to death itself, a different rapport with the Other?[31]

Writing a narrative of a historical figure such as Duleep Singh is itself a bid to come to terms with the failure of narrative and history. "A personal life-narrative is," as Žižek continues, "a *bricolage* of ultimately failed attempts to come to terms with some trauma."[32] In this sense, Duleep Singh, much like Punjab itself, offers only "a failed attempt to displace/obfuscate its constitutive antagonism," Duleep Singh's own impossibility. The failed attempt to drive at the impossibility of Duleep Singh subsists as an opening, refusing to come to terms with closure, as we saw in the organization and networks emergent around Duleep Singh. The question then becomes: How do we drive at the impossible Duleep Singh—a Duleep Singh we can never arrive at? We could try to arrive; we could point to the substantial fullness of a given constellation, to restage a fullness of Duleep Singh in a theater, for example, to turn back to Raz and Singh.

But there is another point of intervention, one that does not settle concepts within an elaborate arrival such as an arrival at Duleep Singh that reinforces him. This intervention would be one that disturbs him by working in the torsion he produces, by working within his inherent impossibility. This book has tried to drive at this opening without giving it place, without mapping it neatly. We do not know who is buried where. Doubt ensues.[33] We cannot capture this doubt by trying to settle our relationships with ghosts, trying to pay our debts. Instead, centering drive in relation to loss, this book has continuously chipped away at Duleep Singh without end, consorting with his fellow travelers. It has offered no clear picture of an "authentic" Duleep Singh but expressed the limits of his historical presence as revealed by the focus on the networks around him and his champions. The book has addressed Duleep Singh with a restlessness, approaching him ceaselessly from different points of departure, fragmenting him without finding anything behind his portrait.

This reading practice need not be oppositional to the Sikh tradition, which is itself not dead but living. Asad has continually asked us to remember that this living nature of a tradition, calling our attention to the inherent impossibility of closure into an essence within the historicity of a tradition. As Asad notes, we cannot write of tradition "as though it was the passing on of an unchanging substance in homogeneous time," since such a rendering "oversimplifies the problem of time's definition of practice, experience, and event." Instead, Asad argues, "in tradition the 'present' is always at the center." In this temporality, "settled cultural assumptions cease to be viable" as peoples "inhabit different kinds of time simultaneously," straddling the gap between experience and expectation.[34] Asad asks us to dwell in this unsettled time and uncompleted history not to suspend historical analysis but to rethink the very parameters of temporality by foregrounding an element of contingency.[35] We must remember what we have *learned* in the Sikh tradition to rethink the trappings of the ego that reinscribe the very contours we wish to erase—the separations that we consider divine gifts.

This ethic is also an orientation that this book has developed through a borrowing from subaltern studies, an intellectual tradition this book has been indebted to even though the tradition itself has been proclaimed lost and "dead."[36] Again the question of loss arises. What do we make of the continually pronounced loss of the subaltern in subaltern studies? The death of the subaltern, which, in turn, led to the death of subaltern studies—an absence that must be recovered and redeemed.[37] It was a recovery required both while alive—a long life, Partha Chatterjee reminds us—and also now in its afterlives.[38] The causes of the death of the subaltern, much like its birth, are overdetermined.[39] Christopher Bayly noted this disappearance early on as a disappearance of subtlety, since naming itself undid the complexity of its human life.[40] For Rosalind O' Hanlon, too, the death of the subaltern arises from the desire to fix the subaltern in a form, which rests upon an essentialism insisting that there is, she writes, "something inherently inextinguishable in the very form of the subaltern's own subjectivity," which she likens to a Hegelian spirit. Within this ideal movement for O'Hanlon, the diagnosis was clear: the subaltern led to "a slow theoretical paralysis" in its attempt to provide an ontology to that which could only be contingent and therefore ontic.[41] In other words, as Jim Masselos writes, the subaltern came to have value, but not subalterns.[42]

Yet, as Gayatri Spivak famously reminds us, the void is the shuttling subaltern rather than a fixed one.[43] In its shuttling, the subaltern refuses to authorize a singular formation though simultaneously, perhaps strategically, incorporated within such histories.[44] Remember that for Spivak the subaltern is not dead, but to repeat, a "violent shuttling," a disappearance in an agonized movement. Is this lack of catharsis a necroidealism, a melancholic attachment? Perhaps I have been too generous in my analysis of Duleep Singh in this book, a generous reading of a failure, but the subaltern appeared as a vertiginous category that eluded both life and death, in which, as Chakrabarty notes, the archaic and modern coincided.[45] Posing questions instead about the meaning of loss and death, we engaged in, to appropriate Rajeswari Sunder Rajan, "a postmortem communication that traverses the boundary between the living and dead."[46] This communication is the work of the drive rather than a desire for a utopian object.[47] In this communication, perhaps, we could reach a point where the "I" began to vanish.[48]

Prophetic Maharaja has foregrounded contingency within a symbolic order—one that is fraught, where time itself cannot be settled—by turning to psychoanalysis, to Talal Asad, and to subaltern studies. In the space of failure there is the possibility for an ethics where the goal is not to create intelligibility by providing an answer to the question "Who am I?" or "Who is Duleep Singh?" through a robust and vigorous methodology. Rather, the book has encircled something that is missed but impossible to forget: that which is at the heart of Duleep Singh but also excluded from him. This strangeness, this abyss, represents the possibility of breaking with shared premises and engaging instead with more difficult questions about justice. It is precisely this vertiginous space that we drove at, constituted against the catharsis demanded by the historical, in which there emerges a possibility for an ethical encounter, a task that upends the incorporative logic of historicity today.[49] By upending, this book has tried to offer another possibility: to learn without closure. In our learning there might be no need to conclude, which means that there is no need to convince, to produce a final conviction about our loss in the carceral operation of history that arrests a community, a tradition, and the very question of sovereignty.[50]

NOTES

INTRODUCTION

1. Numerous scholars have questioned this tendency. Most forcefully, see Stephen Best, "On Failing to Make the Past Present," *Modern Language Quarterly* 73, no. 3 (2012): 453–74; Ethan Kleinberg, Joan Wallach Scott, Gary Wilder, "Theses on Theory and History," *History of the Present* 10, no. 1 (2020): 157–65; and Anjali Arondekar *Abundance: Sexuality's History* (Durham, NC: Duke University Press, 2023).

2. Scholars have challenged such an approach. For one insightful approach, see Manan Ahmed Asif, *The Loss of Hindustan: The Invention of India* (Cambridge, MA: Harvard University Press, 2020). Asif writes, "the history I have sketched here is a prompt to imagine ways forward that do not yield to the majoritarian present, that do not inherit the past as a certainty, and do not romanticize that which is lost" (225).

3. For this project, see the special issue of *Critical Times* that I coedited with Basit Kareem Iqbal. These questions became important to me while reading the work of Gil Anidjar on destruction, as well as conversations with Yannik Thiem and Basit Iqbal. I am grateful for their writing and thinking.

4. Briefly, the Khalsa is essential in understanding the Sikh tradition. The Khalsa became significant when Guru Gobind Singh, the tenth Guru, initiated Sikhs in 1699 who then became designated as Khalsa, a sociopolitical order. As Ganda Singh writes, to use *Khalsa* as a term to address the community "implies the collective, spiritually-directed will [*hukam*] of the community guided by the Guru Granth Sahib" (474). *Khalsa* becomes tied to *Raj* explicitly with Guru Gobind Singh, as we see in Bhai Nand Lal's *Tanakhah-nama* (1695), which states, "the Khalsa shall rule" (*Raj Karega Khalsa*). Thus, although Khalsa Raj signals the rule

of the Khalsa, the constant invocation of *Raj Karega Khalsa* in prayers (*ardas*) within the Sikh tradition continually dislocated the raj itself, as it remained and remains a sovereignty to come. This drive within the Khalsa led to numerous attempts at sovereignty from its inception to the present. See Ganda Singh, "Khalsa," in *Encyclopedia of Sikhism*, ed. Harbans Singh (Patiala: Punjabi University, 2011), 473–74, and Pashaura Singh, "Râj Karegâ Khâlsâ," in *A Dictionary of Sikh Studies* (Oxford: Oxford University Press, 2019), https://www.oxfordreference .com/view/10.1093/acref/9780191831874.001.0001/acref-9780191831874-e-291. I am grateful to Nirvikar Singh for a reminder about the broader commitments of the Khalsa and Khalsa Raj.

5. For cosmopolitan networks, see Seema Alavi, *Muslim Cosmopolitanism in the Age of Empire* (Cambridge, MA: Harvard University Press, 2015). For messianic politics in millenarianism, see Milinda Banerjee, *The Mortal God: Imagining the Sovereign in Colonial India* (Cambridge: Cambridge University Press, 2018), 350.

6. Gil Anidjar, *Blood: A Critique of Christianity* (New York: Columbia University Press, 2016), x.

7. For more on Ranjit Singh, see J. S. Grewal, *The Reign of Maharaja Ranjit Singh: Structure of Power, Economy and Society* (Patiala: Punjabi University, 1981), and Sunit Singh, "The Sikh Kingdom," in *The Oxford Handbook of Sikh Studies*, ed. Pashaura Singh and Louis Fenech (Oxford: Oxford University Press, 2014), 59–69. See also Priya Atwal, *Royals and Rebels: The Rise and Fall of the Sikh Empire* (Oxford: Oxford University Press, 2020).

8. Michael Alexander and Sushila Anand, *Queen Victoria's Maharajah: Duleep Singh 1838–93* (London: Phoenix Press, 1980), 10.

9. An earlier Treaty of Lahore in 1846 and Treaty of Bhyrowal in 1846 had slowly stripped away the power of the state, but the final annexation occurred in 1849.

10. "Lieutenant-Colonel Hon'ble W. E. West to Sir Louis Mallett, CB, Undersecretary of State for India Dated Penrhyn Estate Office, Bangor, north Wales, 12 August 1878," in Measures for Relieving Him his Pecuniary Embarrassments, Foreign Department Political A, August 1879, Nos. 18–20, National Archives of India, New Delhi. Dalhousie had argued that "it cannot be pretended that the loss of his kingdom was felt by him as a misfortune, and his rank among Princes was not so exalted as in itself to call for a stipend of imperial dimensions." See "Affairs of the Maharajah Duleep Singh," India Office Records-L/P&S/18/D18–3, British Library, London.

11. National Archives of India, Foreign Department Political A, August 1879, Nos. 18–20.

12. Duleep Singh, *The Tribune*, June 3, 1886.

13. "Nov. 16, 1886," in Letters from the Earl of Dufferin, Vol. 1, Letters 1–21, India Office Records Mss Eur E243/22: Aug 6th to Dec 21st, 1887, British Library, London.

14. David Scott, "Colonial Governmentality," *Social Text* 43 (1995): 214.

15. Lord Canning to Sir Charles Wood, 22 May 1861, in Royal Archives VIC/ MAIN/N/25. I am grateful to Priya Atwal for sharing these files me.

16. His Highness Maharaja Dhulip Singh, to Earl of Kimberly, Secretary of State for India, Carlton Club, the 8th June 1885, Intention of Maharaja Dhulip Singh to Return to India, Foreign Department Secret I, July 1885, Nos. 23–25, National Archives of India, New Delhi.

17. These Papers Below Relate to the Case of Duleep Singh, Intention of Maharaja Dhulip Singh to visit India, his temporary resistance at Aden, and subsequent return to Europe, Foreign Department Secret I, June 1886, Nos. 12–196, National Archives of India, New Delhi.

18. *The Pioneer*, August 17, 1883. Authors are not listed.

19. Charles Aitchison to C. Grant, 7 August 1883, Objections to Maharaja Dhulip Singh's Proposal to Visit India, Foreign Secret I, December 1883, Nos. 8–17, National Archives of India, New Delhi.

20. D. M. Stewart, C. P. Ilbert, et al. to Earl of Kimberley, Secretary of State for India, Objections to Maharaja Dhulip Singh's Proposal to Visit India, Foreign Secret I, December 1883, Nos. 8–17, National Archives of India, New Delhi.

21. Charles Aitchison to C. Grant, 7 August 1883, Objections to Maharaja Dhulip Singh's Proposal to Visit India, Foreign Secret I, December 1883, Nos. 8–17, National Archives of India, New Delhi.

22. Alavi, *Muslim Cosmopolitanism in the Age of Empire*, 370. Alavi, however, reduces Duleep Singh to these networks. That is, tracing the cosmopolitanism of various émigrés embodied in the nineteenth century, Alavi reveals the wide ranging "transimperial networks" that challenged "the imposed territorially rooted subject identities and borders in Asia" by the British Empire (30). In her conclusion, Alavi turns to Duleep Singh in order to reveal how non-Muslims and Muslims alike used these transimperial Muslim networks to further their causes by relying on this "web of contacts that made borders porous" (401). These networks, Alavi argues, allowed Duleep Singh to develop extensive plans with diverse trans-Asian actors. Accordingly, Alavi concludes, these Muslim cosmopolitans, spread out between empires, were "a critical resource base for all kinds of people who cared to use it" (392). Yet in Alavi's analysis Duleep Singh is reduced to these networks themselves. That is to say, the contestations of what sovereignty would be are lost.

23. Demi-official from Sir John Ware Edgar, KCIE, CSI, Chief Secretary, Bengal Government, Dated the 30 November 1889, Arrest of Abdul Rasul, An Emissary of Maharaja Dalip Singh and His Detention Under Regulation III of 1818, K.W. Secret I, March 1890, Nos. 19–41, National Archives of India, New Delhi.

24. Maharaja Dalip Singh to The Secretary of State for India, 27th July 1890, Affairs of Maharaja Dalip Singh and his Family, K-W Internal A, September 1891, Nos. 55–89, National Archives of India, New Delhi.

25. The biographical literature on Duleep Singh is vast, stretching from the nineteenth century to the present. See especially Lena Login, *Sir Login and Duleep Singh* (London: W. H. Allen & Co., 1890); *Maharaja Duleep Singh Correspondence*, ed. Ganda Singh (Patiala: Punjabi University Patiala, 1977); Michael Alexander and Sushila Anand, *Queen Victoria's Maharajah: Duleep Singh 1838–93* (London: Phoenix Press, 1980); Rishi Ranjan Chakrabarty, *Duleep Singh: The Maharajah of Punjab and the Raj* (Oldbury, UK: D. S. Samara, 1988); *Maharaja Duleep Singh: The Last Sovereign Ruler of the Punjab*, ed. Prithipal Singh Kapur (Amritsar: Shiromani Gurdwara Parbandhak Committee, 1995); Christy Campbell, *The Maharajah's Box: An Imperial Story of Conspiracy, Love, and a Guru's Prophecy* (London: HarperCollins, 2000); and Peter Bance, *Sovereign, Squire and Rebel: Maharajah Duleep Singh and the Heirs of a Lost Kingdom* (London: Coronet House, 2009).

26. In asking the question of fantasy, I am indebted to Joan Wallach Scott's exploration in *The Fantasy of Feminist History* (Durham, NC: Duke University Press, 2011). As Scott writes, "Fantasy can help account for the ways subjects are formed, internalizing and resisting social norms, taking on the terms of identity that endow them with agency. (For that reason it has informed both pessimistic and optimistic theories about human subjectivity.) And it can be used to study the ways in which history—a fantasized narrative that imposes sequential order on otherwise chaotic and contingent occurrences—contributes to the articulation of political identity" (51).

27. Though scholars have noted the importance of the Mughal imperial imagination in shaping, providing continuities for, and challenging colonial rule after the Empire's fall, the Khalsa Raj is conceptualized as lost the moment it ends. The debate around the influence and continuation of Mughal imperial custom is vast and contentious. See Bernard Cohn, "Representing Authority in Victorian India," in *An Anthropologist Among the Historians and Other Essays* (New Delhi: Oxford University Press, 1987), 632–82; Sudipta Sen, *Distant Sovereignty: National Imperialism and the Origins of British India* (New York: Routledge, 2002); Robert Travers, *Ideology and Empire in Eighteenth Century India: The British in Bengal* (Cambridge: Cambridge University Press 2007); and Jon Wilson, *The Domination of Strangers: Modern Governance in Eastern India, 1780–1835* (Basingstoke, UK: Palgrave Macmillan, 2008).

28. Ranajit Guha, "A Conquest Foretold," *Social Text* 54 (1998): 85–99.

29. Gil Anidjar has paid singular attention to precisely this presupposition. Anidjar argues that with the liquidation of Christian theological concepts, community measured through the general kinship of blood becomes central to sovereignty. This liquidation is tied to the Eucharist, to follow Ernst Kantorowicz, particularly when the Eucharist, the blood and flesh of Christ, is no longer tied to the individual but becomes about society in general. It is this rule that emerged from the exception—grace—that holds promise for a harmonious Christian and secured sovereignty. See Anidjar, *Blood*, 66. Ernst H. Kantorowicz, *The King's Two Bodies: A Study in Medieval Political Theology* (Princeton, NJ: Princeton University Press, 2016), 196. Or, as Anidjar writes, "In this development, the theological metamorphosis of blood, the mystical body becomes the body politic, the visible community of Christians" (122).

30. Roberto Esposito, *Communitas: The Origin and Destiny of Community*, trans. Timothy Campbell (Stanford, CA: Stanford University Press, 2010), 2.

31. Caroline Bynum Walker, "Did the Twelfth Century Discover the Individual?," *Journal of Ecclesiastical History* 31, no. 1 (1980): 12, 16.

32. Esposito also sees shifts within *corpus mysticum* as crucial in creating this immunitary paradigm. See Roberto Esposito, *Immunitas: The Protection and Negation of Life*, trans. Zakiya Hanafi (Malden, MA: Polity, 2011), 12. See also Roberto Esposito, *Terms of the Political: Community, Immunity, Biopolitics*, trans. Rhiannon Noel Welch (New York: Fordham University Press, 2013). Esposito still holds on to Christ's sacrifice as a gift. But, as we learn from Anidjar, these ruptures are not so neat. See Anidjar, *Blood*.

33. Esposito, *Terms of the Political*, 15.

34. Esposito, *Communitas*, 6.

35. Anidjar, *Blood*, 66.

36. Anidjar, *Blood*, 96.

37. Partha Chatterjee, *The Nation and Its Fragments: Colonial and Postcolonial Histories* (Princeton, NJ: Princeton University Press, 1993), 236. Anidjar too writes, "the practices of kinship far exceed the matter of blood; but also because all this was not always understood as, much less called, 'consanguinity' or 'Blood.' We nonetheless persist in naming, referring to, kinship and family relations as 'blood'" (96). Anidjar also provides a different reading of community through a brilliant reading of *Moby Dick*, Queequeg, and Ismael in which, though "there is still blood," it "no longer governs—and certainly not rhetorically—the imagined and embodied community" (230). See *Blood*.

38. Jacques Derrida, *Dissemination*, trans. Barbara Johnson (Chicago: University of Chicago Press, 1981), 5.

39. Kapur Singh, "The Church and the State," in *Pārāśarapraśna: The Baisakhi of Gurgobind Singh*, ed. Piar Singh and Madanjit Kaur (Amritsar: Guru Nanak Dev University, 1989), 192–201. For the difficulty of parsing the religious from the political, see Nicholas Dirks, *The Hollow Crown: Ethnohistory of an Indian Kingdom* (Cambridge: Cambridge University Press, 1987), and C. S. Adcock, *The Limits of Tolerance: Indian Secularism and the Politics of Religious Freedom* (Oxford: Oxford University Press, 2014). In relation to Ranjit Singh's empire, the relation between *miri* and *piri* oscillated and remained an irresolvable struggle as institutional checks prevented any singular resolution.

40. Mark C. Taylor, *About Religion: Economies of Faith in Virtual Culture* (Chicago: University of Chicago Press, 1999), 152. Or, as Devin Singh writes, "Monetary overtones emerge noticeable in Christian discourse about the Son as a type of currency in the divine exchange that takes place due to the incarnation, crucifixion, and resurrection of Christ." "Christ as the coin of God," therefore, Singh continues, "comes to the fore as the crucial means of payment in a redemptive exchange" (131). See Devin Singh, *Divine Currency: The Theological Power of Money in the West* (Stanford, CA: Stanford University Press, 2018).

41. Jacques Derrida, *Rogues: Two Essays on Reason*, trans. Pascale-Anne Brault and Michael Naas (Stanford, CA: Stanford University Press, 2005), 101. The very terms of the Khalsa Raj reveal such tensions.

42. Norbert Peabody, *Hindu Kingship and Polity in Precolonial India* (New Delhi: Cambridge University Press, 2006), 8. See also Anne Murphy, *The Materiality of the Past: History and Representation in Sikh Tradition* (Oxford: Oxford University Press, 2012), 12 and 50.

43. Purnima Dhavan, *When Sparrows Became Hawks: The Making of the Sikh Warrior Tradition, 1699–1799* (Oxford: Oxford University Press, 2011), 9, 176. My goal, however, is not to demonstrate how the *Khalsa* itself is fragmented but rather to demonstrate how it troubles historical context itself. That is, rather than give context to the Khalsa to resolve tensions, the Khalsa requires we reconsider context itself, rerouting our very understanding of historicity.

44. For example, see Banerjee, *The Mortal God*, and Caleb Simmons, *Devotional Sovereignty: Kingship and Religion in India* (New York: Oxford University Press, 2020).

45. Kathleen Davis, *Periodization & Sovereignty: How Ideas of Feudalism and Secularization Govern the Politics of Time* (Philadelphia: University of Pennsylvania Press, 2008).

46. Sudipta Sen, "Unfinished Conquest: Residual Sovereignty and the Legal Foundations of the British Empire in India," *Law, Culture and the Humanities* 9, no. 2 (2013): 233.

47. Banerjee, *The Mortal God*, 7.

48. Atwal, *Royal and Rebels*, 34.

49. For example, see Atwal, *Royal and Rebels*, 35–36, 167–69. Atwal brilliantly demonstrates how Ranjit Singh and his family become dominant political players, working through these tensions—tensions that became exacerbated with Ranjit Singh's death. For an earlier time period and these negotiations, see Dhavan, *When Sparrows Became Hawks*, 99–148.

50. Yarimar Bonilla, *Non-Sovereign Futures: French Caribbean Politics in the Wake of Disenchantment* (Chicago: University of Chicago Press, 2015), xiii. On "and," see Jacques Derrida, "Force of Law: The "Mystical Foundation of Authority," in *Acts of Religion*, ed. Gil Anidjar (New York: Routledge, 2002), 231.

51. Bonilla, *Non-Sovereign Futures*, xiii, 10–12. I am grateful to Gil Anidjar for turning my attention here.

52. Again I am grateful to Gil Anidjar for this point, as well as to Basit Iqbal for his refining it.

53. Raymond Gama cited in Bonilla, *Non-Sovereign Futures*, 5. I borrow synchronized clocks from Rebecca Comay, *Mourning Sickness: Hegel and the French Revolution* (Stanford, CA: Stanford University Press, 2011), 4.

54. I thank Basit Iqbal for this suggestion.

55. I want to be clear: this book does not aim to provide resolution in the face of loss. As Rebecca Comay argues, loss eludes being filled, since longing to escape loss can actually cement it, further tethering a person to the very knot they sought to unravel. Comay writes: "The preoccupation with an originary loss ('as such') logically preceding the loss of any determinate object could function equally as a pre-emptive denial of loss which would mask the real inaccessibility of its object by determining it in advance as lost—thus negatively appropriable in its very absence," 89. See Rebecca Comay, "The Sickness of Tradition: Between Melancholia and Fetishism," in *Walter Benjamin and History*, ed. Andrew Benjamin (New York: Continuum, 2005). For attempts to reconstruct Sikh "historical consciousness," see Murphy, *The Materiality of the Past*, 71.

56. Stefania Pandolfo, *Knot of the Soul: Madness, Psychoanalysis, Islam* (Chicago: University of Chicago Press, 2018), 9.

57. The problems with tragedy are manifold and the literature is vast. For one precise examination of the chronopolitical dimensions of tragedy, see Basit Kareem Iqbal, "Asad and Benjamin: Chronopolitics of Tragedy in the Anthropology of Secularism," *Anthropological Theory* 20, no. 1 (2020): 77–96.

58. Campbell, *The Maharajah's Box*, xxvii.

59. Lauren Berlant, *Cruel Optimism* (Durham, NC: Duke University Press, 2011), 123.

60. Berlant, *Cruel Optimism*, 123, 125. As Bonilla writes, disappointment "suggest[s] the success of a new vision, the existence of a new model against which expectations

of what is possible have become recalibrated" (150–51). See Bonilla, *Non-Sovereign Futures*.

61. Slavoj Žižek, *The Sublime Object of Ideology* (London: Verso, 1989), 2. In this sense, as Žižek notes, "knowledge is marked by a lethal dimension: the subject must pay for the approach to it with his own being. In other words, to abolish the misrecognition means at the same time to abolish, to dissolve, the 'substance' which was supposed to hide itself behind the form-illusion of misrecognition," or that which provided consistency (68).

62. Berlant, *Cruel Optimism*, 124.

63. I am grateful to Gil Anidjar for this query and suggestion.

64. Omnia El Shakry made this point in an email communication.

65. I rely largely on English language sources, although I also draw upon Punjabi language primary and secondary source material.

66. Stuart Hall, "Toad in the Garden: Thatcherism Among the Theorists," in *Marxism and the Interpretation of Culture*, ed. Lawrence Grossberg and Cary Nelson (Urbana: University of Illinois Press, 1988), 41.

67. Harleen Kaur and p.s. kehal, "Epistemic Wounded Attachments: Recovering Definitional Subjectivity Through Colonial Libraries," *History and Theory* 62 (2023): 203–24.

68. To be clear: I do not provide indigenous theories of how to deal with loss in order to abscond with an authentic history or authentic sovereign. Instead, my argument is formed in a different problem-space—a space where the outlines of how we articulate loss are already inscribed and, simultaneously, fragmented since they are also marked by the very impossibility of their continual reinscription. Against the thrill of discovery and history, it is this impossibility of circumscribing loss that drives this book and its theoretical register in both Western theory and the Sikh tradition.

69. Puran Singh, *Spirit of the Sikh, Part Two, Volume One* (Patiala: Punjabi University, Patiala, 2002), 227. Puran Singh is reflecting on the Guru Granth Sahib.

70. Brian Keith Axel, *The Nation's Tortured Body: Violence, Representation, and the Formation of a Sikh "Diaspora"* (Durham, NC: Duke University Press, 2001), and Tony Ballantyne, *Between Colonialism and Diaspora: Sikh Cultural Formations in an Imperial World* (Durham, NC: Duke University Press, 2006).

71. It is, as Jacques Lacan asked us to consider, "a palliative for the chaos that ensues owing to the inability of all signifying elements to deal with the hole in existence that has been created by someone's death" (336). See Jacques Lacan, *The Seminar of Jacques Lacan: Book VI Desire and Its Interpretation*, ed. Jacques-Alain Miller, trans. Bruce Fink (Medford, MA: Polity, 2019). There is a crucial difference between Freud and Lacan, as I will show. For Freud, there is a "real" object that is lost; for Lacan the loss is constitutive as lack.

72. Sigmund Freud, "Mourning and Melancholia," in *The Standard Edition of the Complete Psychological Works of Sigmund Freud*, vol. 14, ed. and trans. James Strachey (London: Hogarth Press, 1953), 244. For Lauren Berlant, this kind of allure creates cruel optimism. See Berlant, *Cruel Optimism*.

73. Derek Hook, *(Post)Apartheid Conditions: Psychoanalysis and Social Formation* (New York: Palgrave, 2013), 169.

74. David Scott, *Omens of Adversity: Tragedy, Time, Memory, Justice* (Durham, NC: Duke University Press, 2013), 100.

75. Michel de Certeau, *The Writing of History*, trans. Tom Conley (New York: Columbia University Press, 1988).

76. Lacan, *Desire and Its Interpretation*, 337.

77. Jean Laplanche, *Essays on Otherness*, ed. John Fletcher, trans. Luke Thurston (New York: Routledge, 1999), 249.

78. Ballantyne, *Between Colonialism and Diaspora*, 120, 33.

79. Ballantyne, therefore, to appropriate Anidjar, renders "onto the native his own history (for he will teach the natives how to mourn, what to mourn—a mourning that is not one)"; it matters not whether this history is singular or plural. Gil Anidjar, "Against History," in Marc Nichanian, *The Historiographic Perversion* (New York: Columbia University Press, 2009), 158.

80. "One has to know. One has to know it. One has to have knowledge," writes Derrida. Jacques Derrida, *Specters of Marx: The State of the Debt, the Work of Mourning, and the New International*, trans. Peggy Kamuf (New York: Routledge, 1994), 9.

81. Anidjar, "Against History," 132, 133.

82. For one example of this approach, see Murphy, *Materiality of the Past*.

83. Lacan, *Desire and Its Interpretation*, 336.

84. Freud, "Mourning and Melancholia," 249–50.

85. Juliana Schiesari, *The Gendering of Melancholia: Feminism, Psychoanalysis and the Symbolics of Loss in Renaissance Literature* (Ithaca, NY: Cornell University Press, 1992), 52.

86. Freud's psychoanalytic distinction between mourning and melancholia already initiates melancholia as a multifaceted and not necessarily unifiable set of relationships between a subject and loss. As object-relations psychoanalysis has pointed out, the incorporation of objects and primary identification, hence the process that characterizes melancholia, is foundational in the formation of the ego, which makes mourning possible later on by splitting off an object from the ego. See Judith Butler, *The Psychic Life of Power: Theories in Subjection* (Stanford, CA: Stanford University Press, 1997) 169–70; Freud, "Mourning and Melancholia," 243; and Amy Hollywood, *Acute Melancholia and Other Essays: Mysticism, History, and the Study of Religion* (New York: Columbia University Press, 2016), 83. See also Melanie Klein, "Mourning and Its Relation to Manic-Depressive States," in *Contributions to Psycho-Analysis 1921–1945* (London: Hogarth, 1948), 311–38. Indeed, the process of subjectification is itself centered on, as Paul Verhaeghe clarifies, "the installation of substitute satisfactions, ranging from neurotic symptoms and fantasies to sublimations." See Paul Verhaeghe, "Causation and Destitution of a Pre-ontological Non-entity: On the Lacanian Subject," in *Key Concepts of Lacanian Psychoanalysis*, ed. Dany Nobus (New York: Other Press, 1998), 166.

87. Ranjana Khanna argues that a postcolonial melancholia can offer "the basis for an ethico-political understanding of colonial pasts, postcolonial presents, and utopian futures" (30). See Ranjana Khanna, *Dark Continents: Psychoanalysis and Colonialism* (Durham, NC: Duke University Press, 2003). Indeed, melancholia has been especially generative for scholars. As David L. Eng and David Kazanjian note in *Loss* (Berkeley: University of California Press, 2003), for example, melancholia

constitutes "an ongoing and open relationship with the past" rather than a burial of the past (4).

88. Eng and Kazanjian, *Loss*, 2.

89. For example, see Sigmund Freud, "Beyond the Pleasure Principle," in *The Standard Edition of the Complete Psychological Works of Sigmund Freud*, vol. 18, ed. and trans. James Strachey (London: Hogarth Press, 1955), 7–64.

90. This would be a diachronic analysis—a worthwhile analysis that others have done. With Duleep Singh, see Axel, *The Nation's Tortured Body*. For others, see Harleen Singh, *The Rani of Jhansi* (Cambridge: Cambridge University Press, 2014), and Ramya Sreenivasan, *The Many Lives of a Rajput Queen: Heroic Pasts in India, c. 1500–1900* (Seattle: University of Washington Press, 2007).

91. Comay, "The Sickness of Tradition," 90.

92. Pandolfo, *Knot of the Soul*, 241–42. Also see Nicolas Abraham and Maria Torok, "Mourning or Melancholia: Introjection versus Incorporation," in *The Shell and the Kernel, Vol. 1*, ed. and trans. Nicholas T. Rand (Chicago: University of Chicago Press, 1994).

93. Pandolfo, *Knot of the Soul*, 241–42.

94. Comay, "The Sickness of Tradition," 90: "The structure of melancholia in this way begins to bleed into that of fetishism—the compensatory construction of imaginary unities in response to a traumatic loss ('castration') which structurally can be neither fully acknowledged nor denied." See also Eng and Kazanjian, *Loss*, 2.

95. Of course, fetishism can provide "an opportunity for interpretive openness" (113). See E. L. McCallum, *Object Lessons: How to Do Things with Fetishism* (Albany: SUNY Press, 1999).

96. Stephen Frosh, *Hauntings: Psychoanalysis and Ghostly Transmissions* (New York: Palgrave, 2013). It amounts, as Derek Hook writes, "to a psychotic instance of stasis, one in which the broader libidinal world is stopped, and the melancholic subject (or community) takes itself to the place of the dead" in a fetishistic attachment to an endless present of self-torment (200). See Hook, *(Post)Apartheid Conditions*. Also see Wendy Brown, who draws our attention to attachment to exclusion in *States of Injury: Power and Freedom in Late Modernity* (Princeton, NJ: Princeton University Press, 1995), 73–74.

97. Axel, *The Nation's Tortured Body*, 41, 47.

98. Axel, *The Nation's Tortured Body*, 78.

99. McCallum, *Object Lessons*, xv.

100. In melancholia, as Comay writes, "Reduced to a part-object within the hollow crypt of subjectivity, the object persists as living corpse, at once congealed remains and extruding surplus, whose death accretes like so much cellular efflorescence" (95). See "The Sickness of Tradition."

101. McCallum, *Object Lessons*, 125.

102. There is danger to a promise, of course, which can leave one consuming the past indefinitely. Glossing Nietzsche, Norman Brown writes, "Man's ability to promise involves an unhealthy (neurotic) constipation with the past (the anal character!); he can 'get rid of' nothing. Thus, through the ability to promise the future is bound to the past." Yet this promise need not be calculable, where the ends match the origins. See Norman O. Brown, *Life Against Death: The Psychoanalytical Meaning of History* (Middleton, CT: Wesleyan University Press, 1959).

103. Comay, "The Sickness of Tradition," 90. Also see Dominick LaCapra, *Writing History, Writing Trauma* (Baltimore: Johns Hopkins University Press, 2001).

104. McCallum, *Object Lessons*, 150.

105. Comay, "The Sickness of Tradition," 90.

106. Frantz Fanon, *The Wretched of the* Earth, trans. Constance Farrington (New York: Grove Press, 1968). For example, consider Fanon on oral traditions that were once "filed away as set pieces" relating "inert episodes" (240). I am grateful to Parama Roy for reminding me of this point.

107. See also Michael Taussig, *The Devil and Commodity Fetishism in South America* (Chapel Hill: University of North Carolina Press, 1980), 123–25. Focusing our attention on other forms of life, as this work tries to do, reveals different understandings and relations to loss, which complicates and moves beyond psychoanalytic approaches that can settle the object. Piers Vitebsky, for example, notes resonances between Freud's understanding of mourning and melancholia and Sora systems of belief while arguing there is one crucial difference: "The Sora system may be operated by living actors, yet it is represented equally from the perspective of the dead," whereas for Freud, the dead no longer exist (124). Loss, in this understanding, is not an annihilation that then cultivates fetishistic attachments or a reparative remembering but entails separation that can be brought together by a shaman—a local practice to work through loss. Yet this understanding and practice of loss itself undergoes loss as the Sora world disappears converted into Christianity, and therefore the secular. See Piers Vitebsky, *Living Without the Dead: Loss and Redemption in a Jungle Cosmos* (Chicago: University of Chicago Press, 2017).

108. Maurice Blanchot, *The Book to Come*, trans. Charlotte Mandell (Stanford, CA: Stanford University Press, 2002), 79.

109. Blanchot, *The Book to Come*, 81.

110. Ranajit Guha, *Elementary Aspects of Peasant Insurgency in Colonial India* (Durham, NC: Duke University Press, 1999), 278. See also Prathama Banerjee, *Politics of Time: "Primitives" and History-Writing in a Colonial Society* (New York: Oxford University Press, 2006), 40–49.

111. Silvia Federici, *Caliban and the Witch: Women, the Body, and Primitive Accumulation* (New York: Autonomedia, 2004), 143.

112. Louis E. Fenech, *The Sikh Zafar-namah of Guru Gobind Singh: A Discursive Blade in the Heart of the Mughal Empire* (New Delhi: Oxford University Press, 2013), 104.

113. For example, Timothy Mitchell notes, "Modernity, like capitalism, is defined by its claim to universality, to a uniqueness, unity, and universality that represent the end (in every sense) of history. Yet this always remains an impossible unity, an incomplete universal. Each staging of the modern must be arranged to produce the unified, global history of modernity, yet each requires those forms of difference that introduce the possibility of a discrepancy, that return to undermine its unity and identity" (24). See Timothy Mitchell, "The Stage of Modernity," in *Questions of Modernity*, ed. Timothy Mitchell (Minneapolis: University of Minnesota Press, 2000). For hidden transcripts, see James C. Scott, *Domination and the Arts of Resistance: Hidden Transcripts* (New Haven, CT: Yale University Press, 1990), and chapter 1 of this book. See also Gyan Prakash, *Bonded Histories: Genealogies of Labor Servitude in Colonial India* (Cambridge: Cambridge University Press, 1990), 225.

114. David Marriott, *Whither Fanon? Studies in the Blackness of Being* (Stanford, CA: Stanford University Press, 2018), 312. To take the point further, as Anidjar writes in "Against History," "perhaps, it was never a matter of being against history (as if it were possible)" (159).

115. Though writing about modernity, this might be a way to dwell in what Ananda Abeysekera terms "un-inheriting," which is not reducible to the binaries of receiving/abandoning, remembering/forgetting, embracing/rejecting (3). See Ananda Abeyesekera, *The Politics of Postsecular Religion: Mourning Secular Futures* (New York: Columbia University Press, 2008).

116. Lacan, *Desire and Its Interpretation*, 98.

117. Jacques Lacan, *The Four Fundamental Concepts of Psychoanalysis: Book XI, 1964*(New York: W. W. Norton, 1998), 168.

118. For "blue in the face," see Jacques Lacan, *On Feminine Sexuality, the Limits of Love and Knowledge, Encore, 1972–1973*, ed. Jacques-Alain Miller, trans. Bruce Fink (New York: W. W. Norton, 1998), 58, and *Four Fundamental Concepts*, 214.

119. As Jack Halberstam claims, practicing failure, and being with the losers it produces, can prompt us "to fall short, to get distracted, to take a detour, to find a limit, to lose our way, to forget to avoid mastery" thereby disrupting the fixed stasis of the present. See Jack Halberstam, *The Queer Art of Failure* (Durham, NC: Duke University Press, 2011), 120–21. It is important to recall, however, that Halberstam centers the inadequacy of psychoanalytic inquiry. See, for example, *Skin Shows: Gothic Horror and the Technology of Monsters* (Durham, NC: Duke University Press, 1995).

120. Žižek, *Sublime Object of Ideology*, 192.

121. I borrow ego-assertion and ego-denial from Gurbhagat Singh, who is writing about a different context. Gurbhagat Singh, "Difference and Discourse," *Indian Literature* 35, no. 4 (1992): 121–29.

122. Gurbhagat Singh, *Sikhism and Postmodern Thought* (Amritsar: Naad Pargaas, 2016), 146. J. S. Grewal defines *halemi raj* as a "rule of moderation in which there is no oppression or coercion; an expression used by Guru Arjan for the entire dispensation of Guru Nanak and his successors." See Grewal, *A Study of Guru Granth Sahib: Doctrine, Social Content, History Structure and Status* (Amritsar: Singh Brothers, 2009), 18. Or, as Kapur Singh explicates, "Coercive rule of one people over another was against God's will as now revealed to mankind through Sikhism" (46). See Kapur Singh, *Sikhism for Modern Man*, ed. Madanjit Kaur and Piar Singh (Amritsar: Guru Nanak Dev University Press, 1992).

123. Esposito, *Communitas*, 2.

124. Jacques Derrida, "Faith and Knowledge," in *Acts of Religion*, ed. Gil Anidjar (New York: Routledge, 2002), 87. This is a question of drive. Derrida turns our attention to "that death drive that in silence works on every community, every auto-co-immunity, and in truth constitutes it as such, in its iterability, its heritage, its spectral tradition. Community as common auto-immunity: there is no community that does not maintain its autoimmunity" (87).

125. Centering drive, however, requires (following Lacan) that we "be beyond the instinct to return to a state of equilibrium of the inanimate sphere," which is precisely what transgressions, such as centering impossibility and absence as loss, uphold. See Jacques Lacan, *The Ethics of Psychoanalysis, 1959–1960, Book VII*, ed.

Jacques-Alain Miller, trans. Dennis Porter (New York: W. W. Norton, 1992), 212. For a brilliant reading of desire and drive, see Marika Rose, *A Theology of Failure: Žižek Against Christian Innocence* (New York: Fordham University Press, 2019).

126. I borrow from Sami Khatib, "Melancholia and Destruction: Brushing Walter Benjamin's 'Angel of History' Against the Grain," *Crisis and Critique* 3, no. 2 (2016): 23.

127. For example, see Vasudha Dalmia, *The Nationalization of Hindu Traditions: Bharatendu Harischandra and Nineteenth Century Banaras* (New Delhi: Oxford University Press, 1997); Richard King, *Orientalism and Religion: Post-Colonial Theory, India and the Mystic East* (New York: Routledge, 1999); Gyanendra Pandey, *The Construction of Communalism in Colonial North India*, 2nd ed. (New Delhi: Oxford University Press, 2006); Brian K. Pennington, *Was Hinduism Invented? Britons, Indians, and the Colonial Construction of Religion* (Oxford: Oxford University Press, 2005); Philip C. Almond, *The British Discovery of Buddhism* (Cambridge: Cambridge University Press, 2007); and Teena Purohit, *The Aga Khan Case: Religion and Identity in Colonial India* (Cambridge, MA: Harvard University Press, 2012).

128. Richard Fox, *Lions of the Punjab: Culture in the Making* (Berkeley: University of California, 1985); Harjot Oberoi, *The Construction of Religious Boundaries: Culture, Identity, and Diversity in the Sikh Tradition* (Chicago: University of Chicago Press, 1994); Arvind-Pal Mandair, *Religion and the Specter of the West: Sikhism, India, Postcoloniality, and the Politics of Translation* (New York: Columbia University Press, 2013).

129. Oberoi, *The Construction of Religious Boundaries*, 25.

130. The most prominent "defense" of syncretism in relation to Sikhism comes from Anshu Malhotra in *Piro and the Gulabdasis: Gender, Sect, and Society in Punjab* (New Delhi: Oxford University Press, 2017), 157–61. Farina Mir, on the other hand, cautions against syncretism, not because it destroys the internal coherence of a tradition but because it allows for too much coherence. For example, she argues that syncretism presupposes that "religions in India (primarily Islam and Hinduism, but also Islam and Sikhism) are, *a priori*, in conflict" and/or "it relies on purity or coherence in the traditions that combine, and thereby elides the diversity of thought, opinion, and belief within South Asian Islam, Hinduism, and Sikhism." Mir, *The Social Space of Language: Vernacular Culture in British Colonial Punjab* (Berkeley: University of California Press, 2010), 176–77. Mir elaborates on the problem of syncretism in "Genre and Devotion in Punjabi Popular Narratives: Rethinking Cultural and Religious Syncretism," *Comparative Studies in Society and History* 48, no. 3 (2006): 727–58.

131. For a heterogenous past in Punjab, see Mir, *The Social Space of Language*; Timothy S. Dobe, *Hindu Christian Faqir: Modern Monks, Global Christianity, and Indian Sainthood* (Oxford: Oxford University Press, 2015); and Malhotra, *Piro and the Gulabdasis*. For an important critique of heterogeneity as an essentialism, see David Scott, *Formations of Ritual: Colonial and Anthropological Discourses on the Sinhala Yaktovil* (Minneapolis: University of Minnesota Press, 1994), and *Refashioning Futures: Criticism after Postcoloniality* (Princeton, NJ: Princeton University Press, 1999).

132. This is a continually articulated problem in relation to Sikhs in particular. For example, Veena Das writes, "A narrative of Sikh history in terms of a series of systematic dualisms separating the Sikh self from the Hindu other could not be built without a systematic 'forgetting' of the close relations between Hindus and Sikhs in everyday life, especially the bonds of language, common mythology, shared worship, and the community created through exchanges" (115). See Veena Das, *Life and Words: Violence and the Descent Into the Ordinary* (Berkeley: University of California Press, 2007).

133. This is a revised but borrowed formulation from Omnia El Shakry.

134. Eric L. Santner, *Stranded Objects Mourning, Memory, and Film in Postwar Germany* (Ithaca, NY: Cornell University Press, 1993), 151.

135. See Talal Asad, *The Idea of an Anthropology of Islam* (Washington, DC: Georgetown University Center for Contemporary Arab Studies, 1986), and Alasdair C. MacIntyre, *After Virtue: A Study in Moral Theory* (Notre Dame, IN: University of Notre Dame Press, 1981), 222. See also Omnia El Shakry, "Inwardness: Comparative Religious Philosophy in Modern Egypt," *Journal of the American Academy of Religion* 90, no. 2 (2022): 450–72. For example, Asad's foundational work demonstrates that tradition is neither a static nor homogenous inheritance of content but rather embodies "continuities of conflict" not merely tied to contextual reasoning.

136. Omnia El Shakry, "Rethinking Arab Intellectual History: Epistemology, Historicism, Secularism," *Modern Intellectual History* 18, no. 2 (2021): 547–72.

137. Samira Haj, *Reconfiguring Islamic Tradition: Reform, Rationality, and Modernity* (Stanford, CA: Stanford University Press, 2008), 4–5.

138. Scholars of South Asia have explored Asad's notion of tradition. Anand Pandian compellingly reveals tradition's "fragmentary form," which highlights the "impossibility of a whole and seamless horizon of experience rather than sustaining the possibility of its reconstruction." However, "such impossibility of coherence to which cultural fragments often testify," Pandian continues, "does not annul the persistence and vitality of tradition" (470). Leela Prasad also demands that we reflect on how even though codified forms of tradition, such as shastras [remembered literature], can be quite specific in their pursuit to order all possibilities within complexities of the time, individuals engage in "an intriguing process that does not disturb *theoretically* the intrinsic immutability associated with shastric knowledge (considered to be of divine origins), but witnesses continually the adaptation of shastra in practice" (135). Naveeda Khan too recommends that we contemplate how "religious argumentation may be seen as expressive of ongoing striving" in which experimentation is not about innovation or self-fashioning, but about "revisiting and reinhabiting theological conundrums through words and practices" (11). See Anand Pandian, "Tradition in Fragments: Inherited Forms and Fractures in the Ethics of South India," *American Ethnologist* 35, no. 3 (2008): 466–80. Leela Prasad, *Poetics of Conduct Oral Narrative and Moral Being in a South Indian Town* (New York: Columbia University Press, 2006); Naveeda Khan, *Muslim Becoming: Aspiration and Skepticism in Pakistan* (Durham, NC: Duke University Press, 2012).

139. MacIntyre, *After Virtue*, 223. MacIntyre writes, "It is rather the case that an adequate sense of tradition manifests itself in a grasp of those future possibilities

which the past has made available to the present. Living traditions, just because they continue a not-yet-completed narrative, confront a future whose determinate and determinable character, so far as it possesses any, derives from the past."

140. Khan, *Muslim Becoming*, 7. The contradiction between Khan's use of Deleuze to foreground becoming and my reading of Lacan and Žižek might appear to collapse under its own conceptual weight. But, as Aaron Schuster argues, this opposition might not be as clean as it first appears, for, as he notes, perhaps we can think of a "less positive and less affirmationist Deleuze to abjure the all too easy opposition between negativity, impossibility, castration, and lack versus creativity, difference, and becoming" in order to "interpret Deleuze's philosophy as an extended and highly original attempt to think negativity and the violence of the negative *differently* (45). See Aaron Schuster, *The Trouble with Pleasure: Deleuze and Psychoanalysis* (Cambridge, MA: MIT Press, 2016). See also Andrew Culp, *Dark Deleuze* (Minneapolis: University of Minnesota Press, 2016).

141. I owe this understanding of *naam* and *maryada* to Jagdish Singh, according to whom *maryada* forms the unformable through its limiting gestures. Moreover, I borrow "play of modalities" from Katharine Ewing, who clarifies the play between the symbolic and the Real, writing, "I see the experiencing subject as moving among different modalities and an array of desires." See Katherine Pratt Ewing, *Arguing Sainthood: Modernity, Psychoanalysis, and Islam* (Durham, NC: Duke University Press, 1997), 197.

142. Creativity, however, is not merely the new and "unattached to older forms of reasoning." See Haj, *Reconfiguring Islamic Tradition*, 33.

143. Slavoj Žižek, *The Plague of Fantasies* (London: Verso, 1997), 13.

144. Gayatri Chakravorty Spivak, "In a Word: Interview," in *Outside in the Teaching Machine* (New York: Routledge, 1993), 21.

145. Spivak, "In a Word," 21.

146. I borrow "grasping and un-grasping" from Gayatri Chakravorty Spivak, *A Critique of Postcolonial Reason: Toward a History of the Vanishing Present* (Cambridge, MA: Harvard University Press, 1999), 242.

147. Gil Anidjar, "Sapientia," *Identities: Journal for Politics, Gender and Culture*, April 14, 2020, https://identitiesjournal.edu.mk/index.php/IJPGC/announcement /view/36.

1. COMMUNITY

1. I borrow this from Gil Anidjar, *Blood: A Critique of Christianity* (New York: Columbia University Press, 2016), 34. This remains a central question for scholars of Sikh studies, even in their search for fluidity.

2. For these changes, see David Gilmartin, "Environmental History, Biradari, and the Making of Pakistani Punjab," in *Punjab Reconsidered: History, Culture, and Practice*, ed. Anshu Malhotra and Farina Mir (New Delhi: Oxford University Press, 2012), 289–319 and David Gilmartin, *Blood and Water: The Indus River Basin in Modern History* (Berkeley: University of California Press, 2015).

3. Partha Chatterjee, *The Nation and Its Fragments: Colonial and Postcolonial Histories* (Princeton, NJ: Princeton University Press, 1993), 236.

4. See Shail Mayaram, *Against History, Against State: Counterperspectives from the Margins* (New York: Columbia University Press, 2003).

5. I draw on Georges Sorel with the recognition that Sorel's "revisionist impulse" opens, as George Ciccariello-Maher writes, "an important space for contingency, uneven development, and autonomous struggles that points toward decolonization and liberation from orthodox stageism" (43). Sorel's moves, in other words, allow us to draw together different identities "to accommodate a move across the 'colonial difference'" (45). For more on this reading of Sorel, see George Ciccariello-Maher, *Decolonizing Dialectics* (Durham, NC: Duke University Press, 2017).

6. Georges Sorel, *Reflections On Violence*, ed. and trans. Jeremy Jennings (Cambridge: Cambridge University Press, 1999), 116, 28.

7. I follow Jean-Luc Nancy, who argues that myth is interrupted by its myth, for "the word 'myth' itself designates the absence of what it names. This is what constitutes the interruption: *'myth' is cut off from its own meaning, on its own meaning, by its own meaning*. If it even still has a proper meaning" (52). See Jean-Luc Nancy, *The Inoperative Community*, ed. Peter Connor, trans. Peter Connor et al. (Minneapolis: University of Minnesota Press, 1991), 52–57.

8. Roberto Esposito, *Communitas: The Origin and Destiny of Community*, trans. Timothy Campbell (Stanford, CA: Stanford University Press, 2010), 8.

9. This could be seen as functioning as a precursor to fascism. Sorel is often seen as a precursor to fascism in his rejection of the individualist and rationalist aspects of modernity, as Zeev Sternhell argues. But Sorel's work rejects such conflation with fascism. As Ciccariello-Maher argues, "by claiming Sorel as a fascist precursor, Sternhall has miraculously transformed him into his opposite" (41). This is the case because Sorel rejects social harmony, the biologized unity of the state, and theorizes proletarian struggles as seeking the destruction of the state. See Ciccariello-Maher, *Decolonizing Dialectics*, and Zeev Sternhell, Mario Sznajder, and Maia Ashéri, *The Birth of Fascist Ideology: From Cultural Rebellion to Political Revolution* (Princeton, NJ: Princeton University Press, 1994).

10. Nancy, *The Inoperative Community*, 15. For example, Nancy argues "a community is not a project of fusion, or in some general way a productive or operative project— nor is it a *project* at all" (15). One can see this Duleep Singh in diasporic renderings that look to find a find redemption for their own being. And Duleep Singh becomes capable, though at first lost in the sins of empire, of reclaiming a known and enunciable Sikh identity in order to redeem the entirety of Punjab.

11. This play within community related to myth, prophecy, and loss is not an abstraction—conceptual parameters I impose from the West—but a premise within the Sikh tradition. Jagdish Singh, for example, argues the experience of double death is central to *Sikhi*, which first annihilates the subject, and then tribal notions of community itself through *shabad*. This double death, in my reading, first results in the death of the individual subject through the idea of Duleep Singh and then, after this death, death through *shabad*, destroying the bonds of a singular known community in the recognition of *sarbat da bhala* (welfare for all). This would be the *sangat*, the community. Jagdish Singh made this point in a conversation, for which I am grateful.

12. James C. Scott, *Domination and the Arts of Resistance: Hidden Transcripts* (New Haven, CT: Yale University Press, 1990).

13. Ranajit Guha, "Gramsci in India: Homage to a Teacher," in *The Small Voice of History*, ed. Partha Chatterjee (Delhi: Permanent Black, 2009), 370.

14. Ranajit Guha, "Chandra's Death," in *Subaltern Studies V: Writings on South Asian History and Society*, ed. Ranajit Guha (Delhi: Oxford University Press, 1987), 142.

15. Chatterjee, *The Nation and Its Fragments*, 26.

16. For example, Scott writes, "The fact that social criticism remains ideologically limited can never, I am convinced, justify the conclusion that the group which makes that criticism is prevented by a hegemonic ideology from consciously formulating a more far-reaching critique." Scott, *Domination and the Arts of Resistance*, 92.

17. Gayatri Chakravorty Spivak, "Subaltern Studies: Deconstructing Historiography," in *In Other Worlds: Essay In Cultural Politics* (New York: Routledge, 1988), 201.

18. Scott, *Domination and the Arts of Resistance*, 28, 25. My goal is not to establish Duleep Singh's intent, to determine its strategic or authentic nature, but to think about how his discourse affirmed a particular discursive formation.

19. Petition from Duleep Singh, India Office Records L/P&S/18/D24: 29th March 1882, British Library, London.

20. Scott, *Domination and the Arts of Resistance*, 79. In the South Asian context, Douglas Haynes shows how "the language of constitutional principle was not a rigid framework predetermining all potential expression but one that allowed a wide variety of expression within its limitations" (ix). See Douglas E. Haynes, *Rhetoric and Ritual in Colonial India: The Shaping of a Public Culture in Surat City, 1852–1928* (Berkeley: University of California Press, 1991).

21. No. 126 Maharajah Duleep Singh to the Secretary of State (Marquis of Hartington), 16th April 1882, Correspondence Relative to the Maharajah Duleep Singh (1849–1886), India Office Records L/P&S/18/D25, British Library, London.

22. No. 131 Maharajah Duleep Singh to the Secretary of State (Marquis of Hartington), 25th July 1882, Correspondence Relative to the Maharajah Duleep Singh (1849–1886).

23. For example, the state recognized that Duleep Singh's allowance was low especially since the terms were set in 1862 and required an elite lifestyle from Singh. But still the appraisals on his property revealed that Duleep Singh was "one of the strictest preservers of winged game in the country," and therefore "there can be little doubt that the preservation of game, carried on as it is by the Maharajah *does* interfere with the letting of his farms, and keeps down the rental." The key became to locate Duleep Singh's personal financial failures—failures located in productivity of his landed estates. See India Office Records R/1/1/62.

24. Affairs of the Maharajah Duleep Singh (Continuation of Memorandum, dated 4th December 1885), Maharajah Dhuleep Singh, India Office Records L/P&S/18/D18-4, British Library, London.

25. "*The Times*, August 31st, 1882," in *Maharaja Duleep Singh Correspondence*, ed. Ganda Singh (Patiala: Punjabi University Patiala, 1977), 98, 101.

26. Memorandum, 15th June 1887, India Office Records L/P&S/18/D152, British Library, London.

27. "*The Times*, August 31st, 1882," 101.

28. Queen Victoria to Maharaja Duleep Singh, 5th November, 1882 as cited in Michael Alexander and Sushila Anand, *Queen Victoria's Maharajah: Duleep Singh 1838–93* (London: Phoenix Press, 1980), 166.

29. Affairs of the Maharajah Duleep Singh (Continuation of Memoranda, dated 16th September 1875, 6th February 1877, and 22nd June 1882), Maharajah Dhuleep Singh, India Office Records L/P&S/18/D18-4, British Library, London.

30. Note to Secretary of State, 3rd August 1883, Objections to Maharaja Dhulip Singh's Proposal to Visit India, Foreign Department Secret I, December 1883, Nos. 8–17, National Archives of India, New Delhi.

31. Charles Aitchison to C. Grant, 7 August 1883, Objections.

32. Aitchison to Grant, Objections. For the post–Ranjit Singh disintegration of the Sikh Empire, see Fauja Singh, ed., *Maharaja Kharak Singh* (Patiala: Punjabi University, Patiala, 1977), and Khushwant Singh, *The Fall of the Kingdom in Punjab* (Delhi: Penguin, 2014).

33. Aitchison to Grant, Objections.

34. Manu Goswami, *Producing India: From Colonial Economy to National Space.* (Chicago: University of Chicago Press, 2004), 135.

35. For example, see Ashis Nandy, "History's Forgotten Doubles," *History and Theory* 34, no. 2 (1995): 44–66, Dipesh Chakrabarty, *Provincializing Europe: Postcolonial Thought and Historical Difference* (Princeton, NJ: Princeton University Press, 2000), Prathama Banerjee, *Politics of Time: "Primitives" and History-Writing in a Colonial Society* (Oxford: Oxford University Press, 2006).

36. Aitchison to Grant, Objections.

37. Aitchison to Grant, Objections.

38. Colonel G. Gordon Young to W. M. Young, 30th July 1883, Objections.

39. S. C Bayly, 9th August 1883, Objections.

40. Ranajit Guha argues that the pressures of such insurgency required both the colonial state and elite discourse to "reduce the semantic range of many words and expressions, and assign to them specialized meanings in order to identify peasants as rebels and their attempt to turn the world upside down as crime." Guha, *Elementary Aspects of Peasant Insurgency in Colonial India* (Durham, NC: Duke University Press, 1999), 17.

41. Aitchison to Grant, Objections.

42. W. O. Clarke to G. Knox, 4th August 1883, Objections.

43. Letter Enclosed in W. O. Clarke to G. Knox, 4th August 1883, Objections.

44. S. C. Mittal, *Freedom Movement in Punjab (1905–29)* (Delhi: Concept Publishing Company, 1977), 24. Bengalis had taken numerous positions in Punjab, since the state determined Punjabis did not have the capacity to so. This created anxieties in the population. For example, General Dillon relayed, "the editor of the little Rawal Pindi paper" had mentioned "the discontent of the educated Punjabis to find the Bengalis sitting in this greater number of the little posts in the Punjab to which Punjabis naturally aspired." See India Office Records R/1/1/62. See also Kenneth Jones, "The Bengali Elites in Post-Annexation Punjab: An Example of Inter-Regional Influence in Nineteenth-Century India," *Indian Economic & Social History Review* 3, no. 4 (1966): 376–95, and Nina Puri, *Political Elite and Society in the Punjab* (New Delhi: Vikas Publishing House, 1985).

45. Daniel Argov, *Moderates and Extremists in the Indian Nationalist Movement, 1883–1920* (Bombay: Asia Publishing House, 1967), 6–7.

46. Anil Seal, *The Emergence of Indian Nationalism: Competition and Collaboration in the Later Nineteenth Century* (Cambridge: Cambridge University Press, 1971), 217.

47. Dewan Narendra Nath as cited in Argov, *Moderates and Extremists in the Indian Nationalist Movement*, 14.

48. Kenneth Jones, *Arya Dharm: Hindu Consciousness in 19th-Century Punjab* (Delhi: Manohar, 1976), 243. The other incidents included the white protests against the Ilbert Bill. As Jones writes, "The Ilbert Bill, which threatened the privileges of the white ruling class, united all 'natives' in a common front against the bill's opponents" (243). Furthermore, it is important to note Banerjea specifically used "Indian" to cultivate national unity. Seal writes, "the decision to call the new association Indian, and not the Bengal" was significant. See Seal, *The Emergence of Indian Nationalism*, 252.

49. Annual Report of the Indian Association for 1883 as cited by R. C. Majumdar, *History of the Freedom Movement in India, Volume 1* (Calcutta: Firma K. K. Mukhopadhyay, 1962), 377.

50. As Lacan writes in *Ethics of Psychoanalysis*, "As far as desires are concerned, come back later. Make them wait" (315; see also 212).

51. Sanjay Seth, "Rewriting Histories of Nationalism: The Politics of 'Moderate Nationalism' in India, 1870–1905," *American Historical Review* 104, no. 1 (1999): 108. Seth writes, "This gap did not simply operate as an external cause, shaping the discourse of moderate nationalism; it occupied a prominent place in that discourse. Drawing attention to the gap was part of the discursive strategy of moderate nationalism; it was part of the nationalist case as to why British rule needed to take a different form, one in which the Indian elites would play a greater role in administering the country." Also see Sukanya Bannerjee, *Becoming Imperial Citizens: Indians in the Late-Victorian Empire* (Durham, NC: Duke University Press, 2010).

52. I borrow the co-concealment of race and religion from Gil Anidjar, *Semites: Race, Religion, Literature* (Stanford, CA: Stanford University Press, 2008), 27–28.

53. Sudipta Kaviraj, *The Imaginary Institution of India* (Delhi: Permanent Black, 2010), 7. Or, in Seth's terms, "Nationalist historiography homogenizes the history of nationalism, either because it stumbles over the first step—its blinkered vision results in its only identifying one form of imagining the nation—or because, in telling the story of Indian nationalism, it assimilates all other forms of national imagining to this one form" (114). Nationalism also homogenizes all possible imaginings, even those outside its contours. locating them within its broader narrative. See Seth, "Rewriting Histories of Nationalism."

54. Sumit Sarkar, *Writing Social History* (Delhi: Oxford University Press, 1998), 363.

55. Kaviraj asks us to question the construction of such an Indian "we," noting how Bengalis entered "into narrative contract with communities who had nothing really to do with them in the past, constantly gerrymandering the boundaries of their national collective self." Kaviraj, *Imaginary Institution of India*, 183.

56. Seth asks that we "acknowledge and embrace the possibility of many histories, and thus also of many ways of being Indian." "Rewriting Histories of Nationalism," 116.

57. Bernard Cohn, *Colonialism and Its Forms of Knowledge: The British in India* (Princeton, NJ: Princeton University Press, 1996). Thomas Metcalf, too, notes how "the peoples of India were defined by unchanging racial and cultural identities" in the British commitment of scientific understanding (117). In Punjab, this extended to tribes as well as officials believed they could "harness the Punjab's distinctive social forms, above all in the settlement of canal colonies, to the creation of a prosperous land" (129). See Thomas Metcalf, *Ideologies of the Raj* (Cambridge: Cambridge University Press, 1995).

58. Karuna Mantena, *Alibis of Empire: Henry Maine and the Ends of Liberal Imperialism* (Princeton, NJ: Princeton University Press, 2010), 11. Partha Chatterjee, too, notes, "One of the fundamental elements in the colonial conceptualization of India as a 'different' society was the fixed belief that the population was a mélange of communities." *The Nation and Its Fragments*, 223.

59. Lepel Griffin to Lord Dufferin, June 21st 1885, Letters to Viceroy from Persons in India, India Office Records Mss Eur F130/40A: 1885, British Library, London.

60. Griffin to Lord Dufferin, June 21st 1885.

61. For example, Mantena notes how Alfred Lyall was concerned "with the cumulative impact of Western education on the transformation of religious belief. The spread of English education seemingly induced a kind of religious malaise and spiritual unrest among the most advanced native populations." This unrest challenged triumphant narratives of secular teleology, and instead "Lyall argued that without knowing the end point of the current spiritual interregnum, British rule unwittingly advanced the prospects of new and potentially more threatening religious formations." Mantena, *Alibis of Empire*, 168.

62. Clarke to Knox, 4th August 1883.

63. John H. Herdon to C. Brune, 5th August 1883, Objections.

64. C. Brune enclosed in Aitchison to Grant, Objections.

65. Viceroy to Secretary of State, London, 16th August 1883, Objections.

66. Memorandum, 15th June 1887.

67. Clarke to Knox, 4th August 1883. The footnote reads "The Akalis are Sikh zealots living at, or attached to, the give Sikh 'Takhts' (chief Sikh temples) viz., the Akalbunga at Amritsar; the temple at Anandpur in the Hoshiarpur district; that at Mukatsar, in the Firozpur district, at Patna in Bengal, and at Apchalnagar, near Hyderabad in the Deccan. They chiefly live at the last named place." See Memorandum, 15th June 1887.

68. Viceroy to Secretary of State, London, 16th August 1883. The lieutenant governor had said the same to the viceroy in an earlier correspondence. In a telegram on August 16, 1883, the viceroy noted to the secretary of state that the "Lieutenant Governor of Punjab considers that paper is not of great importance, but it indicates use that might be made of Duleep Singh's name." See No. 149 Telegram from Viceroy to Secretary of State, 16th August 1883, Correspondence Relative to Maharajah Duleep Singh (1849–1886), India Office Records L/P&S/18/D/25, British Library, London.

69. "Viceroy to Secretary of State, London, 16th August 1883," in Objections to Maharaja Dhulip Singh's Proposal to Visit India, National Archives of India, Foreign Secret I, December 1883, Nos. 8–17.

70. Memorandum of information relating to the case of Maharaja Dalip Singh, which exists in the Punjab secretariat and Central Police Office, Special Branch, which

has not been communicated to the Government of India, Proceedings of Maharaja Dalip Singh, his advances to Russia, and feeling in the army and Native States regarding him, India Office Records R/1/1/62, British Library, London.

71. Jacques Lacan, "Seminar on 'The Purloined Letter,'" in *Écrits*, ed. and trans. Bruce Fink (New York: W. W. Norton, 2002), 19. This incompatibility and foreignness, Lacan reminds us, is "proven by the fact that possession of the letter is impossible to bring forward publicly as legitimate" (19–20). Though Lacan's early seminar is interested in, as Žižek notes, "a senseless, 'mechanical' symbolic order regulating the subject's innermost self-experience," I invoke this reading through the later Lacan, who demands we consider the Real in the process of subjectification. Žižek reveals how the "traumatic presence of the Real" interrupts "the smooth running of the symbolic circuit" through the letter turned object of desire (23). See Slavoj Žižek, *Enjoy Your Symptom!: Jacques Lacan in Hollywood and Out* (New York: Routledge, 1992). For different readings of Lacan's seminal work, see John P. Muller and William J. Richardson, eds., *The Purloined Poe: Lacan, Derrida, and Psychoanalytic Reading* (Baltimore: Johns Hopkins University Press, 1988).

72. Memorandum, 15th June 1887.

73. Memorandum, 15th June 1887.

74. Memorandum, 15th June 1887.

75. C. A. Bayly argues that the position of Persian eroded as a state language in part because of political danger. Bayly writes, "Political suspicion also played an important part [in eroding Persian's position]. In the mind of some officials, Persian was the language of dissidence and its suppression was therefore desirable on political grounds." C. A. Bayly, *Empire and Information: Intelligence Gathering and Social Communication in India, 1780–1870* (Cambridge: Cambridge University Press, 1996), 286.

76. Extract enclosed in Letter from Charles Aitchison to H. M Durand, 8th August 1885, Maharaja Dhulip and Major Evans Bell's Book "The Annexation of the Punjab," Foreign Department Secret I, August 1885, Nos. 17–21, National Archives of India, New Delhi.

77. Maharaja Dhulip Singh to Sardar Jee, 28th June 1885, "The Annexation of the Punjab."

78. So though blood is, Anidjar writes, "only one name among many in an economy of terms and symbols—'natural' or not—that have appealed to the collective imagination," we keep speaking of kinship, now ethnicity or, perhaps, culture, as a blood relation. Anidjar, *Blood*, 96.

79. Chand Kaur was the wife of Kharak Singh, Duleep Singh's half-brother, who initially succeeded Maharaja Ranjit Singh. For the *misl* system, see Indu Banga, *The Agrarian System of Sikhs* (New Delhi: Manohar Publications, 1978). Maharaja Dhulip Singh to Sardar Jee, 28th June 1885, "The Annexation of the Punjab."

80. For more on Duleep Singh's conversion, see chapter 3.

81. W. Coldstream to Elsmie, 28th November 1885, Intention of Maharaja Dhulip Singh to visit India, his temporary resistance at Aden, and subsequent return to Europe, Foreign Department Secret I, June 1886, Nos. 12–196, National Archives of India, New Delhi.

82. Memorandum, 15th June 1887. For more on ethical practice in relation to Duleep Singh, see chapter 3.

83. K. W. No. 2: C. L. Tupper to H. M. Durand, 6th October 1885, Intention.

84. C. L. Tupper to H. M. Durand, 12th December 1885, Intention.

85. No. 20, Foreign Department Proceedings B, January 1887, Punjab State Archives, Chandigarh.

86. Edward Royle, *Victorian Infidels: The Origins of the British Secularist Movement, 1791–1866* (Manchester: Manchester University Press, 1974).

87. Evans Bell, *The Annexation of the Punjaub and the Maharaja Duleep Singh* (London: Trüber & Co., 1882), 4, 88, 78.

88. Tupper to Durand, 12th December 1885.

89. Scott, *Domination and the Arts of Resistance*, 8, 18.

90. Tupper to Durand, 12th December 1885.

91. G. S. Forbes to W. M. Young, 15th June, 1886, Translation and circulation by Sardar Thakur Singh, Sindhanwalia, of Major Evans Bell's work, India Office Records R/1/1/30, British Library, London.

92. Young wrote, "I have to report that the English edition of the book is known to have been in the hands of the following persons: —Chanda Singh—Student, Buta Singh—of Lahore, Sardar Thakur Singh—Sindhanwalia, Harkishan Das—Parohit, Sher Singh—Naib Tehsildar, Natha Singh—Subadar, Sarup Singh—of Fatehgarh, Ram Singh—Jotshi, Jamiot Rai—of Shahgarib, Ganda Singh-of Kohat, Muhammad Hossain—Moulvi, Pratap Singh—Granthi." W. M. Young to G. S. Forbes, 18th June, 1886, in Translation and circulation.

93. Coldstream to Elsmie, 28th November 1885.

94. Memorandum, 15th June 1887.

95. C. L. Tupper to H. M. Durand, 28th December 1885, Intention.

96. Sardar Attar Singh, to Private Secretary to His Honor the Lieutenant-Governor Punjab, August 9 1887, Proceedings of Maharaja Dalip Singh, his advances to Russia, and feeling in the army and Native States regarding him, India Office Records R/1/1/62, British Library, London.

97. Ranajit Guha, *Dominance Without Hegemony: History and Power in Colonial India* (Cambridge, MA: Harvard University Press, 1997), 162. For example, Prachi Deshpande notes how the proliferation of new history textbooks sought to "reorder a new generation's historical imagination by giving the new political and geographical realities in the subcontinent deep roots in antiquity. In doing so, they simultaneously sought to erase older existing imaginations and conceptual frameworks about the past as illegitimate as indicative of a lack of historical consciousness" (85). See Prachi Deshpande, *Creative Pasts: Historical Memory and Identity in Western India, 1700–1960* (Delhi: Permanent Black, 2007).

98. Seth, "Rewriting Histories of Nationalism," 79, 92, 106. The literature on temporality is vast. For understandings on different temporal forms, see Reinhart Koselleck, *Futures Past: On the Semantics of Historical Time*, trans. Keith Tribe (Cambridge, MA: MIT Press, 1985); Jacques Derrida, *Specters of Marx: The State of Debt, the Work of Mourning and the New International*, trans. Peggy Kamuf (New York: Routledge, 1994); Achille Mbembe, *On the Postcolony* (Berkeley: University of California Press, 2001); Ruth Mas, "On the Apocalyptic Tones of Islam in Secular Time," in *Secularism and Religion Making*, ed. Arvind-Pal S. Mandair and Markus Dressler (Oxford: Oxford University Press, 2011), 87–103.

99. Michel Foucault reminds us how "the author allows a limitation of the cancerous and dangerous proliferation of significations within a world where one is thrifty not only with one's resources and riches but also with one's discourse and their significations. The author is the principle of thrift in the proliferation of meaning." Foucault, "What Is an Author?," in *Aesthetics, Methods, and Epistemology*, ed. James D. Faubian (New York: New Press, 1998), 221.

100. Maurice Blanchot, *The Space of Literature*, trans. Ann Smock (Lincoln: University of Nebraska Press, 1982), 193.

101. Blanchot, *The Space of Literature*, 193. To reiterate, this is not the matter of a critical reading practice, in which the reader becomes the authority and then can determine the authenticity of the text itself. Rather, as Blanchot argues, "a genuine reading never puts the genuine book into question. But neither does it submit to the 'text'" (194). Though Blanchot references reading in relation to literary works, consigning nonliterary works to a known "tightly woven net of determined significations," it is precisely the impossibility of an historical known, crowded as the landscape was with different historical imaginations, that allows us to read Bell's work through the "strange liberty" provided by literary reading (194–95). See Blanchot, *The Space of Literature*.

102. Nicholas B. Dirks, *Castes of Mind: Colonialism and the Making of Modern India* (Princeton, NJ: Princeton University Press, 2001), 83. For problem-space, see David Scott, *Refashioning Futures: Criticism After Postcoloniality* (Princeton, NJ: Princeton University Press, 1999).

103. See Guha, *Dominance Without Hegemony*. The shift to modern historiography, as Prachi Deshpande, aptly notes, "also involved the complex survival of earlier forms and their content in the new archive." Deshpande, *Creative Pasts*, 124.

104. From Home Department, No. 83, 13th January 1886, Note from Forbes, Translation and circulation.

105. G. S. Forbes to Secretary, 8th June 1886, Translation and circulation.

106. Farina Mir, *The Social Space of Language: Vernacular Culture in British Colonial Punjab* (Berkeley: University of California Press, 2010), 194, 185.

107. I follow C. S. Adcock's work, which pays "attention to the fractured politics of Hindu unity," which in turn "helps to break down the clear opposition that Tolerance narratives imply between the Arya Samaj and the Indian National Congress." Adcock, *The Limits of Tolerance: Indian Secularism and the Politics of Religious Freedom* (New York: Oxford University Press, 2014), 12.

108. Forbes to Secretary, 8th June 1886.

109. From Home Department, No. 83, 13th January 1886, Note from Forbes, Translation and circulation.

110. Extract from demi-official letter from W. M. Young to Secretary, Translation and circulation.

111. Forbes to Secretary, 8th June 1886.

112. Brian Keith Axel, *The Nation's Tortured Body: Violence, Representation, and the Formation of a Sikh "Diaspora"* (Durham, NC: Duke University Press, 2001), 41, 57.

113. Extract from Abstract of Political Intelligence, Punjab Police, No. 10, 13th March 1886, Intention.

114. Jacques Derrida argues that the "conditions of possibility of the gift designate simultaneously the conditions of the impossibility of the gift." Derrida, *Given Time: I. Counterfeit Money*, trans. Peggy Kamuf (Chicago: University of Chicago Press, 2004), 11.
115. Derrida, *Given Time*, 12.
116. Within such a logic, in which failure, the wound itself, as Žižek argues, "contains liberatory potential" (138). In other words, as Žižek writes, "the very obstacle to full assertion of our identity opens up the space for it (148). Slavoj Žižek, *Absolute Recoil: Towards a New Foundation of Dialectical Materialism* (New York: Verso, 2014).
117. Here I follow Shoshana Felman, who argues that Lacan provides opportunity to rethink the analytical reference of a text beyond the author by demonstrating how situating "the object of analysis" is "not necessarily to recognize a *known*, to find an answer, but also, and perhaps more challenging, to locate an *unknown*, to find a question" (153). See Muller and Richardson, *The Purloined Poe*, 133–56.

2. THE PUBLIC

1. A. P. MacDonnell, to Secretary to the Government of the Punjab, A Scurrilous Article Relating to the Income Tax, Home Department Public Proceedings, August 1887, Nos. 66–69, National Archives of India, New Delhi.
2. Amelia Bonea, *The News of Empire: Telegraphy, Journalism, and the Politics of Reporting in Colonial India, c. 1830–1900* (Delhi: Oxford University Press, 2016), 24.
3. Response by H. M. Durand to Mr. Irwin's Note, Proceedings of Maharaja Dalip Singh, his advances to Russia, and feeling in the army and Native States regarding him. India Office Records R/1/1/62, British Library, London.
4. J. Barton Scott and Brannon D. Ingram, "What Is a Public? Notes from South Asia," *South Asia: Journal of South Asian Studies* 38, no. 3 (2015): 361.
5. Jürgen Habermas, *The Structural Transformation of the Public Sphere: An Inquiry Into A Category of Bourgeois Society*, trans. Thomas Burger (Cambridge, MA: MIT Press, 1991), 104. Habermas's work considers the shifts within this concept of publicness historically, most notably how this ideal of critical deliberation, and its emancipatory potential, remained compromised in the modern period as the public transformed to include mass culture. It is difficult therefore to reify the conceptual logic Habermas deploys as the emergence and sustenance of the public sphere at large.
6. For one example, see Michael Warner, *Publics and Counterpublics* (New York: Zone Books, 2005). Warner adeptly reveals Habermas's neglect of how "some publics are defined by their tension with a larger public" since "their participants are marked off from persons or citizens in general." For Warner, this conflictual public is "structured by alternative dispositions or protocols, making different assumptions about what can be said or what goes without say," enabling a "horizon of opinion and exchange"—what Warner deems a counterpublic, destabilizing the very public Habermas delineates in his work (57).

7. For comprehensive insight into this literature, see Scott and Ingram, "What Is a Public?"

8. Scott and Ingram, "What is a Public? Notes from South Asia," 358.

9. This typology is not exact, for scholars have thoroughly highlighted the heterogeneity of the public. To take one example, Rama Sundari Mantena argues that "in nineteenth-century India, the formation of vernacular public spheres occasioned and conditioned the proliferation of political subjectivities" (1682–1705). Mantena, "Vernacular Publics and Political Modernity: Language and Progress in Colonial South India," *Modern Asian Studies* 47, no. 5 (2013): 1682. This is an important insight, allowing us to consider manifold modes of subjectivity instituted within the colony as well as their concomitant forms of ethical engagement cultivated in the subcontinent into the present.

10. See, for example, C. A. Bayly, *Empire & Information: Intelligence Gathering and Social Communication, 1780–1870* (Delhi: Cambridge University Press, 1999). As Bayly writes, India was "not qualitatively different from other societies with emergent public spheres" (182).

11. Sandria Freitag, *Collective Action and Community: Public Arenas and the Emergence of Communalism in North India* (Berkeley: University of California Press, 1989), 284.

12. Partha Chatterjee, *The Nation and Its Fragments: Colonial and Postcolonial Histories* (Princeton, NJ: Princeton University Press, 1993), 74, 147, 237–38.

13. Sandria Freitag, "Postscript: Exploring Aspects of 'the Public' from 1991 to 2014," *South Asia: Journal of South Asian Studies* 38, no. 3 (2015): 512–23.

14. For example, see Dipesh Chakrabarty, *Provincializing Europe: Postcolonial Thought and Historical Difference* (Princeton, NJ: Princeton University Press, 2000), and Chatterjee, *The Nation and Its Fragments.*

15. Sandria Freitag, "Introduction: 'The Public' and Its Meanings in Colonial South Asia," *South Asia: Journal of South Asian Studies* 14, no. 1 (1991): 1.

16. Jodi Dean, "Publicity's Secret," *Political Theory* 29, no. 5 (2001): 629.

17. Scott and Ingram, "What Is a Public?," 359.

18. Michael Taussig too reminds us how the public secret is a presupposition that guarantees society. A public secret, which Taussig defines as "that which is generally known, but cannot be articulated" (5), is the basis of the society at large where one learns what the acceptable parameters of knowledge are, that is, where one learns to "know what not to know" (2). Though this public secret has its own inherent transgression, inviting its own defacement, this transgression creates further enchantment and transformation rather than its annulment. In the colony this dissimulation becomes murky since the colonized are not seen to have the capacity for a nonliteral being and instead exist as failing mimetic reproductions. Within this logic, the public secret, alongside its revelation and concealment, are strictly managed through the regulatory apparatus of the state in order to assuage both possible transgressions and contradictions. See Michael Taussig, *Defacement: Public Secrecy and the Labor of the Negative* (Stanford, CA: Stanford University Press, 1999).

19. Dean, "Publicity's Secret," 630, 632.

20. J. Barton Scott, "How to Defame a God: Public Selfhood in the Maharaj Libel Case," *South Asia: Journal of South Asian Studies* 38, no. 3 (2015): 392.

21. Dean, "Publicity's Secret," 628.

22. Dean, "Publicity's Secret," 647.

23. Anjali Arondekar, *For the Record: On Sexuality and the Colonial Archive in India* (Durham, NC: Duke University Press, 2009), 4.

24. Gayatri Chakravorty Spivak, *A Critique of Postcolonial Reason: Toward a History of the Vanishing Present* (Cambridge, MA: Harvard University Press, 1999), 242.

25. No. 181 Maharaja Duleep Singh to the Secretary of State, 2nd November 1885, Correspondence Relative to the Maharajah Duleep Singh (1849–1886), India Office Records L/P&S/18/D25, British Library, London.

26. No. 191 Copy of Sikh Prophecy forwarded by Maharajah Duleep Singh to Sir. O. Burne After an Interview on 2nd January 1886, Correspondence Relative to the Maharajah Duleep Singh (1849–1886), India Office Records L/P&S/18/D25, British Library, London.

27. No. 206 Interview of Sir O. Burne with the Maharajah, 24th March 1886, Correspondence Relative to the Maharajah Duleep Singh (1849–1886), India Office Records L/P&S/18/D25, British Library, London.

28. No. 190 Claims of Maharajah Duleep Singh, Memorandum of Conversation between Maharaja Duleep and Sir Owen Burne, 29th, January 1886, India Office Records L/P&S/18/D25, British Library, London.

29. Balbinder Singh Bhogal, "Gur-Sikh Dharm," in *History of Indian Philosophy*, ed. Purushottama Bilimoria (London: Routledge, 2017), 493.

30. Memorandum, 15th June 1887, India Office Records L/P&S/18/D152, British Library, London.

31. No. 214 Telegram from Secretary of State (Earl of Kimberley to Viceroy, March 31st, 1886), Correspondence Relative to the Maharajah Duleep Singh (1849–1886), India Office Records L/P&S/18/D25, British Library, London.

32. Enclosure 2 Telegram from Viceroy to Resident, Aden April 15th 1886, Correspondence Relative to the Maharajah Duleep Singh (1849–1886), India Office Records L/P&S/18/D25, British Library, London.

33. G. S. Forbes to Secretary, 29th October 1885, Foreign Department, Secret I June 1886, Nos. 12–196, National Archives of India, New Delhi.

34. Memorandum of information which has been supplied to the Foreign office with regard to the case of Maharaja Duleep Singh, Proceedings of Maharaja Dalip Singh, his advances to Russia, and feeling in the army and Native States regarding him, India Office Records R/1/1/62, British Library, London.

35. Extract from Abstract of Political Intelligence, Punjab Police, dated the 1st May 1886" in Foreign Department, Secret I June 1886, Nos. 12–196, National Archives of India, New Delhi.

36. Memorandum supplied to the Foreign office.

37. Sanjay Seth, "Rewriting Histories of Nationalism: The Politics of 'Moderate Nationalism' in India, 1870–1905," *American Historical Review* 104, no. 1 (1999): 111n49.

38. *The Tribune*, August 4, 1883.

39. *The Pioneer*, August 9, 1883.

40. *The Tribune*, August 11, 1883.

41. See Edwin Hirschmann, *White Mutiny: The Ilbert Bill Crisis in India and Genesis of the Indian National Congress* (New Delhi: Heritage, 1980), and Mrinalini Sinha,

Colonial Masculinity: The "Manly Englishman" and the "Effeminate Bengali" in the Late Nineteenth Century (New York: St. Martin's Press, 1995), 33–34.

42. *The Tribune*, August 11, 1883.

43. Thomas Metcalf, *Ideologies of the Raj* (Cambridge: Cambridge University Press, 1995), 200–201.

44. Lord Ripon as cited in Metcalf, *Ideologies of the Raj*, 201. Also see Anil Seal, *The Emergence of Indian Nationalism: Competition and Collaboration in the Later Nineteenth Century* (Cambridge: Cambridge University Press, 1971), 148.

45. Sinha, *Colonial Masculinity*, 38. Or, as Partha Chatterjee contends in relation to Lord Ripon, "The question was not, as some historians have supposed, whether Ripon was 'too weak a man' to carry out the liberal mission of making Indians fit for modern government. What his 'failure signaled was the inherent impossibility of completing the project of the modern state without superseding the condition of colonial rule" (21). See Chatterjee, *The Nation and Its Fragments*.

46. *The Tribune*, August 11, 1883.

47. *The Pioneer*, August 8, 1883.

48. Note by the Secretary to the Government of Punjab, W. M. Young 16th June 1887, India Office Records L/P&S/18/D152, British Library, London.

49. Note by the Secretary to the Government of Punjab, W. M. Young.

50. Minute by His Honor the Lieutenant-Governor of Punjab, J. B. Lyall 18th June 1887, India Office Records L/P&S/18/D152, British Library, London.

51. General Channer to General Dillon, 6th February 1887, Proceedings of Maharaja Dalip Singh.

52. Summary of Correspondence: Section 1-Popular Feeling about Dalip Singh's expected arrival in India, Proceedings of Maharaja Dalip Singh.

53. Chatterjee, *The Nation and Its Fragments*, 224.

54. Minute by the Lieutenant-Governor of Punjab, J. B. Lyall.

55. Note by the Secretary to the Government of Punjab, W. M. Young.

56. Papers connected to Dalip Singh, Proceedings of Maharaja Dalip Singh.

57. Mary Poovey, *Making A Social Body: British Cultural Formation, 1830–1864* (Chicago: University of Chicago Press, 1995), 11.

58. Lt.-Colonel G. C. Ross, Commandment, 16th Bengal Cavalry to Major General W. K. Elles, Adjutant-General in India, Proceedings of Maharaja Dalip Singh.

59. General Dillon to General Sir F. Roberts, 11th February, 1887, Proceedings of Maharaja Dalip Singh.

60. General Channer to General Dillon, 6th February 1887, Proceedings of Maharaja Dalip Singh.

61. In relation to the bazaar, see chapter 4.

62. But this is not to say the press was undivided; N. G. Barrier discloses how in nineteenth-century Punjab the press became increasingly divided among communal lines. My concern is with the instability within such categorical formations. See N. Gerald Barrier and Paul Wallace, *The Punjab Press, 1880–1905* (East Lansing: Michigan State University Press, 1970).

63. Memorandum, 15th June 1887, India Office Records L/P&S/18/D152, British Library, London.

64. Maharaja Leaves Aden and Proceeds to Paris, Affairs of the Maharajah Duleep Singh, India Office Records L/P&S/18/D83, British Library, London.

65. *The Tribune*, August 4, 1883.

66. Officials recognized the difficulties of this possibility because it would be too inconvenient, especially because of climate. The concern was that Duleep Singh would not be able to live in South India after living in a cool and temperate climate for so many years. This was all moot, since Duleep Singh was eventually arrested in Aden for issuing a rebellious proclamation.

67. Memorandum, 15th June 1887.

68. *The Tribune*, April 17, 1886.

69. Extract from Abstract of Political Intelligence, Punjab Police, No. 22, dated 12th June 1886, Foreign Department, Secret I June 1886, Nos. 12–196, National Archives of India, New Delhi.

70. Memorandum, 15th June 1887.

71. Memorandum, 15th June 1887.

72. Extract from Abstract of Political Intelligence, Punjab Police, No. 18, dated 8th May 1886, Foreign Department, Secret I June 1886, Nos. 12–196, National Archives of India, New Delhi.

73. G. R. Irwin to C. L. Tupper, 10th January 1889, Warrants for the Detention of Jiwan Singh and Pertab Singh, India Office Records R/1/1/95, British Library, London.

74. Memorandum, 15th June 1887.

75. Notes by Assistant General Superintendent, 17th June 1896, Petition from Sardar Dyal Singh Majithia, for permission to adopt a successor to his jagir, refused, K. W. Secret I, August 1896, Nos. 5–21, National Archives of India, New Delhi.

76. This seems to be Bannerjee's conjecture that he was the initial reason for Majithia's *Tribune*, though Bannerjee was indeed quite helpful in providing logistical help early on. Surendranath Banerjee, "The Pure Gold," in *Sardar Dyal Singh Majithia as Seen by His Contemporaries*, ed. Ihsan H. Nadiem (Lahore: Dyal Singh Research & Cultural Forum, 2011), 50.

77. A. B. Barnard to F. B. Peacock, 9th April 1887, Proceedings of Maharaja Dalip Singh.

78. Memorandum written by Donald McCracken of information relating to the case of Maharaja Duleep Singh in Punjab Secretariat and Central Police Office, Special Branch, Proceedings of Maharaja Dalip Singh.

79. Chatterji would go on to become the Vice Chancellor of Punjab University. For more on Chatterji, see Ayesha Jalal, *Self and Sovereignty: Individual and Community in South Asian Islam Since 1850* (New York: Routledge, 2000), 135–36.

80. Protul Chandra Chatterjee, "A Liberal Helper," in Nadiem, *Sardar Dyal Singh Majithia as Seen by His Contemporaries*, 70.

81. Notes by Assistant General Superintendent, 17th June 1896, Petition from Sardar Dyal Singh Majithia, for permission to adopt a successor to his jagir, refused, K. W. Secret I, August 1896, Nos. 5–21, National Archives of India, New Delhi.

82. A. B. Bernard to H. M. Durand, Police Office, Calcutta, 4th June 1887, Proceedings of Maharaja Dalip Singh.

83. Madhvi Yasin, *British Paramountcy in Kashmir, 1876–1894* (Delhi: Atlantic Publishers, 1984), 63.

84. Bernard to Durand, 4th June 1887.

85. Bernard to Durand, 4th June 1887.

86. Extract from Punjab Police Abstract, September 3rd 1887, Movements of certain emissaries of Maharaja Dalip Singh and Sardar Thakur Singh, and alleged disaffection of a portion of the Native Army, India Office Records R/1/1/67, British Library, London.

87. *Aftab-i-Hind*, 28th August 1886 qtd in Memorandum, 15th June 1887, India Office Records L/P&S/18/D152, British Library, London.

88. Translation of an article in the '*Rahbar-i-Hindi*' newspaper, Lahore, dated May 1887, A Scurrilous Article.

89. Minute by the Lieutenant-Governor of Punjab, J. B. Lyall.

90. Dalip Singh's Case as stated by himself, Memorandum, 15th June 1887.

91. Singh's Case as stated by himself.

92. Extract from the Tribune, Saturday the 11th June 1887, Memorandum, 15th June 1887, India Office Records L/P&S/18/D152, British Library, London.

93. Note by the Secretary to the Government of Punjab, W. M. Young.

94. Minute by the Lieutenant-Governor of Punjab, J. B. Lyall.

95. H. C. Fenshawe to H. S. Barner, Punjab Civil Secretariat, 22nd April 1986, Petition from Sardar Dyal Singh Majithia.

96. Minute by the Lieutenant-Governor of Punjab, J. B. Lyall.

97. Extract from Report on Native Papers for the week ending the 25th June 1887, Seditious Article in the 'Dhumketu' in favor of Maharaja Dalip Singh, India Office Records R/1/1/64, British Library, London.

98. Extract from Report on Native Papers, Seditious Article.

99. H. M. Durand to Viceroy, 4th July 1887, Seditious Article.

100. P. D. Henderson to H. M. Durand, 2nd July 1887, Seditious Article.

101. Durand to Viceroy, 4th July 1887, Seditious Article.

102. Note by the Secretary to the Government of Punjab, W. M. Young.

103. Memorandum, 15th June 1887, India Office Records L/P&S/18/D152, British Library, London.

104. K. W. No. 2: Memorandum, Memo. On the intrigues of Maharaja Dalip Singh, and issue of warrants for the arrest of certain emissaries of His Highness, India Office Records R/1/1/68, British Library.

105. As Harleen Kaur and p.s. kehal correctly recognize, this leads to wounded attachments that do not question the epistemological structure of recovery—repair, renegotiation, and repudiation—that further binds one to the archive. Kaur and kehal, "Epistemic Wounded Attachments: Recovering Definitional Subjectivity through Colonial Libraries," *History and Theory* 62 (2023): 203–24.

106. K. W. No. 2: Memorandum.

107. File Submitted to Chief Secretary, enclosed G. R. Irwin to the Government of Bengal, 4th March 1887, Proceedings of Maharaja Dalip Singh.

108. *Beaver* Office, 2nd April 1887, Memo. On the Intrigues of Maharaja Dalip Singh.

109. K. W. No. 2: Memorandum, Memo. On the Intrigues of Maharaja Dalip Singh.

110. The memorandum notes that Mukherjee was only trying to swindle money out of Duleep Singh for retirement. See K. W. No. 2: Memorandum.

111. Col. P. D. Henderson to H. M. Durand, 22nd August 1887, Proceedings and arrest of Arur Singh *alias* Pertap Singh, an emissary sent by Maharaja Dalip Singh from Moscow, India Office Records R/1/1/65, British Library, London.

112. Re: Arur Singh, Inspector of Calcutta Police, 6th August 1887, Proceedings and arrest of Arur Singh.

113. J. Ware Edgar to H. M. Durand, 7th August 1887, on board Yacht Rhotas, Bhagalpur, Proceedings and arrest of Arur Singh.

114. Confidential Report by A. B. Barnard, Deputy Commissioner of Police, Calcutta, 7th August 1887, Proceedings and arrest of Arur Singh.

115. H. M. Durand to J. Ware Edgar, 10th August 1887, Proceedings and arrest of Arur Singh.

116. Telegram, Thugee to Foreign Secretary, 24th August 1887, Proceedings and arrest of Arur Singh.

117. Henderson to Durand, Proceedings and arrest of Arur Singh. "Peach" is an obsolete term to denote an informant.

118. Major R. B. Burnaby, Commandant, Chunar to His Highness Maharaja Duleep Singh, 8th September 1887, Proceedings and arrest of Arur Singh.

119. Eventually, Aziz-ud-din, a British agent heavily involved in Duleep Singh's surveillance, extracted information from Arur Singh by becoming friends with him. This information was not related to Mukherjee but was tied to the Native States and their relation to intrigue.

120. Colonel P. D. Henderson to Sir J. Ware Edgar, November 12th 1889, Arrest of Abdul Rasul, an Emissary of Maharaja Dalip Singh and his detention under Regulation III of 1818, K. W. Secret I, March 1890, Nos. 19–41, National Archives of India, New Delhi.

121. J. Lambert, Deputy Commissioner of Police, Calcutta to Chief Secretary to the Government of Bengal, 30th November 1889, Arrest of Abdul Rasul.

122. Private Secretary to the Governor-General, 11th August, 1887, Proceedings and arrest of Arur Singh.

123. A. B. Barnard to H. M. Durand, 13th September 1887, Enquiries Made By A Person From Pondicherry Regarding Arur Singh, an Emissary of Dalip Singh, K. W. Secret I, December 1887, Nos. 32–34, National Archives of India, New Delhi.

124. Arondekar, *For the Record*, 12.

125. Demi-Official from Colonel W. I. Bax, Commanding, 11th Bengal Lancers to Major-General W. K. Elles, CB, Adjutant-General, 11th June 1887, Proceedings of Maharaja Dalip.

126. Gayatri Chakravorty Spivak, *In Other Worlds: Essays in Cultural Politics* (New York: Routledge, 1987), 214.

3. CONVERSION

1. Jacques Rancière, *Proletarian Nights: The Workers' Dream in Nineteenth-Century France*, trans. John Drury (London: Verso, 2012), 11.

2. Slavoj Žižek argues, for example, "the subject itself is nothing but the failure of symbolization, of its own symbolic representation." See Žižek, "Class Struggle or Postmodernism?: Yes, Please!" in *Contingency, Hegemony, Universality: Contemporary Dialogues on the Left*, ed. Judith Butler, Ernesto Laclau, and Slavoj Žižek (London: Verso, 2000), 120.

3. The point is not to make Oedipus the crucial premise or harnessing Duleep Singh to the yoke of an originary absence. For this critique, see Gilles Deleuze and Felix Guattari, *Anti-Oedipus: Capitalism and Schizophrenia*, trans. Robert Hurley, Mark Sem, and Helen R. Lane (Minneapolis: University of Minnesota Press, 2003), 45–50.

4. Slavoj Žižek, as quoted in Adrian Johnson, *Žižek's Ontology: A Transcendental Materialist Theory of Subjectivity* (Evanston, IL: Northwestern University Press, 2008), 42. See Joan Copjec, *Imagine There's No Woman: Ethics and Sublimation* (Cambridge, MA: MIT Press, 2004), 93.

5. Slavoj Žižek, *How To Read Lacan* (New York: W. W. Norton, 2007), 34. Žižek, however, cautions us to not locate the Real as the numinous, since "the Real is not the external In-itself that eludes the symbolic grasp, that the symbolic can only encircle in an inconsistent and antinomic way; the Real is nothing but the gap or antagonism that thwarts the symbolic from within—the symbolic touches the Real in a totally immanent way. We are thus led back to the key paradox of the Real: it is not the inaccessible In-itself, it is simultaneously the Thing-in-itself and the obstacle which prevents our access to the Thing-in-itself." The absent center, the Real, then is not simply excluded from symbolic coordinates as an inaccessibility. Rather, the Real is "an effect of the symbolic, not in the sense of performativity, of the 'symbolic construction of reality,' but in the totally different sense of a kind of ontological 'collateral damage' of symbolic operations: the process of symbolization is inherently thwarted, doomed to fail, and the Real is this immanent failure of the symbolic. The circular temporality of the process of symbolization is crucial here: the Real is the effect of the failure of the symbolic to reach (not the In-itself, but) itself, to fully realize itself, but this failure occurs because the symbolic is thwarted in itself" (959). For more, see Slavoj Žižek, *Less Than Nothing: Hegel and the Shadow of Dialectical Materialism* (London: Verso, 2012). Or, as Adrian Johnston succinctly notes, there is "a constant, continual process of reciprocal modification [that] links disparate orders/registers," creating a tethering that never allows for subjectivity to achieve "a self-relating autonomy in relation to its ontological underbelly." Adrian Johnston, *Žižek's Ontology: A Transcendental Materialist Theory of Subjectivity* (Evanston, IL: Northwestern University Press, 2008), 274.

6. Michael Taussig, *Shamanism, Colonialism, and the Wild Man: A Study in Terror and Healing* (Chicago: University of Chicago Press, 1987), 121. Taussig notes that although "terror thrives on the production epistemic murk" it all requires "hermeneutic violence, that creates feeble fictions in the guise of realism, objectivity, and the like, flattening contradiction and systemizing chaos" (132).

7. Michel Foucault, "Nietzsche, Genealogy, History," in *Aesthetics, Method, and Epistemology*, ed. James D. Faubion (New York: New Press, 1998), 371. It is important to note that I follow Asad's revision of Foucault through Alasdair MacIntyre so as not to deny the foundational unity of the Sikh tradition. This is productive tension within Asad's work. For more, see Asad, "The Trouble of Thinking: An Interview with Talal Asad," in *Powers of the Secular Modern: Talal Asad and His Interlocutors*, ed. David Scott and Charles Hirschkind (Stanford, CA: Stanford University Press, 2006), 243–303. Asad further considers these questions in *Secular Translations: Nation-State, Modern Self, and Calculative Reason* (New York: Columbia University Press, 2018).

8. Taussig, *Shamanism, Colonialism, and the Wild Man*, 121.

9. Whereas conversion marks a movement between positions, as Daniel Colucciello Barber writes, reversion signals a rejection of the dualism central to conversion. Barber, "The Immanent Refusal of Conversion," *Journal for Cultural and Religious Theory* 13, no. 1 (2014): 149.

10. Charles Taylor, *Philosophical Arguments* (Cambridge, MA: Harvard University Press, 1995), 228.

11. Peter van der Veer, "Introduction," in *Conversion to Modernities: The Globalization of Christianity*, ed. Peter van der Veer (New York: Routledge, 1996), 6.

12. Talal Asad, "Comments on Conversion," in van der Veer, *Conversion to Modernities*, 263.

13. Gurinder Singh Mann, for example, notes the innovation of *pahul* in the Sikh tradition was "marked by humility and spirit of warm welcome toward those who decided to join the Sikh community" (495). See Gurinder Singh Mann, "Conversion to Sikhism," in *The Oxford Handbook of Religious Conversion*, ed. Lewis R. Rambo and Charles E. Farhadian (Oxford: Oxford University Press, 2014).

14. For this form of religiosity and the disciplinary regime it entailed after the Reformation, see Wolfgang Reinhard, "Reformation, Counter-Reformation, and the Early Modern State a Reassessment," *Catholic Historical Review* 75, no. 3 (1989): 383–404; Ronnie Po-Chia Hsia, *Social Discipline in the Reformation: Central Europe, 1550–1750* (London: T. J. Press, 1989); and Talal Asad, *Genealogies of Religion: Discipline and Reasons of Power in Christianity and Islam* (Baltimore: Johns Hopkins University Press, 1993).

15. Barber, "The Immanent Refusal of Conversion."

16. For example, Kapur Singh writes, *Sikhi* "does assert that the basic sickness of the human soul arises out of its individuation, its involution, and descent from the universal Spirit" (61). This descent, however, is not a dualism; rather, as Kapur Singh continues, "Sikhism, while accepting that the personal aspect of the absolute reality is singular, declares this Person to be the Universal Mind of which all other finite minds are but emanations. These finite minds are at each moment one with the Universal Mind, the essence of their finitude being eliminative and not productive. That what makes a mind finite and distinguished from the Universal Mind is, what has been eliminated out of it, and not what has been produced by it. It is this Universal Mind which Sikhism holds as the absolute Reality, and it is from this doctrine that the basic teachings of Sikhism, which essentially aim at the destruction of the self-centredness of the individual mind, arise" (87). See Kapur Singh, *Me Judice* (Amritsar: B. Chattar Singh Jiwan Singh, 2003).

17. Naindeep Singh Chann, "Rahit Literature," in *Brill's Encyclopedia of Sikhism Online*, ed. Knut A. Jacobsen et al. (Leiden: Brill, 2017), 183–91. This shift away from practices occurs once private belief becomes hegemonic, which creates conditions where, as Talal Asad writes, "the concept of *practices* was partly subordinated to the concept of *propositions*" (276). Asad, "Comments on Conversion."

18. Guru Granth Sahib, 555. I invoke such a reading not to deny the unity of the Sikh tradition but to consider organization of difference outside the logic of inner and outer that *Sikhi* asks us to question. Metaphors about the failure of a checklist or maps to discover enlightenment and redemption, central teachings prior to *Sikhi*, are challenged by the Guru Granth Sahib.

19. Arvind-Pal Singh Mandair, "Shabad (Word)," in *Sikhism: Encyclopedia of Indian Religions*, ed. Arvind-Pal Singh Mandair (Dordrecht: Springer, 2017), https://link .springer.com/referenceworkentry/10.1007/978-94-024-0846-1_486.

20. Karl Marx, "Chapter 1: The Commodity," in *Capital: A Critique of Political Economy, Volume 1*, trans. Ben Fowkes (New York: Penguin Books, 1976), 125–77.

21. Tony Ballantyne, *Between Colonialism and Diaspora: Sikh Cultural Formations in an Imperial World* (Durham, NC: Duke University Press, 2006), 93.

22. Asad, "Comments on Conversion," 265.

23. Memorandum, 15th June 1887, India Office Records L/P&S/18/D152, British Library, London.

24. Extract from Abstract of Political Intelligence, Punjab Police, No. 18, dated the 8th May 1886, Intention of Maharaja Dhulip Singh to visit India, his temporary resistance at Aden, and subsequent return to Europe, Foreign Department Secret I, June 1886, Nos. 12–196, National Archives of India, New Delhi.

25. Memorandum, 15th June 1887.

26. Memorandum, 15th June 1887.

27. Extract from Abstract of Political Intelligence, Punjab Police, No. 11, dated the 20th March 1886.

28. Partha Chatterjee, "Women and the Nation," in *The Nation and Its Fragments: Colonial and Postcolonial Histories* (Princeton, NJ: Princeton University Press, 1993), and Lata Mani, *Contentious Traditions: The Debate on Sati in Colonial India* (Berkeley: University of California Press, 1998).

29. Enclosure No. 1, Memo. On the intrigues of Maharaja Dalip Singh, and issue of warrants for the arrest of certain emissaries of His Highness, India Office Records R/1/1/68, British Library, London.

30. Enclosure No. 3, Memo. On the intrigues of Maharaja Dalip Singh.

31. "Letter from Lord Dalhousie to Sir George Couper, 3rd March 1851," in *Private Letters of Marquess of Dalhousie*, ed. J. G. A. Baird (London: William Blackwood and Sons, 1910), 156.

32. Minute by the Honourable J. Lowis, 14th September 1853, Proceedings of Maharaja Dalip Singh, his advances to Russia, and feeling in the army and Native States regarding him, India Office Records R/1/1/62, British Library, London.

33. C. Grant to Sir C. Aitchison, 7th August 1883, in Objections to Maharaja Dhulip Singh's Proposal to Visit India, Foreign Department Secret I, December 1883, Nos. 8–17, National Archives of India, New Delhi. As we saw in chapter 1, however, the colonial state remained fearful at the unpredictability embedded within the community.

34. Extract from a letter from Colonel Bonness Fischer, British Consular Agent, Pondicherry, dated 5th March 1887 in Movements of Sardar Thakur Singh Sindhanwalia, an agent of Maharaja Dalip Singh, K. W. Secret I, August 1887, Nos. 15–51, National Archives of India, New Delhi.

35. Gauri Viswanathan, *Outside the Fold: Conversion, Modernity, and Belief* (Princeton, NJ: Princeton University Press, 1998), 14.

36. Enclosure No. 3, Memo. On the intrigues of Maharaja Dalip Singh.

37. Rupa Viswanath, "The Emergence of Authenticity Talk and the Giving of Accounts: Conversion as Movement of the Soul in South India, ca. 1900," *Comparative Studies in Society and History* 55, no. 1 (2013): 120–41.

38. For a brilliant review that challenges attempts to determine modern from traditional, see Talal Asad, "Politics and Religion in Islamic Reform: A Critique of Kedouries's Afgani and Abduh," *Review of Middle East Studies* 2 (1976): 13–22.
39. Extract from Abstract of Political Intelligence, Punjab Police, No. 18, dated the 8th May 1886.
40. Catherine Hall, *Civilising Subjects: Metropole and Colony in the English Imagination 1830–1867* (Chicago: University of Chicago Press, 2002), 92.
41. Jean Comaroff and John Comaroff, *Of Revelation and Revolution: Christianity, Colonialism, and Consciousness in South Africa* (Chicago: University of Chicago Press, 1991), 1:251, 245.
42. Asad, "Comments on Conversion," 264–65. See also Viswanath, "Emergence of Authenticity Talk."
43. Asad, "Comments on Conversion," 265.
44. Ruth Marshall, *Political Spiritualities: The Pentecostal Revolution in Nigeria* (Chicago: University of Chicago Press, 2009), 57, 64.
45. Timothy Dobe, *Hindu Christian Faqir: Modern Monks, Global Christianity, and Indian Sainthood* (New York: Oxford University Press, 2015), 105.
46. Viswanathan, *Outside the Fold*, xvi, 17.
47. Viswanathan, *Outside the Fold*, 110, 176.
48. Viswanathan, *Outside the Fold*, 240.
49. Maharaja Duleep Singh to Earl of Kimberley, 11th March 1886, Intention of Maharaja Dhulip Singh to visit India.
50. H. M. Durand to the Viceroy, April 14th, 1886, Intention of Maharaja Dhulip Singh to visit India.
51. C. L. Tupper to H. M. Durand, 6th October 1885, Intention of Maharaja Dhulip Singh to visit India.
52. C. L. Tupper to H. M. Durand, 12th October 1885, Intention of Maharaja Dhulip Singh to visit India.
53. Tupper to Durand, 12th October 1885.
54. Confession of Jawala Singh, son of Desa Singh, caste Jhiwar, age 52 years of Raja Sansi in the Amritsar District in Memo. On the intrigues of Maharaja Dalip Singh.
55. Extract from Abstract of Political Intelligence, Punjab Police, No. 16, dated the 24th April, 1886, Intention of Maharaja Dhulip Singh to visit India.
56. Memorandum, 15th June 1887.
57. Michel de Certeau, *The Practice of Everyday Life*, trans. Steven F. Rendall (Berkeley: University of California Press, 1984), 21, xiv.
58. Saba Mahmood, *Politics of Piety: The Islamic Revival and the Feminist Subject* (Princeton, NJ: Princeton University Press, 2005), 27.
59. Adrian Johnston, *Badiou, Žižek, and Political Transformations: The Cadence of Change* (Evanston, IL: Northwestern University Press, 2008), 110.
60. Edward Pluth, "Against Spontaneity: Badiou, Lacan, and Žižek on the Act," *International Journal of Žižek Studies* 1, no. 2 (2007): 20–21.
61. Peter Gratton, "Change We Can't Believe In: Adrian Johnston on Badiou, Žižek, & Political Transformation," *International Journal of Žižek Studies* 4, no. 3 (2007): 2 and 14. What constitutes an act is a highly contested question. See Slavoj Žižek, *The Ticklish Subject: The Absent Centre of Political Ontology* (London: Verso, 1999); Edward Pluth, *Signifiers and Acts: Freedom in Lacan's Theory of the Subject* (Albany:

SUNY Press, 2007); Johnston, *Badiou, Žižek, and Political Transformations*; Slavoj Žižek, *Less Than Nothing: Hegel and the Shadow of Dialectical Materialism* (London: Verso, 2012).

62. Kapur Singh, *Pārāśarapraśna: The Baisakhi of Guru Gobind Singh* (Amritsar: Guru Nanak Dev University, 2001), 48.

63. Puran Singh, *Spirit of the Sikh: Part II Volume Two* (Patiala: Publication Bureau Punjabi University, Patiala, 2017), 256.

64. Puran Singh, *The Book of Ten Masters* (Patiala: Patiala Punjabi University, Patiala Publication Bureau, 1981), 117.

65. Extract from Abstract of Political Intelligence, Punjab Police No. 18, 8th May 1886, Intention of Maharaja Dhulip Singh to visit India.

66. The state noted "(I) Sardar Thakur Singh Sindhanwalia; (2) Sardar Gurbachan Singh, his son (3) Sardar Narinder Singh, another son of Sardar Thakur Singh (4) Sardar Bakshish Singh, (5) Partab Singh; (6) Parohit Harkishen Das; (7) Harnam Singh, Granthi; (8) Hira Singh; (9) Jamiat Rai," National Archives of India, Foreign Department Secret I, June 1886, Nos. 12–196.

67. Kapur Singh, *Pārāśarapraśna*, 278, 279.

68. Puran Singh, *Spirit of the Sikh*, 100.

69. Memorandum, 15th June 1887.

70. I follow Taussig, who notes how though the shaman in his context is woven into a "colonial construction of determinism's Otherness in which savagery and racism are tightly knotted," this very Otherness is "mobilized in creative deployments" which produce opportunity through a transcription "into a domain of chance and perhapsness." This "domain of chance foregrounds the epistemic murk of sorcery where contradiction and ambiguity in social relations undermine his steadfastness in a weltering of signs cracking the divine and the natural apart from one another and into images from which . . . obtuse meaning erupts into play." Taussig, *Shamanism, Colonialism, and the Wild Man*, 465.

71. Memorandum, 15th June 1887.

72. Extract from Abstract of Political Intelligence, Punjab Police, No. 12. March 27th 1886, Intention of Maharaja Dhulip Singh to visit India.

73. For example, see Neeladri Bhattacharya, "Remaking Custom: The Discourse and Practice of Colonial Codification," in *Tradition, Ideology and Dissent: Essays in Honour of Romila Thapar*, ed. R. Champakalakshmi and Sarvepalli Gopal (Delhi: Oxford University Press, 1996), and Nicholas Dirks, *The Hollow Crown: The Ethnohistory of an Indian Kingdom* (Cambridge: Cambridge University Press, 1988).

74. Memorandum, 15th June 1887.

75. Telegram May 14th 1886, From Lieutenant-Governor, to Foreign Simla, Intention of Maharaja Dhulip Singh to visit India.

76. Lieutenant-Governor Aitchison, Lahore to Foreign Secretary, Simla, 14th May 1886, Intention of Maharaja Dhulip Singh to visit India.

77. Telegram from Viceroy to Resident at Aden, 8th May 1886, Intention of Maharaja Dhulip Singh to visit India.

78. Telegram from Maharaja Dhulip Singh, Aden to Viceroy at Simla, 12th May 1886, Intention of Maharaja Dhulip Singh to visit India.

79. Telegram from Viceroy to Resident at Aden, 15th May 1886, Intention of Maharaja Dhulip Singh to visit India.

80. Nandini Chatterjee, *The Making of Indian Secularism: Empire, Law and Christianity, 1830–1960* (New York: Palgrave Macmillan, 2011), 78.

81. Telegram from Viceroy to Resident at Aden, 15th May 1886.

82. Telegram from Viceroy to Resident at Aden, 15th May 1886.

83. Brigadier General A. S. T. Hogg at Aden to H. M. Durand, 25th May 1886, Intention of Maharaja Dhulip Singh to visit India.

84. Telegram from Political, Bombay to Foreign, Simla, 10th June 1886, Intention of Maharaja Dhulip Singh to visit India.

85. Extract from Abstract of Political Intelligence No. 25, 3rd July 1886, Intention of Maharaja Dhulip Singh to visit India.

86. Memorandum, 15th June 1887.

87. Memorandum, 15th June 1887.

88. W. Mackworth Young to H. M. Durand, 31st May 1886, Intention of Maharaja Dhulip Singh to visit India. The preceding quotation is also from this source.

89. Puran Singh, *Spirit of the Sikh*, 256–58.

90. Marx, *Capital*, 163–77.

91. Slavoj Žižek, *The Sublime Object of Ideology* (London: Verso, 1989), 26.

92. Memorandum, 15th June 1887.

93. W. Coldstream to Elsmie, 28th November 1885, Intention of Maharaja Dhulip Singh to visit India.

94. Extract from Abstract of Political Intelligence, Punjab Police No. 18, 8th May 1886, Intention of Maharaja Dhulip Singh to visit India.

95. Žižek, *Sublime Object of Ideology*, 51.

96. Tsing writes about how *matsutake* "begins and ends its life as a gift," for example. Anna Tsing, *The Mushroom at the End of the World* (Princeton, NJ: Princeton University Press, 2015), 128.

97. C. A. Bayly, "The Origins of Swadeshi (Home Industry): Cloth and Indian Society, 1700–1930," in *The Social Life of Things: Commodities in Cultural Perspective*, ed. Arjun Appadurai (Cambridge: Cambridge University Press, 1986), 285–321.

98. Jacques Derrida, *Specters of Marx: The State of Debt, the Work of Mourning and the New International*, trans. Peggy Kamuf (New York: Routledge, 1994), 151.

99. Appadurai, *The Social Life of Things*, 13, 57, 22.

100. Memorandum, 15th June 1887.

101. Colonel P. D. Henderson to Foreign Secretary, 10th June 1887 in Proceedings of Maharaja Dalip Singh, his advances to Russia, and feeling in the army and Native States regarding him, India Office Records R/1/1/62, British Library, London.

102. Memorandum, 15th June 1887.

103. G. R. Irwin to Under-Secretary, 7th July 1888, Proceedings of Maharaja Dalip Singh and his arrival at Paris, India Office Records R/1/1/90, British Library, London.

104. Note on 6th September 1888, Proceedings of Maharaja Dalip Singh and his arrival at Paris.

105. We must recall, as Yarimar Bonilla argues, that "disappointment proves that apathy has not settled in." Bonilla, *Non-Sovereign Futures: French Caribbean Politics in the Wake of Disenchantment* (Chicago: University of Chicago Press, 2015), 172.

4. RUMORS

1. Ranajit Guha, *Elementary Aspects of Peasant Insurgency in Colonial India* (Durham, NC: Duke University Press, 1999), 13.

2. Allen Feldman, "Violence and Vision: The Prosthetics and Aesthetics of Terror," *Public Culture* 10, no. 1 (1997): 29.

3. James C. Scott, *Domination and the Arts of Resistance: Hidden Transcripts* (New Haven, CT: Yale University Press, 1990), 151–52.

4. Guha, *Elementary Aspects of Peasant Insurgency*, 253, 257, 259.

5. Guha, *Elementary Aspects of Peasant Insurgency*, 260.

6. Gayatri Chakravorty Spivak, *In Other Worlds: Essay In Cultural Politics* (New York: Routledge, 1988), 213, 215. Jacques Derrida, too, notes that privileging speech functions "to confine writing to a secondary and instrumental function: translator of a full speech that was fully present (present to itself, to its signified, to the other, to the very condition of the theme of presence in general)." Derrida, *Of Grammatology*, trans. Gayatri Chakravorty Spivak (Baltimore: Johns Hopkins University Press, 1997), 8.

7. Spivak, *In Other Worlds*, 254.

8. Guha, *Elementary Aspects of Peasant Insurgency*, 264.

9. Luise White, *Speaking with Vampires: Rumor and History in Colonial Africa* (Berkeley: University of California Press, 2000), 83, 85.

10. Homi Bhabha, *Location of Culture* (New York: Routledge, 1994), 207.

11. Talal Asad, *Genealogies of Religion: Discipline and Reasons of Power in Christianity and Islam* (Baltimore: Johns Hopkins University Press, 1993), 210.

12. Bhabha, *Location of Culture*, 210.

13. Jennifer Wenzel, *Bulletproof: Afterlives of Anticolonial Prophecy in South Africa and Beyond* (Chicago: University of Chicago Press, 2009), 3.

14. Richard Fox, *Lions of the Punjab: Culture in the Making* (Berkeley: University of California, 1985), 13.

15. Copy of a Letter from Duleep Singh to Ketkoff, Proceedings of Maharaja Dalip Singh, his advances to Russia, and feeling in the army and Native States regarding him, India Office Records R/1/1/62, British Library, London.

16. Extract from Political Abstract of Intelligence, Punjab Police, No. 3, 22nd January 1887, Proceedings of Maharaja Dalip Singh, his advances to Russia, and feeling in the army and Native States regarding him, India Office Records R/1/1/62, British Library, London.

17. Sir R. B. Morier, Her Majesty's Ambassador at St. Petersburgh to the Marquis of Salisbury, K.G., Secretary of State for Foreign Affairs, September 20th, 1887, Proceedings of Maharaja Duleep Singh at Moscow, K. W. Secret I, December 1883, Nos. 8–17; Foreign Department K. W. Secret I, January 1888, Nos. 8–13, National Archives of India, New Delhi.

18. Mark Condos, *The Insecurity State: Punjab and the Making of Colonial Power in British India* (Cambridge: Cambridge University Press, 2017), 69.

19. India Office Records L/P&S/18/D152. For more on the Kukas historically, see Fauja Singh, *Kuka Movement: An Important Phase in Punjab's Role in India's Struggle for Freedom* (Delhi: Motilal Banarsidass, 1965) and, in the present, see Joginder

Singh, *The Namdhari Sikhs: Their Changing Social and Cultural Landscape* (Delhi: Manohar, 2013).

20. *Bhogs* are the end ceremonies of the *akhand* paths, which is the continuous reading of the *granth* (Sikh scriptures) from beginning to end. Memorandum, 15th June 1887, India Office Records L/P&S/18/D152, British Library, London.

21. Memorandum, 15th June 1887.

22. Memorandum, 15th June 1887. Ram Singh, the founder of the Namdhari sect, was the first to engage in such boycotts in the South Asian subcontinent against colonial rule, although in this reading Orthodox Khalsa Sikhs are involved as well.

23. Guha, *Elementary Aspects of Peasant Insurgency*, 258.

24. Dipesh Chakrabarty, *Habitations of Modernity: Essays in the Wake of Subaltern Studies* (Chicago: University of Chicago Press, 2002).

25. Sudipta Sen, *Empire of Free Trade: The East India Company and the Making of the Colonial Marketplace* (Philadelphia: University of Pennsylvania Press, 1998), 119.

26. Chakrabarty, *Habitations of Modernity*, 76.

27. Guha, *Elementary Aspects of Peasant Insurgency,* 258–259.

28. Memorandum, 15th June 1887.

29. C. L. Tupper To H. M. Durand, Lahore, December 12th, 1885, Intention of Maharaja Dhulip Singh to visit India, his temporary resistance at Aden, and subsequent return to Europe, Foreign Department Secret I, June 1886, Nos. 12–196, National Archives of India, New Delhi.

30. Memorandum, 15th June 1887.

31. These are different modes of expression, and I do not mean to collapse their distinction.

32. Joginder Singh, "Namdhari Sikhs of Punjab: Historical Profile," *Journal of Punjab Studies* 21, no. 2 (2014): 274.

33. Michael Nijhawan, *Dhadi Darbar: Religion, Violence, and the Performance of Sikh History* (Delhi: Oxford University Press, 2006), 100. Nijhawan reminds us that this interpretative creativity against submission to a religious tradition is not to "let the notion of free will and rational choice enter through the backdoor, simply because this would be required for writing a coherent historiography according to the principles of Enlightenment discourse."

34. Memorandum, 15th June 1887. The *barah mah* is reprinted in full form in Jaswinder Singh, *Kuka Movement: Freedom Struggle in Punjab* (New Delhi: Atlantic Publishers and Distributors, 1985), 296–308.

35. I borrow this from Frank Ruda, *Abolishing Freedom: A Plea for a Contemporary Use of Fatalism* (Lincoln: University of Nebraska Press, 2016), 10.

36. Memorandum, 15th June 1887.

37. Memorandum, 15th June 1887.

38. Bishen Singh, Arora of Kabul, Kuka Suba, Gurcharn Singh's Reported Intention to Go to Central Asia, Memorandum on Russian Intrigues in India, Foreign Department Secret F, August 1889, Nos. 114–115, National Archives of India, New Delhi.

39. Bishen Singh, Gurcharn Singh's Reported Intention.

40. Bishen Singh, Gurcharn Singh's Reported Intention.

41. Bishen Singh, Gurcharn Singh's Reported Intention.

42. This understanding allows us to consider how, as Virinder Kalra argues "the dhadi tradition went from being a heteroreligious form to being closely concomitant with Sikhs" without positing loss and a search for whispers (133). For this heteroreligious approach, see Varinder Kalra, *Sacred and Secular Musics: A Postcolonial Approach* (London: Bloomsbury, 2015). The second quotation is at 65.

43. Farina Mir, *The Social Space of Language: Vernacular Culture in British Colonial Punjab* (Berkeley: University of California Press, 2010), 120.

44. Memorandum, 15th June 1887.

45. Mir, *The Social Space of Language*, 25.

46. Memorandum, 15th June 1887.

47. Ann Laura Stoler, "'In Cold Blood': Hierarchies of Credibility and the Politics of Colonial Narratives," *Representations* 37 (1992): 182.

48. Secretary's Note, H. M. Durand 4th July 1887, Proceedings of Maharaja Dalip Singh, his advances to Russia, and feeling in the army and Native States regarding him, India Office Records R/1/1/62, British Library, London.

49. Memorandum, 15th June 1887.

50. Memorandum by Munshi Aziz-ud-din, Derah Dun, April 9th, 1887, Proceedings of Maharaja Dalip Singh.

51. Parama Roy, *Indian Traffic: Identities in Question in Colonial and Postcolonial India* (Berkeley: University of California Press, 1998), 31.

52. H. M. Durand to Colonel Sir E. R. C. Bradford, May 2nd, 1887, Proceedings of Maharaja Dalip Singh.

53. Colonel P. D. Henderson to the Foreign Secretary, 11th June 1887, Proceedings of Maharaja Dalip Singh.

54. Roy, *Indian Traffic*, 31.

55. Simanti Dutta, *Imperial Mappings in Savage Spaces: Baluchistan and British India* (Delhi: B. R. Publishing Corporation, 2002), 41.

56. Minute by His Honor the Lieutenant-Governor of Punjab, J. B. Lyall, 18th June 1887, India Office Records L/P&S/18/D152, British Library, London.

57. Mrinalini Sinha, *Colonial Masculinity: The "Manly Englishman" and "The Effeminate Bengali" in the Late Nineteenth Century* (New York: St. Martin's Press, 1995).

58. Minute by the Lieutenant-Governor of Punjab, 18th June 1887.

59. Minute by the Lieutenant-Governor of Punjab, 18th June 1887.

60. Minute by the Lieutenant-Governor of Punjab, 18th June 1887.

61. Minute by the Lieutenant-Governor of Punjab, 18th June 1887.

62. Minute by the Lieutenant-Governor of Punjab, 18th June 1887.

63. I follow Mahmood Mamdani's distinction in the present day in *Good Muslim, Bad Muslim: America, the Cold War, and the Roots of Terror* (New York: Doubleday, 2004). I borrow an atrophying information order from Parama Roy, *Alimentary Tracts: Appetites, Aversions, and the Postcolonial* (Durham, NC: Duke University Press, 2010), 52.

64. Minute by the Lieutenant-Governor of Punjab, 18th June 1887.

65. Arjun Appadurai, *Modernity At Large: Cultural Dimensions of Globalization* (Minneapolis: University of Minnesota Press, 1996), 76.

66. Minute by the Lieutenant-Governor of Punjab, 18th June 1887.

67. Condos, *The Insecurity State*, 179.

68. Memorandum, 15th June 1887.

69. Spivak, *In Other Worlds*, 213.

70. Memorandum, 15th June 1887.

71. Memorandum, 15th June 1887.

72. Extract from Political Abstract of Intelligence, Proceedings of Maharaja Dalip Singh.

73. Homi Bhabha, "In a Spirit of Calm Violence," in *After Colonialism: Imperial Histories and Postcolonial Displacements*, ed. Gyan Prakash (Princeton, NJ: Princeton University Press, 1995), 334. Earlier, I cited *Location of Culture*, and within it the essay "By Bread Alone: Signs of Violence in the Mid-Nineteenth Century." There are minor differences in the two texts.

74. C. L. Tupper to H. M. Durand, Lahore, December 12th, 1885, Intention of Maharaja Dhulip Singh to visit India, his temporary resistance at Aden, and subsequent return to Europe, Foreign Department Secret I, June 1886, Nos. 12–196, National Archives of India, New Delhi.

75. Memorandum, 15th June 1887.

76. Extract from Political Abstract of Intelligence, Proceedings of Maharaja Dalip Singh.

77. Roy, *Alimentary Tracts*, 33.

78. Tupper to Durand, Lahore, December 12th, 1885.

79. Spivak, *In Other Worlds*, 213.

80. Bhabha, *Location of Culture*, 200.

81. Bhabha, *Location of Culture*, 207.

82. Ashis Nandy, "Oppression and Human Liberation: Towards a Third World Utopia," *Alternatives* 4, no. 2 (1978): 179.

83. Talal Asad, "The Idea of an Anthropology of Islam," *Occasional Paper Series* (Washington, DC: Georgetown University Center for Contemporary Arab Studies, 1986), and Alasdair C. MacIntyre, *After Virtue: A Study in Moral Theory* (Notre Dame, IN: University of Notre Dame Press, 1981), 222.

84. Omnia El Shakry, "Rethinking Arab Intellectual History: Epistemology, Historicism, Secularism," *Modern Intellectual History* 18, no. 2 (2021): 564.

85. See Rajbir Singh Judge, "There Is No Colonial Relationship: Antagonism, Sikhism, and South Asian Studies" *History and Theory* 57, no. 2 (June 2018): 193–215.

86. Ashis Nandy, "History's Forgotten Doubles," *History and Theory* 34, no. 2 (1995): 66.

87. Nandy, "History's Forgotten Doubles," 66.

88. Extract from Political Abstract of Intelligence, Punjab Police, No. 34, dated the 4th September 1886, Rumoured Recruitment of Sikhs for the Russian Army, Foreign Department, Secret F September 1887, Nos. 1–7, National Archives of India, New Delhi.

89. Memorandum, 15th June 1887.

90. Spivak, *In Other Worlds*, 213.

91. All quotations in this paragraph are from Memorandum, 15th June 1887.

92. All quotations in this paragraph are from Memorandum, 15th June 1887.

93. Memorandum, 15th June 1887.

94. Memorandum, 15th June 1887.

95. Memorandum, 15th June 1887.
96. *The Pioneer*, "Thursday, the 1st July 1886," in Objections of Her Majesty's Agent and Consul-General, Egypt to Maharaja Dhalip Singh Visiting Egypt, Foreign Department. K. W. Secret-I, August 1886, Nos. 15–19, National Archives of India, New Delhi.
97. Extract from Political Abstract of Intelligence, Proceedings of Maharaja Dalip Singh.
98. Memorandum, 15th June 1887; Extract from Political Abstract of Intelligence, 19th February 1887, Proceedings of Maharaja Dalip Singh.

5. REFORM

1. Harbans Singh, *The Heritage of the Sikhs* (New Delhi: Manohar, 1983), 210.
2. Kenneth W. Jones, *Socio-Religious Reform Movements in British India* (Cambridge: Cambridge University Press, 1989), 109.
3. Jagjit Singh. *Singh Sabha Lehar* (Amritsar: Guru Ramdas Printing Press, 1941), 13. Singh writes: "Sikh dharm di asli maryada kaaim karna si." We can then conceptualize this as an attempt to institute a limit through the very constitution of a border, a riverbank, in relation to *naam*.
4. Harjot Oberoi, *The Construction of Religious Boundaries: Culture, Identity, and Diversity in the Sikh Tradition* (Chicago: University of Chicago Press, 1994), 296.
5. Norman Gerald Barrier, *The Sikhs and their Literature: A Guide to Tracts, Books and Periodicals, 1849–1919* (Delhi: Manohar Book Service, 1970), xxv. For example, *The Tribune*, on February 16, 1881, reported, "It is said that the Singh Sabha at Umritsur has been split into different sections on account of the religious difference which exists among its Sikh Members."
6. Teja Singh, "The Singh Sabha Movement," in *The Singh Sabha and Other Socio-Religious Movements in the Punjab,1850–1925*, ed. Ganda Singh (Patiala: Publication Bureau Punjabi University, Patiala, 1997), 32.
7. It is, of course, as Partha Chatterjee writes, "hardly surprising to discover that the ideology which shaped and gave meaning to the various collective acts of the peasantry was fundamentally *religious*" (31). Partha Chatterjee, "Agrarian Relations and Communalism in Bengal, 1926–1935," in *Subaltern Studies I: Writings on South Asian History and Society*, ed. Ranajit Guha (New Delhi: Oxford University Press, 1982), 9–38.
8. The literature is vast. For example, see Jones, *Socio-Religious Reform Movements*, and Bernard Cohn, "The Census, Social Structure and Objectification in South Asia," in *An Anthropologist Among the Historians and Other Essays* (Delhi: Oxford University Press, 1987), 224–54.
9. For a heterogenous past in Punjab, see Farina Mir, *The Social Space of Language: Vernacular Culture in British Colonial Punjab* (Berkeley: University of California Press, 2010); Timothy S. Dobe, *Hindu Christian Faqir: Modern Monks, Global Christianity, and Indian Sainthood* (Oxford: Oxford University Press, 2015); and Anshu Malhotra, *Piro and the Gulabdasis: Gender, Sect, and Society in Punjab* (New Delhi: Oxford University Press, 2017). For an important critique of heterogeneity as an essentialism, see David Scott, *Formations of Ritual: Colonial and*

Anthropological Discourses on the Sinhala Yaktovil (Minneapolis: University of Minnesota Press, 1994), and *Refashioning Futures: Criticism After Postcoloniality* (Princeton, NJ: Princeton University Press, 1999).

10. Oberoi, *The Construction of Religious Boundaries*, 375. Tony Ballantyne is an exception, arguing that we need to pay attention the debates and contestations around Duleep Singh. But, he concludes, "a more detailed assessment of the response to Dalip Singh's life and death could be assembled." This is an attempt toward this assessment. Ballantyne, *Between Colonialism and Diaspora: Sikh Cultural Formations in an Imperial World* (Durham, NC: Duke University Press, 2006), 100.

11. For example, see the Akali agitations that emerged in the 1920s about what constituted the relation between *miri-piri* (spiritual and temporal). In other words, self-governance central to the Akali movement, too, has a long presence within the Sikh tradition as questions of reform in gurdwara management and education remained central to considering the relation between *Sikhi* and the state, the relation between *miri* and *piri*. For a counter-reading, see Richard Fox, *Lions of the Punjab: Culture in the Making* (Berkeley: University of California Press, 1985). Fox argues that it was British colonialism that "set in motion confrontation over cultural meanings and religious organizations between temple managers and Singh reformers, which led reformers to look for converts in the rural areas" (182).

12. Scott, *Formations of Ritual*, xviii.

13. Anand Pandian, "Tradition in Fragments: Inherited Forms and Fractures in the Ethics of South India," *American Ethnologist* 35, no. 3 (2008): 470.

14. Talal Asad, *Genealogies of Religion: Discipline and Reasons of Power in Christianity and Islam* (Baltimore: Johns Hopkins University Press, 1993), 210.

15. Kapur Singh, "The Church and the State," in *Pārāśarapraśna: The Baisakhi of Gurgobind Singh*, ed. Piar Singh and Madanjit Kaur (Amritsar: Guru Nanak Dev University, 1989), 192–201.

16. C. S. Adcock, *The Limits of Tolerance: Indian Secularism and the Politics of Religious Freedom* (Oxford: Oxford University Press, 2014), 47. On this shift of tradition in South Asia, see Fox, *Lions of the Punjab*; Vasudha Dalmia, *The Nationalization of Hindu Traditions: Bharatendu Harischandra and Nineteenth Century Banaras* (New Delhi: Oxford University Press, 1997); Richard King, *Orientalism and Religion: Post-Colonial Theory, India and The Mystic East* (New York: Routledge, 1999); Brian K. Pennington, *Was Hinduism Invented? Britons, Indians, and the Colonial Construction of Religion* (Oxford: Oxford University Press, 2005); Teena Purohit, *The Aga Khan Case: Religion and Identity in Colonial India* (Cambridge, MA: Harvard University Press, 2012). For an excellent challenge to this understanding of reform, see Shruti Patel, "Beyond the Lens of Reform: Religious Culture in Modern Gujarat," *Journal of Hindu Studies* 10, no. 1 (2017): 47–85. For an account on how an earlier Sikh past was conceptualized through the trope of reform, which collapsed Sikhism into Hinduism within colonial logics, see Brian Hatcher, "Situating the Swaminarayan Tradition in the Historiography of Modern Hindu Reform," in *Swaminarayan Hinduism: Tradition, Adaptation and Identity*, ed. Raymond Brady Williams and Yogi Trivedi (New Delhi: Oxford University Press, 2016), 6–37.

17. See Singh, *The Heritage of the Sikhs*. See also Gurdarshan Singh Dhillon, "Origin and Development of the Singh Sabha Movement: Constitutional Aspects," in *The*

Singh Sabha and Other Socio-Religious Movements in the Punjab,1850–1925, ed. Ganda Singh (Patiala: Publication Bureau Punjabi University, Patiala, 1997), 45–58. Reform implies this very notion. As Brian Pennington argues, "the idea of reform functions by means of an idiom of return or correction. Reform implies a tradition gone astray, one that must be directed back into the channels of its original inspiration" (155). Pennington, "Reform and Revival, Innovation and Enterprise A Tale of Modern Hinduism," in *The Protestant Reformation in a Context of Global History Religious Reforms and World Civilizations*, ed. Heinz Schilling and Silvana Seidel Menchi (Berlin: Duncker & Humblot, 2017), 149–69.

18. Oberoi, *Construction of Religious Boundaries*; Arvind-Pal Mandair, *Religion and the Specter of the West: Sikhism, India, Postcoloniality, and the Politics of Translation* (New York: Columbia University Press, 2013).

19. Though perfectibility is located in a now past *Sikhi*, the goal remains to accelerate toward a future expectation broken from present experience. Put differently, this is a temporality without limit, a promise of rupture. See Reinhart Koselleck, *Futures Past: On the Semantics of Historical Time*, trans. Keith Tribe (New York: Columbia University Press, 2004). This desire to recover what is now lost to provide an authentic historical representation remains a central historiographical thrust in Sikh Studies. To give one example, Arvind Mandair argues we must break out of the ontotheological schema to inaugurate a new moment. My concern is with the very impossibility of such authenticity. See Mandair, *Religion and the Specter of the West*.

20. Harbans Singh, "Origin of the Singh Sabha," in *The Singh Sabha and Other Socio-Religious Movements in the Punjab,1850–1925*, ed. Ganda Singh (Patiala: Publication Bureau Punjabi University, Patiala, 1997), 30.

21. Nripinder Singh, *The Sikh Moral Tradition* (Delhi: Manohar, 2008), 269.

22. Oberoi, *Construction of Religious Boundaries*, 32, 33, 315, 25.

23. As Samira Haj writes in relation to reform in the Islamic tradition, "Various actors failed to carry out their 'prescribed' roles as reformers or as traditionalists" because "the actors involved in responding to day-to-day realities on the ground found themselves shifting positions that in many ways defied simply causal explanations." Haj, *Reconfiguring Islamic Tradition: Reform, Rationality, and Modernity* (Stanford, CA: Stanford University Press, 2008), 186–87. In a contrasting theoretical approach, Murphy argues, "Reform as a whole was also a colonial project" (151). Murphy, "The Formation of the Ethical Sikh Subject in the Era of British Colonial Reform," *Sikh Formations* 11, nos. 1–2 (2015): 149–59. Or consider the work of Mandair. He writes: Trumpp's translation functioned to "demarcate conceptual boundaries for the study of Sikhism" that provided a "framework that interpreters could contest but never remain outside of" (191–92). In the latter approaches, cause and effect are neatly demarcated. See Mandair, *Religion and the Specter of the West*.

24. Talal Asad, *Secular Translations: Nation-State, Modern Self, and Calculative Reason* (New York: Columbia University Press, 2018), 95. James Laidlaw, in relation to the Jain tradition, too, notes how people "hold values which are in irreducible conflict," making the task of easily identifying "logical consistency" difficult since it "takes work to create, reproduce, and maintain." Laidlaw, *Riches and Renunciation: Religion, Economy and Society Among the Jains* (Oxford: Oxford University Press, 1995), 22.

25. Talal Asad, *Genealogies of Religion: Discipline and Reasons of Power in Christianity and Islam* (Baltimore: Johns Hopkins University Press, 1993), 210.

26. Anand Pandian, "Tradition in Fragments: Inherited Forms and Fractures in the Ethics of South India," *American Ethnologist* 35, no. 3 (2008), 470. In relation to Islam, SherAli Tareen astutely rejects the utility of such binary constructions that are the products of Western scholarship on Islam. Instead, he argues for a conceptual approach that views rival narratives on the boundaries of religion as competing political theologies. Tareen, *Defending Muhammad in Modernity* (Notre Dame, IN: University of Notre Dame Press, 2020).

27. On learning, I follow Gil Anidjar, who writes: "learning—the deceptively simple task of taking a step toward a knowledge of self or other—does mean exposing oneself to an enormous mass of unknowns. To uncertainty and to incompleteness. Or to denial, and to the possibility of failure. Is there, in fact, a self? And is it ours? Can we really know ourselves?" We should recall here Sikh itself means learner. Anidjar, "Sapientia," *Identities: Journal for Politics, Gender and Culture*, April 14, 2020. https://identitiesjournal.edu.mk/index.php/IJPGC/announcement/view/36.

28. Gil Anidjar, "Homo Discens," *Critical Times* 3, no. 3 (2020): 443–49.

29. See Sigmund Freud, "The Interpretation of Dreams [Second Part] and On Dreams," in *The Standard Edition of the Complete Psychological Works of Sigmund Freud*, vol. 5, ed. and trans. James Strachey (London: Hogarth, 1953). Noting the limits of interpretation, Freud writes, "This is the dream's navel, the spot where it reaches down into the unknown. The dream-thoughts to which we are led by interpretation cannot, from the nature of things, have any definite endings; they are bound to branch out in every direction into the intricate network of our world of thought. It is at some point where this meshwork is particularly close that the dream-wish grows up, like a mushroom out of its mycelium" (525). Said otherwise, there is no final interpretation, no final word to determine an objective essence to a dream. A mushroom itself does not have a seed from where we can trace an origin and, therefore, teleology.

30. Anna Lowenhaupt Tsing, *The Mushroom at the End of the World: On the Possibility of Life in Capitalist Ruins* (Princeton, NJ: Princeton University Press, 2015), 50 and 137.

31. Slavoj Žižek, *Less Than Nothing: Hegel and the Shadow of Dialectical Materialism* (London: Verso, 2012), 467.

32. Talal Asad, "Thinking About Tradition, Religion, and Politics in Egypt Today," *Critical Inquiry* 42, no. 1 (2015): 167.

33. Though there are similarities with J. Barton Scott's notion of a "reform assemblage," which he defines as "an open-ended network of unstable elements" that "operated according to principles of connection, heterogeneity, and multiplicity," my concern is with how this heterogeneity itself was a struggle that created order, created orthodoxy. Scott, *Spiritual Despots: Modern Hinduism and the Genealogies of Self-Rule* (Chicago: University of Chicago Press, 2016), 90.

34. I borrow "framework of inquiry" from Samira Haj. See *Reconfiguring Islamic Tradition*, 4–5.

35. Singh, "The Church and the State," 192–201.

36. For more on Ranjit Singh, see J. S. Grewal, *The Reign of Maharaja Ranjit Singh: Structure of Power, Economy and Society* (Patiala: Punjabi University, 1981), and,

more recently, Sunit Singh, "The Sikh Kingdom," in *The Oxford Handbook of Sikh Studies*, ed. Pashaura Singh and Louis Fenech (Oxford: Oxford University Press, 2014), 59–69. For the difficulties in maintaining the Khalsa Raj and conflicts that arose within, see Priya Atwal, *Royals and Rebels: The Rise and Fall of the Sikh Empire* (Oxford: Oxford University Press, 2020), 74, as well as Kapur Singh, *Me Judice* (Amritsar: B. Chattar Singh Jiwan Singh, 2003), 369. The problem is a broader one, of course. As Partha Chatterjee writes, "the same set of ethical norms or religious practices which justify existing relations of domination also contain, in a single dialectical unity, the justification for legitimate revolt" (338). Chatterjee, "More on Modes of Power and the Peasantry," in *Subaltern Studies II: Writing on South Asian History and Society*, ed. Ranajit Guha (New Delhi: Oxford University Press, 1983), 311–49.

37. I borrow from Shahid Amin, "Gandhi as Mahatma: Gorakhpur District, Eastern UP, 1921–2," in *Subaltern Studies III: Writings on South Asian History and Society* (New Delhi: Oxford University Press, 1984), 55.

38. Omnia El Shakry, *The Great Social Laboratory: Subjects of Knowledge in Colonial and Postcolonial Egypt* (Stanford, CA: Stanford University Press, 2007), 14.

39. Sardar Attar Singh, to Private Secretary to His Honor the Lieutenant-Governor Punjab, August 9th, 1887, Proceedings of Maharaja Dalip Singh, his advances to Russia, and feeling in the army and Native States regarding him. India Office Records R/1/1/62, British Library, London.

40. Hatcher, "Situating the Swaminarayan Tradition," 19. In relation to how martial theory oscillated between loyalty and sedition in relation to Sikhs, see Gajendra Singh, *The Testimonies of Indian Soldiers and the Two World Wars: Between Self and Sepoy* (New York: Bloomsbury, 2014).

41. Memorandum, 15th June 1887, India Office Records L/P&S/18/D152, British Library, London.

42. The literature on the paradoxes of the policy on non-interference is vast; as scholars have noted, its rhetorical force rarely matched its application. For example, Nicholas Dirks, *The Hollow Crown: The Ethnohistory of an Indian Kingdom* (Cambridge: Cambridge University Press, 1988); C. S. Adcock, *The Limits of Tolerance: Indian Secularism and the Politics of Religious Freedom* (New York: Oxford University Press, 2014); Mitra Sharafi, *Law and Identity in Colonial South Asia: Parsi Legal Culture, 1772–1947* (Cambridge: Cambridge University Press, 2014).

43. Mark Condos, *The Insecurity State: Punjab and the Making of Colonial Power in British India* (Cambridge: Cambridge University Press, 2017), 102. For how this was gendered, see Mrinalini Sinha, *Colonial Masculinity: The 'Manly Englishman' and the 'Effeminate Bengali' in the Late Nineteenth Century* (Manchester: Manchester University Press, 1995).

44. Note by the Secretary to the Government of Punjab, W. M. Young 16th June 1887, India Office Records L/P&S/18/D152, British Library, London.

45. Note by W. M. Young.

46. Memorandum, 15th June 1887.

47. Memorandum, 15th June 1887.

48. On the imaginary threat, see Condos, *The Insecurity State*. The recent focus on the colonial state's anxiety, however, have removed the possibility of a subaltern

resistance since the overwrought focus, following C. A. Bayly, is on how religion, rumors, and threats were "more often reflections of the weakness and ignorance of the colonisers than a gauge of hegemony" (143). This reading can reduce attempts to organize against colonial rule as apparitions in colonial minds. See C. A. Bayly, *Empire and Information: Intelligence Gathering and Social Communication in India, 1780–1870* (Cambridge: Cambridge University Press, 1996). Instead I accord with Gyan Prakash in considering how even though these efforts did not radically change "the relations of power that is no reason to conclude these that these challenges were insignificant" (225). Prakash, *Bonded Histories: Genealogies of Labor Servitude in Colonial India* (Cambridge: Cambridge University Press, 1990).

49. Ranajit Guha, "The Prose of Counter-Insurgency," in *Subaltern Studies Vol. II: Writings on South Asian History and Society*, ed. Ranajit Guha (Delhi: Oxford University Press, 1983), 1–42. Yet this inseparability of religion and politics cannot be reduced to the coupling of the religious within the modern state form, which is, after all, a distinct historical formation. See Haj, *Reconfiguring the Islamic Tradition*, 18.

50. Memorandum by Munshi Aziz-ud-din, Derah Dun, April 9th, 1887, Proceedings of Maharaja Dalip Singh, his advances to Russia, and feeling in the army and Native States regarding him. India Office Records R/1/1/62, British Library, London.

51. Sindhanwalia, for example, would mark his letters with a seal bearing the inscription "Akal Sahai" following Maharaja Ranjit Singh's days.

52. To the Private Secretary to His Excellency the Viceroy and Governor General of India from Thakur Singh Sindhanwalia, Pondicherry, dated 27th January 1887, Movements of Sardar Thakur Singh Sindhanwalia, an agent of Maharaja Dalip Singh, K. W. Secret I, August 1887, Nos. 15–51, National Archives of India, New Delhi.

53. To the Private Secretary from Thakur Singh Sindhanwalia, 27th January 1887.

54. From Sardar Thakur Singh Sindhanwalia, to J. B. Lyall, Lieutenant-Governor of Punjab, Pondicherry, dated 15th March 1887, Movements of Sardar Thakur Singh Sindhanwalia.

55. Note by R. B., January 5th 1887, Movements of Sardar Thakur Singh Sindhanwalia.

56. H. M. Durand to A. P. MacDonnell, Simla, dated May 6th 1887, Movements of Sardar Thakur Singh Sindhanwalia.

57. Harjot Singh Oberoi, "Bhai, Babas, and Gyanis: Traditional Intellectuals in 19th Century Punjab," *Studies in History* 2, no. 2 (1980): 62.

58. Extract from a letter from Colonel Bonness Fischer, British Consular Agent, Pondicherry, dated 5th March 1887 in Movements of Sardar Thakur Singh Sindhanwalia.

59. Even Duleep Singh, whose entire resistance is reduced to his immense pecuniary embarrassments, recognized both the horror and essential character of money. He wrote when asking for money from Sindhanwalia: "Let some money from the Native Princes and have it sent to me, so that I may use it in bribing the Russian officials. Wicked as it may look one cannot get on in this world without it." See K. W. 2 Memorandum, Memo. On the intrigues of Maharaja Dalip Singh, and issue of warrants for the arrest of certain emissaries of His Highness, India Office Records R/1/1/68, British Library, London.

60. Hussein Ali Agrama, *Questioning Secularism: Islam, Sovereignty, and the Rule of Law in Modern Egypt* (Chicago: University of Chicago Press, 2012), 33.

61. For example, Agrama notes "as a result, religious claims are viewed with both suspicion and anxiety; suspicion that they are really claims of political power or personal gain, and anxiety about the wider political ramifications of allowing such claims to be used in this way." Agrama, *Questioning Secularism*, 33.

62. One can detect this suspicion today as historians try to determine the "real" nature of the Singh Sabha.

63. No. 83 Memorandum, P. D. Henderson, Warrants for the Detention of Jiwan Singh alias Karam Singh and Pertab Singh, Giani, emissaries of Maharaja Dalip Singh, and particulars of intrigues being carried on His Highness's Behalf, India Office Records R/1/1/95, British Library, London.

64. Bayly, *Empire and Information*, 6.

65. For the individual bourgeois self and determining authentic religious meaning in a tradition, see Charles Taylor, *Sources of the Self: The Making of the Modern Identity* (Cambridge, MA: Harvard University Press, 1992); Brian Hatcher, *Bourgeois Hinduism, or, The Faith of the Modern Vedantists: Rare Discourse from Early Colonial Bengal* (Oxford: Oxford University Press, 2008). This produced the religious elites as untrustworthy figures, which coalesced in the figure of the Brahmin and *mullah* in colonial India. See Lata Mani, *Contentious Traditions: The Debate on Sati in Colonial India* (Berkeley: University of California Press, 1998); Robert Yelle, *The Language of Disenchantment: Protestant Liberalism and Colonial Discourse in British India* (Oxford: Oxford University Press, 2013); Scott, *Spiritual Despots*.

66. No. 83 Memorandum, Henderson.

67. Note by the Secretary to the Government of Punjab, W. M. Young 16th June 1887 in India Office Records L/P&S/18/D152, British Library, London.

68. No. 83 Memorandum, Henderson.

69. No. 83 Memorandum, Henderson.

70. Purnima Dhavan, *When Sparrows Became Hawks: The Making of the Sikh Warrior Tradition, 1699–1799* (Oxford: Oxford University Press, 2011), 176.

71. K.W. 2 Memorandum, Memo. On the intrigues of Maharaja Dalip Singh. The colonial state recorded the names of 1. Bhagat Singh, Garanthi of Golden Temple, Amritsar 2. Narang Singh, Garanthi of Golden Temple, Amritsar 3. Hira Singh, Garanthi of Golden Temple, Amritsar 4. Choti Sarkar Sodhi of Anandpur 5. Majhli Sarkar, " "6. Gulab Singh, Garanthi of Patna 7. Bhagat Singh, Garanthi of Patna 8. Nann Singh, Garanthi of Nander, Deccan 9. Gian Singh, Akali, Fakir of Nander.

72. For cosmopolitan networks in relation to Duleep Singh, see Seema Alavi, *Muslim Cosmopolitanism in the Age of Empire* (Cambridge, MA: Harvard University Press, 2015).

73. Chatterjee, "Agrarian Relations and Communalism in Bengal," 31.

74. Extract from a Letter from Major-General M. Dillon to Sir F. Roberts, dated Murree, the September 1887, Proceedings of Maharaja Dalip Singh and Jamal-ud-din, an Afghan Sheikh in Moscow, India Office Records R/1/1/66, British Library, London.

75. K. W. 2 Memorandum, Memo. On the intrigues of Maharaja Dalip Singh.

76. Colonel F. E. Hastings, Commanding 2nd Sikhs to Major-General W. K. Elles, C. B., Adjutant-General in India, Edwardesbad, 10th June 1887, Proceedings of

Maharaja Dalip Singh, his advances to Russia, and feeling in the army and Native States regarding him. India Office Records R/1/1/62, British Library, London.

77. *Khalsa Akhbar*, June 1st, 1887.

78. Rachel Sturman, *The Government of Social Life in Colonial India: Liberalism, Religious Law, and Women's Rights* (Cambridge: Cambridge University Press, 2012), 204. For Oberoi, this technological shift explains the hegemony of Khalsa normative values.

79. Memorandum on the "Khurshed-i-Khalsa" by the Officer in Charge of the Special Branch of the Central Police Office, dated Lahore, the 25th November 1885, Intention of Maharaja Dhulip Singh to visit India, his temporary resistance at Aden, and subsequent return to Europe, Foreign Department Secret I, June 1886, Nos. 12–196, National Archives of India, New Delhi.

80. Translation of a notice circulated by the Khalsa Diwan, Lahore, October 23rd, 1885, Intention of Maharaja Dhulip Singh to visit India.

81. Memorandum, 15th June 1887.

82. Translation of a notice circulated by the Khalsa Diwan, October 23rd, 1885, Intention of Maharaja Dhulip Singh to visit India.

83. Memorandum, 15th June 1887.

84. Translation of a notice circulated by the Khalsa Diwan, Lahore, February 8th, 1886, Intention of Maharaja Dhulip Singh to visit India.

85. Memorandum, 15th June 1887.

86. Translation of a notice circulated by the Khalsa Diwan, Lahore, April 1886, Intention of Maharaja Dhulip Singh to visit India.

87. Memorandum, 15th June 1887. See also *Khalsa Akhbar*, April 16, 1887.

88. Translation of a notice circulated by the Khalsa Diwan, Lahore, April 1886, Intention of Maharaja Dhulip Singh to visit India.

89. W. M. Young to H. M. Durand, Lahore, 24th May 1886, Intention of Maharaja Dhulip Singh to visit India.

90. Note by G. S. Forbes, May 28th, 1886, Intention of Maharaja Dhulip Singh to visit India.

91. *The Pioneer*, May 20, 1886.

92. Memorandum, 15th June 1887.

93. Memorandum, 15th June 1887.

94. If the Khalsa *panth* is a unity, as a *sangat*, *alhida* reminds us that one can become disjointed from within.

95. A copy of the *hukamnama* is printed in Singh, *Singh Sabha Lahir*, 35.

96. Dhavan notes this tension as does Kapur Singh. See Dhavan, *When Sparrows Became Hawks*, and Singh, "The Church and the State."

97. *Khalsa Akhbar*, 16 April 1887. The translations are mine.

98. Extract enclosed in Letter from Charles Aitchison to H.M Durand, 8th August 1885, Maharaja Dhulip and Major Evans Bell's Book "The Annexation of the Punjab," Foreign Department Secret I, August 1885, Nos. 17–21, National Archives of India, New Delhi. For more, see chapter 1.

99. Memorandum, 15th June 1887.

100. C. L. Tupper to H. M. Durand, 28th December 1885, Intention of Maharaja Dhulip Singh to visit India.

101. Sardar Attar Singh, to Private Secretary to His Honor the Lieutenant-Governor Punjab, August 9th, 1887, Proceedings of Maharaja Dalip Singh.

102. Singh to Private Secretary, Proceedings of Maharaja Dalip Singh.

103. Singh to Private Secretary, Proceedings of Maharaja Dalip Singh.

104. *Khalsa Akhbar*, July 1st, 1887. The translations are mine.

105. Singh, to Private Secretary, Proceedings of Maharaja Dalip Singh.

106. Copy of a Communication from Bhai Gurmukh Singh, Secretary to the Khalsa Diwan and Assistant Professor of the Oriental College, Lahore, to the Private Secretary to his Honor the Lieutenant-Governor, Punjab, dated the 25th November 1886, Proceedings of Maharaja Dalip Singh.

107. Copy of a Communication from Bhai Gurmukh Singh.

108. Memorandum, 15th June 1887.

109. Douglas McCracken to Foreign Secretary, February 28th, 1889, Warrants for the Detention of Jiwan Singh alias Karam Singh and Pertab Singh, Giani, emissaries of Maharaja Dalip Singh, and particulars of intrigues being carried on His Highness's Behalf, India Office Records R/1/1/95, British Library, London.

110. For more on this case, see Oberoi, *Construction of Religious Boundaries*.

111. *Madras Mail*, March 10, 1888.

112. *The Civil Military Gazette*, quoted in P. D. Henderson to Foreign Secretary, April 30th, 1888, Particulars of interviews with Abdul Rasul, an emissary of Maharaja Dalip Singh at Cairo, India Office Records R/1/1/82, British Library, London.

113. Henderson, July 1st 1888, Particulars of interviews with Abdul Rasul. Henderson wrote, "a perusal of the printed paper in the file about Bawa Khem Singh will lead to an impression that there is some ground for a distrust which this spontaneous mention of him by a confidant of Dalip Singh must tend to deepen."

114. Note by Henderson, 2nd August 1888, Particulars of interviews with Abdul Rasul.

115. David Arnold, "Bureaucratic Recruitment and Subordination in Colonial India: The Madras Constabulary, 1857–1947," in *Subaltern Studies IV: Writings on South Asian History and Society*, ed. Ranajit Guha (Delhi: Oxford University Press, 1985), 2.

116. Verne Dusenbury, "The Word as Guru: Sikh Scripture and the Translation Controversy," *History of Religions* 31, no. 4 (1992): 401.

117. Gayatri Chakravorty Spivak, "Can the Subaltern Speak?," in *Marxism and the Interpretation of Culture*, ed. Lawrence Grossberg and Cary Nelson (Urbana: University of Illinois Press, 1988), 284, 297.

118. Ethan Kleinberg, *Haunting History: For a Deconstructive Approach to the Past* (Stanford, CA: Stanford University Press, 2017), 1.

119. Ranajit Guha, "On Some Aspects of the Historiography of Colonial India," in *Subaltern Studies I: Writings on South Asian History and Society*, ed. Ranajit Guha (New Delhi: Oxford University Press, 1982), 4.

120. Memorandum, 15th June 1887.

121. Extract from Political Abstract of Intelligence, Punjab Police, no. 3, Dated the 22nd January 1887, Proceedings of Maharaja Dalip Singh.

122. Memorandum, 15th June 1887.

123. Memorandum, 15th June 1887.

124. Oberoi, *Construction of Religious Boundaries*, 303, 298. For another work that takes the *Khalsa Akhbar* at face value, see Louis Fenech, *Martyrdom in the Sikh Tradition: Playing the "Game of Love"* (Delhi: Oxford University Press, 2000).

125. Ranajit Guha contends that the pressures of insurgency required both the colonial state and elite discourse "reduce the semantic range of many words and expressions, and assign to them specialized meanings in order to identify peasants as rebels and their attempt to turn the world upside down as crime." Guha, *Elementary Aspects of Peasant Insurgency in Colonial India* (Durham, NC: Duke University Press, 1999), 17. The British, however, did try to limit the possible meaning of Duleep Singh, designing a specific role for him to play, as Atwal explains—a meaning that shifted as geopolitical concerns changed. See Atwal, *Royal and Rebels*, 198.

126. Memorandum, 15th June 1887.

127. Memorandum, 15th June 1887.

128. Oberoi, *Construction of Religious Boundaries*, 298.

129. The Arya Samaj, too, deployed this logic. See Adcock, *Limits of Tolerance*, 107.

130. Memorandum, 15th June 1887.

131. For example, when considering ethics and lived aspects of reform, Anne Murphy argues that "the terrain for this exploration of the ethical is the flourishing new print environment of the late nineteenth- and early twentieth-century Punjab." Murphy then highlights the importance of one text by Mohan Singh Vaid. See Murphy, "Formation of Ethical Sikh Subject," 152.

132. Florenica Mallon, *Peasant and Nation: The Making of Postcolonial Mexico and Peru* (Berkeley: University of California Press, 1995), 11.

133. Memorandum, 15th June 1887.

134. Oberoi, *The Construction of Religious Boundaries*, 33.

135. Arvind-Pal Mandair is a slight exception to this rule. Although he pinpoints Trumpp's translation as site of colonial inauguration, he also notes how such an inauguration can never be fully complete. See Arvind-Pal Singh Mandair, *Religion and the Specter of the West: Sikhism, India, Postcoloniality, and the Politics of Translation* (New York: Columbia University Press, 2013). For a more in-depth discussion of Mandair's work that is not possible here, see Rajbir Singh Judge, "The Multiple Horizons of Sikh Orthodoxy: Tradition, Fantasy, and Modern Temporality. Review Essay of Arvind Mandair, *Religion and the Specter of the West: Sikhism, India, Postcoloniality, and the Politics of Translation*," *Journal of Sikh and Punjab Studies* 23, nos. 1–2 (2016): 181–92.

136. Spivak, "Can the Subaltern Speak?," 287.

137. Ananda Abeysekara, *The Politics of Postsecular Religion: Mourning Secular Futures* (New York: Columbia University Press, 2008), 218.

CONCLUSION

1. The preceding quotations are from Deepa Alexander, "On King and Country: Bringing Alive 'The Black Prince,'" *The Hindu*, July 6, 2017, http://www.thehindu.com/entertainment/movies/director-kavi-raz-on-the-black-prince/article19224119.ece.

2. Deepa Alexander, "On King and Country," *The Hindu, Metro Plus*, July 8, 2017. http://www.thehindu.com/todays-paper/tp-features/tp-metroplus/on-king-and -country/article19237378.ece.

3. Shashank Bengali, "A New Film Tells the Story of the Sikh Boy Ruler Who Was Ripped from His Kingdom and Transformed Into an English Aristocrat," *Los Angeles Times*, July 14, 2017, http://www.latimes.com/world/asia/la-fg-india-black -prince-film-20170714-story.html.

4. Lee Edelman, *No Future: Queer Theory and the Death Drive* (Durham, NC: Duke University Press, 2004).

5. "Sikh Period Drama 'The Black Prince' to Make Digital Debut April 10," *India West*, April 3, 2018, http://www.indiawest.com/entertainment/global/sikh-period -drama-the-black-prince-to-make-digital-debut/article_a5ce93f6-378f-11e8-90d5 -d774865b0774.html.

6. Bengali, "New Film."

7. Ranajit Guha, "A Conquest Foretold," *Social Text* 54 (1998): 92.

8. Slavoj Žižek, "Class Struggle or Postmodernism? Yes Please!," in *Contingency, Hegemony, Universality: Contemporary Dialogues on the Left*, ed. Judith Butler, Ernesto Laclau, and Slavoj Žižek (London: Verso, 2000), 125.

9. Guha, "A Conquest Foretold," 96, 94.

10. See Johannes Fabian, *Time and the Other: How Anthropology Makes Its Object* (New York: Columbia University Press, 1983).

11. Slavoj Žižek, *Less Than Nothing: Hegel and the Shadow of Dialectical Materialism* (New York: Verso, 2012), 651.

12. Karl Marx, "Preface to the First Edition," in *Capital: A Critique of Political Economy*, trans. Ben Fowkes (New York: Penguin Books, 1976), 1:91.

13. I borrow "accumulation by dispossession" from David Harvey. See Harvey, *The New Imperialism* (Oxford: Oxford University Press, 2003). For an important critique of Harvey's analysis, see Navyug Gill, "Accumulation by Attachment: Colonial Benevolence and the Rule of Capital in Nineteenth-Century Panjab," *Past & Present* 256, no. 1 (2022): 203–38. For more on time, see Ranajit Guha, *Dominance Without Hegemony: History and Power in Colonial India* (Cambridge, MA: Harvard University Press, 1997), 13–20, 178. As Guha argues, "the striving to cope with and make up for such inadequacy and incompleteness constitutes for each of them its historic project and the condition of all its dynamism" (178). One moment of coping can lie in the nation-state. For example, Partha Chatterjee writes, capitalist society has the ability "to reunite capital and labor ideologically at the level of the political community of the nation, borrowing from another narrative the rhetoric of love, duty, welfare and the like" (235–236). See Chatterjee, *The Nation and Its Fragments: Colonial and Postcolonial Histories* (Princeton, NJ: Princeton University Press, 1993).

14. Sami Khatib, "No Future: The Space of Capital and the Time of Dying," in *Former West: Art and the Contemporary After 1989*, ed. Maria Hlavajova and Simon Sheikh (Cambridge, MA: MIT Press, 2017), 649.

15. I borrow "illusory wholeness" and "originary plentitude" from Saidiya Hartman. See Hartman, *Scenes of Subjection: Terror, Slavery, and Self-Making in Nineteenth-Century America* (Oxford: Oxford University Press, 1997), 74.

16. For this project, see Anne Murphy, *The Materiality of the Past: History and Representation in Sikh Tradition* (Oxford: Oxford University Press, 2012).

17. I borrow "orthopedics" from Jacques Lacan, who mocked the centrality of an "orthopedics of the ego" among psychoanalysts. See Lacan, *Seminar III: The Psychoses, 1955–1956*, ed. Jacques-Alain Miller, trans. Russell Grigg (New York: W. W. Norton, 1993), 235.

18. Gil Anidjar, "Against History," in Marc Nichanian, *The Historiographic Perversion* (New York: Columbia University Press, 2009), 518.

19. Prathama Banerjee, *Politics of Time: "Primitives" and History-Writing in a Colonial Society* (Oxford: Oxford University Press, 2006), 20.

20. Jacques Derrida, *Archive Fever: A Freudian Impression*, trans. Eric Prenowitz (Chicago: University of Chicago Press, 1996), 68.

21. Gary Wilder, "From Optic to Topic: The Foreclosure Effect of Historiographic Turns," *American Historical Review* 117, no. 3 (2012): 723–45.

22. Alexander Kojève, *Introduction to the Reading of Hegel: Lectures on the Phenomenology of Spirit*, trans. James H. Nichols (Ithaca, NY: Cornell University Press, 1980), 159. Indeed, as Kojève argues in his infamous footnote, after the end of history, "men would construct their edifices as works of art as birds build their nests and spiders spin their webs, would perform musical concert after the fashion of frogs and cicadas, would play like young animals, and would indulge in love like adult beasts" (159).

23. Wilder, "From Optic to Topic," 730.

24. Žižek, "Class Struggle or Postmodernism?," 94.

25. Hartman, *Scenes of Subjection*, 77.

26. This might mean that we too might have to refuse, to follow Partha Chatterjee, to engage in "reasonable discourse." See Chatterjee, "Religious Minorities and the Secular State: Reflections on an Indian Impasses," *Public Culture* 8, no 1 (1995): 11–39.

27. Hartman, *Scenes of Subjection*, 75.

28. Dominick LaCapra, *Writing History, Writing Trauma* (Baltimore: Johns Hopkins University Press, 2001), 48.

29. I borrow "*homo historicus*" from Denise Ferreira Da Silva. *Homo historicus* is, as she writes, "the transparent I, the self-determined subject of universality." Da Silva, *Toward a Global Idea of Race* (Minneapolis: University of Minnesota Press, 2007), 88.

30. Talal Asad, *Formations of the Secular: Christianity, Islam, Modernity* (Stanford, CA: Stanford University Press, 2003), 223.

31. Michel de Certeau, *The Writing of History*, trans. Tom Conley (New York: Columbia University Press, 1987), 5.

32. Žižek, "Class Struggle or Postmodernism?," 125.

33. Jacques Derrida, *Specters of Marx: The State of Debt, the Work of Mourning and the New International*, trans. Peggy Kamuf (New York: Routledge, 1994), 9.

34. Asad, *Formations of the Secular*, 222.

35. Žižek, *Less Than Nothing*, 223.

36. Partha Chatterjee. "After Subaltern Studies," *Economic and Political Weekly* 47, no. 35 (2012): 44–49.

37. As Guha writes, "We want to emphasize [rebel consciousness's] sovereignty, its consistency, and its logic in order to compensate for its absence from the literature." See Ranajit Guha, *Elementary Aspects of Peasant Insurgency in Colonial India* (Durham, NC: Duke University Press, 1999), 13.

38. Partha Chatterjee, for example, notes, "If one thinks of the coming and going of intellectual fashions, 30 years is an unusually long time for a school or trend to stay in or around the limelight." Chatterjee, "After Subaltern Studies," 44.

39. Ranajit Guha, "Subaltern Studies Projects for Our Time and Their Convergence," in *The Small Voice of History*, ed. Partha Chatterjee (Delhi: Permanent Black, 2009), 347.

40. Bayly argues, "the rhetorical devices of 'subaltern' and 'peasant resistance' often impede them in this more subtle analysis." See C. A. Bayly, "Rallying Around the Subaltern," *Journal of Peasant Studies* 16, no. 1 (1988): 120.

41. Rosalind O'Hanlon, "Recovering the Subject: Subaltern Studies and Histories of Resistance in Colonial South Asia," *Modern Asian Studies* 22, no. 1 (1988): 222, 218. Dipesh Chakrabarty responds to this critique in *Subaltern Studies Vol. IV: Writings on South Asian History and Society*, ed. Ranajit Guha (Delhi: Oxford University Press, 1985), 364–76.

42. Jim Masselos, "The Dis/appearance of Subalterns: A Reading of a Decade of Subaltern Studies," *South Asia: Journal of South Asian Studies* 15, no. 1 (1992): 125.

43. Gayatri Chakravorty Spivak, "Can the Subaltern Speak?" in *Marxism and the Interpretation of Culture*, ed. Lawrence Grossberg and Cary Nelson (Urbana: University of Illinois Press, 1988), 306.

44. For example, Shahid Amin notes, "The was thus no single authorized version of the Mahatma to which the peasants of eastern UP and north Bihar may be said to have subscribed in 1921." See Amin, "Gandhi as Mahatma: Gorakhpur District, Eastern U.P., 1921–2," in *Subaltern Studies Vol. III: Writings on South Asian History and Society*, ed. Ranajit Guha (Delhi: Oxford University Press, 1984), 55.

45. Dipesh Chakrabarty, "Subaltern Studies in Retrospect and Reminiscence," *South Asia: Journal of South Asian Studies* 38, no. 1 (2015): 13. Spivak writes, "[Freud] predicates a history of repression that produces the final sentence," one with a double origin: "one hidden in the amnesia of the infant, the other lodged in our archaic past." Spivak, "Can the Subaltern Speak?," 297.

46. Rajeswai Sunder Rajan, "Death and the Subaltern," in *Can the Subaltern Speak?: Reflections on the History of an Idea*, ed. Rosalind C. Morris (New York: Columbia University Press, 2010), 117.

47. Even though Chandra's death troubles such historical methodology, see Ranajit Guha, "Chandra's Death," in *Subaltern Studies V: Writings on South Asian History and Society*, ed. Ranajit Guha (Delhi: Oxford University Press, 1987).

48. Stefania Pandolfo, *Impasse of the Angels* (Chicago: University of Chicago Press, 1997), 11.

49. Here I follow Omnia El Shakry, who reminds us that "psychoanalysis may continue to offer, one, although not the only possible, outlet to the maladies of our time, an ethical stance in which we not only subject ourselves and our drives to

radical critique but simultaneously open ourselves up to an ethical encounter with the Other." See El Shakry, *The Arabic Freud: Psychoanalysis and Islam in Modern Egypt* (Princeton, NJ: Princeton University Press, 2017), 115.

50. David Marriott, *Whither Fanon? Studies in the Blackness of Being* (Stanford, CA: Stanford University Press, 2018), 312.

BIBLIOGRAPHY

ARCHIVES

British Library, London
National Archives of India, New Delhi
Punjab State Archives, Chandigarh

BOOKS AND ARTICLES

Abeysekara, Ananda. *The Politics of Postsecular Religion: Mourning Secular Futures.* New York: Columbia University Press, 2008.

Abraham, Nicolas, and Maria Torok. *The Shell and the Kernel, Vol. 1.* Ed. and trans. Nicholas T. Rand. Chicago: University of Chicago Press, 1994.

Adcock, C. S. *The Limits of Tolerance: Indian Secularism and the Politics of Religious Freedom.* New York: Oxford University Press, 2014.

Agrama, Hussein Ali. *Questioning Secularism: Islam, Sovereignty, and the Rule of Law in Modern Egypt.* Chicago: University of Chicago Press, 2012.

Alavi, Seema. *Muslim Cosmopolitanism in the Age of Empire.* Cambridge, MA: Harvard University Press, 2015.

Alexander, Michael, and Sushila Anand. *Queen Victoria's Maharajah: Duleep Singh 1838–93.* London: Phoenix Press, 1980.

Almond, Philip C. *The British Discovery of Buddhism.* Cambridge: Cambridge University Press, 2007.

Amin, Shahid. "Gandhi as Mahatma: Gorakhpur District, Eastern UP, 1921–2." In *Subaltern Studies III: Writings on South Asian History and Society,* ed. Ranajit Guha, 1–61. New Delhi: Oxford University Press, 1984.

Anidjar, Gil. "Against History." Afterword to Marc Nichanian, *The Historiographic Perversion*. New York: Columbia University Press, 2009.

——. *Blood: A Critique of Christianity*. New York: Columbia University Press, 2016.

——. "Homo Discens." *Critical Times* 3, no. 3 (2020): 443–49.

——. "Sapientia." *Identities: Journal for Politics, Gender and Culture*. April 14, 2020. https://identitiesjournal.edu.mk/index.php/IJPGC/announcement/view/36.

——. *Semites: Race, Religion, Literature*. Stanford, CA: Stanford University Press, 2008.

Appadurai, Arjun. "Introduction: Commodities and the Politics of Value." In *The Social Life of Things: Commodities in Cultural Perspective*, ed. Arjun Appadurai, 3–63. Cambridge: Cambridge University Press, 1986.

——. *Modernity At Large: Cultural Dimensions of Globalization*. Minneapolis: University of Minnesota Press, 1996.

Argov, Daniel. *Moderates and Extremists in the Indian Nationalist Movement, 1883–1920*. Bombay: Asia Publishing House, 1967.

Arnold, David. "Bureaucratic Recruitment and Subordination in Colonial India: The Madras Constabulary, 1857–1947." In *Subaltern Studies IV: Writings on South Asian History and Society*, ed. Ranajit Guha, 1–53. Delhi: Oxford University Press, 1985.

Arondekar, Anjali. *Abundance: Sexuality's History*. Durham, NC: Duke University Press, 2023.

——. *For the Record: On Sexuality and the Colonial Archive in India*. Durham, NC: Duke University Press, 2009.

Asad, Talal. "Comments on Conversion." In *Conversion to Modernities: The Globalization of Christianity*, ed. Peter van der Veer, 263–73. New York: Routledge, 1996.

——. *Formations of the Secular: Christianity, Islam, Modernity*. Stanford, CA: Stanford University Press, 2003.

——. *Genealogies of Religion: Discipline and Reasons of Power in Christianity and Islam*. Baltimore: Johns Hopkins University Press, 1993.

——. *The Idea of an Anthropology of Islam*. Washington, DC: Georgetown University Center for Contemporary Arab Studies, 1986.

——. "Politics and Religion in Islamic Reform: A Critique of Kedouries's Afgani and Abduh." *Review of Middle East Studies* 2 (1976): 13–22.

——. *Secular Translations: Nation-State, Modern Self, and Calculative Reason*. New York: Columbia University Press, 2018.

——. "Thinking About Tradition, Religion, and Politics in Egypt Today." *Critical Inquiry* 42, no. 1 (2015): 166–214.

——. "The Trouble of Thinking: An Interview with Talal Asad." In *Powers of the Secular Modern: Talal Asad and His Interlocutors*, ed. David Scott and Charles Hirschkind, 243–303. Stanford, CA: Stanford University Press, 2006.

Asif, Manan Ahmed. *The Loss of Hindustan: The Invention of India*. Cambridge, MA: Harvard University Press, 2020.

Atwal, Priya. *Royals and Rebels: The Rise and Fall of the Sikh Empire*. Oxford: Oxford University Press, 2020.

Axel, Brian Keith. *The Nation's Tortured Body: Violence, Representation, and the Formation of a Sikh "Diaspora."* Durham, NC: Duke University Press, 2001.

Baird, J. G. A., ed. *Private Letters of Marquess of Dalhousie*. London: William Blackwood and Sons, 1910.

Ballantyne, Tony. *Between Colonialism and Diaspora: Sikh Cultural Formations in an Imperial World*. Durham, NC: Duke University Press, 2006.

Bance, Peter. *Sovereign, Squire and Rebel: Maharajah Duleep Singh and the Heirs of a Lost Kingdom*. London: Coronet House, 2009.

Banerjee, Milinda. *The Mortal God: Imagining the Sovereign in Colonial India*. Cambridge: Cambridge University Press, 2018.

Banerjee, Prathama. *Politics of Time: "Primitives" and History-Writing in a Colonial Society*. Oxford: Oxford University Press, 2006.

Banga, Indu. *The Agrarian System of Sikhs*. New Delhi: Manohar Publications, 1978.

Bannerjee, Sukanya. *Becoming Imperial Citizens: Indians in the Late-Victorian Empire*. Durham, NC: Duke University Press, 2010.

Barber, Daniel Colucciello. "The Immanent Refusal of Conversion." *Journal for Cultural and Religious Theory* 13, no. 1 (2014): 142–50.

Barrier, N. Gerald, and Paul Wallace. *The Punjab Press, 1880–1905*. East Lansing: Michigan State University Press, 1970.

——. *The Sikhs and Their Literature: A Guide to Tracts, Books and Periodicals, 1849–1919*. Delhi: Manohar Book Service, 1970.

Bayly, C. A. *Empire and Information: Intelligence Gathering and Social Communication in India, 1780–1870*. Cambridge: Cambridge University Press, 1996.

——. "The Origins of Swadeshi (Home Industry): Cloth and Indian Society, 1700–1930." In *The Social Life of Things: Commodities in Cultural Perspective*, ed. Arjun Appadurai, 285–321. Cambridge: Cambridge University Press, 1986.

——. "The Pre-History of 'Communalism'? Religious Conflict in India, 1700–1860." *Modern Asian Studies* 19, no. 2 (1985): 177–203.

——. "Rallying Around the Subaltern." *Journal of Peasant Studies* 16, no. 1 (1988): 110–20.

Bell, Evans. *The Annexation of the Punjaub and the Maharaja Duleep Singh*. London: Trüber & Co., 1882.

Berlant, Lauren. *Cruel Optimism*. Durham, NC: Duke University Press, 2011.

Best, Stephen. "On Failing to Make the Past Present." *Modern Language Quarterly* 73, no. 3 (2012): 453–74.

Bhabha, Homi. "In a Spirit of Calm Violence." In *After Colonialism: Imperial Histories and Postcolonial Displacements*, ed. Gyan Prakash, 326–43. Princeton, NJ: Princeton University Press, 1995.

——. *The Location of Culture*. New York: Routledge, 1994.

Bhattacharya, Neeladri. "Predicaments of Secular Histories." *Public Culture* 20, no. 1 (2008): 57–73.

——. "Remaking Custom: The Discourse and Practice of Colonial Codification." In *Tradition, Ideology and Dissent: Essays in Honour of Romila Thapar*, ed. R. Champakalakshmi and Sarvepalli Gopal, 20–51. Delhi: Oxford University Press, 1996.

Bhogal, Balbinder Singh. "Gur-Sikh Dharm." In *History of Indian Philosophy*, ed. Purushottama Bilimoria, 487–95. London: Routledge, 2017.

Blanchot, Maurice. *The Book to Come*. Trans. Charlotte Mandell. Stanford, CA: Stanford University Press, 2002.

——. *The Space of Literature*. Trans. Ann Smock. Lincoln: University of Nebraska Press, 1982.

Bonea, Amelia. *The News of Empire: Telegraphy, Journalism, and the Politics of Reporting in Colonial India, c. 1830–1900*. Delhi: Oxford University Press, 2016.

Bonilla, Yarimar. *Non-Sovereign Futures: French Caribbean Politics in the Wake of Disenchantment*. Chicago: University of Chicago Press, 2015.

Brown, Norman O. *Life Against Death: The Psychoanalytical Meaning of History*. Middleton, CT: Wesleyan University Press, 1959.

Brown, Wendy. *States of Injury: Power and Freedom in Late Modernity*. Princeton, NJ: Princeton University Press, 1995.

Butler, Judith. *The Psychic Life of Power: Theories in Subjection*. Stanford, CA: Stanford University Press, 1997.

Campbell, Christy. *The Maharajah's Box: An Imperial Story of Conspiracy, Love, and a Guru's Prophecy*. London: HarperCollins, 2000.

Chakrabarty, Dipesh. *Habitations of Modernity: Essays in the Wake of Subaltern Studies*. Chicago: University of Chicago Press, 2002.

——. "Invitation to a Dialogue." In *Subaltern Studies Vol. IV: Writings on South Asian History and Society*, ed. Ranajit Guha, 364–76. Delhi: Oxford University Press, 1985.

——. *Provincializing Europe: Postcolonial Thought and Historical Difference*. Princeton, NJ: Princeton University Press, 2000.

——. "Subaltern Studies in Retrospect and Reminiscence." *South Asia: Journal of South Asian Studies* 38, no. 1 (2015): 10–18.

Chakrabarty, Rishi Ranjan. *Duleep Singh: The Maharajah of Punjab and the Raj*. Oldbury, UK: D. S. Samara, 1988.

Chann, Naindeep Singh. "Rahit Literature." In *Brill's Encyclopedia of Sikhism Online*, ed. Knut A. Jacobsen et al., 183–91. Leiden: Brill, 2017.

Chatterjee, Nandini. *The Making of Indian Secularism: Empire, Law and Christianity, 1830–1960*. New York: Palgrave Macmillan, 2011.

Chatterjee, Partha. "After Subaltern Studies." *Economic and Political Weekly* 47, no. 35 (2012): 44–49.

——. "Agrarian Relations and Communalism in Bengal, 1926–1935." In *Subaltern Studies I: Writings on South Asian History and Society*, ed. Ranajit Guha, 9–38. New Delhi: Oxford University Press, 1982.

——. "More on Modes of Power and the Peasantry." In *Subaltern Studies II: Writing on South Asian History and Society*, ed. Ranajit Guha, 311–49. New Delhi: Oxford University Press, 1983.

——. *The Nation and Its Fragments: Colonial and Postcolonial Histories*. Princeton, NJ: Princeton University Press, 1993.

——. "Religious Minorities and the Secular State: Reflections on an Indian Impasses." *Public Culture* 8, no 1 (1995): 11–39.

——. "Secularism and Toleration." *Economic and Political Weekly* 29, no. 28 (1994): 1768–77.

Ciccariello-Maher, George. *Decolonizing Dialectics*. Durham, NC: Duke University Press, 2017.

Cohn, Bernard. *An Anthropologist Among the Historians and Other Essays*. New Delhi: Oxford University Press, 1987.

——. *Colonialism and Its Forms of Knowledge: The British in India*. Princeton, NJ: Princeton University Press, 1996.

Comaroff, Jean, and John Comaroff. *Of Revelation and Revolution: Christianity, Colonialism, and Consciousness in South Africa, vol. 1.* Chicago: University of Chicago Press, 1991.

Comay, Rebecca. *Mourning Sickness: Hegel and the French Revolution.* Stanford, CA: Stanford University Press, 2011.

——. "The Sickness of Tradition: Between Melancholia and Fetishism." In *Walter Benjamin and History,* ed. Andrew Benjamin, 88–101. New York: Continuum, 2005.

Condos, Mark. *The Insecurity State: Punjab and the Making of Colonial Power in British India.* Cambridge: Cambridge University Press, 2017.

Copjec, Joan. *Imagine There's No Woman: Ethics and Sublimation.* Cambridge, MA: MIT Press, 2004.

Culp, Andrew. *Dark Deleuze.* Minneapolis, University of Minnesota Press, 2016.

Da Silva, Denise. *Toward a Global Idea of Race.* Minneapolis: University of Minnesota Press, 2007.

Dalmia, Vasudha. *The Nationalization of Hindu Traditions: Bharatendu Harischandra and Nineteenth Century Banaras.* New Delhi: Oxford University Press, 1997.

Das, Veena. *Life and Words: Violence and the Descent Into the Ordinary.* Berkeley: University of California Press, 2007.

Davis, Kathleen. *Periodization & Sovereignty: How Ideas of Feudalism and Secularization Govern the Politics of Time.* Philadelphia: University of Pennsylvania Press, 2008.

de Certeau, Michel. *The Practice of Everyday Life.* Trans. Steven F. Rendall. Berkeley: University of California Press, 1984.

——. *The Writing of History.* Trans. Tom Conley. New York: Columbia University Press, 1988.

Dean, Jodi. "Publicity's Secret." *Political Theory* 29, no. 5 (2001): 624–50.

Deleuze, Gilles, and Félix Guattari. *Anti-Oedipus: Capitalism and Schizophrenia.* Trans. Robert Hurley, Mark Sem, and Helen R. Lane. Minneapolis: University of Minnesota Press, 2003.

Derrida, Jacques. *Archive Fever: A Freudian Impression.* Trans. Eric Prenowitz. Chicago: University of Chicago Press, 1996.

——. *Dissemination.* Trans. Barbara Johnson. Chicago: University of Chicago Press, 1981.

——. "Faith and Knowledge: The Two Sources of 'Religion' at the Limits of Reason Alone." In *Acts of Religion,* ed. Gil Anidjar, 40–101. New York: Routledge, 2002.

——. "Force of Law: The "Mystical Foundation of Authority," in Anidjar, *Acts of Religion,* 230–98.

——. *Given Time: I. Counterfeit Money.* Trans. Peggy Kamuf. Chicago: University of Chicago Press, 2004.

——. *Of Grammatology.* Trans. Gayatri Chakravorty Spivak. Baltimore: Johns Hopkins University Press, 1997.

——. *Rogues: Two Essays on Reason.* Trans. Pascale-Anne Brault and Michael Naas. Stanford, CA: Stanford University Press, 2005.

——. *Specters of Marx: The State of Debt, the Work of Mourning and the New International.* Trans. Peggy Kamuf. New York: Routledge, 1994.

Deshpande, Prachi. *Creative Pasts: Historical Memory and Identity in Western India, 1700–1960.* Delhi: Permanent Black, 2007.

Dhavan, Purnima. *When Sparrows Became Hawks: The Making of the Sikh Warrior Tradition, 1699–1799*. Oxford: Oxford University Press, 2011.

Dirks, Nicholas. *Castes of Mind: Colonialism and the Making of Modern India*. Princeton, NJ: Princeton University Press, 2001.

——. *The Hollow Crown: The Ethnohistory of an Indian Kingdom*. Cambridge: Cambridge University Press, 1988.

Dobe, Timothy. *Hindu Christian Faqir: Modern Monks, Global Christianity, and Indian Sainthood*. New York: Oxford University Press, 2015.

Dusenbury, Verne. "The Word as Guru: Sikh Scripture and the Translation Controversy." *History of Religions* 31, no. 4 (1992): 385–402.

Dutta, Simanti. *Imperial Mappings in Savage Spaces: Baluchistan and British India*. Delhi: B. R. Publishing, 2002.

Edelman, Lee. *No Future: Queer Theory and the Death Drive*. Durham, NC: Duke University Press, 2004.

El Shakry, Omnia. *The Arabic Freud: Psychoanalysis and Islam in Modern Egypt*. Princeton, NJ: Princeton University Press, 2017.

——. *The Great Social Laboratory: Subjects of Knowledge in Colonial and Postcolonial Egypt*. Stanford, CA: Stanford University Press, 2007.

——. "Inwardness: Comparative Religious Philosophy in Modern Egypt." *Journal of the American Academy of Religion* 90, no. 2 (2022): 450–72.

——. "Rethinking Arab Intellectual History: Epistemology, Historicism, Secularism." *Modern Intellectual History* 18, no. 2 (2021): 547–72.

Eng, David L., and David Kazanjian, eds. *Loss*. Berkeley: University of California Press, 2003.

Esposito, Roberto. *Communitas: The Origin and Destiny of Community*. Trans. Timothy Campbell. Stanford, CA: Stanford University Press, 2010.

——. *Immunitas: The Protection and Negation of Life*. Trans. Zakiya Hanafi. Malden, MA: Polity, 2011.

——. *Terms of the Political: Community, Immunity, Biopolitics*. Trans. Rhiannon Noel Welch. New York: Fordham University Press, 2013.

Ewing, Katherine Pratt. *Arguing Sainthood: Modernity, Psychoanalysis, and Islam*. Durham, NC: Duke University Press, 1997.

Fabian, Johannes. *Time and The Other: How Anthropology Makes Its Object*. New York: Columbia University Press, 1983.

Fanon, Frantz. *The Wretched of the Earth*. Trans. Constance Farrington. New York: Grove Press, 1968.

Federici, Silvia. *Caliban and the Witch: Women, the Body, and Primitive Accumulation*. New York: Autonomedia, 2004.

Feldman, Allen. "Violence and Vision: The Prosthetics and Aesthetics of Terror." *Public Culture* 10, no. 1 (1997): 24–60.

Felman, Shoshana. "On Reading Poetry: Reflections on the Limits and Possibilities of Psychoanalytical Approaches." In *The Purloined Poe: Lacan, Derrida, and Psychoanalytic Reading*, ed. John P. Muller and William J. Richardson, 133–56. Baltimore: Johns Hopkins University Press, 1988.

Fenech, Louis. *Martyrdom in the Sikh Tradition: Playing the Game of Love*. New Delhi: Oxford University Press, 2000.

——. *The Sikh Zafar-namah of Guru Gobind Singh: A Discursive Blade in the Heart of the Mughal Empire.* New Delhi: Oxford University Press, 2013.

Foucault, Michel. "Nietzsche, Genealogy, History." In *Aesthetics, Method, and Epistemology*, ed. James D. Faubion, 369–91. New York: New Press, 1998.

——. *Subjectivity and Truth Lectures at the Collège de France, 1980–1981.* Ed. Frédéric Gros. Trans. Graham Burchell. London: Palgrave Macmillan, 2017.

——. "What Is an Author?" In *Aesthetics, Methods, and Epistemology*, ed. James D. Faubion, 205–21. New York: New Press, 1998.

Fox, Richard. *Lions of the Punjab: Culture in the Making.* Berkeley: University of California Press, 1985.

Freitag, Sandria. *Collective Action and Community: Public Arenas and the Emergence of Communalism in North India.* Berkeley: University of California Press, 1989.

——. "Crime in the Social Order of Colonial North India." *Modern Asian Studies* 25, no. 2 (May 1991): 227–61.

——. "Enactments of Ram's Story and the Changing Nature of 'The Public' in British India." *South Asia: Journal of South Asian Studies* 14, no. 1 (1991): 65–90.

——. "Introduction: 'The Public' and Its Meanings in Colonial South Asia." *South Asia: Journal of South Asian Studies* 14, no. 1 (1991): 1–13.

——. "Postscript: Exploring Aspects of 'the Public' from 1991 to 2014." *South Asia: Journal of South Asian Studies* 38, no. 3 (2015): 512–23.

Freud, Sigmund. *Beyond the Pleasure Principle.* In *The Standard Edition of the Complete Psychological Works of Sigmund Freud*, vol. 18, ed. and trans. James Strachey, 7–64. London: Hogarth, 1955.

——. "The Interpretation of Dreams [Second Part] and On Dreams." In *The Standard Edition of the Complete Psychological Works of Sigmund Freud*, vol. 5, ed. and trans. James Strachey. London: Hogarth, 1953.

——. "Mourning and Melancholia." In *The Standard Edition of the Complete Psychological Works of Sigmund Freud*, vol. 14, ed. and trans. James Strachey, 243–58. London: Hogarth, 1953.

Frosh, Stephen. *Hauntings: Psychoanalysis and Ghostly Transmissions.* New York: Palgrave, 2013.

Gill, Navyug. "Accumulation by Attachment: Colonial Benevolence and the Rule of Capital in Nineteenth-Century Panjab." *Past & Present* 256, no. 1 (2022): 203–38.

Gilmartin, David. *Blood and Water: The Indus River Basin in Modern History.* Berkeley: University of California Press, 2015.

——. "Environmental History, Biradari, and the Making of Pakistani Punjab." In *Punjab Reconsidered: History, Culture, and Practice*, ed. Anshu Malhotra and Farina Mir, 289–319. New Delhi: Oxford University Press, 2012.

Goswami, Manu. *Producing India: From Colonial Economy to National Space.* Chicago: University of Chicago Press, 2004.

Gratton, Peter. "Change We Can't Believe In: Adrian Johnston on Badiou, Žižek, & Political Transformation." *International Journal of Žižek Studies* 4, no. 3 (2007): 1–15.

Grewal, J. S. *The Reign of Maharaja Ranjit Singh: Structure of Power, Economy and Society.* Patiala: Punjabi University, 1981.

——. *A Study of Guru Granth Sahib: Doctrine, Social Content, History Structure and Status.* Amritsar: Singh Brothers, 2009.

Guha, Ranajit. "Chandra's Death." In *Subaltern Studies V: Writings on South Asian History and Society*, ed. Ranajit Guha, 135–65. Delhi: Oxford University Press, 1987.

——. "A Conquest Foretold." *Social Text* 54 (1998): 85–99.

——. *Dominance Without Hegemony: History and Power in Colonial India*. Cambridge, MA: Harvard University Press, 1997.

——. *Elementary Aspects of Peasant Insurgency in Colonial India*. Durham, NC: Duke University Press, 1999.

——. "Gramsci in India: Homage to a Teacher." In *The Small Voice of History*, ed. Partha Chatterjee, 361–70. Delhi: Permanent Black, 2009.

——. "On Some Aspects of the Historiography of Colonial India." In *Subaltern Studies I: Writings on South Asian History and Society*, ed. Ranajit Guha, 1–8. New Delhi: Oxford University Press, 1982.

——. "The Prose of Counter-Insurgency." In *Subaltern Studies II: Writings on South Asian History and Society*, ed. Ranajit Guha, 1–40. New Delhi: Oxford University Press, 1983.

——. "Subaltern Studies Projects for Our Time and Their Convergence." In *The Small Voice of History*, ed. Partha Chatterjee, 346–60. Delhi: Permanent Black, 2009.

Habermas, Jürgen. *The Structural Transformation of the Public Sphere: An Inquiry Into A Category of Bourgeois Society*. Trans. Thomas Burger. Cambridge, MA: MIT Press, 1991.

Haj, Samira. *Reconfiguring Islamic Tradition: Reform, Rationality, and Modernity*. Stanford, CA: Stanford University Press, 2008.

Halberstam, Jack. *The Queer Art of Failure*. Durham, NC: Duke University Press, 2011.

——. *Skin Shows: Gothic Horror and the Technology of Monsters*. Durham, NC: Duke University Press, 1995.

Hall, Catherine. *Civilising Subjects: Metropole and Colony in the English Imagination 1830–1867*. Chicago: University of Chicago Press, 2002.

Hall, Stuart. "Toad in the Garden: Thatcherism among the Theorists." In *Marxism and the Interpretation of Culture*, ed. Lawrence Grossberg and Cary Nelson, 35–57. Urbana: University of Illinois Press, 1988.

Hartman, Saidiya. *Scenes of Subjection: Terror, Slavery, and Self-Making in Nineteenth-Century America*. Oxford: Oxford University Press, 1997.

Harvey, David. *The New Imperialism*. Oxford: Oxford University Press, 2003.

Hatcher, Brian. *Bourgeois Hinduism, or, The Faith of the Modern Vedantists: Rare Discourse from Early Colonial Bengal*. Oxford: Oxford University Press, 2008.

——. "Situating the Swaminarayan Tradition in the Historiography of Modern Hindu Reform." *Swaminarayan Hinduism: Tradition, Adaptation and Identity*, ed. Raymond Brady Williams and Yogi Trivedi, 6–37. New Delhi: Oxford University Press, 2016.

Haynes, Douglas E. *Rhetoric and Ritual in Colonial India: The Shaping of a Public Culture in Surat City, 1852–1928*. Berkeley: University of California Press, 1991.

Hirschmann, Edwin. *White Mutiny: The Ilbert Bill Crisis in India and Genesis of the Indian National Congress*. New Delhi: Heritage, 1980.

Hollywood, Amy. *Acute Melancholia and Other Essays: Mysticism, History, and the Study of Religion*. New York: Columbia University Press, 2016.

Hook, Derek. *(Post)Apartheid Conditions: Psychoanalysis and Social Formation*. New York: Palgrave, 2013.

Hsia, Ronnie Po-Chia. *Social Discipline in the Reformation: Central Europe, 1550–1750*. London: T. J. Press, 1989.

Iqbal, Basit Kareem. "Asad and Benjamin: Chronopolitics of Tragedy in the Anthropology of Secularism." *Anthropological Theory* 20, no. 1 (2020): 77–96.

Iqbal, Basit Kareem, and Rajbir Singh Judge, eds. "The Destruction of Loss." *Critical Times* 6, no. 2 (2023).

Jalal, Ayesha. *Self and Sovereignty: Individual and Community in South Asian Islam Since 1850*. New York: Routledge, 2000.

Johnston, Adrian. *Badiou, Žižek, and Political Transformations: The Cadence of Change*. Evanston, IL: Northwestern University Press, 2008.

——. *Žižek's Ontology: A Transcendental Materialist Theory of Subjectivity*. Evanston, IL: Northwestern University Press, 2008.

Jones, Kenneth. *Arya Dharm: Hindu Consciousness in 19th-Century Punjab*. Delhi: Manohar, 1976.

——. "The Bengali Elites in Post-Annexation Punjab: An Example of Inter-Regional Influence in Nineteenth-Century India." *Indian Economic & Social History Review* 3, no. 4 (1966): 376–95.

——. *Socio-Religious Reform Movements in British India*. Cambridge: Cambridge University Press, 1989.

Judge, Rajbir Singh. "The Multiple Horizons of Sikh Orthodoxy: Tradition, Fantasy, and Modern Temporality." *Journal of Sikh and Punjab Studies* 23, nos. 1–2 (2016): 181–92.

——. "There Is No Colonial Relationship: Antagonism, Sikhism, and South Asian Studies." *History and Theory* 57, no. 2 (June 2018): 193–215.

Kalra, Virinder Singh. "Locating the Sikh Pagh." *Sikh Formations* 1, no. 1 (2005): 75–92.

——. *Sacred and Secular Musics: A Postcolonial Approach*. London: Bloomsbury, 2015.

Kantorwicz, Ernst H. *The King's Two Bodies: A Study in Medieval Political Theology*. Princeton, NJ: Princeton University Press, 2016.

Kapur, Prithipal Singh, ed. *Maharaja Duleep Singh: The Last Sovereign Ruler of the Punjab*. Amritsar: Shiromani Gurdwara Parbandhak Committee, 1995.

Kaur, Harleen, and p.s. kehal. "Epistemic Wounded Attachments: Recovering Definitional Subjectivity Through Colonial Libraries." *History and Theory* 62 (2023): 203–24.

Kaviraj, Sudipta. *The Imaginary Institution of India*. Delhi: Permanent Black, 2010.

Khan, Naveeda. *Muslim Becoming: Aspiration and Skepticism in Pakistan*. Durham, NC: Duke University Press, 2012.

Khanna, Ranjana. *Dark Continents: Psychoanalysis and Colonialism*. Durham, NC: Duke University Press, 2003.

Khatib, Sami. "Melancholia and Destruction: Brushing Walter Benjamin's 'Angel of History' Against the Grain." *Crisis and Critique* 3, no. 2 (2016): 21–39.

——. "No Future: The Space of Capital and the Time of Dying." In *Former West: Art and the Contemporary After 1989*, ed. Maria Hlavajova and Simon Sheikh, 639–52. Cambridge, MA: MIT Press, 2017.

King, Richard. *Orientalism and Religion: Post-Colonial Theory, India and The Mystic East*. New York: Routledge, 1999.

Klein, Melanie. *Contributions to Psycho-Analysis 1921–1945*. London: Hogarth, 1948.

Kleinberg, Ethan. *Haunting History: For a Deconstructive Approach to the Past*. Stanford, CA: Stanford University Press, 2017.

Kleinberg, Ethan, Joan Wallach Scott, and Gary Wilder. "Theses on Theory and History." *History of the Present* 10, no. 1 (2020): 157–65.

Kojève, Alexander. *Introduction to the Reading of Hegel: Lectures on the Phenomenology of Spirit*. Trans. James H. Nichols. Ithaca, NY: Cornell University Press, 1980.

Koselleck, Reinhart. *Futures Past: On the Semantics of Historical Time*. Trans. Keith Tribe. New York: Columbia University Press, 2004.

——. *The Practice of Conceptual History: Timing History, Spacing Concepts*. Trans. Todd Samuel Presner et al. Stanford, CA: Stanford University Press, 2002.

Lacan, Jacques. *The Ethics of Psychoanalysis*. Ed. Jacques-Alain Miller. Trans. Dennis Porter. New York: W. W. Norton, 1992.

——. *The Four Fundamental Concepts of Psychoanalysis*. Ed. Jacques-Alain Miller. Trans. Alan Sheridan. New York: W. W. Norton, 1978.

——. *On Feminine Sexuality, the Limits of Love and Knowledge, Encore*. Ed. Jacques-Alain Miller. Trans. Bruce Fink. New York: W. W. Norton, 1998.

——. *The Seminar of Jacques Lacan, Book III: The Psychoses, 1955–1956*. Ed. Jacques-Alain Miller. Trans. Russell Grigg. New York: W. W. Norton, 1993.

——. *The Seminar of Jacques Lacan, Book VI: Desire and Its Interpretation*. Ed. Jacques-Alain Miller. Trans. Bruce Fink. Medford, MA: Polity, 2019.

——. "Seminar on 'The Purloined Letter.'" In *Écrits*, ed. and trans. Bruce Fink, 6–48. New York: W. W. Norton, 2002.

LaCapra, Dominick. *Writing History, Writing Trauma*. Baltimore: Johns Hopkins University Press, 2001.

Laidlaw, James. *Riches and Renunciation: Religion, Economy and Society Among the Jains*. Oxford: Oxford University Press, 1995.

Laplanche, Jean. *Essays on Otherness*. Ed. John Fletcher. Trans. Luke Thurston. New York: Routledge, 1999.

Login, Lena. *Sir Login and Duleep Singh*. London: W. H. Allen & Co., 1890.

MacIntyre, Alasdair C. *After Virtue: A Study in Moral Theory*. Notre Dame, IN: University of Notre Dame Press, 1981.

Mahmood, Saba. *Politics of Piety: The Islamic Revival and the Feminist Subject*. Princeton, NJ: Princeton University Press, 2005.

Majumdar, R. C. *History of the Freedom Movement in India, Volume 1*. Calcutta: Firma K. K. Mukhopadhyay, 1962.

Malhotra, Anshu. *Piro and the Gulabdasis: Gender, Sect, and Society in Punjab*. New Delhi: Oxford University Press, 2017.

Mallon, Florenica. *Peasant and Nation: The Making of Postcolonial Mexico and Peru*. Berkeley: University of California Press, 1995.

Mamdani, Mahmood. *Good Muslim, Bad Muslim: America, the Cold War, and the Roots of Terror*. New York: Doubleday, 2004.

Mandair, Arvind-Pal Singh. *Religion and the Specter of the West: Sikhism, India, Postcoloniality, and the Politics of Translation*. New York: Columbia University Press, 2013.

——. "Shabad (Word)." In *Sikhism: Encyclopedia of Indian Religions*, ed. Arvind-Pal Singh Mandair. Dordrecht: Springer, 2017. https://link.springer.com/referenceworkentry/10.1007/978-94-024-0846-1_486.

Mani, Lata. *Contentious Traditions: The Debate on Sati in Colonial India*. Berkeley: University of California Press, 1998.

Mann, Gurinder Singh. "Conversion to Sikhism." In *The Oxford Handbook of Religious Conversion*, ed. Lewis R. Rambo and Charles E. Farhadian, 488–507. Oxford: Oxford University Press, 2014.

Mantena, Karuna. *Alibis of Empire: Henry Maine and the Ends of Liberal Imperialism*. Princeton, NJ: Princeton University Press, 2010.

Mantena, Rama Sundari. "Vernacular Publics and Political Modernity: Language and Progress in Colonial South India." *Modern Asian Studies* 47, no. 5 (2013): 1678–705.

Marriott, David. *Whither Fanon? Studies in the Blackness of Being*. Stanford, CA: Stanford University Press, 2018.

Marshall, Ruth. *Political Spiritualities: The Pentecostal Revolution in Nigeria*. Chicago: University of Chicago Press, 2009.

Marx, Karl. *Capital: Volume 1: A Critique of Political Economy*. Trans. Ben Fowkes. New York: Penguin Books, 1976.

Mas, Ruth. "On the Apocalyptic Tones of Islam in Secular Time." In *Secularism and Religion Making*, ed. Arvind-Pal S. Mandair and Markus Dressler, 87–103. Oxford: Oxford University Press, 2011.

Masselos, Jim. "The Dis/appearance of Subalterns: A Reading of a Decade of Subaltern Studies." *South Asia: Journal of South Asian Studies* 15, no. 1 (1992): 105–25.

Mayaram, Shail. *Against History, Against State: Counterperspectives from the Margins*. New York: Columbia University Press, 2003.

Mbembe, Achille. *On the Postcolony*. Berkeley: University of California Press, 2001.

McCallum, E. L. *Object Lessons: How to Do Things with Fetishism*. Albany: SUNY Press, 1999.

Metcalf, Thomas R. *The Aftermath of Revolt: India, 1857–1870*. Princeton, NJ: Princeton University Press, 1964.

——. *Ideologies of the Raj*. Cambridge: Cambridge University Press, 1995.

Mir, Farina. "Genre and Devotion in Punjabi Popular Narratives: Rethinking Cultural and Religious Syncretism." *Comparative Studies in Society and History* 48, no. 3 (2006): 727–58.

——. "Imperial Policy, Provincial Practices: Colonial Language Policy in Nineteenth-Century India." *Indian Economic & Social History Review* 43, no. 4 (2006): 100–126.

——. *The Social Space of Language: Vernacular Culture in British Colonial Punjab*. Berkeley: University of California Press, 2010.

Mitchell, Timothy. *Colonizing Egypt*. Berkeley: University of California Press, 1991.

——. "The Stage of Modernity." In *Questions of Modernity*, ed. Timothy Mitchell, 1–34. Minneapolis: University of Minnesota Press, 2000.

Mittal, S. C. *Freedom Movement in Punjab (1905–29)*. Delhi: Concept Publishing Company, 1977.

Muller, John P., and William J. Richardson, eds. *The Purloined Poe: Lacan, Derrida, and Psychoanalytic Reading*. Baltimore: Johns Hopkins University Press, 1988.

Murphy, Anne. "The Formation of the Ethical Sikh Subject in the Era of British Colonial Reform." *Sikh Formations* 11, nos. 1–2 (2015): 149–59.

——. *The Materiality of the Past: History and Representation in Sikh Tradition*. Oxford: Oxford University Press, 2012.

Nadiem, Ihsan H., ed. *Sardar Dyal Singh Majithia as Seen by His Contemporaries.* Lahore: Dyal Singh Research & Cultural Forum, 2011.

Nancy, Jean-Luc. *The Inoperative Community.* Ed. Peter Connor. Trans. Peter Connor, Lisa Garbus, Michael Holland, and Simona Sawhney. Minneapolis: University of Minnesota Press, 1991.

Nandy, Ashis. "History's Forgotten Doubles." *History and Theory* 34, no. 2 (1995): 44–66.

——. "Oppression and Human Liberation: Towards a Third World Utopia." *Alternatives* 4, no. 2 (1978): 165–80.

Nijhawan, Michael. *Dhadi Darbar: Religion, Violence, and the Performance of Sikh History.* Delhi: Oxford University Press, 2006.

Oberoi, Harjot. "Bhai, Babas, and Gyanis: Traditional Intellectuals in 19th Century Punjab." *Studies in History* 2, no. 2 (1980): 33–62.

——. *The Construction of Religious Boundaries: Culture, Identity, and Diversity in the Sikh Tradition.* Chicago: University of Chicago Press, 1994.

O'Hanlon, Rosalind. "Recovering the Subject: Subaltern Studies and Histories of Resistance in Colonial South Asia." *Modern Asian Studies* 22, no. 1 (1988): 189–224.

Pandey, Gyanendra. *The Construction of Communalism in Colonial North India,* 2nd ed. New Delhi: Oxford University Press, 2006.

Pandian, Anand. "Tradition in Fragments: Inherited Forms and Fractures in the Ethics of South India." *American Ethnologist* 35, no. 3 (2008): 466–80.

Pandolfo, Stefania. *Impasse of the Angels.* Chicago: University of Chicago Press, 1997.

——. *Knot of the Soul: Madness, Psychoanalysis, Islam.* Chicago: University of Chicago Press, 2018.

Patel, Shruti. "Beyond the Lens of Reform: Religious Culture in Modern Gujarat." *Journal of Hindu Studies* 10, no. 1 (2017): 47–85.

Peabody, Norbert. *Hindu Kingship and Polity in Precolonial India.* New Delhi: Cambridge University Press, 2006.

Pennington, Brian K. "Reform and Revival, Innovation and Enterprise: A Tale of Modern Hinduism." In *The Protestant Reformation in a Context of Global History Religious Reforms and World Civilizations,* ed. Heinz Schilling and Silvana Seidel Menchi, 149–69. Berlin: Duncker & Humblot, 2017.

——. *Was Hinduism Invented? Britons, Indians, and the Colonial Construction of Religion.* Oxford: Oxford University Press, 2005.

Pluth, Edward. "Against Spontaneity: Badiou, Lacan, and Žižek on the Act." *International Journal of Žižek Studies* 1, no. 2 (2007): 1–29.

——. *Signifiers and Acts: Freedom in Lacan's Theory of the Subject.* Albany: SUNY Press, 2007.

Poovey, Mary. *Making A Social Body: British Cultural Formation, 1830–1864.* Chicago: University of Chicago Press, 1995.

Prakash, Gyan. *Bonded Histories: Genealogies of Labor Servitude in Colonial India.* Cambridge: Cambridge University Press, 1990.

Prasad, Leela. *Poetics of Conduct: Oral Narrative and Moral Being in a South Indian Town.* New York: Columbia University Press, 2006.

Puri, Nina. *Political Elite and Society in the Punjab.* New Delhi: Vikas Publishing House, 1985.

Purohit, Teena. *The Aga Khan Case: Religion and Identity in Colonial India*. Cambridge, MA: Harvard University Press, 2012.

Rajan, Rajeswai Sunder. "Death and the Subaltern." In *Can the Subaltern Speak?: Reflections on the History of an Idea*, ed. Rosalind C. Morris, 117–38. New York: Columbia University Press, 2010.

Rancière, Jacques. *Proletarian Nights: The Workers' Dream in Nineteenth-Century France*. Trans. John Drury. London: Verso, 2012.

Reinhard, Wolfgang. "Reformation, Counter-Reformation, and the Early Modern State a Reassessment." *Catholic Historical Review* 75, no. 3 (1989): 383–404.

Rose, Marika. *A Theology of Failure: Žižek Against Christian Innocence*. New York: Fordham University Press, 2019.

Roy, Parama. *Alimentary Tracts: Appetites, Aversions, and the Postcolonial*. Durham, NC: Duke University Press, 2010.

——. *Indian Traffic: Identities in Question in Colonial and Postcolonial India*. Berkeley: University of California Press, 1998.

Royle, Edward. *Victorian Infidels: The Origins of the British Secularist Movement, 1791–1866*. Manchester: Manchester University Press, 1974.

Ruda, Frank. *Abolishing Freedom: A Plea for a Contemporary Use of Fatalism*. Lincoln: University of Nebraska Press, 2016.

Santner, Eric L. *Stranded Objects Mourning, Memory, and Film in Postwar Germany*. Ithaca, NY: Cornell University Press, 1993.

Sarkar, Sumit. *Writing Social History*. Delhi: Oxford University Press, 1998.

Schiesari, Juliana. *The Gendering of Melancholia: Feminism, Psychoanalysis and the Symbolics of Loss in Renaissance Literature*. Ithaca, NY: Cornell University Press, 1992.

Schuster, Aaron. *The Trouble with Pleasure: Deleuze and Psychoanalysis*. Cambridge, MA: MIT Press, 2016.

Scott, David. "Colonial Governmentality." *Social Text* 43 (1995): 191–220.

——. *Formations of Ritual: Colonial and Anthropological Discourses on the Sinhala Yaktovil*. Minneapolis: University of Minnesota Press, 1994.

——. *Omens of Adversity: Tragedy, Time, Memory, Justice*. Durham, NC: Duke University Press, 2013.

——. *Refashioning Futures: Criticism After Postcoloniality*. Princeton, NJ: Princeton University Press, 1999.

Scott, J. Barton. "How to Defame a God: Public Selfhood in the Maharaj Libel Case." *South Asia: Journal of South Asian Studies* 38, no. 3 (2015): 387–402.

——. *Spiritual Despots: Modern Hinduism and the Genealogies of Self-Rule*. Chicago: University of Chicago Press, 2016.

Scott, J. Barton, and Brannon D. Ingram. "What Is a Public? Notes from South Asia." *South Asia: Journal of South Asian Studies* 38, no. 3 (2015): 357–70.

Scott, James C. *Domination and the Arts of Resistance: Hidden Transcripts*. New Haven, CT: Yale University Press, 1990.

Scott, Joan Wallach. *The Fantasy of Feminist History*. Durham, NC: Duke University Press, 2011.

Seal, Anil. *The Emergence of Indian Nationalism: Competition and Collaboration in the Later Nineteenth Century*. Cambridge: Cambridge University Press, 1971.

Sen, Sudipta. *Distant Sovereignty: National Imperialism and the Origins of British India*. New York: Routledge, 2002.

——. *Empire of Free Trade: The East India Company and the Making of the Colonial Marketplace*. Philadelphia: University of Pennsylvania Press, 1998.

——. "Unfinished Conquest: Residual Sovereignty and the Legal Foundations of the British Empire in India." *Law, Culture and the Humanities* 9, no. 2 (2013): 227–42.

Seth, Sanjay. "Rewriting Histories of Nationalism: The Politics of 'Moderate Nationalism' in India, 1870–1905." *American Historical Review* 104, no. 1 (1999): 95–116.

Sharafi, Mitra. *Law and Identity in Colonial South Asia: Parsi Legal Culture, 1772–1947*. Cambridge: Cambridge University Press, 2014.

Simmons, Caleb. *Devotional Sovereignty: Kingship and Religion in India*. New York: Oxford University Press, 2020.

Singh, Devin. *Divine Currency: The Theological Power of Money in the West*. Stanford, CA: Stanford University Press, 2018.

Singh, Fauja. *Kuka Movement: An Important Phase in Punjab's Role in India's Struggle for Freedom*. Delhi: Motilal Banarsidass, 1965.

——, ed. *Maharaja Kharak Singh*. Patiala: Punjabi University, Patiala, 1977.

Singh, Gajendra. *The Testimonies of Indian Soldiers and the Two World Wars: Between Self and Sepoy*. New York: Bloomsbury, 2014.

Singh, Ganda. "Khalsa." In *Encyclopedia of Sikhism*, ed. Harbans Singh, 473–74. Patiala: Punjabi University, 2011.

——, ed. *Maharaja Duleep Singh Correspondence*. Patiala: Punjabi University Patiala, 1977.

——, ed. *Private Correspondence Relating to the Anglo-Sikh Wars*. Amritsar: Sikh History Society, 1955.

Singh, Gurbhagat. *Sikhism and Postmodern Thought*. Amritsar: Naad Pargaas, 2016.

Singh, Harbans. *The Heritage of the Sikhs*. New Delhi: Manohar, 1983.

Singh, Harleen. *The Rani of Jhansi*. Cambridge: Cambridge University Press, 2014.

Singh, Jagjit. *Singh Sabha Lahir*. Amritsar: Guru Ramdas Printing Press, 1941.

Singh, Jaswinder. *Kuka Movement: Freedom Struggle in Punjab*. New Delhi: Atlantic Publishers and Distributors, 1985.

Singh, Joginder. *The Namdhari Sikhs: Their Changing Social and Cultural Landscape*. Delhi: Manohar, 2013.

——. "Namdhari Sikhs of Punjab: Historical Profile." *Journal of Punjab Studies* 21, no. 2 (2014): 267–97.

Singh, Kapur. *Me Judice*. Amritsar: B. Chattar Singh Jiwan Singh, 2003.

——. *Pārāśarapraśna: The Baisakhi of Gurgobind Singh*. Ed. Piar Singh and Madanjit Kaur. Amritsar: Guru Nanak Dev University, 1989.

——. *Sikhism for Modern Man*. Ed. Madanjit Kaur and Piar Singh. Amritsar: Guru Nanak Dev University Press, 1992.

Singh, Khushwant. *The Fall of the Kingdom in Punjab*. Delhi: Penguin Books, 2014.

Singh, Nripinder. *The Sikh Moral Tradition*. Delhi: Manohar, 2008.

Singh, Pashaura. "Rāj Karegā Khālsā." In *A Dictionary of Sikh Studies*. Oxford University Press, https://www.oxfordreference.com/view/10.1093/acref/9780191831874.001 .0001/acref-9780191831874-e-291.

Singh, Puran. *The Book of Ten Masters*. Patiala: Punjabi University, Patiala Publication Bureau, 1981.

——. *Spirit of the Sikh: Part II, Volume Two*. Patiala: Publication Bureau Punjabi University, Patiala, 2017.

Singh, Sunit. "The Sikh Kingdom." In *The Oxford Handbook of Sikh Studies*, ed. Pashaura Singh and Louis E. Fenech, 59–69. Oxford: Oxford University Press, 2016.

Singh, Teja. "The Singh Sabha Movement." In *The Singh Sabha and Other Socio-Religious Movements in the Punjab, 1850–1925*, ed. Ganda Singh, 31–44. Patiala: Publication Bureau Punjabi University, Patiala, 1997.

Sinha, Mrinalini. *Colonial Masculinity: The "Manly Englishman" and The "Effeminate Bengali" in the Late Nineteenth Century*. New York: St. Martin's Press, 1995.

Sorel, Georges. *Reflections on Violence*. Ed. and trans. Jeremy Jennings. Cambridge: Cambridge University Press, 1999.

Spivak, Gayatri Chakravorty. "Can the Subaltern Speak?" In *Marxism and the Interpretation of Culture*, ed. Lawrence Grossberg and Cary Nelson, 271–313. Urbana: University of Illinois Press, 1988.

——. *A Critique of Postcolonial Reason: Toward a History of the Vanishing Present*. Cambridge, MA: Harvard University Press, 1999.

——. *In Other Worlds: Essays in Cultural Politics*. New York: Routledge, 1988.

——. *Outside in the Teaching Machine*. New York: Routledge, 1993.

——. "Scattered Speculations on the Subaltern and the Popular." *Postcolonial Studies* 8, no.4 (2005): 475–86.

Sreenivasan, Ramya. *The Many Lives of a Rajput Queen: Heroic Pasts in India, c. 1500–1900*. Seattle: University of Washington Press, 2007.

Sternhell, Zeev, Mario Sznajder, and Maia Ashéri. *The Birth of Fascist Ideology: From Cultural Rebellion to Political Revolution*. Princeton, NJ: Princeton University Press, 1994.

Stoler, Ann Laura. "'In Cold Blood': Hierarchies of Credibility and the Politics of Colonial Narratives." *Representations* 37 (1992): 151–89.

Sturman, Rachel. *The Government of Social Life in Colonial India: Liberalism, Religious Law, and Women's Rights*. Cambridge: Cambridge University Press, 2012.

Tareen, SherAli. *Defending Muhammad in Modernity*. Notre Dame, IN: University of Notre Dame Press, 2020.

Taussig, Michael. *Defacement: Public Secrecy and the Labor of the Negative*. Stanford, CA: Stanford University Press, 1999.

——. *The Devil and Commodity Fetishism in South America*. Chapel Hill: University of North Carolina Press, 1980.

——. *Shamanism, Colonialism, and the Wild Man: A Study in Terror and Healing*. Chicago: University of Chicago Press, 1987.

Taylor, Charles. *Philosophical Arguments*. Cambridge, MA: Harvard University Press, 1995.

——. *Sources of the Self: The Making of the Modern Identity*. Cambridge, MA: Harvard University Press, 1992.

Taylor, Mark C. *About Religion: Economies of Faith in Virtual Culture*. Chicago: University of Chicago Press, 1999.

Travers, Robert. *Ideology and Empire in Eighteenth Century India: The British in Bengal*. Cambridge: Cambridge University Press 2007.

Tsing, Anna Lowenhaupt. *The Mushroom at the End of the World: On the Possibility of Life in Capitalist Ruins*. Princeton, NJ: Princeton University Press, 2015.

Van der Veer, Peter, ed. *Conversion to Modernities: The Globalization of Christianity.* New York: Routledge, 1996.

——. *Imperial Encounters: Religion and Modernity in India and Britain.* Princeton, NJ: Princeton University Press, 2001.

Verhaeghe, Paul. "Causation and Destitution of a Pre-ontological Non-entity: On the Lacanian Subject." In *Key Concepts of Lacanian Psychoanalysis*, ed. Dany Nobus, 164–89. New York: Other Press, 1998.

Viswanath, Rupa. "The Emergence of Authenticity Talk and the Giving of Accounts: Conversion as Movement of the Soul in South India, ca. 1900." *Comparative Studies in Society and History* 55, no. 1 (2013): 120–41.

Viswanathan, Gauri. *Outside the Fold Conversion, Modernity, and Belief.* Princeton, NJ: Princeton University Press, 1998.

Walker, Caroline Bynum. "Did the Twelfth Century Discover the Individual?" *Journal of Ecclesiastical History* 31, no. 1 (1980): 1–17.

Warner, Michael. *Publics and Counterpublics.* New York: Zone Books, 2005.

Wenzel, Jennifer. *Bulletproof: Afterlives of Anticolonial Prophecy in South Africa and Beyond.* Chicago: University of Chicago Press, 2009.

White, Luise. *Speaking with Vampires: Rumor and History in Colonial Africa.* Berkeley: University of California, 2000.

Wilder, Gary. "From Optic to Topic: The Foreclosure Effect of Historiographic Turns." *American Historical Review* 117, no. 3 (2012): 723–45.

Wilson, Jon. *The Domination of Strangers: Modern Governance in Eastern India, 1780–1835.* Basingstoke, UK: Palgrave Macmillan, 2008.

Yasin, Madhvi. *British Paramountcy in Kashmir, 1876–1894.* Delhi: Atlantic Publishers, 1984.

Yelle, Robert. *The Language of Disenchantment: Protestant Liberalism and Colonial Discourse in British India.* Oxford: Oxford University Press, 2013.

Žižek, Slavoj. *Absolute Recoil: Towards a New Foundation of Dialectical Materialism.* New York: Verso, 2014.

——. "Class Struggle or Postmodernism?: Yes, Please!" in *Contingency, Hegemony, Universality: Contemporary Dialogues on the Left*, ed. Judith Butler, Ernesto Laclau, and Slavoj Žižek, 90–135. London: Verso, 2000.

——. *Enjoy Your Symptom!: Jacques Lacan in Hollywood and Out.* New York: Routledge, 1992.

——. *How to Read Lacan.* New York: W. W. Norton, 2007.

——. *Less Than Nothing: Hegel and the Shadow of Dialectical Materialism.* London: Verso, 2013.

——. *Looking Awry: An Introduction to Jacques Lacan Through Popular Culture.* Cambridge, MA: MIT Press, 1991.

——. *The Plague of Fantasies.* London: Verso, 1997.

——. *The Sublime Object of Ideology.* London: Verso, 1989.

——. *The Ticklish Subject: The Absent Centre of Political Ontology.* London: Verso, 1999.

INDEX

GPSR Authorized Representative: Easy Access System Europe, Mustamäe tee 50, 10621 Tallinn, Estonia, gpsr.requests@easproject.com